R01030 79863

LB 2328 .D55 1996

Dimensions of the community college.

$40.00

CHICAGO PUBLIC LIBRARY
SOCIAL SCIENCES AND HISTORY
400 S. STATE ST.   60605

BAKER & TAYLOR

DIMENSIONS OF THE COMMUNITY COLLEGE

GARLAND STUDIES IN HIGHER EDUCATION
VOLUME 6
GARLAND REFERENCE LIBRARY OF SOCIAL SCIENCE
VOLUME 1075

GARLAND STUDIES IN HIGHER EDUCATION

This series is published in cooperation with the Program in Higher Education, School of Education, Boston College, Chestnut Hill, Massachusetts.

PHILIP G. ALTBACH, *Series Editor*

THE SOCIAL ROLE OF HIGHER
EDUCATION
Comparative Perspectives
edited by Ken Kempner
and William Tierney

DIMENSIONS OF THE
COMMUNITY COLLEGE
*International, Intercultural, and
Multicultural Perspectives*
edited by Rosalind Latiner Raby
and Norma Tarrow

THE LIBERAL ARTS COLLEGE
ADAPTING TO CHANGE
The Survival of Small Schools
by Gary Bonvillian
and Robert Murphy

REFORM AND CHANGE
IN HIGHER EDUCATION
International Perspectives
edited by James E. Mauch and
Paula L.W. Sabloff

SCIENCE AND TECHNOLOGY IN
CENTRAL AND EASTERN EUROPE
The Reform of Higher Education
edited by A.D. Tillett
and Barry Lesser

CHINA'S UNIVERSITIES, 1895–1995
A Century of Cultural Conflict
by Ruth Hayhoe

THE FUNDING OF
HIGHER EDUCATION
International Perspectives
edited by Philip G. Altbach and
D. Bruce Johnstone

JESUIT EDUCATION AND SOCIAL
CHANGE IN EL SALVADOR
by Charles J. Beirne

HIGHER EDUCATION IN CRISIS
*New York in National
Perspective*
edited by William C. Barba

DIMENSIONS OF THE COMMUNITY COLLEGE
INTERNATIONAL, INTERCULTURAL, AND MULTICULTURAL PERSPECTIVES

EDITED BY
ROSALIND LATINER RABY
NORMA TARROW

GARLAND PUBLISHING, INC.
NEW YORK AND LONDON
1996

Copyright © 1996 by Rosalind Latiner Raby and Norma Tarrow
All rights reserved

Library of Congress Cataloging-in-Publication Data

Dimensions of the community college : international, intercultural, and multicultural perspectives / edited by Rosalind Latiner Raby, Norma Tarrow.
    p.   cm. — (Garland reference library of social science ; v. 1075.
Garland studies in higher education ; v. 6)
    Includes bibliographical references and index.
    ISBN 0-8153-1343-8 (alk. paper)
    1. Community colleges—Cross-cultural studies. 2. Multicultural education—Cross-cultural studies. I. Raby, Rosalind Latiner. II. Tarrow, Norma Bernstein. III. Series: Garland reference library of social science ; v. 1075. IV. Series: Garland reference library of social science. Garland studies in higher education ; vol. 6.
LB2328.D55   1996
378'.052—dc20   96-3231
                                                                                     CIP

Printed on acid-free, 250-year-life paper
Manufactured in the United States of America

Contents

List of Maps, Figures, and Tables	ix
Series Editor's Preface	xi
Preface	xiii
Introduction Norma Tarrow	xv

Part I
Dimensions of U.S. and Canadian Community Colleges

Introduction to Part I	3
Chapter 1 International, Intercultural, and Multicultural Dimensions of Community Colleges in the United States Rosalind Latiner Raby	9
Chapter 2 Community Self-Help International Development Projects: A Humanistic Perspective Jean Cook	37

CHAPTER 3
FROM AID TO TRADE: NEW TRENDS
IN INTERNATIONAL EDUCATION IN CANADA
Daniel Schugurensky and Kathy Higgins   53

CHAPTER 4
WEAVING THE AMERICAN TAPESTRY: MULTICULTURAL
EDUCATION IN COMMUNITY COLLEGES
Naomi Okumura Story   79

CHAPTER 5
INTERNATIONALIZING THE CURRICULUM:
IDEALS VS. REALITY
Rosalind Latiner Raby   111

CHAPTER 6
STUDY ABROAD IN THE PACIFIC ISLANDS:
MORE THAN AN INTERNATIONAL EXPERIENCE
Sharon Narimatsu and Robert W. Franco   145

CHAPTER 7
REFORM AND QUALITY ASSURANCE IN BRITISH
AND AMERICAN HIGHER EDUCATION
Ruth Burgos-Sasscer and David Collins   159

CHAPTER 8
BUILDING CONSENSUS FOR INTERNATIONAL
AND MULTICULTURAL PROGRAMS:
THE ROLE OF PRESIDENTIAL LEADERSHIP
Evan S. Dobelle and James H. Mullen   175

PART II
DIMENSIONS OF COMMUNITY COLLEGES ABROAD

INTRODUCTION TO PART II   195

CHAPTER 9
CULTURE, TECHNOLOGY, DEVELOPMENT:
PARTNERS WITH A PRICE TAG
Mathilda Esformes Harris   211

CHAPTER 10
THE ROLE OF THE COMMUNITY COLLEGE
IN COUNTERING CONFLICT IN MULTICULTURAL
SOCIETIES
Cornelia H. van der Linde   239

CHAPTER 11
ASSESSING THE RELEVANCE OF AMERICAN
COMMUNITY COLLEGE MODELS IN JAPAN
Tina Yamano and John N. Hawkins   259

CHAPTER 12
EGYPTIAN COMMUNITY COLLEGES: A CASE STUDY
Amin A. Elmallah, Kal Gezi, and Hassan Abdel Hamid Soliman   273

CHAPTER 13
MICHLALOT EZORIYOT — REGIONAL COLLEGES
IN ISRAEL: CHALLENGES, PROMISES,
AND PROSPECTS OF AN ALTERNATIVE MODEL
IN HIGHER EDUCATION
Yaacov Iram   291

CHAPTER 14
A REVIEW OF COMMUNITY COLLEGE
DEVELOPMENT IN SOUTH AFRICA
Mbuyiselwa Silas Zuma   303

CONTRIBUTORS   327

INDEX   331

List of Maps, Figures, and Tables

Maps

7   Map 1. Locations of Case Studies Discussed in Part I

7   Map 2. Regions of the World Related to Part I Case Studies

208 Map 3. Regions of the World Related to Part II Case Studies

Figures

16 Figure 1. Four Phases of Community College IIMEP Development

23 Figure 2. Configuration of Three Levels

43 Figure 3. Triangulation Metaphor

177 Figure 4. Internal Consensus

185 Figure 5. External Consensus

275 Figure 6. Educational System in Egypt

305 Figure 7. Schematic Representation of the Educational System in South Africa in 1993

Tables

29 Table 1. California Colleges for International Education: Numbers of Nontraditional Study-Abroad Programs

29 Table 2. California Colleges for International Education: IIMEP Activities

124 Table 3. CCIE—Internationally Oriented Classes Introduced in 1993 and 1994

197 Table 4. Community College Models

278 Table 5. Ma'ahad of Social Service, Alexandria: 1992 Curriculum

279 Table 6. Commercial Ma'ahad, Tanta: 1992 Curriculum

279 Table 7. Technical and Industrial Ma'ahad, Alexandria: 1992 Curriculum

279 Table 8. Hotel and Tourism Ma'ahad, Port Said: 1992 Curriculum

Series Editor's Preface

Higher education is a multifaceted phenomenon in modern society, combining a variety of institutions and an increasing diversity of students, a range of purposes and functions, and different orientations. The series combines research-based monographs, analyses, and discussions of broader issues and reference books related to all aspects of higher education. It is concerned with policy as well as practice from a global perspective. The series is dedicated to illuminating the reality of higher and postsecondary education in contemporary society.

Philip G. Altbach
Boston College

Preface

Dimensions of the Community College: International, Intercultural, and Multicultural Perspectives blends the theoretical and pragmatic analyses of international, intercultural, and multicultural education programs in American community colleges and their models abroad. This publication is pertinent to those who desire a conceptual understanding of the issues at hand and to those who need a more functional approach to support, maintain, and expand existing programs at their own colleges. Indeed, community colleges have an obligation of informing students about peoples, cultures, and relationships on the local, national, and international level. As the Commission on the Future of Community Colleges stated in *Building Communities for a New Century* (Washington, D.C.: American Association of Community and Junior Colleges, 1988), "In the century ahead, parochialism is not an option." Many community colleges, nationwide and abroad, are actively involved in a variety of aspects of international, intercultural, and multicultural education, through which they share everything from technology to institutional expertise. This is a subject demanding attention because of its proclivity and prominence worldwide.

This book contains two parts. The first examines a variety of international and intercultural/multicultural educational programs (IIMEPs) in selected North American community colleges. Each chapter examines a particular IIMEP, either as a case study or as part of a multicollege comparison. Although there is tremendous diversity among community college IIMEPs, only a representative few were included in this book. Each chapter either shows a novel application of a specific program or describes program-oriented issues that are currently under debate.

The second part explores how the U.S. community college model is used, transplanted, or imposed upon other nations in the world. Some chapters in this section are case studies of a single country, while other chapters take a comparative approach to analyze theoretical concepts. Throughout both parts, case studies portray a cross section of the world and provide a balance between industrialized and developing countries. The international community college dimensions in the industrialized countries of Canada, Great Britain, Israel, Japan, and the United States are discussed, and regions of Africa (South Africa, Sierra Leone, and Egypt), Europe (Eastern Europe, Great Britain, Greece, and Russia), North America (United States and Canada), and Asia (Israel, India, Thailand, Japan, and Polynesia) are highlighted. The solicited chapters provide a broad view of the world community, illustrating both the desired and unforeseen effects of the community college model worldwide. Rather than limiting itself to detailed case-descriptions of community college models, this publication seeks theoretical commonalities that can then be augmented in future publications.

The book is an outcome of the 1993 Western Regional Conference of the Comparative and International Education Society. One theme of that conference was "Internationalism and Multiculturalism in the Community College." The authors are experienced in analyzing the role of the particular aspect of community college international, intercultural/multicultural education on which their chapters focus.

A debt of appreciation is due to Garland Publishing and to Philip Altbach for his insightful editorial comments. Special gratitude is given to Lilian Mazariegos and the entire staff at the Institute for International Programs of the Los Angeles Community College District for their assistance during the course of editing this book. Finally, the editors would like to express their sincerest love and appreciation to our families for their continued strength and conviction, especially in 1993 and 1994, during two of California's worst natural disasters. We dedicate this book to our families.

Introduction

Norma Tarrow

> Education that teaches us to celebrate rather than condemn cultural diversity; to understand rather than undermine differing traditions and beliefs; to respect rather than revile mankind's infinite societal variations—such education may not be enough to preserve man's precarious perch on planet Earth, but surely the educational effort must be made. (Ernest Boyer [former U.S. Commissioner of Education] 1979, 14–19)

Several years ago, Rosalind Latiner Raby and I recognized the need for a volume that would fill the void in the literature for a blend of theoretical and pragmatic analysis of international education programs in U.S. community colleges and their models abroad, that would recognize the symbiotic relationship between such programs and newer intercultural/multicultural education efforts, and that would provide a conceptual underpinning for more functional approaches guiding such programs. Ours was a dual effort involving (1) the 1993 Western Regional Conference of the Comparative and International Education Society, which featured invited papers on specific issues, case studies, and regions, and (2) the publication of a book based on those papers.

When we divided up the tasks involved, I am sure that Rosalind Raby, as senior editor, had no idea of the complexities and complications that would be involved. In the face of incredible adversities and accommodating to the individuality of contributors, she has carried this project through to completion with patience and integrity.

And now to the task at hand. What will this book do for you the reader, most probably a college faculty member or administrator, community leader, policymaker, or student? Part I of this chapter will provide a brief review and expansion of some new but generally accepted or acceptable ideas. Part II will permit more extensive consideration of major nonconsensual issues, and part III will provide conclusions.

PART I: CONSENSUAL CONCEPTS

In this part, a variety of concepts relating to international and intercultural/multicultural education that are consensually acknowledged by educational practitioners and researchers in the field are examined.

Definitions and Program Development

In chapter 1, Raby clearly defines and traces the development of the fields of international and intercultural/multicultural education, as well as the various programs included in each field, and presents our thesis that community colleges, by virtue of the populations they serve both in the United States and abroad, have a special mandate to attend to these fields. Further, in the context of increasingly pluralistic societies and an increasingly interdependent world, such programs must be viewed not as peripheral to the mission of community colleges but as integrated into the total fabric of the institution, with benefits at the individual, community, and world levels.

As early as 1979, the President's Commission on Foreign Language and International Studies urged a special effort in community colleges to increase the international/intercultural dimension. And in 1988, the Commission on the Future of Community Colleges of the American Association of Community and Junior Colleges expressed grave concern over the ignorance of the vast majority of community college students with regard to the heritage of others in our multicultural society and to the international issues related to increasing global interdependence (Commission on the Future of Community Colleges 1988).

Academic Infusion

The importance of the infusing international intercultural/multicultural concepts into all aspects of the college and into all courses, rather than using them as an isolated addendum to the curriculum, is strongly made by Raby in chapter 5. Success is most assured when this infusion approach is combined with joint classes, new classes, new degree programs, special speakers or programs, faculty development efforts, and institutional affiliations, a viewpoint also articulated by Fersh (1990).

This emphasis on academic aspects for the greatest long-term effect is also supported by Backman (1984). In regard to infusion into courses or programs, he calls for incentives and support to internationalize (or interculturalize/multiculturalize) courses by such techniques as adding non-Western material or providing comparative approaches. He also suggests area studies, intercultural studies, the establishment of a major or a minor or a concentration, as well as the expansion of library support for these fields. Further, he stresses the needs to go beyond humanities and social sciences and include all disciplines and involve a critical mass of articulate faculty. However, he does not ignore the many other aspects of international and intercultural/multicultural educational programs (IIMEPs), such as enrollment of foreign students, student exchange, study abroad, faculty exchanges, faculty development (including release time, summer stipends, travel support, support for faculty exchange, and grant writing), programs related to English language development, international (and multicultural) activities, outreach activities (including community and business advisory and support groups), and development-assistance projects (Backman 1984).

Components Assuring Success

Raby has described the components she views as essential to assure success in the implementation of international programs (which, as Story has pointed out, are pertinent to multicultural efforts as well) at the community college level: Greenfield has also addressed these issues, identifying the following components:

- A commitment from the board of trustees via a supportive policy statement.
- Inclusion of international [and intercultural/multicultural][1] education in the mission-and-goals statement of the college.
- A process of ongoing involvement of interested faculty and staff.
- An adequate structure to administer or coordinate programs and resources with qualified, knowledgeable personnel. *A full-time director or at least a faculty member with substantial release time, a clearly visible office, and clerical support are absolutely necessary, as are funds for publicity, program development, and travel.* (emphasis added)
- A good public information system to keep the college and community aware of the program and its activities.
- Participation by community advisory and support groups.
- A strong commitment by the president and key academic leaders and interested faculty. (Greenfield 1990, 3)

Role of Administrators

The significance of the role of top-level community college administrators in initiating, promoting, and maintaining IIMEPs is certainly stressed by Dobelle and Mullen in chapter 8. In chapter 7, Burgos-Sasscer and Collins carry this further with their emphasis on the value of administrative exchanges, as well as the expansion of the influence of these administrators as a consequence of career changes. Certainly, having the support of a college president is invaluable in terms of budget allocation, program support, and program development. But perhaps both sets of authors place too much emphasis on the role of the president. She or he can provide leadership, but little will be accomplished unless both *internal* (students, faculty unions, administrators) and *external* (board of trustees, community and local business leaders) consensus is gained and the fact that change in one sector involves change in the others is recognized. The process may require starting with a few committed members in each group (for example, faculty members in key roles) who can help nurture a core group, who patiently encourage faculty development efforts, and who offer collegial leadership within curriculum, fiscal, and governance committees or bodies. Backman (1984) specifically suggests a campuswide committee appointed by the president or by the vice president of academic affairs, with a highly respected faculty member as chair.

With a similar process taking place in other involved constituencies, the college president's interests in international and intercultural/multicultural education can be transformed into effective programs. In the final analysis, while there is no sure prescription for building this consensus, successful examples exist that can serve as models for other institutions. The right model must come to each institution in its own time and as the result of much internal soul-searching, after conflict has been overcome, and after cooperation and commitment have been built. It must be based on the full acceptance of international and intercultural/multicultural programs as central, rather than peripheral, to the mission of the community college.

Nontraditional Study Abroad

Since 1981, the National Association of Foreign Student Affairs (NAFSA) has had a clear set of guidelines to assure the academic viability of study-abroad programs. Although there is general agreement that such programs provide an invaluable means of learning a foreign language and understanding another culture, Narimatsu and Franco (chapter 6) have provided a model for programs that can go far beyond this traditional interpretation. Such a model can include revitalization of a culture and an impetus for reform (social, political, educational, or a combination of the three). Its contribution to rediscovering and reaffirming one's heritage, to self-exploration, and to self-discovery has clear implications for the agenda of both internationalists and interculturalists/multiculturalists. Spofford (1990) points out, however, that such programs require more sophisticated recruitment, student selection, and orientation than have been utilized for traditional study-abroad programs—a difficult prospect in an age of shrinking resources.

Transfer of the U.S. Model

According to Yamano and Hawkins (chapter 11), transfer of the American community college model abroad appears to involve one of four configurations:

1. Adoption of the institutional, political, and economic patterns of the lender;
2. A totally exploitative relationship between lending and borrowing institutions in a dominant-subordinate environment;
3. Complete autonomy of the borrowing nation, leading to a measure of self-reliance and independence;
4. Reciprocity and cooperative participation between lending and borrowing institutions, with mutual benefit accruing to each.

Japan provides an example of the problematic outcomes of creating a college for profit without a full understanding of local culture. Even the terminology for the community college model depicts this lack of understanding. The term *komyuniti kareji* is a transliteration of the English term *community college*, yet the more usable term *tanki daigaku* (junior college) does not depict the community college model in its entirety. Despite the rationale that (primarily male) students were being prepared for transfer to U.S. four-year institutions, these programs failed when they maintained a totally American character. Transference of the U.S. model (based on the philosophy of access and equality) was distorted into a two-tier, gender-segregated system and provides an example of unsuccessful transfer.

Descriptive chapters by Iram (chapter 13) and the team of Elmallah, Gezi, and Soliman (chapter 12) provide examples of the transfer of the American model to the Middle East, in particular, to Israel and Egypt. In contrast to Japan, Israel provides an example of the successful implementation of the *michlalot ezoriyot*, the community (or regional) college based on a combination of the U.S. "multipurpose," the European "specialized," and the British "binary" models. As in the United States, the michlalot ezoriyot is the greatest provider of some form of higher education to subordinate groups in society, although the participation rate of ethnic and racial minorities is still low and the attrition rate of these minorities is high in relation to their representation in the general population. Israel is still struggling with the transition from "elite" to "mass" higher education. This has been, and continues to be, a divisive issue in both Western industrialized, as well as emerging developing, nations.

Egypt provides an example where partial and sensitive transfer of the U.S. model *may* work in the form of the *ma'ahad* (community college). The authors makes some specific recommendations based on the U.S. model, including:

- Development of a master plan for higher education, coordinating the missions of the university, the higher ma'ahad, and the two-year (community college) ma'ahad and providing for articulation and collaboration;
- Building of closer relationships with business and community agencies;
- Adoption of the U.S. concept of open access for all students, in the effort to democratize education.

Yet they point out that certain aspects of the U.S. model (such as the concept of local control; the emphasis on experimentation, innovation, and nontraditional offerings; the valuing of faculty research; and the relatively generous allocation of resources) will not transfer successfully.

In chapter 14, Zuma traces the development of a South African community college system, arguing that the South African heritage can be retained while the U.S. community college model is adapted to meet local needs and provide empowerment in the community environment. Issues of equity, productivity, and illiteracy will need to be addressed. Conceptual partnerships between South African and U.S. colleagues and institutions (including the term *community college* itself), are seen as the key to long-term educational and even societal stability as South Africa adapts to the radical changes brought by the end of apartheid. In chapter 10, van der Linde compares the success of U.S., Canadian, and Malaysian institutions with that of South African institutions in the provision of constructive training for employment and life skills. Again, the emphasis is on conceptual partnership between developed and developing countries' community college models.

As Raby points out in the introduction to part II, however, "the ideal that relaxed requirements and equitable access lead to academic or vocational opportunities and that education at a community college provides the foundation for economic or political reform is dubious at best." The world recession has brought with it the privatization of community colleges, increased tuition, or both, thus altering the accessibility ideal. As pressure has mounted for international and multicultural efforts to be somewhat self-supporting, many community colleges have become involved in exporting their model and utilizing the resources thus gained for such purposes. Raby discusses the problems that arise from this process on the financial, academic, and philosophical levels. This leads us to consideration of the first of the nonconsensual issues discussed by several authors and from varying perspectives.

PART II: CONTROVERSIAL CONCEPTS

The chapters in this publication illuminate several debates current in the field of community college international, intercultural, and multicultural education. These debates range from the purpose of international development—and hence, the direction U.S. community colleges should take in this direction—to the definitional components regarding the terms *international, intercultural,* and *multicultural* and their application.

Impetus for Transfer and Development Projects

There appears to be general agreement that the approach to the transfer of the community college model, as well as to international development activities undertaken by a given community college, is determined by whether the impetus is financial, cultural, or ethical. Harris (chapter 9) views the exporting of American community college models to non-Western societies as an extreme form of neocolonialism. Such export is inevitably accompanied by Western cultural, linguistic, and moral codes, which may not coincide with those of the receiving country and may stifle their attempts at maintaining their own cultural, linguistic, and moral identity and autonomy. The educational needs of developing countries (reaching women, rural populations, groups underrepresented in higher education, and groups of new immigrants and the "new majority" in urban areas) and the anxiety about becoming involved in technology transfers all point to the community college as one means of providing education for those who otherwise could not obtain it. Contrasting the "technological mind" with "traditional wisdom," she decries the pursuit of the former to the detriment or exclusion of the latter.

Development Concerns

Harris provides an illuminating discussion of the "development" model, which reached its zenith in the 1960s and 1970s and was funded by such agencies as U.S. AID (Agency for International Development). Such programs often view tradition as the antithesis of modernization and development, the road to which is defined by the Western country or institution offering assistance through agricultural or technological projects as well as through introduction of the community college model. Critics point to an agenda other than the strictly humanitarian one, to the arrogant furthering of a dependency model, and to the lack of attention to creating alternative models that would be more appropriate to the needs of poorer countries.

In chapter 2, Cook describes ongoing projects at Sinclair Community College based on international community service experience. Their emphasis is on self-help projects to improve the quality of life and promote educational reform. Although Cook and her colleagues obviously believe strongly in their humanitarian approach, in the current climate of criticism of Western-dominated development projects and the current era of fiscal constraints this model is increasingly difficult to promote.

Canadian institutions, funded by such agencies as the Canadian International Development Agency (CIDA), have long been in the forefront of implementing, consulting for, and monitoring development projects. In chapter 3, Schugurensky and Higgins claim that this paradigm is being replaced by a global marketplace paradigm. The emphasis has changed from providing assistance in areas such as education and health (as at Sinclair College) to promotion of trade (as at Grant MacEwan College). The clientele has therefore also changed from the less developed countries to those in the Pacific Rim and Eastern Europe, and will probably soon expand to include the enlarging South and Central American membership of the North American Free Trade Alliance (NAFTA). The funding source has also changed from government agencies such as CIDA to the generation of sources of revenue through cost-recovery projects by international education offices. This privatization model, based on an entrepreneurial mentality, is changing from a college-driven to an industry-driven model. The concept that profit encourages international activities appears to be realistic now and for the future both in Canada and in the United States with its Republican-controlled Congress. After years of expansion, contraction and cutbacks will lead to downsizing and greater selectivity. Whether development efforts are based on humanitarian or entrepreneurial objectives, there is certainly a need to consider whether they are a form of neocolonialism that can result in heightened conflict and loss of autonomy.

Multicultural or Intercultural Education

In chapter 4, Story points out that programs offered under the umbrella of "multicultural education" range from marginalized activities to comparative studies of various cultures and, at a greater extreme, the consideration of issues leading to the empowerment of subgroups and the promotion of social change and reform. She states that the level of sophistication of an institution's interpretation of multicultural education is dependent on the organizational leadership of the administration, the cultural environment of the faculty, and the "voice of the local community." More important, any assessment of the success or failure of multicultural education is obviously hampered by the lack of consensus on its definition.

The distinction between multicultural and intercultural arrived at by the Council of Europe (Rey 1992) would be most helpful here. After many years of developing programs across national borders to deal with linguistic and cultural, immigrant and indigenous minorities, the council limits the use of the word *multicultural* to the description of a situation. Thus, a heterogeneous or pluralistic society can be described as multicultural. However, in terms of *processes* or *programs* designed to deal with a multicultural society, the council prefers the term *intercultural*, implying *interaction* between dominant and subordinate groups, where both groups make concessions and the resultant change occurs in both, not just in the subordinate group. The intercultural dialectic acknowledges the need to address inequities, which multicultural education may, but does not necessarily, address. While the multicultural dialectic may choose to limit itself to "safe topics" such as cultural heroes and holidays, the intercultural approach *must* deal with issues (such as stereotyping, prejudice, discrimination, racism, segregation, slavery, immigration, and equal opportunity) affecting social interaction and justice. Such an approach clearly has implications for the empowerment of subordinate groups and for social policy and change. Such an approach would not content itself with "multicultural" food or dance festivals but would infuse these social (and political/economic) issues into all aspects of academic and campus life. Such an approach is clearly appropriate not just for the American community college, not just for American education in general, but also for multicultural societies and community colleges dealing with similar issues all over the world.

Rhetoric and Reality

The dichotomy between ideals and the reality of implementation pervades both multicultural/intercultural and international education efforts. In chapter 1, Raby, noting that community colleges have been involved in internationalizing efforts for over twenty years, proffers several hypotheses to account for their limited success. In terms of fostering intercultural learning and activities, there seems to be general agreement that community colleges are in a unique position. They are more flexible and open to change than are four-year colleges and universities, serve a larger proportion of minority students, and serve increasing numbers of foreign students. For those in terminal programs, the community college represents the last chance for formal education to make an impact. For those transferring to four-year colleges, their community college experiences may represent the last opportunity to have diversified courses and experiences before entering into their concentration or fields of study. The community college is more responsive to local control, to local issues, to its responsibility in the building of community, and to empowering its students to be competitive in the global economy.

Yet community colleges lag behind the four-year colleges in implementing international and multicultural requirements. As they move in this direction, will they follow the lead of the four-year universities in focusing, in Story's words, "on global multiculturalism rather than on domestic diversity"? Obviously the former is easier and safer to carry off. It is much more comfortable to concern oneself with starving children in Africa than with those on the streets of American cities. As conservative forces edge out liberal voices, will there be funding for faculty development, for multidimensional student support services, for curriculum innovation? Can the community college's programs rise above "political correctness" by celebrating *diversity* as well as *unity* and by emphasizing commonalities and interdependency between "American" and "other" cultures and between American and global issues? Will there be a move towards the development of national standards or guidelines for community colleges (such as those NCATE [National Credential Association for Teachers in Education] has effectively implemented, requiring all accredited teacher-training programs to include a strong multicultural dimension)? Will community colleges content themselves with marginalized multicultural activities or "add-ons" or infuse *inter*cultural and international perspectives into all aspects of college life? Will they be satisfied with programs to strengthen racial or ethnic identity or move on to those that improve community relations; fill voids in cultural and international knowledge; help people relate to other cultures; support interracial, interethnic, and international agendas and issues; and cooperate with universities to develop future community college faculty representing all segments of society and committed to a democratic, pluralistic society? Will community and business leaders, faculty, students, and boards of trustees prioritize intercultural and international education and activities in their policy and mission statements and then back up the policy with the resources and effort needed to assure that the rhetoric of such statements is carried out in course syllabi, library holdings, student services, new programs, and admissions and hiring procedures?

Multicultural vs. International Education

It frequently appears that supporters of multicultural/intercultural education line up on one side while those committed to international education line up on the other side of the college campus. Each views the other as a threat and, more important, a competitor in the struggle to corner increasingly scarce resources. Often they do not recognize the extent of their common goals and their need to cooperate in convincing those who control the purse strings of the priority of those goals in societies where minorities are becoming the "new majority" and where increasingly restrictive immigration policies, narrow political agendas, ethnocentrism, and racial and ethnic violence are coming to the fore. Enrollment of foreign students—once recognized as having a major positive economic impact on the community, contributing to the strengthening of international ties, providing diverse viewpoints that benefited the typical American close-to-home community college student, and often educating students who would subsequently rise to influential positions in their own countries—is now subject to intense criticism and scrutiny. One has to look not only at policies such as California's recently adopted Proposition 187 but also at similar policies in the United Kingdom, France, and Spain to realize the international implications of multiculturalism, to fully understand how international programs and intercultural/multicultural programs should blend into what we have termed IIMEPs.

On a positive note, Broward Community College in Florida is among the first to recognize the symbiotic relationship between international and multicultural/intercultural education and has mandated an "international/intercultural general education requirement for all Associate of Arts degree students." Courses certified as meeting this requirement meet one of three goals:

1. A fundamental understanding of the key elements of global and national interdependence;
2. A deeper knowledge and understanding of other cultures;
3. General competency in a second language as a basis for the fuller comprehension of other cultures and of one's own culture in the global context.

Institutional Obstacles to IIMEP

Obviously, unanimous consensus on the value of IIMEPs does not exist. Five major obstacles to the development and implementation of such programs were described and analyzed by Backman (1984):

1. Lack of institutional commitment from top administrators;
2. Faculty opposition;
3. Lack of attention to IIMEPs in the institutional mission statement;
4. Current institutional structure (new programs seen as a threat);

5. Inadequate funding.

Both Backman (1984) and Greenfield (1990) suggest means of dealing with these obstacles that are equally valid for supporters of any innovation, in any era, and at any type of academic institution. At the four-year university with which I have been affiliated, effective approaches have included:

- Enlightening of administrators;
- Commitment to IIMEPs as an important criterion in the selection process for new administrators and faculty;
- Campuswide faculty committees, under the leadership of highly respected colleagues;
- Incentives for course revision;
- Travel funds for faculty and administrators;
- Faculty exchange programs;
- Cooperative development of mission statements at the level of individual schools and in the university as a whole;
- Curriculum efforts involving the creation of interdisciplinary courses and programs;
- Support for grant writing;
- Utilization of discretionary funds by deans or the academic vice president, to serve as seed money for new projects;
- Involvement in broad-based regional consortia with two-year and four-year institutions.

Raby's California case study of international programs and Story's comparative examples of multicultural programs further highlight ways of overcoming negative forces (such as natural resistance to change, ethnocentrism, and competition for scarce resources) hindering development, to define IIMEPs and the symbiotic relationship between multicultural and international education comprehensively, and to make IIMEPs part of the mission statement of colleges at the campus, district, state, national, and international level.

PART III: CONCLUSIONS

As you, the reader, approach this varied volume, it might be helpful to consider that three rubrics cut through both the international and multicultural/intercultural programs at U.S. community colleges and programs based on transfer of the U.S. community college model abroad:

1. *Economic*. Without sufficient finances, programs, and activities, colleges

cannot be built nor sustained. In keeping with today's emphasis on international business, trade agreements, technological transfers, etc., community colleges and their programs need to be entrepreneurial, drawing on different funding sources and serving a different clientele from that in the past. Community colleges are definitely an export item, but will have to be creative in locating and using resources for this purpose.

2. *Cultural.* In both developing and industrialized countries, there is a strong interest in U.S. community colleges. The philosophy behind community colleges is sound and their ideals (democracy, access, equality) are valid as long as respect for local culture is prioritized. If this is the case, the consequences can only benefit society in terms of increased education, training, and intercultural and international literacy based on active and participatory program planning and learning. There is certainly increased sensitivity to avoiding the creation of neocolonial dependency models!

3. *Ethical.* There is concern, on the part of some, about U.S. colleges doing international development for "business" reasons. This is definitely the trend of the future. Community colleges and their development projects are an export item, and often, the resources gained from such programs are the major source of funding of IIMEPs on community college campuses.

Change has been slow, but more and more, based on a variety of motivations, colleges are acknowledging the need and supporting the change. More colleges belong to interinstitutional international consortia, have internationalized aspects of their curriculum, and have expanded intercultural, multicultural, and international programs in the United States and throughout the world. True, they do not guarantee social reform and may lose their attraction, but by then, large numbers of young people will have been influenced by, and will continue to influence others with, an international and intercultural/multicultural perspective.

As we close this introduction, we note with some optimism, in the second half of the 1990s, the policy statement of the community college previously cited for its unique approach of combining international intercultural/multicultural education efforts, which is a model emulated by many others:

> Broward Community College recognizes the importance of providing for students an international and intercultural dimension. As citizens of the United States and as inhabitants of planet Earth, today's students will be confronted throughout their lives with issues that transcend national boundaries. So interconnected is the political and

economic world that some understanding of current issues and the events that shape them, as well as an appreciation for other cultures and customs throughout the world, is now basic to good citizenship. This has become an essential aspect of today's curriculum. It is further recognized that community colleges have a major responsibility in providing an international/intercultural dimension because of the increasing numbers of students for whom the community college will provide their only college-level educational experience. Moreover, the nature of the community college, and its emphasis on serving a local constituency, requires that the global agenda be addressed. (Broward Community College 1991, 9, quoted in King and Fersh 1992, 28)

NOTES

1. Brackets added.

REFERENCES

Backman, E.L. "Internationalizing the Campus: A Strategy for the 1980s." In E.L. Backman (ed.), *Approaches to International Education.* New York: Macmillan, 1984.

Boyer, E.L. "Keynote Speech at the Annual AACJC Convention." *Community and Junior College Journal* 49, no. 6 (1979): 14–19.

Commission on the Future of Community Colleges. *Building Communities for a New Century.* Washington, D.C.: American Association of Community and Junior Colleges, 1988.

Fersh, S.H. "Adding an International Dimension to the Community College: Examples and Implication." In R.K. Greenfield (ed.), *Developing International Education Programs.* New Directions for Community Colleges Series No. 70. San Francisco: Jossey-Bass, 1990.

Greenfield, Richard K. (ed.). *Developing International Education Programs.* New Directions for Community Colleges Series No. 70. San Francisco: Jossey-Bass, 1990).

King, Maxwell C., and Seymour H. Fersh. *Integrating the International/Intercultural Dimension in the Community College.* Washington, D.C.: Association of Community College Trustees, Community Colleges for International Development, 1992.

Rey, Madaline. "Council for Cultural Cooperation Report." Council of Europe, 1992.

Spofford, W.K. "The Effective Development of Nontraditional Study-Abroad Programs." In R.K. Greenfield (ed.), *Developing International Education Programs.* New Directions for Community Colleges Series No. 70. San Francisco: Jossey-Bass, 1990.

Part I
Dimensions of U.S. and Canadian Community Colleges

Introduction to Part I

In the last quarter of the twentieth century, an international, intercultural, and multicultural revolution has significantly transformed the technological, political, economic, and social variables that define how countries interact. There is thus a recognized need for establishing an internationally, interculturally/multiculturally literate generation that can deal with the complexities of our world.

> Our society needs education and understanding about the world as never before because its complexities and interrelationships economically, socially, and politically are even more dramatic and manifest than they were during the Cold War. (McGrath 1993, 112)

Educational institutions, including community colleges, respond to this type of educational reform by creating, implementing, and evaluating policies that highlight international and intercultural/multicultural educational programs (IIMEPs) and disseminate that knowledge throughout the campus and the community. Over the past few decades, these policies have not only have impacted community colleges in the United States but have affected community college variations found abroad.

Post–World War II, traditional four-year universities were criticized for being unable to meet the needs of a changing economy and society. The U.S. community college, in part, evolved, as a "feeder" institution to provide educational opportunities for students (a) who did not fit the "traditional" profile, (b) who lacked a sufficient academic background for entrance to four-year universities, or (c) who could not afford university tuition. The resulting community college countered the notion of higher education as a venture intended for only the few. Contemporary U.S. community colleges are publicly supported institutions that are accredited to award the associate degree as the highest degree. These institutions combine introductory-level academic transfer programs, adult basic educational programs, remedial education, vocational/technical educational programs, and community services (Cohen and Brawer 1982). Since passage of the 1965 Higher Education Act, the number of community colleges has doubled and in 1992 constituted 40 percent of all U.S. institutions of higher education (Adelman 1992).

Frequently, community college IIMEPs are peripheral to the mission of the college and are marginal in the larger educational scheme. However, since 1975, the proliferation of IIMEP efforts has encouraged significant educational reform, nationally as well as worldwide. In community college literature, two distinct yet related disciplines have emerged: international education and intercultural/multicultural education. Among the latter, the two terms *intercultural* and *multicultural* are often used synonymously. In the introduction to this book, Tarrow defines these terms and discusses means by which they can be used in the future. While intercultural/multicultural programs focus on domestic pluralism, international programs emphasize global relationships. Both share the goal of accelerating knowledge about, and encouraging cross-cultural communication that enhances, cultural, ethnic, class, and gender relationships among divergent groups. Both also—either independently or jointly—work to entrench policy in college mission statements, which helps secure implementation of international and intercultural/multicultural literacy skills.

Community college IIMEP efforts are diverse and have been well documented as unique entities in previous publications. The chapters in part I highlight a specific IIMEP, and they help define unique trends pertaining to educational reform. Each chapter provides a theoretical discussion of a specific program supported by a North American community college case study. In the process, variables that account for successful programs—those that underscore elements of failure and those that describe the principal goals and features of that program within the college structure—are presented. Finally, the chapters in part I present both the problems that proponents of international and intercultural/multicultural education face and the options they might select to resolve their difficulties.

Significant patterns connect the chapters in part I. Raby provides general paradigms for historical and theoretical analysis of IIMEPs. One common pattern is the role of community college administrators as significant factors in initiating, promoting, and maintaining IIMEPs. Burgos-Sasscer and Collins, as well as Dobelle and Mullen, define unique aspects of administrators in IIMEPs, for it is the administrator who prompts reform in terms of budget allocation, program support, and program development. Furthermore, it is common for administrators to change colleges in their pursuit of occupational advancement. As such, within a few years, a single administrator can influence many different colleges where she/he works. As Dobelle and Mullen maintain, presidential leadership is the glue for maintaining consensus for IIMEP educational reform. Their case studies of Middlesex College and City College of San Francisco support the important role of presidents in initiating and maintaining the internal and external consensus that is essential for perpetuation of IIMEPs.

A second pattern highlights a single case study that has had a significant impact on other community colleges and may influence other similar programs in the future. Burgos-Sasscer and Collins present the Truman-Sandwell administrative exchange, which sets the precedent for exchanges that go beyond student/faculty boundaries. Since the Truman-Sandwell exchange, several other "administrator exchanges" have occurred in North American community colleges, most of which share commonalities discussed in this chapter. With its novel approach to the promotion of cultural rejuvenation, Narimatsu and Franco's case study redefines traditional study-abroad programs. This chapter may change the raison d'être for community college study-abroad programs. Finally, Cook's case study of international development programs sponsored by Sinclair Community College illustrates that a single college can successfully engage in nonprofit international development programs with some degree of success.

On the surface, many chapters seem to deal with either international or intercultural/multicultural issues. However, another pattern occurs in which the two themes overlap. For example, Narimatsu and Franco discuss revitalization of the rich multicultural heritage of Polynesian students and faculty through an international program; Raby and Story illustrate the balance of these terms in the curriculum and in the overall college; Dobelle and Mullen describe the effects of a multicultural student body and community on international consensus. In part II, this pattern emerges again as Harris depicts intercultural/multicultural misunderstanding as an element of cultural imperialism in international development projects, as van der Linde delineates similar effects for a multicultural society in flux, and as the various case studies portray the effects of a multicultural community on community college models abroad.

The final pattern pairs chapters to demonstrate alternative views of a type of program. The chapter by Burgos-Sasscer and Collins is paired with the one by Narimatsu and Franco because they both illustrate unique byproducts of international and intercultural/multicultural programs. The chapter by Schugurensky and Higgins is paired with that by Cook because they present two conflicting viewpoints pertaining to international development programs as currently used by community colleges. Whereas Higgins and Schugurensky advocate a change from a humanist to a privatization model, Cook advocates the humanist perspective in light of changing economic world connections. The two chapters provide different theoretical perspectives for a similar type of activity. There are also interesting ties between these chapters and the Dobelle and Mullen chapter, which illustrates how both the privatization and humanist perspectives are needed to ensure a building of consensus for IIMEPs. Story (chapter 4) and Raby (chapter 5) present a comparative review of multicultural and international programs, respectively. Both identify variables necessary for successful programs, and both chapters define the dichotomy between the ideals of these programs and the reality of implementing these ideals. Finally, the opening chapter by Raby and the closing chapter by Dobelle and Mullen identify elements that support successful IIMEPs. While Raby emphasizes a holistic approach, Dobelle and Mullen concentrate on the role of a single player, the president/chancellor.

Map 1 identifies the locations within North America of the case studies discussed in Part I. Map 2 identifies the regions of the world that have a connection with these case studies.

REFERENCES

Adelman, C. *The Way We Are: The Community College as American Thermometer.* U.S. Department of Education. Washington, D.C.: U.S. Government Printing Office, 1992.

Cohen, A.M., and F.B. Brawer. *The American Community College.* San Francisco: Jossey-Bass, 1982.

McGrath, C. Peter. *An American Imperative.* New York: The Johnson Foundation, 1993. Cited by Frederick C. Kintzer in "Higher Education Approaches the 21st Century: New Perspectives on Nonuniversities," speech presented at Nova Southeastern University, August 1994.

MAP 1. Locations of Case Studies Discussed in Part I

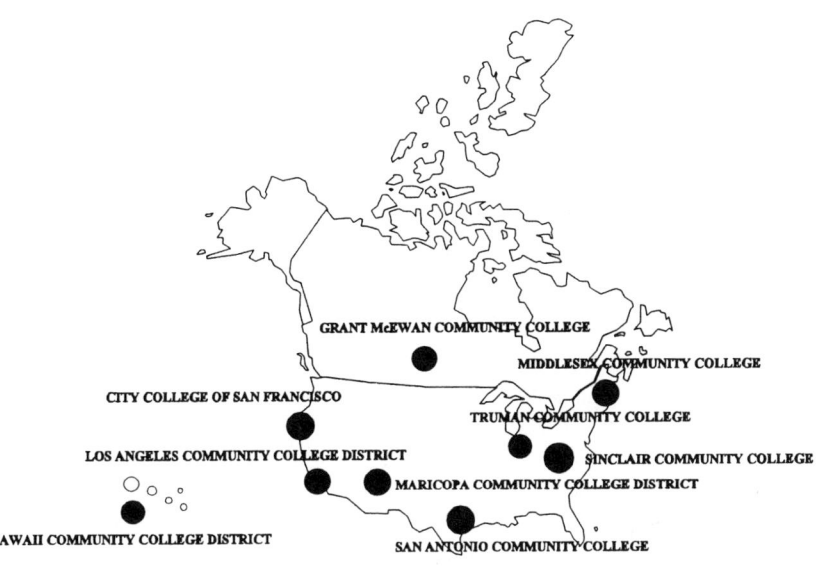

MAP 2. Regions of the World Related to Part I Case Studies

1 International, Intercultural, and Multicultural Dimensions of Community Colleges in the United States

Rosalind Latiner Raby

INTERNATIONAL, INTERCULTURAL, AND MULTICULTURAL EDUCATIONAL PROGRAMS
An array of socioeconomic, political, and technological revolutions underscores the twentieth century, a period of tremendous fluctuation and change. The international, intercultural, and multicultural revolution has transformed global relationships profoundly by merging issues with theories, strategies with policies, and economies with politics. Reverberating down from this revolution is the critical need to cultivate adults who are internationally, interculturally, and multiculturally competent to deal with the new complexities of our world. An international, intercultural, and multicultural literacy is contingent upon the ability to reconcile conflicting ideologies by understanding multiple perspectives and by respecting relative differences.

Economic, political, technological, environmental, and sociocultural ties forge relationships that are outside national control. It is precisely these relationships that U.S. institutions of higher education, including community colleges, recognize as important educational components. Two-year community (and former junior) colleges provide personalized instruction in liberal arts, science, and technology and also offer extracurricular activities. Technical colleges specialize in vocational education that prepares students for midlevel technical employment. U.S. community colleges educate students to participate in the modern work force, provide in-service training (and retraining), prepare students to transfer to a four-year college or university to complete a bachelor's degree, and grant short-cycle certificates and the two-year associate-of-arts degree. Community colleges accentuate personal improvement despite educational background, age, or socioeconomic status. All students over age 17 are eligible to enroll, which allows the student population to mirror the multicultural and multiethnic mixture of the local community.

In 1994 over 1,200 American community colleges enrolled 43 percent of all higher education students and served 51 percent of all noncredit adult and continuing education students. In addition, 51 percent of all domestic students and 25 percent of all international students at four-year colleges were transfer students from community colleges. The ERIC Clearinghouse for Community Colleges maintains that nationally over the past five years, a consistent 23–24 percent of community college students transfer to four-year universities (Cohen 1993). In 1993 50 percent of California State University and 20 percent of University of California bachelor's degree recipients were community college transfers. Nationally in 1992, 6 million students enrolled in credit courses and 4 million in noncredit, continuing education courses (California Postsecondary Education Committee 1992).

Despite the complete general education offered at community colleges, there remains a critical need for international, intercultural, and multicultural courses and experiences. This is true for transfer as well as for nontransfer students. For transfer students, there is no guarantee that their upper-division courses will have an international, intercultural, or multicultural focus, and therefore, for both transfer and nontransfer students, their introduction to these fields will be obtained at the community college.

In 1984 the Commission on International Education of the American Council on Education reported that "international education programs are no longer optional for community colleges, they have become integral" (King and Fersh 1983). These words were reiterated by the Commission on the Future of Community Colleges in their report "Building Communities: A Vision for a New Century" (1988) and in a report given at the November 1994 American Council on International Intercultural Education/Stanley Foundation Leadership Retreat and titled "Building the Global Community: The Next Step" (Elsner, Tsunoda, and Korbel 1994). Indeed, the sentiment involved remains irrefutable today, especially in light of the culturally pluralistic and internationally dependent society in which we live.

Community college international and intercultural/multicultural education programs (IIMEPs) mirror program components found in four-year universities, including differentiation between (a) inter/multicultural[1] and (b) international programs. These two components are often placed under the rubric of global education even though they may take separate but not necessarily conflicting directions. In community college literature, including the recent "Building the Global Community: The Next Step," a draft policy that seeks to define the direction and implementation of strategies for community college IIMEPs, the terms *intercultural* and *multicultural* are used synonymously (Elsner, Tsunoda, and Korbel 1994). Throughout this book, the terms will also be used interchangeably, but a detailed discussion of their profound differences is found in Tarrow's introduction to this book.

In community colleges, inter/multicultural education advances bilingual education, ethnic studies, and foreign language programs. International education fosters study abroad, faculty exchange, international students, international development, and internationalization of the curriculum programs. Inter/multicultural programs stress the interaction of many cultures within a domestic setting, with the educational focus on pluralism at the microlevel. International programs accent the interaction of different cultures on a global scale, with the educational focus on pluralism at the macrolevel. Despite rivalry in political and budget power struggles, both programs have begun to discern conceptual similarities and appreciate one another's theoretical differences. Collaboration encourages innovative attempts to promote a single agenda harmoniously, and "it has become abundantly clear that our domestic well-being is linked inextricably to the new world conditions" (ACE 1993, 1; Smithee 1991).

Since the mid-1980s, U.S. IIMEPs have been fueled by a changing college environment that reflects a permanent multicultural society. In particular, IIMEPs support the (a) induction of refugees or immigrants who require language services, (b) transformation of the community into an international frontier that demands special skills, and (c) servicing of a multicultural population that possesses varying interests. Many community colleges convey a strong commitment to international and inter/multicultural education based on the premise that such education is itself valid. Scanlon (1990) and King and Fersh (1992) define three main rationales for why community colleges promote IIMEPs. First, the political rationale born during the cold war and sustained in the post–cold-war era perceives IIMEPs as a pragmatic tool for national security. Second, since the late 1980s and the end of the cold war, the economic rationale recognizes IIMEPs as a means to promote international trade and, hence, as a requirement to ensure a competitive edge in the world market economy. Finally, throughout the decades, the humanist rationale promotes IIMEPs as a process for understanding other languages and cultures, which eventually contributes toward the building of tolerance and peace. While these rationales differ in emphasis, they all highlight the importance of IIMEPs as a critical part of the American community college experience.

Regardless of intent or rationale, and despite an almost inbred provincialism, IIMEPs continue to make tremendous strides in American community colleges (Elsner, Tsunoda, and Korbel 1994). Growth is encouraged out of concerns that students are unable to deal with various contemporary global agendas, as well as from conditions mandating that colleges educate internationally and inter/multiculturally competent citizens. Revisions of community college policy and mission statements support IIMEPs as a means for preparing students for their future political, economic, and moral roles in society. Nonetheless, there is more rhetoric about than implementation of these programs, and the incongruence of this is explored in subsequent chapters of this book.

Profile of International and Multicultural Education Programs

Community colleges in the United States sponsor several types of IIMEPs, many of which are found at four-year institutions and some of which are elaborated upon in subsequent chapters in this book. Some IIMEPs highlight classroom instruction, others emphasize off-campus programs, while still others employ a combination of different types of pedagogy. In 1991 the American Council on International/Intercultural Education (ACIIE) defined international and multicultural education as follows:

> (a) *international education*: the teaching of students and the community about other countries including culture, language, political and social systems, the economic interdependence of countries and how the importance of having this awareness through teaching causes better understanding about our own country and the similarities and differences with others;
>
> (b) *multicultural education*: the greater understanding of other cultures, the recognition, acceptance and understanding of the multicultural diversity within the American culture. In practice it involves course work, seminars, personnel training and community service activities designed to heighten awareness of this diversity. (ACIIE 1991, 7)

The combination of the two "form the seamless web that many refer to as global," with international education "engag[ing] Americans in contact with individuals and institutions outside our borders" and intercultural (multicultural) education "focus[ing] on undertakings which deal with the rich diversity of cultures within the U.S." (Elsner, Tsunoda, and Korbel 1994, 2). There are a variety of IIMEPs offered at community colleges, the most popular of which are defined below.

FACULTY/STAFF EXCHANGE PROGRAMS

Faculty and short-term administrative exchanges are the direct transfer of positions between faculty members or administrators from a U.S. institution and those from an overseas institution. Beyond the mere transfer of positions, these exchanges provide a framework for academic, personal, and cultural experiences. Students benefit by having the opportunity to study with a foreign educator. When families are involved, a total life experience is felt. The actual number of annual community college participants is small, but the effect is substantial when they return to their classrooms and their campuses. Fulbright Faculty Exchanges and Scholar-in-Residence awards help accommodate some of the financial needs required by exchanges.

INTERNATIONAL STUDENTS PROGRAMS

International students are germane to the community college mission, since they provide an academic and a cultural richness not found elsewhere. The presence of international students alters domestic students' perceptions and understanding of a world society, serves as a human resource in both class discussions and student activities, and becomes the basis for friendships that often filter into future social, political, and economic relationships. International students take courses that will enhance their careers, business, or transfer education, and the enrollment levels in many of these courses are low for the college in general. In addition, international student nonresident tuition is particularly attractive during times of fiscal difficulty and becomes an occasional form of export education. The importance attributed to international students by individual campuses correlates with the numbers enrolled, which range from a few dozen to over 1,000. In 1993 U.S. community colleges enrolled over 60,000 international students (Zikopoulos 1993).

STUDENT STUDY-ABROAD PROGRAMS

Study-abroad programs encourage development of international and inter/multicultural understanding through participant observation. These short-term summer or semester-length college-credit classes in foreign locations usually concentrate on foreign language instruction as well as on humanities, arts, social sciences, natural history, and occupational fields. These programs are distinct from study tours in that they have a university-accredited curriculum, provide funding for the community college, and are academic in content. In keeping with the community college "open door" philosophy, study-abroad programs include all ages, aptitudes, and backgrounds and do not sacrifice academic standards. Several studies confirm that students (especially minority students) who participate in study-abroad programs exhibit definite changes in perception and attitude towards global relationships and demonstrate increased levels of political concern and that many claim this educational venture to be the most dramatic of their life

(Carew 1993). Faculty and student support of study abroad often becomes the foundation of a college's international efforts.

INTERNATIONAL CURRICULUM PROGRAMS

Community colleges continue to broaden the international and inter/multicultural perspectives of staff and students by introducing international and inter/multicultural elements into classes, programs, and majors. The accentuation of foreign language and area studies programs exemplifies this direction. All disciplines (academic as well as technical) not only can, but should, include international and multicultural perspectives and themes. Curricular modifications assist staff and students to transcend their own cultural conditioning and to become more knowledgeable about and sensitive to other cultures. Professional development activities further promote creation of new modules, classes, and programs as well as introduce innovative teaching methodologies in the classroom. The ultimate internationalized curriculum includes certificate and A.A. degree programs in international studies, multicultural studies, international business, and the like.

INTERNATIONAL DEVELOPMENT PROGRAMS

International development programs include bilateral agreements that provide technical, language, and knowledge transfers to other countries. International relationships are often initiated by delegations that visit American community colleges to learn about the inner workings of the college. Together, U.S. colleges and those from abroad design and implement curriculum reform. The emphasis is primarily on technical, vocational, or occupational assistance that encourages midlevel manpower training in foreign institutes. Development programs support IIMEPs on-campus through staff development and exchanges. One variation of the international development program, the Foreign Contract Education Program, enables foreign nationals to complete American accredited college courses in their home country. Although prevalent at the university level, these ventures are relatively new to community colleges. In general, development programs allow community colleges to formulate new initiatives and programs that train professionals and nonacademics to carry out future political, economic and social transformations.

INTER/MULTICULTURAL STUDIES AND RELATED PROGRAMS

Inter/multicultural education includes new courses in interculturalism, multiculturalism and ethnic studies, bilingual, ESL (for international students and recent immigrants), and foreign language programs that explore pluralistic relationships through examination of ethnic, religious, racial, and gender issues. Inter/multicultural education increases cross-cultural sensitivity within one's own community, preserves minority identities and highlights the inter/multicultural diversity that exists within the American culture across time and space. A national average of American community colleges indicates that 22 percent of all students are minorities: 10 percent are African Americans, 7 percent are Hispanic, 4 percent are Asian Americans, and 1 percent are Native Americans (King and Fersh 1992, 31). Diversifying the curriculum and hiring minority administrators and faculty are an integral part of inter/multicultural programs. In light of recent global ethnic unrest, new educational policies now contain explicit inter/multicultural educational components.

INTERNATIONAL RELATIONS, PARTNERSHIPS, AND SERVICES

International relations and services support consortia membership and community organizations. National consortia include the ACIIE, the National Association for Foreign Student Affairs (NAFSA), the Institute of International Education (IIE), the College Consortium for International Studies (CCIS), and Community Colleges for International Development (CCID). Colleges maintain relationships with local chapters of the World Affairs Council, the World Trade Association, Sister Cities International, City Councils for International Visitors, and Rotary International. Ties with local businesses serve as the foundation of many of these programs.

Historical Framework

Institutionalization of IIMEPs in U.S. universities began after World War II in the form of study-abroad and area studies programs. Repercussions from the launching of Sputnik, the Vietnam War, popularization of the Peace Corps, and heightened ethnic movements profoundly raised American consciousness of world affairs. As four-year university IIMEPs evolved, community college developments were negligible. Both the embryonic state of the community college system and the philosophy that these colleges were not appropriate mechanisms for IIMEPs impeded development. Hess (1982) claims that prior to 1967 no American community college had established IIMEPs, yet by 1992, the majority had procured at least some IIMEP connections (Greenfield 1990; King and Fersh 1992). The process of transforming IIMEPs from negligible to integral parts of American community colleges consisted of four phases (see figure 1).

By 1977, IIMEPs were fully recognized as important components of community colleges (Shannon 1978). The American Association of Community Colleges (AACC) established an International/Intercultural Committee (IIC) with sixty-five initial members, whose board of directors fully supported international and inter/multicultural programs. Recognition came in 1978, when the U.S. Commissioner of Education report stated that "community colleges should lead the way in rebuilding our commitment to international education" (Boyer 1979, 14).

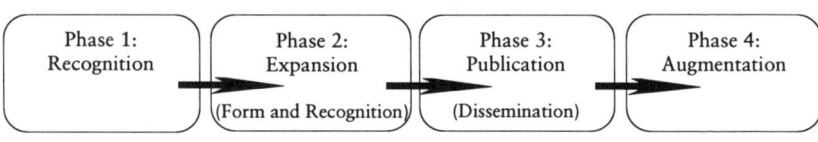

FIGURE 1. Four Phases of Community College IIMEP Development

PHASE 1: RECOGNITION

The first phase of development was when community colleges were characterized as plausible receptacles for IIMEPs. The negative stereotype that IIMEPs were superfluous to community colleges was countered by the reality that colleges (a) served an increasingly international and multicultural community, (b) taught employable skills for entry into a job market whose global context has changed dramatically, and (c) provided students with increased understanding and sensitivity on issues of local, national, and international importance. In 1971 the AACC established an office for IIMEPs, and despite adversities, IIMEPs solidified as a facet of the community college.[2]

The recognition of community colleges as recipients of federal grant programs allowed for lucrative support and validation for IIMEPs in community colleges. In 1972 the U.S. Office of Education's Institute of International Studies awarded its first Group Project Abroad Grant to a community college. The inclusion of section 603 in the Title VI National Defense Education Act also acknowledged community colleges. By 1976 over a dozen colleges received federal funding to pioneer a structure for community college IIMEPs (Fersh and Greene 1984). By 1994 the U.S. Information Agency and the Bureau of Educational and Cultural Affairs provided numerous educational programs intended for community colleges (Koltai 1993).

Full recognition, however, did not materialize until IIMEPs were actually implemented at community colleges. This implementation directly confronted the traditional premise that IIMEPs were the sole realm of the university. In 1969 Rockland Community College opened an office coordinating study-abroad programs, the success of which inspired other colleges to pursue similar options. By 1973 the tristate consortium CCIS pioneered cooperative study-abroad efforts and subsequently expanded nationwide to allow broader numbers of students to benefit from study abroad.[3] Rockland and Brevard community colleges implemented an internationalized curriculum by expanding language and civilization courses and by incorporating them into study-abroad courses. A parallel growth in multicultural education resulted in the establishment of ethnic studies and bilingual education departments and majors nationwide. International development programs materialized in 1973 but were not fully recognized until 1976, when CCID was formed. Finally, two surveys (1974, 1977) identified and highlighted the benefits of having international students at community colleges. A formal liaison between NAFSA and the AACC subsequently focused efforts on supporting this relationship (Diener and Kerr 1979).

PHASE 2: EXPANSION

The second phase of development involved expanding interest in and adoption of IIMEPs nationwide. Shannon's 1977 survey of 1,200 community colleges indicates that 300 (25 percent) made some commitment to international and inter/multicultural education. The increased availability of federal, state, and private corporation grants further advanced existing IIMEPs. Whether their observations were real or perceived, national publications concluded that by the end of the 1980s, many community colleges were involved in one or more facets of IIMEPs (Commission on the Future of Community Colleges 1988). By 1990 all community colleges of the League for Innovation Institutions had extensive and well-established IIMEPs (Patterson 1990).

Expansion transpired on various levels beginning with the establishment of on-campus committees and international education offices, some with full-time directors. Support networks enabled colleges to expand study-abroad programs, departmentalize multicultural programs, and adopt non-Western perspectives in civilization, history, and literature classes. El Paso Community College was one of the first to institutionalize bilingual and multicultural opportunities. Finally, state and regional consortia emerged as a support network for initiating or expanding IIMEPs.[4]

Several national publications accentuated and thereby validated the pivotal role IIMEPs played in community colleges. In 1978 the U.S. Commissioner of Education stressed the community college as a leader in "rebuilding our commitment to international education" (Boyer 1979, 14). The 1979 report "Strength through Wisdom: A Critique of U.S. Capability" identified IIMEPs as important prerequisites for national security, noting the potential of community colleges to introduce large numbers of adults to world cultures. Warnings were made that without IIMEPs, international incompetency would increase and would endanger America's future. The report recommended that community colleges "have a central role [to] enlarge their international commitment and engage in the staff development necessary to strengthen their contribution to foreign language and area studies" (Perkins 1979, 1–2, 75, 161). In *Expanding the International Dimension of Higher Education* Burn specifically included community colleges as a significant player in promoting IIMEPs (Burn 1980, 23). She noted that over 50 percent of all first-year university students were community college transfer students and that in order for these students to compete effectively in the university setting, their pretransfer preparation should include international and inter/multicultural competency. Both of the abovementioned publications proposed that community colleges establish and maintain quality IIMEPs to prepare students for future roles in society. Despite recommendations for reform, the Council on Learning Report (1981) confirmed that only 5 percent of all undergraduate courses actually stressed international and inter/multicultural concerns.

The 1980 adoption of Concurrent Resolution 601(a) by Congress further supported the increased presence of IIMEPs at community colleges as the study of foreign languages, cultures, and international studies expanded at all levels of education (Fersh and Greene 1984). In 1982 the AACC reconfirmed that "education for international/intercultural understanding has thus become imperative for Americans" (*AACJC IIC Newsletter* 1982, 1–2). In retrospect, the pioneering colleges of the 1970s became role models, in both form and print, for colleges undergoing the tremendous changes that were to take place in the 1980s.

PHASE 3: PUBLICATION

From 1979 to 1989, numerous academic publications defined the role of IIMEPs in community colleges, accentuated the importance of IIMEPs for those still suspicious of the international and inter/multicultural agenda, and furnished guidelines for colleges interested in creating new or expanding existing IIMEPs. The majority of these publications promoted "how to" descriptions of preexisting individual IIMEPs. Resource sharing became the foundation upon which many colleges were able to establish their own IIMEPs without "reinventing the wheel." Two special issues of *Journal* (1989, 1990) highlighted this pragmatic approach.

The decade culminated in the publication of "Building Communities: A Vision for a New Century" (1988), which was a product of the Commission on the Future of Community Colleges Report. This report defined a theoretical and philosophical purpose for community college IIMEPs as "an obligation to keep students informed about people and cultures other than their own" (2). By 1989, the mere volume of publications placed community colleges in their own niche in IIMEP literature and rendered them academically valid by the federal government, academicians, and community college administration and faculty.[5] However, in this wealth of literature, critical analysis and conceptualization of the theoretical understanding of this IIMEP phenomenon and its application at the college and community levels was and continues to be lacking.

Solidification of IIMEPs in community colleges coincided with an explicit increase in community college receipt of Title VI, Title VIB, and other private, federal, state, and local grants (Fersh and Greene 1984; King and Fersh 1992).[6] These grants were accompanied by the national dissemination of publications that described completed projects and provided guidelines for duplication, especially in internationalizing general and business curricula. Through various public policy and mission statements, the ACIIE officially encouraged colleges to establish clear institutional goals and policies that advocated the value of an international and inter/multicultural dimension throughout the entire college, became an important clearinghouse for new publications, and served as a valuable link to federal and foreign government offices (AACJC 1985, 1988, 1989, 1991).

PHASE 4: AUGMENTATION

By 1990 numerous community colleges had made comprehensive attempts to establish IIMEPs permanently on their campuses. Phase 4 includes augmentation of study-abroad options and initiation of less popular but equally important IIMEPs. Traditional study-abroad programs have concentrated on foreign language/civilization instruction in Western Europe. Alternative approaches augmented these programs by expanding course offerings to other disciplines and geographic areas, including Africa, Asia, and Latin America.

Diversification occurred in technical assistance programs, international student programs, faculty exchanges, and contract education programs. An American Council of Education 1992 survey of sixty randomly selected community colleges indicated that 70 percent had international contacts; 50 percent had international business, internationalization-of-curriculum, and study-abroad programs; 30 percent had sister-city relations; and 15 percent belonged to international consortia. These programs are offered throughout the world with 40 percent in the newly independent states of Eurasia and former Eastern European countries, 33 percent in Latin America, 30 percent in China, 29 percent in Europe, 11 percent in Africa, and 5 percent in the Middle East (Harris 1993). Furthermore, each program supports another. International development is linked with faculty development and can produce study-abroad and faculty exchange options. International and inter/multicultural literacy efforts affect curriculum as classes infuse non-Western perspectives into lesson plans and new classes are created with international themes. At many colleges, the traditional IIMEP foundation, which stressed study-abroad programs, is now incorporating a holistic approach that encompasses many international endeavors; certificate/A.A. degree programs and partnerships between international business organizations and community colleges are also drawn into these interrelationships.[7]

As a result of two decades of discussion, IIMEPs are being accepted as an important part of the agendas and mission statements of many districts and many individual colleges. At community colleges, all levels (from trustees to students) continue to confirm the importance of IIMEPs, even in times of fiscal difficulty (Fersh and Furlow 1993; Raby 1994). Since 1990, there has also been a significant rise in the number of community colleges awarded grants that directly or indirectly address international and inter/multicultural competency. The National Security Education Act (1991) stressed the need for increased opportunities for community college study abroad, foreign language, and area specialist training. Many university-affiliated institutions (such as the Intercultural Studies Institute, the University of Hawaii Asian Studies Institute, and the University of California, Los Angeles International Seminars) now include and encourage community college faculty participation. Finally, a "blueprint for the future"—a draft policy that will (1) clarify community college goals in IIMEP education, (2) explore how IIMEP themes and concepts can be integrated into community college education, (3) determine what each college can offer to the domain of IIMEPs, and (4) envision imaginative responses to fund IIMEPs in times of shrinking resources—has been initiated (Elsner, Tsunoda, and Korbel 1994, 2).

With the current changing political climate, however, the fate of IIMEPs is in jeopardy. Severe budget cuts affect "periphery programs" such as IIMEPs. Antagonistic feelings between disciplines and territorialism over limited resources further impede future endeavors. Such conflicts result in the resurfacing of the archaic notion that community colleges are inappropriate places for international and inter/multicultural education. The escalating cost of supporting IIMEPs results in a reduced number of programs and fewer participants. The recent worldwide recession has affected the number of students and faculty who can afford to travel abroad and the number of international students who can afford to attend American community colleges. Previous gains (such as newly created specific offices with full-time directors or deans and consortia membership) are also at risk. Furthermore, while international and inter/multicultural proponents are recognizing conceptual similarities, heightened competition (real or perceived) for limited funds impedes collaboration. Examples of collaboration are found in chapters 4 and 8. In California, DeAnza Community College's offering of A.A. degree programs in international studies, intercultural studies, or a combination of the two is one example of the two constituencies working together for a common goal. The foundation of international development programs has changed from being "an historic opportunity to apply our ideals, our sense of decency and our humanitarian impulse to the repair of the world" to one that addresses "a so-called privatization [so that] community colleges can cooperate with business and industry for competing in the international market" (Koltai 1993, 2–6). The future and consequences of community colleges as "the best and most useful export product in the field of education; training and human resources development" (Koltai 1993, 7) is examined in part II of this book.

Nonetheless, while the future remains uncertain, many colleges still exhibit solid commitment to IIMEPs. In 1994 the CCID consisted of twenty-one members and forty-seven affiliates in the United States and Canada, while the ACIIE included over 150 members.

INTERNATIONAL AND MULTICULTURAL COMPETENCY

In light of recent social and economic events, community colleges recognize the need to include international or inter/multicultural competency as a key element of their missions. For students to work and live effectively in an increasingly international and multicultural world, they must understand, without bias, the histories, goals, and values (i.e., the cultures) of the world community. Such understanding forms the basis for international and inter/multicultural competency. This competency requires more than simple awareness; it demands a deep understanding of the world and of the interrelationships that exist between different cultures:

> where people begin to think in international and inter-cultural terms; where differences in response can be anticipated and understood merely as differences and not as right and wrong reactions; where one is constantly conscious of the different meanings and interpretations of the same words and expressions by people whose minds are conditioned by other languages. (Bhatia, 1985)

As students gain this competency, they become empowered with knowledge that assists them in all future endeavors (Council on Learning 1981; CAFLIS 1989; American Association of State Colleges and Universities 1988).

Based on Honigmann's heuristic tripartite model that interprets any given social situation by how it is affected by overlapping cultural components, international and inter/multicultual competency impacts three interconnected levels: individual, community/societal, and global (Honigmann 1959). Figure 2 depicts a configuration of these components.

Individual Level

The community college exists as an important yet often untapped educational source for establishing international and inter/multicultural competency in a wide range of individuals. Educating the individual—be it student, teacher, administrator, or trustee—is the foundation upon which international competency is built.

IIMEPs are created for and by individuals. At present, 22 percent of all community college students belong to ethnic minorities: 10 percent African American, 7 percent Hispanic, 4 percent Asian American, and 1 percent Native American (Fersh and Furlow 1993, 11). The widening of student interests forces colleges to expand beyond provincial concerns and offer IIMEPs relevant to contemporary needs. A growing ethnic diversity among faculty is also significant. In California in 1993, 42.7 percent of all full-time faculty were women; 4.9 percent, Asian/Pacific Islander; 6.0 percent, African American; and 8 percent, Hispanic (California Community Colleges 1993). Faculty and administrators who participate in various IIMEPs experience personal growth, which increases their own level of competency and, in turn, affects their relationships with other faculty and students. As entire disciplines become internationalized, even greater numbers of students are affected. Individuals who participate in one IIMEP may later be inclined to become involved in other IIMEPs as well.

Debate continues regarding the value to students of acquiring international and inter/multicultural knowledge. Many studies demonstrate a decreasing interest in fostering international and inter/multicultural competency. This point of view is expressed in the American Council of Education's 1987 survey of 1,311 community colleges. Although 47 percent of college presidents considered international competency to be important, 86 percent of the colleges did not belong to international consortia and 51 percent did not require international and inter/multicultural components in their general education curriculum. Of those colleges that did require this

FIGURE 2. Configuration of Three Levels

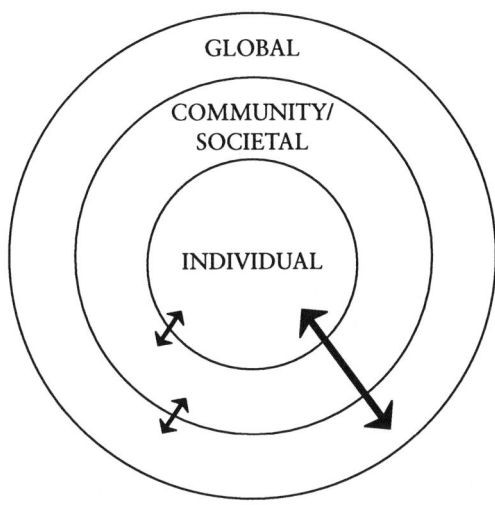

component, 72 percent offered Western civilization or history courses, 37 percent offered world civilization or history courses, 18 percent offered non-Western civilization or history courses, and 6 percent offered "other" international courses (Barrows 1981; Commission on the Future of Community Colleges 1988). However, both a 1990 survey of thirty-eight national colleges and a 1993 survey of fifty-three California colleges indicate that IIMEPs are becoming significantly more prevalent than earlier studies have indicated (Patterson 1990; Raby 1993).[8]

Nonetheless, the inadequate level of knowledge regarding the interdependent world remains a major concern for the 1990s, as "young Americans have less and less knowledge of and interest in foreign places. Practically all that young Americans have today is an unsubstantial awareness that there are many cultures" (Bloom 1987, 34–35). The 1991 National Security Education Act specifically states that "our ignorance of world cultures and languages represents a threat to our ability to remain a world leader." ("National Security Education Act" 1991, A53) This lack will affect the future interactions of college graduates.

Community/Societal Level

Community colleges serve the needs of local/regional communities within a specific geographic region and are designed to meet community needs (Hollinshead 1936). Indeed, community colleges in the United States have an "outstanding record of responding to society's needs" (Koltai 1993, 6). However, it is now necessary to redefine the concept of "community," since it has evolved to refer also to a community of interests in terms of services provided. Such interests correspond to a socioeconomic and political milieu that is both international and inter/multicultural. Competency in these areas serves the community when community colleges produce graduates who are (a) economically skilled to work in a global market, (b) politically empowered to participate in society, and (c) morally adept to function in society. The global economy demands that community colleges educate students who can compete in these new global contexts. For example, technical training, tourism, allied health fields, and international business all meet needs expressed by an evolving community. Our country demands informed citizens who are sensitive to issues of local, national, and international importance. Politicians supporting the Freedom Exchange Act (1992) further contend that American security and prosperity depend upon such a level of sensitivity. Finally, a more empathetic citizen enhances the community by maintaining cohesive relationships, by working successfully with different ethnic groups, and by forming a foundation on which a thriving community can exist (Raby 1990).

The expansion of "community" is quite apparent in California. Despite an abysmal budget crisis, the California Postsecondary Education Commission nonetheless reports that because the multicultural character of California's population is growing rapidly and because it is less expensive to educate students in community colleges, most of future enrollment growth will occur in California community colleges (California Postsecondary Education Commission 1994, 3).

There are direct correlations between the type of IIMEPs initiated at a college and the immediate communities that support that college. New majors, courses, and extracurricular activities reflect international and inter/multicultural trends within the community itself. Intensive English-language programs flourish as colleges accommodate refugees, immigrants, and international students, all of whom are members of the community. The presence of foreign-born and international students reflects the larger ethnic populations living near colleges. Multiethnic communities support local business constituencies, which often have international connections. The popularity of ethnic studies, inter/multicultural and international studies, and international business classes reflects the need for students to learn about different cultures so that they can assist in building a more harmonious and economically prosperous community.

Global Level

Rapid economic development and global telecommunications impact the way business is conducted and the manner in which political events are conceived and interpreted. Increasingly, national socioeconomic, security, and environmental policies not only affect others but are also influenced by them. As Fersh and Furlow (1993) note, international literacy is a prerequisite for enabling people to consider positively the ethnic variations that exist within each individual community. It is not uncommon for community colleges to have student representatives from numerous countries. Indeed, Broward Community College (Florida) has the largest number of international students of any two- or four-year college or university in the country, the Mesa Community College (Arizona) student body represents 126 countries, and the Los Angeles Community College District student body represents 101 countries (Raby 1994; Elsner, Tsunoda, and Korbel 1994). Consequently, the global village scenario is actualizing interrelationships that have become fundamental parts of our lives.

The new global dimension of IIMEPs includes past contributions (such as bringing international students and scholars to local colleges, sending U.S. students and scholars abroad, and promoting institutional exchanges with international institutions). However, as Tsunoda acknowledges, we must add an "application of international education back home to the communities around us. There is a pressing need for higher education to contribute toward strengthening the social fabric of our multicultural society, toward involving our students and ourselves in service to our communities and as individuals in these groups to assume greater sense of social responsibility and conscience" (Tsunoda 1994).

Academic integrity requires that all academic and technical college courses present updated and accurate information that includes reference to international and inter/multicultural interrelationships. Ignoring these areas not only limits the quality of information but also constitutes irresponsible education. For example, teaching nursing without acknowledging health issues that arise from migration, transmission of AIDS, and travel is negligent. Teaching biology without assessing international environmental impacts is also remiss. International events affect local businesses and tourism that help support local communities. Community college graduates need to support and enhance these and other relationships. The influx of Japanese language and civilization classes is indicative of this phenomenon. Finally, first-hand experiences obtained through participation in many IIMEPs personally affect not only the individual but also the college itself as future international and inter/multicultural endeavors are solidified. International development projects, student and faculty exchanges, contract education, and sister-city relationships all establish bonds between the campus and the global community that are dynamic and increase in intensity over time.

CALIFORNIA COLLEGES FOR INTERNATIONAL EDUCATION: A CASE STUDY

Since 1960, Californian educational and political leaders have built a community college system emulated by other states and, consequently, by other countries worldwide (California Higher Education Policy Center 1994, 23). A case study of the Californian community college system is indicated precisely because of its diversity and recognition. California supports 107 community colleges, which have 70,000 full- and part-time staff members and enroll over 1.3 million students in a state where one in seventeen adults is a community college student. These colleges vary in size, location, and venue, yet combined, they reflect a multiethnic and culturally diverse state. In the 1992–1993 academic year 300,299 (19.9 percent) of California community college students were Hispanic (other than Filipino), 177,762 (11.8 percent) were Asian American or Pacific Islander, 109,373 (7.2 percent) were African American, and 16,848 (1.1 percent) were American Indian/Alaskan Native. In addition, there were 216,000 international students attending California community colleges.[9] California community colleges offer a variety of opportunities for a significant proportion of the society to develop international or inter/multicultural competency. In the early 1970s, there were a sizable number of both inter/multicultural educational opportunities and occasional study-abroad and faculty exchange programs. By the late 1970s, the number of colleges offering study-abroad programs increased, yet neither the quality nor sustainability of these programs was assured. A number of California community colleges have in the 1980s and 1990s received Title VI and Title VIB grants to create exemplary international studies and international business programs. Nonetheless, strong anti-international sentiments prevailed, which threatened the expansion of IIMEPs. The founding of California Colleges for International Education (CCIE) in 1983 helped the process of enlightening and supporting numerous colleges in their international and inter/multicultural education efforts.

An examination of CCIE's evolution mirrors the developmental matrix presented in the beginning of this chapter. The growth of CCIE corresponds to phase 2, expansion. From 1988 to 1994, CCIE membership grew from thirty-one to fifty-seven colleges. Furthermore, the CCIE's original mission, the assurance of high academic standards for study-abroad programs, evolved into its current mission, to (a) encourage development of international and inter/multicultural perspectives in community colleges, (b) increase awareness and encouragement of international development through technical education, (c) promote opportunities for sharing international and inter/multicultural expertise, (d) form liaisons between national organizations and consortia involved in international and inter/multicultural education activities, and (e) provide an international and inter/multicultural education resource for the office of the California community colleges' chancellor.

The sharing of CCIE member colleges' guidelines, procedures, and reports on initiating and expanding IIMEPs reflects phase 3, publication. Finally, the diversification of CCIE programs reflects phase 4, augmentation. Whereas the majority of CCIE colleges once introduced IIMEPs solely through study-abroad programs, in the past three years the concentration on internationalizing curriculum (especially in regard to international business) has assured the prominence of these programs. Several CCIE members are involved in the California network of International Trade Development Centers, and are active members of CCID, International Consortium for Education and Economic Development (ICEED), and Community Colleges International (CCI).[10] Finally, the augmentation phase supports the inclusion of IIMEPs in college/district and state mission statements. Included among the latter is the basic agenda of the California community colleges' board of governors, which mandates a diversified curriculum that comprehensively analyzes the cultures and economics of other nations and California's potential role in international activities (Board of Governors 1990). Table 1 depicts significant regional variations in the number of nontraditional study-abroad efforts, and table 2 portrays the growth of other forms of IIMEPs at CCIE member colleges (Raby 1989–1993).

It must be noted that CCIE represents slightly over half of all California community colleges and that several nonmember colleges also offer IIMEPs. A 1990 survey of all colleges in the state indicates that among non-CCIE colleges, twenty (19 percent) offer study-abroad programs, eighteen (17 percent) offer international and inter/multicultural core-curriculum courses, one college offers an A.A. degree in international studies, and one college offers an international business program (*Directory of International and Intercultural Study Resources* 1990). Despite the strong presence of IIMEPs throughout California, there are thirty-two colleges (30 percent) that do not offer any IIMEPs. More importantly, an acute budget crisis, which is estimated to last through 1996, is forcing many active colleges to decrease institutional support, to make IIMEPs accountable for their own budget, and in some instances, to temporarily curtail IIMEPs' activities altogether. Despite financial problems, the need to maintain IIMEPs as a means of increasing awareness and supporting international competency remains considerable.

FUTURE CONCERNS FOR IIMEPs

According to Hess (1982), the primary components of thriving community college IIMEPs include (1) support from chief administrative officers, (2) commitment from faculty, and (3) a specific coordinator. Greenfield appends this list with (a) board-of-trustees commitment through supportive policy or mission statements, (b) continuing involvement by faculty and staff, (c) funding to support a visible office, clerical staff, publicity, and travel, (d) community and support-group participation, and (e) a public information system (Greenfield 1990). Enlightened trustee, administrative, and faculty support (including academic senate and department chairs), plus an adeptly managed office, enables community colleges to prevail over the many challenges facing international and inter/multicultural education. As IIMEPs become entrenched in educational philosophy and in the mission statements at the district and individual college levels, programs may be provided with the necessary resources and nonfinancial support essential for growth and survival.

The description of the California case study suggests that four additional components are necessary for the success of IIMEPs. First is the ability to overcome negative forces that hinder development (such as resistance to change, parochialism in educational policy structure, and ethnocentric perceptions of the world, which many disciplines and faculty currently display. Indeed, as Koltai (1993) noted, the liberal faculty of the 1960s have become the liberal administrators of the 1990s. However, the 1990s faculty are now more conservative, and since they want to preserve the status quo, they have become suspicious of change. Faculty negativism and apathy make internationalization and inter/multiculturalization difficult. Outreach programs can counter these negative forces by gradually encouraging faculty to participate in IIMEPs. However, progress in this regard has been excruciatingly slow, and this obstacle has proven to be the most difficult to overcome.

The second component is the need to define IIMEPs comprehensively. Despite recent advances, confusion remains as to what international education includes and how it can work harmoniously with inter/multicultural education. Many college administrators and faculty still need to be reminded that IIMEPs are more than just a way for selected faculty members to travel abroad. This perception is not only narrow but also potentially harmful for future IIMEP development. The ambiguity about defining community college IIMEPs has also contributed to a scarcity of critical scholarship and debate on community college IIMEPs and their applications. This in turn undermines the assessment of the new initiatives and ongoing activities of community college IIMEPs on particular campuses. An integral definition that systematically accounts for program diversity is hence required.

TABLE 1. California Colleges for International Education: Numbers of Nontraditional Study-Abroad Programs

Region	1989		1990		1991		1992		1993	
	SE	SU	SE	SU	SE	SU	SE	SU	SE	SU
Europe	13	18	20	27	22	29	34	32	29	30
Asia	5	2	1	6	2	6	2	7	4	9
Australia/South Pacific	0	2	2	1	1	3	0	5	0	4
Latin America	2	12	4	18	4	11	6	21	11	22
Africa	0	3	0	0	0	2	0	3	0	2
Total	20	37	27	52	29	51	42	68	44	67

SE=Fall and spring semester programs
SU=Summer programs and winter/spring break programs

TABLE 2. California Colleges for International Education: IIMEP Activities

	1989	1990	1991	1992	1993
Faculty seminars	—	—	—	1	4
Teacher exchanges	4	5	7	5	10
International students	10	13	24	22	50
International development	3	5	9	6	14
A.A. Degree/certificate programs	4	7	5	13	23*
Number of CCIE colleges	31	46	48	50	52

* Some are in the planning stage.

The third component highlights the raison d'être for IIMEPs. Although IIMEPs have always been in the "business" of generating funds, the "business" end has not been exploited or overtly publicized. Rather, IIMEPs have been valued as a means for academic, humanistic, and individual growth. The 1990s have brought privatization into central focus, since community colleges are more frequently providing their services for a price and using that money to help finance programs that are not income-generating. As a result, community colleges cooperate with, and become subordinate to, the interests of enterprises that function in the international market. Indeed, the community college has become a "most useful export product in the field of education: training and human resources development" (Koltai 1993, 7). These conflicting ideologies undermine the original mission of community colleges, yet clearly reflect the needs and priorities of the 1990s. The dichotomy of interests is explored in several chapters of this book.

The final component is to ensure that international and inter/multicultural education is indeed part of the community college mission at national, state, district, and individual college levels. This assures support from trustees, administration, faculty, and students and is the first step towards ultimate acceptance. However, colleges need also to go beyond the mission's rhetoric and assure implementation of its components throughout the curriculum and the campus at large. Recognition from the academic community and transfer of the credits of IIMEP courses, programs, and degrees to four-year universities are also crucial for future success. It is both exciting as well as distressing that a November 1994 gathering of the elite of community college IIMEPs met to debate and produce a new national policy that defines, guides, and facilitates IIMEP implementation. Indeed, this gathering debated new and important issues, such as the needs and expectations of community college graduates as defined by the global community and the actions, roles, and leadership needed for the effective advancement of IIMEPs in a climate of limited resources. However, considerable time is still being spent on reiterating past concerns, such as defining IIMEPs and highlighting obstacles for faculty and students. While the meeting itself demonstrates that there is tremendous support among community colleges, private and public business, government, and private funding sources, the fact that many issues are still being debated after twenty years of discussion is not encouraging.

In conclusion, as we enter into the next century, comprehensive community college IIMEPs remain not only essential but critical. As previously indicated, IIMEPs are no longer optional, they are integral to the success and mission of community colleges nationwide. Especially in times of fiscal difficulty, this integral nature must be respected and protected.

NOTES

1. For purposes of logistics the terms *intercultural* and *multicultural* will be merged as "inter/multicultural."

2. Prior to 1992, the AACC was known as the American Association of Community and Junior Colleges (AACJC). From its founding in 1975 until 1991, the American Council on International/Intercultural Education (ACIIE) was known as the International/Intercultural Consortium of the American Association of Community and Junior Colleges. Since 1994, the AACC has had a Commission on International/Intercultural Services and a director of academic, student, and international services, and one of its affiliate councils is the ACIIE. The ACIIE provides an outlet for the sharing of information and resources, represents its community college membership on national task forces and commissions, and enables the networking process to persist.

3. The original CCIS members were Mercer Community College, N.J., Harrisburg Community College, Pa.; and Rockland Community College, N.Y. In 1992 there were 150 participating community colleges.

4. The National Consortia include the ACIIE; CCID; and CCIS, which provides opportunities for international faculty seminars and student study abroad. State

or regional consortia include FCCHE (Florida), NJCCIIE (New Jersey), PIN (Minnesota), PNIIEC (Washington), CCIE (California), TCCCIE (Texas), consortia in Illinois and Michigan, the Northwest Consortia, and the Southwest Consortia.

5. Partial listing of 1979–1989 publications: King, Maxwell, and Robert L. Breuder (eds.), *Advancing International Education*, New Directions for Community Colleges Series (San Francisco: Jossey-Bass, No. 26, 1979); *Community and Junior College Journal* (March 1979); Pusch, Margaret, *Multicultural Education* (Yarmouth, Me.: Intercultural Press, 1979); Diener, T. J., and L. Keer (1979); Terrell, R., *Faculty Exchange Programs*, San Francisco, March 30–April 2, 1980 (ERIC Document Reproduction Service No. ED 188-724); Fersh, Seymour, and Edward Fitchen (eds.), *The Community College and International Education: A Report of Progress* (Cocoa, Fla.: Brevard Community College, 1981); Fersh, Seymour, "The Community College and the World Community," *Community College Frontiers*, Summer 9(4) (1981); Council on Learning. *National Task Force Statement on Education and the World View* (New Rochelle, N.Y.: Change Magazine Press, 1981); Educational Testing Service, *College students' knowledge and beliefs: A survey of global understanding* (New Rochelle, N.Y.: Change Magazine Press, 1981); McDonnel, L.M., S.E. Berryman, and D. Scott, *Federal Support for International Studies: The Role of NDEA Title VI* (Santa Monica, Cal.: Rand Publication Series, 1981); Hess, Gerhard, *Freshmen and Sophomores Abroad: Community Colleges and Overseas Academic Programs* (New York: Teachers College Press, 1982); Adams, A.H., and G. Earwood, *Internationalizing the Community College*, ISHE Fellows Program Research Report No. 2. (Tallahassee, Fla.: Institute for Studies in Higher Education, 1982); Lamar, Johnson B. (1982); King, Maxwell, and Seymour Fersh, "International Education and the U.S. Community College: From Optimal to Integral," *Junior College Resource Review* (Spring 1983); Fersh, Seymour, and William Greene (1984); Backman, E.L., *Approaches to International Education* (New York: American Council on Education/Macmillan, 1984); American Association of Community and Junior Colleges, *Statement on the Role of International/Intercultural Education in Community Colleges* (adopted by AACJC board of directors, April 1985); Mahoney, James R., and Clyde Sakamoto, *International Trade Education: Issues and Programs* (1985); Giammarella, M., "A Profile of the Foreign Student at a Public Two-Year College: The Borough of Manhattan Community College Response to the Financial Problems of Foreign Students" *Community Review* 7 (1986); Fifeld, Mary, and Clyde Sakamoto (eds.), *The Next Challenge: Balancing International Competition and Cooperation* (Washington, D.C.: American Association of Community and Junior Colleges, 1987); Wurzel, Jaime, *Toward Multiculturalism: A Reader in Multicultural Education* (Yarmouth, Me.: Intercultural Press, 1988); B.J. Ebersole, "International Education: Where and How Does It Fit in Your College?" (*Community, Technical and Junior College Journal* 1989: 29–31); King, M.C., and S.H. Fersh, "International Education: Its Future Is Now," (*Community, Technical and Junior College Journal* 59, no. 3, 1989: 28–29).

6. From 1972 to 1993, Title VI and Title VIB grants were awarded to seventy-three community colleges. Many individual colleges received more than one grant and/or both Title VI and Title VIB grants.

7. The following colleges all have exemplary international business programs that have emerging relationships with state departments of commerce: Bergen College (New Jersey), Central Piedmont (North Carolina), Chicago Loop College (Illinois), Coast College (California), Dallas County Community College District (Texas), Humber College (Ontario), Kirkwood College (Iowa), Miami-Dade Community College District (Florida), Pima College, (Arizona), Portland College (Oregon), St. Louis College (Missouri), and Coastline District and Vista College (California).

8. The *Patterson Directory* indicated that of the colleges surveyed: 96 percent had international student programs, 73 percent had study-abroad programs, 63 percent had faculty exchange programs, 50 percent offered noncredit international business courses, 40 percent offered internationalized general curriculum courses, and 33

percent offered A.A. degree programs in international business. Among CCIE colleges, 96 percent offer cultural anthropology courses, 93 percent offer non-European history courses, 85 percent offer cultural geography and ethnic studies courses, 74 percent offer international business courses, 66 percent offer non-European humanities courses, 54 percent offer international relations courses, and 50 percent offer courses in intercultural communications and multicultural studies.

9. The 1993–1994 academic year numbers show similar statistics, but are not as accurate because of an 18.6 percent unknown/nonrespondent rate (as opposed to 4.1 percent in 1992 and 5.8 percent in 1991) (Sacramento: California Higher Education Policy Center, May 3, 1994).

10. The California International Trade Development Centers system includes the following colleges: Citrus College, Coastline College (with a high-technology emphasis), Fresno College, Los Angeles Southwest College, Merced College (with an agriculture emphasis), Oxnard College, Riverside College (with an African emphasis), Sacramento City College (with an Asian emphasis), Southwestern College, and Vista College (with an Eastern European emphasis). The following centers have been instrumental in the development of A.A. degree programs in international business at their respective colleges and are also members of CCIE: Coastline College, Oxnard College, Vista College, and Fresno College.

International development programs are exemplified by Yosemite district's nationally renowned Cooperative Association of States for Scholarships (CASS)—which are offered to socioeconomically disadvantaged, talented students from Central American and the Caribbean—and the East Central European Scholarship Program (ECESP), offered to students from Poland, Czechoslovakia, and Hungary to study management, economics, and agro-technology. Other notable international development programs are in the Coast, San Diego, and Los Angeles districts, which are involved in the national ICEED programs; Los Angeles district has an ongoing ESL program in Salamanca (Spain), Shanghai (China), and Vladivostok (Russia) and contract education programs in Japan and Australia. The newly formed CCI is working on a consortia level towards international development projects, primarily in Eastern Europe and Russia.

REFERENCES

American Association of Community and Junior Colleges (AACJC). "Statement on the Role of International/Intercultural Education in Community Colleges." Adopted by AACJC Board of Directors. Washington, D.C., April 1985.

———. "Mission Statement." Adopted by AACJC Board of Directors. *AACJC Public Policy Agenda.* Washington, D.C., April 1988.

———. "Policy Statements of the American Association of Community and Junior Colleges." *Membership Directory.* Washington, D.C.: AACJCP, 1989.

———. A Summary of Selected National Data Pertaining to Community, Technical and Junior Colleges. Washington, D.C.: AACJC, 1991. Quoted in King and Fersh 1992, pp. 9, 31.

"AACJC Board Adopts Statements on the Role of International/Intercultural Education in the Community College." *AACJC International/Intercultural Consortium Newsletter (AACJC IIC Newsletter).* May 1982.

American Association of State Colleges and Universities. "Incorporating an International Dimension in Colleges and Universities." *Guidelines: Incorporating an International Dimension in Colleges and Universities.* Washington, D.C.: American Association of State Colleges and Universities, 1988.

American Council on Education (ACE). "A National Interest and International Dimensions of Higher Education in a Post War Era." ACE Monograph Bulletin. Washington, D.C.: ACE, 1993.

———. "Survey of Undergraduate International Studies (1986–1987)." *Higher Education Panel Survey Number 76.* 1988.

American Council on International Intercultural Education (ACIIE). "Mission Statement." As approved by the ACIIE Executive Board in Kansas City. *AACJC Public Policy Agenda*. Kansas City, April 11, 1991.

Barrows, Thomas. *College Students' Knowledge and Beliefs: A Survey of Global Understanding*. New Rochelle, N.Y.: Change Magazine Press, 1981.

Bhatia, V.N. "The Use of the Curriculum in Internationalizing the University." *Journal of the AIERA* 5, no. 1 (Spring 1985).

Bloom, A. *The Closing of the American Mind: How Higher Education Has Failed Democracy and Impoverished the Souls of Today's Students*. New York: Simon and Schuster, 1987.

Board of Governors. California Community Colleges. *The Basic Agenda*. Sacramento: Community College League of California, 1992.

Boyer, E.L. "Keynote Speech at the Annual AACJC Convention." *AACJC Journal* 49, no. 6 (1979): 14–19.

Bradley, Bill, and Jim Heach. "Freedom Exchange Act." S. 2777, H.R. 5353. Washington, D.C., 1992.

Burn, Barbara. *Expanding the International Dimension of Higher Education*. Washington, D.C.: Carnegie Council on Policy Studies, 1980.

California Community Colleges. "Staffing and Salaries Report: Management Information Services." Sacramento: Chancellor's Office, California Community Colleges, 1993.

California Community Colleges. "Unduplicated Headcount for Fall 1991 through Fall 1993: Management Information Services." Sacramento: Chancellor's Office, California Community Colleges, 1994.

California Higher Education Policy Center. *Time for Decision: California's Legacy and the Future of Education: A Report with Recommendations*. San Jose: California Higher Education Policy Center, 1994.

California Postsecondary Education Commission. "Population Growth, Local Needs Push Districts to Plan More Centers, Campuses." *The News: Community College League of California* (January–February 1994): 1–3.

California Postsecondary Education Committee. "Critical Issues Draft Language, November 11, 1992." Sacramento, November 1992.

Carew, Joy Gleason. "For Minority Students, Study Abroad Can Be Inspiring and Liberating." *Chronicle of Higher Education* 3 (January 6, 1993): 11.

Coalition for the Advancement of Foreign Languages and International Studies (CAFLIS). A Plan of Action for International Competence: A Key to America's Future. Washington, D.C.: CAFLIS, 1989.

Cohen, Arthur. "Talk on Community Colleges." Comparative and International Education Society Western Regional Conference, Los Angeles, 1993.

Commission on the Future of Community Colleges. *Building Communities: A Vision of a New Century*. Washington D.C.: American Association of Community and Junior Colleges, 1988.

Community College League of California. "Capitol Report: December 20, 1993." 1993.

Community, Technical and Junior College Journal. (December 1988–January 1989).

———. (August/September 1990).

Council on Learning. "Statement and Recommendations on American Responsibilities as a Global Power and Appropriate Educational Directions." *National Task Force Statement on Education and the World View*. New Rochelle, N.Y.: Change Magazine Press, 1981.

Diener, T.J., and L. Kerr. "Institutional Responsibilities to Foreign Students." *New Directions for Community Colleges* 7 no. 2 (1979): 49–57.

Directory of International and Intercultural Study Resources. San Francisco: The Center for International Education, Communication and Development of City College of San Francisco, 1990.

Elsner, Paul A., Joyce S. Tsunoda, and Linda A. Korbel. "Building the Global Community: The Next Step." *Points of Departure for the American Council on International Intercultural Education/Stanley Foundation Leadership Retreat,* Washington, D.C., November 28–30, 1994.

Elsner, Paul A., and Joyce Tsunoda. "International Education and Multiculturalism in the Community College" Position Paper, Washington, D.C.: ACIIE, June 1994.

Fersh, Seymour, and Richard H. Furlow (eds.). *The Community College and International Education: A Report of Progress.* Vol. III. Glen Ellyn, Ill.: College of Dupage, 1993.

Fersh, Seymour, and William Greene (eds.). *The Community College and International Education: A Report of Progress.* Vol. II. Fort Lauderdale, Fla.: Broward Community College, 1984.

Greenfield, Richard K. *Developing International Education Programs.* New Directions for Community Colleges Series No. 70. San Francisco: Jossey-Bass, 1990.

Harris, Mathilda. "Keynote Address to the Comparative and International Education Society Western Region Conference." Los Angeles, November 5–6, 1993.

Hess G. *Freshmen and Sophomores Abroad: Community Colleges and Overseas Academic Programs.* New York: Teachers College Press, 1982.

"Higher Education Act Reauthorization." *Toward Human Resource Development.* Washington, D.C.: ACCT/AACJC, 1991.

Hollinshead, B.S. "The Community College Program." *Junior Community College Journal* 7 (1936): 166–84.

Honigman, John J. *The World of Man.* New York: Harper, 1959.

King, Maxwell, and Robert L. Breuder (eds.). *Advancing International Education.* New Directions for Community Colleges Series No. 26. San Francisco: Jossey-Bass, 1979.

King, Maxwell C., and Seymour H. Fersh. "International Education and the U.S. Community College: From Optional to Integral." *ERIC Junior College Resource Review* (Spring 1983).

———. *Integrating the International/Intercultural Dimension in the Community College.* Washington, D.C.: Association of Community College Trustees and Community Colleges for International Development, 1992.

Koltai, Leslie. "Are There Challenges and Opportunities for American Community Colleges on the International Scene?" Keynote Address at the Comparative and International Education Society Western Region Conference, Los Angeles, November 5–6, 1993.

Lamar, Johnson B. (ed.). *General Education in Two-Year Colleges.* New Directions for Community Colleges Series No. 40. San Francisco: Jossey-Bass, 1982.

"National Security Education Act of 1991." *The Chronicle of Higher Education* (December 4, 1991): A53–A55.

Patterson, Judith. Directory of International Education Resources: At League for Innovation Institutions, 1990. Charlotte, N.C.: International Business Center, Central Piedmont Community College, 1990.

Perkins, James. "Strength through Wisdom: A Critique of U.S. Capability. A Report to the President from the President's Commission on Foreign Language and International Studies." Washington, D.C.: President's Commission on Foreign Language and International Studies, 1979.

Raby, Rosalind Latiner. *California Colleges for International Education Annual Reports: 1988–1989; 1989–1990; 1990–1991; 1991–1992; 1992–1993; 1993–1994.* Los Angeles: 1989; 1990; 1991; 1992; 1993; 1994 (respectively).

———. "Internationalizing the California Community College Curriculum." *Global Pages* 8, no. 1 (Spring 1990): 6–8.

———. "Identity and Community through Community College International Education." *Comparative and International Education Society Newsletter.* Tallahassee, Fla.: Florida State University Learning Systems Institute Press, 1993.

Scanlon, David G. "Lessons for the Past in Developing International Education in

Community Colleges." *Developing International Education Programs.* New Directions for Community Colleges Series No. 70. San Francisco: Jossey-Bass, 1990.

Shannon, William. *A Survey of International/Intercultural Education in Two-Year Colleges—1976.* La Plata, Md.: Charles County Community College, 1978.

Smithee, Michael. *Association of International Education* 42, no. 6 (April/May 1991): 1–4.

Tsunoda, Joyce. "Address to the Association of International Education Administrators Annual Conference at Tokai University." Honolulu, Hawaii, February 5, 1994.

Zikopoulos, Marianthi (ed.). *Open Doors 1991/1992: Report on International Educational Exchange.* New York: Institute of International Education Publications, 1993.

2 COMMUNITY SELF-HELP INTERNATIONAL DEVELOPMENT PROJECTS

A Humanistic Perspective

Jean Cook

As we approach the twenty-first century, we see a significant shift in the political and social geography of the developing countries in the world. The dismantling of communist regimes, the devolution of colonialism, and the push towards privatization have heightened America's responsibilities both in developing countries and at home. Diverse opportunities now exist for U.S. community colleges to become involved in assisting the movement of developing countries toward greater self-reliance, in improving the quality of life, in promoting educational reform, and in implementing new technological and educational services.

In this chapter, the means by which community colleges engage in international development projects is explored from the humanistic perspective. In particular, the benefits incurred from community self-help development programs and the use of these programs to assist countries in their movement toward sustainability are highlighted. The case studies stem from two externally funded international development projects involving Sinclair Community College (Ohio) faculty and administrators: (a) the University Development Linkages Project (UDLP) in India, funded by the U.S. Agency for International Development, and (b) the Society Taking Active Responsibility for International Self-Help (STARFISH) projects in Sierra Leone.

Community Self-Help Development: A Theoretical and Pragmatic Concept

The phrase "community self-help development" denotes organized efforts to improve the quality of life for persons in the communities in which they live. This is mainly achieved by overcoming residents' apathy through an emphasis on self-help (Clinard 1989). In this way, citizens participate in activities designed to improve the quality of their lives through the maximum use of their personal initiative and available community resources. According to a United Nations report:

> Community development is a complex of processes made up of two essential elements: the participation by the people themselves in efforts to improve their level of living with as much reliance as possible on their own initiative; and the provisions of technical and other service in ways which encourage initiative, self-help and mutual help and make these more effective. (United Nations 1960, 1)

Since World War II, the United Nations has actively employed community self-help development projects as part of their international development and peacekeeping activities (United Nations 1960). The term *self-help* is about people, organizations, leadership, culture, trust, commitment, and responsibility. People experience "self-help" when they are able to do a task by themselves, unaided by others. Self-help takes place when individuals do something, understand, and realize something new, so that they make the experience a part of their own reality. The learning process is concrete, highly participatory, experiential, and highly pertinent to their lives. A major book on this subject, *The Power to Change* (Fernando 1992), is an anthology of stories that documents exciting successful self-help projects. Some of these projects were developed through a villager's initiative, while others were coaxed into existence through volunteer efforts. It is the spirit of these international development self-help projects that Sinclair Community College strives to recreate and sustain.

Fernando depicts several projects. One type is Colombo's oldest rural women's organization, Lanka Mahila Samithi (LMS). At LMS centers women learn how to provide safe water and sanitation, obtain job skills, cook healthy meals, and protect the environment. Many LMS workers are villagers who were trained at these centers. Upon completion of the program, the women return to their villages and help build up the villagers' sense of self-reliance. Their work is monitored by LMS field coordinators, and it has taken almost sixty years to build a sense of trust between rural women and the organization (Fernando 1992).

Another project is the Society for the Promotion of Area Resource Centres (SPARC) (Mahila Milan) in Bombay. SPARC was initiated in 1988. Its purpose is to help slum women become more self-reliant by empowering them to deal with Indian bureaucracy and authority figures. For example, before SPARC was founded, these women were unable to take a sick child to the hospital or get their ration cards on time, since they did not know how to fill out the correct forms (Gahlot 1992). Similarly, in Indonesia the spirit of *gotong royong* (mutual help) is the basis of volunteerism. Traditionally, mutual help had been a universal phenomenon, but social and economic changes dampened the spirit of helping one's neighbor willingly and spontaneously in the event of an accident, disaster, sickness, or death. Today, gotong royong is being carried out through private voluntary nonprofit organizations.

Community self-help initiatives in developing countries are affected by cultural mores intertwined with colonialism, poverty, and family traditions. Because of the poverty and economic difficulties in developing countries, the flow of the hard currency needed to purchase machinery, equipment, and computers from overseas is severely limited. The result is that technology plays a minimal role, while the inhabitants concentrate on their familiar and present mode of work and life in order to survive. Even when a new technology such as the automobile enters the mainstream, it does not push out the old. One still sees the automobile and the bullock cart traveling side by side on a national highway.

Furthermore, creative decision making and problem solving are limited by the general population's respect for their community's mores and for the dictates of family traditions. Consequently, people are conditioned not to want to make independent decisions that go against commonly accepted practices. Today, television brings the influence of the Western world to the most distant of all rural villages. Village youngsters are seeking changes for themselves while continuing to acquiesce to an older person's wishes. For example, in India, "under the same roof, members of a family may seemingly live so blinded to each other that each member seems to belong to a different century" (Seth 1989).

The emphasis of self-help international development programs is on assistance to those countries that are coming to terms with their colonial legacy, which emphasized dependency instead of self-reliance. In the two cases under study, India and Sierra Leone, people were accustomed to doing a task simply because they were told, and they did not rely on their own decision-making skills. This behavior is rapidly changing today in both a quiet and explosive manner. The international development humanist perspective maintains that the United States in general, and community colleges in particular, have a genuine desire to support the transition of developing countries from colonialism to self-reliance.

COMMUNITY COLLEGES AND INTERNATIONAL DEVELOPMENT

In community colleges, the term *international development* is ascribed to the offering of technical training and the performance of consulting tasks in developing countries. *International education* is generally defined as courses, programs, and activities that increase awareness in an individual about the global world. In the United States, the consortium Community Colleges for

International Development (CCID) helps coordinate and support the international development activities of sixty community colleges nationwide in a number of international locations. Created in 1976, CCID has a combined enrollment of more than 750,000 students in its member institutions, which include those colleges offering more than 350 programs in technical or vocational subjects plus university-parallel and community service programs. CCID member colleges deliver technical training, consult on projects, create international student and faculty exchanges, host international visitors, and conduct international conferences and seminars. By joining CCID, community college chancellors or presidents make a formal commitment for themselves and their institutions to international development programs that benefit other countries as well as those of their own employees.

International awareness through international development and education activities is a high priority at Sinclair Community College, located in Dayton, Ohio. This is demonstrated by Sinclair's active membership in CCID, a college budget supporting an international education committee, and its staff development policies, which encourage faculty and student involvement. Although college policies do not explicitly weigh international involvement as criteria for hiring, promotion, and tenure, such involvement is nonetheless encouraged. Through participation in various international development programs, Sinclair is generally recognized to be in the national forefront of educational leadership and innovation. Sinclair is also a member of the League for Innovation in the Community Colleges, a coalition of the twenty U.S. community colleges that are most noted for creative and innovative leadership and faculty.

Sinclair Community College, like many community colleges, relies solely on external grant funds and not on community or state funds to support its international development activities. Such a policy substantially affects the types of opportunities utilized by a college's faculty and staff. In the aftermath of the cold war, even though internationalization is a realistic part of everyday life, the United States has turned inwards, attending a plethora of domestic issues rather than concentrating its efforts on foreign assistance. The reasons for this change in policy are varied, yet the result is that it is now imperative for those interested in participating in international development projects to secure financing from external funding sources.

New Global Models for Community Self-Help International Programs

The Center for Vocational Education (CVE) in Madras, India, and STAR-FISH in Sierra Leone, West Africa, are two international development projects with which Sinclair Community college faculty are involved and are global models of their kind. Both projects receive community and business donations. STARFISH is funded by a mining corporation located in Sierra Leone and through Dayton-area community donations. However, most of the funding for Sinclair Community College's involvement in the CVE comes through the UDLP of the U.S. Agency for International Development. The STARFISH model and algorithm proposal process for new projects are being replicated by Sinclair Community College in the Madras project.

STARFISH

The nonprofit organization STARFISH is dedicated to helping people help themselves. Its purpose is to provide, through a clearinghouse operation, short-term volunteer opportunities to individuals willing to lend their time and talents in the empowerment of some of the world's least powerful people, with an emphasis on improving the quality of village life for over 2,000 mining employees.

STARFISH began through the independent efforts of Joseph Giardullo, professor of nursing at Sinclair Community College. Joseph served as a volunteer team leader with Operation Crossroads Africa in the summer of 1986, giving immunizations to villagers and their children in remote areas of Sierra Leone. Because college students were used as manpower, Operation Crossroads Africa limited its projects to the summer months and no plans were made to return to these remote villages to administer booster shots. Joseph convinced Operations Crossroads Africa to allow him to raise funds privately, and under these auspices, he returned to the same villages in Sierra Leone to administer the necessary boosters in December 1986.

During the early months of 1987, Joseph and Dayton-area volunteers began to explore the possibilities of creating a new nonprofit organization to address the ongoing needs of the people of Sierra Leone. While this new nonprofit's beginnings would be concentrated in Sierra Leone, the concept of assisting in development activities in other countries was incorporated.

On December 11, 1987, STARFISH was officially incorporated as a nonprofit corporation by the state of Ohio. In 1991 it was established as a subsidiary of an international mining corporation in Sierra Leone and became a non-governmental organization (NGO) in Sierra Leone. In 1992 the total revenues for STARFISH were over $400,000, which was obtained through corporate and community donations. The organization is governed by a board of trustees, who implement the charter and by-laws. In the United States, it is administered by a full-time executive director and by part-time administrative and clerical staff, including Dayton-area volunteers. College student interns are used in a volunteer capacity on a full-time basis at various times throughout the year. The interns assist the organization with office operations and research information needed by the professional volunteers traveling to Sierra Leone to implement identified projects.

Even though STARFISH is a separate organization from Sinclair, it is the ultimate example of how Sinclair faculty and students remain true to the philosophy of the college's founder, David A. Sinclair: "Find the need and endeavor to meet it." The "can do" attitude reflected by Joseph and his colleagues is epitomized in the STARFISH organization.

The STARFISH Model

Using the triangulation metaphor, STARFISH's community self-help international development model has three key players: an educational institution, an independent private nonprofit voluntary agency, and the for-profit sector (see figure 3).

All three groups are critical to the success of the model. The first group, an educational institution such as Sinclair Community College, provides volunteers to assist in international development projects. The faculty, staff, and student volunteers not only see what life is like outside the United States but also enrich their own lives by having an opportunity to give of themselves to others.

The following are some examples of what Sinclair faculty have achieved: Radiology faculty Denise Moore, Lee Shadle, and Beverly Van Den Einde, along with their radiology students, obtained donated X-ray equipment from Dayton-area hospitals; oversaw the transportation of the equipment; installed the equipment at a health clinic in Sierra Leone; and provided training and follow-up activities for rural X-ray technicians. Linda Eads, of the nursing faculty, designed a minor-surgery room and procured medical supplies, linens, operating room gowns, sutures, masks, etc., for physicians at clinics at the hospitals of Sierra Rutile, Serabu, Mattru, and Njala University College. Other Dayton-area volunteers are currently involved in projects to change agricultural practices; improve surgical techniques; develop a curriculum on the value of wells, latrines, and personal hygiene; construct a model latrine; reduce occupational injuries; install solar lights; and conduct an assessment of needs at Njala University College.

The second group, the voluntary organizations, has the infrastructure to operate at the grass-roots level in developing countries and has a good understanding of what works best in assistance projects, and it can apply donor money most efficiently and reliably. Data from a Carnegie Commission report (1992) indicate that U.S. private voluntary organizations engaged in international development projects "tripled between 1973 and 1989, and

FIGURE 3. Triangulation Metaphor

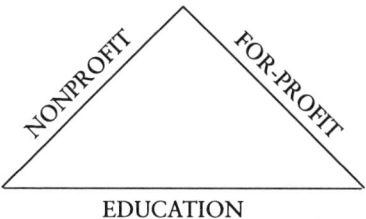

U.S. Government funds allocated for their support increased seventeenfold."

Voluntary organizations in the United States, working with their counterparts in the developing world, are able to design and conduct such workable projects as the international development projects regularly funded by U.S. Rotary Clubs. A major concern of American donors is how to ensure that their donated funds are actually spent on a specific project. STARFISH has almost eliminated that problem because of its active presence in Sierra Leone in a newly built Distribution Center at Sierra Rutile. The staff at the center oversee the import, storage, distribution, and purchase of supplies for STARFISH and other voluntary agencies.

For the third group, the American private for-profit sector, operating in a developing country contributes to global prosperity as well as to that of the developing country and of the United States; but business will grow and prosper only if its workers are literate, healthy, and technologically competent.

The STARFISH model works when the "gatekeepers"—the leaders in educational institutions, voluntary agencies, and the for-profit sector who make or remove barriers for their employees to participate in field experiences in developing countries—lead where others are timid. The gatekeepers must be creative and committed in their dedication to international development partnerships. When gatekeepers respond to the developing country's changing circumstances and emerging opportunities in an adaptive, flexible manner, then their employees/volunteers have unprecedented opportunities for personal and professional growth. Without informed, flexible, committed leaders as gatekeepers, the STARFISH model is nonfunctional. By combining their efforts, all three groups—education, nonprofit, and for-profit—accomplish more than they could achieve separately.

USING AN ALGORITHM FOR PROJECT PLANNING

To bring its Sierra Leone constituents to make a mutually agreed-upon decision about a project, STARFISH initiated an algorithm proposal process in 1991. The algorithm flowchart is a tool to evaluate the appropriateness of proposed development projects and to formulate STARFISH's policy on aid and development while ensuring the cost-effectiveness and consistency of the projects.

Every volunteer submitting a proposal for a STARFISH development project subjects the project's ideas to a series of questions in the algorithm. Each proposal must be submitted on a special form and must include answers to criteria on acceptance and nondependency. The criteria for acceptance are whether the project promotes the STARFISH mission by being culturally acceptable and having a strong self-help component, being environmentally sound and educational, helping the underprivileged, and benefiting the majority of the Sierra Leonean community.

About 80 percent of the algorithm covers nondependency criteria. Because Sierra Leone has limited technological resources, the supplies and equipment involved in the project must be appropriate and made or partly made in Sierra Leone. If the resources are not available in Sierra Leone, then cost reduction or other modifications must be made to enhance the long-term sustainability, nondependency, and affordability of the project.

In addition, a specific person in Sierra Leone must be committed to the project, actively involved in planning and implementation, and willing to accept responsibility for the project. In this way, sustainability comes to the fore, since the people of Sierra Leone have accepted their responsibilities prior to the start of the project. When the indigenous population is not fully committed or actively involved in the project, then a plan or incentive to find such a person must be implemented. Most of the projects involve furthering food production and farming, developing an industry, or making significant contributions to health, education, or both. All projects must have a plan for continued monitoring, continued evaluation, and future planning. Final project approval is given by the STARFISH board of trustees in Dayton, Ohio.

The algorithm format was used to evaluate a proposal to fund the construction of a new well and a large latrine in Moriba Town. The initial plans were modified during extensive discussions among all the parties concerned, both in the United States and in Sierra Leone. The project called for the use of a large quantity of soap for a hand-washing educational project in the elementary schools. At first, the soap was to be donated by schoolchildren in the United States and transported free by a corporate sea container to Sierra Leone. The algorithm process identified a self-dependency component of using imported soap from the United States. Consequently, a decision was made to use soap made in the villages, thereby promoting the growth of small soap-making industries.

CASE STUDY: SIERRA LEONE, WEST AFRICA

The work on projects in the Kono Region in Sierra Leone began in 1986, one year prior to the incorporation of STARFISH. The earliest projects concentrated on health-care and community-development services and training at Manjama and Koidu. As STARFISH activities became established, the private and corporate donor base grew significantly. An example of the work accomplished in the Kono Region is the development of a birthing clinic, which required volunteer expertise in such tasks as tiling the clinic to maintain cleanliness, renovation of the physical structure, installation of solar equipment to ensure reliable energy, and the delivery of pharmaceutical and medical supplies to enable the clinic to start a cost-recovery medicine program.

Many of the STARFISH volunteers came from Sinclair's Allied Health faculty or were second-year students, community persons, health professionals, and other educators in the Dayton area. For example, during the holiday and summer breaks of 1988–92, groups of Sinclair faculty and students worked at the health clinic at the mining site in Sierra Leone and assisted with the building of a new wing at the health clinic, stocked the pharmacy with donated drugs, installed donated X-ray equipment from a Dayton hospital, financed the trip to Sierra Leone through personal fund-raising activities, trained a West African midwife and a STARFISH project manager at Sinclair Community College, and housed the West Africans in private Dayton homes. These experiences provided valuable lessons about public service and valuable cross-cultural experiences for both the American and African students and faculty.

The volunteer work generated such local interest in Sierra Leone that an additional eight faculty members from six Dayton-area colleges and universities conducted an assessment of the needs of Njala University College during the summer of 1990. (Njala is located about 120 miles inland from the coast of Sierra Leone.) Njala faculty, STARFISH volunteers, and mining company employees used their human and physical resources for local economic development projects and for the sake of personal and professional development.

The UDLP

The purpose of the UDLP, which is funded through the U.S. Agency for International Development (U.S. AID), is to internationalize U.S. higher educational institutions by linking them with foreign higher educational institutions. The UDLP is not a "grant" but a "cooperative agreement" in which the U.S. and foreign educational institutions mutually agree on the implementation of the agreement's objectives and allocation of funds.

Unlike STARFISH, which is a separate organization from Sinclair and receives its funding from the private sector, the UDLP project in Madras, India, is the culmination of several years of effort by Sinclair Community College and the Eastern Iowa Community College District, in conjunction with CCID, to work with Indian educators and clergy.

Sinclair is the lead institution and fiscal agent for $750,000 in UDLP funds and $750,000 in community college matching funds covering a five-year span from October 1, 1992, through September 30, 1997. The goal is to provide operational, logistical, and programmatic support to the Center for Vocational Education (CVE), so that by September 30, 1997, it becomes a proactive, self-sufficient, prototype institution for the offering of vocational and technical education in India.

Small teams of community college faculty and administrators travel to India for different six-week periods during each year of the project. The team members are drawn from the sixty community colleges belonging to CCID. Each team member has individual objectives and areas of expertise. In the following list, each team member's name is linked to an area of expertise: Nancy Lloyd Pfahl, College of DuPage (fund-raising and grants development); Jean Cook, Jim Houdeshell, and Tom Singer, Sinclair Community College (project management, construction trades, and quality control); Linda Hoodgenjik, Spokane Community College (geriatric home health care); David Streifford, St. Louis Community College (computer training and video development); and Jon Ryan, Eastern Iowa Community College District (small business development).

During 1994–97, fifteen additional community college individuals will make up new project teams. An open application process takes place each summer. The applications are reviewed by a committee at Sinclair Community College and Eastern Iowa Community College. The applications are then sent to the CVE's director in Madras for his review with the CVE's Advisory Committee. Their recommendations are reviewed at Sinclair and Eastern Iowa, and applicants are notified. A discussion of the time frame for a visit to Madras and specific project objectives then takes place with the UDLP project director in Dayton. Appropriate travel and financial arrangements follow.

CASE STUDY: MADRAS, INDIA
The Madras project is the culmination of several years of efforts by the author and the CVE director during her 1991 and 1992 visits to India as a lec-

turer in the Fulbright program and during numerous meetings and planning sessions with college administration at Sinclair Community College, the Eastern Iowa Community College District, and CCID. The UDLP links Sinclair Community College, Eastern Iowa Community College and CCID with the CVE, the A.M. Jain College, Stella Maris College, Madras Christian College, and Loyola College in Madras. Three offices have been established for this project: Sinclair Community College (project director, Dr. Jean Cook), Eastern Iowa Community College (assistant project director, Ed Stoessel), and in Madras (director of the CVE, Adrian J. Almeida).

The UDLP funds provide for the expansion of the CVE in Madras. The CVE developed out of volunteer efforts by its director, Adrian J. Almeida, and his community associates to connect government and private funding groups with volunteer agencies that could either provide or oversee that the appropriate training programs were initiated and implemented.

The community college project teams provide technical assistance to the CVE to develop its infrastructure (building refurbishment implementation of management systems and fiscal controls); initiate a human resource development plan to include the curricula and delivery systems (location, equipment, teachers, etc.) necessary for fifteen vocational and technical training programs; implement a master plan for a resource development office (contract training, grants development, fund-raising, public relations), in association with the National Council for Research and Development (NCRD) (Pfahl and Cook 1993); conduct a national train-the-trainer conference on the CVE's model approach to polytechnics, technical teacher-training institutes, industrial training institutes, and universities in India; and raise funds to ensure that the CVE is financially, logistically, and programmatically self-sufficient when U.S. AID funds end in 1997 (Herbkersman and Cook 1991).

The 1992–93 project team presented four workshops on grant writing and project management, developed a resource development plan, and oversaw both the refurbishment of the building housing the CVE and the initiation of project management tasks. The 1993–94 team used their technical expertise in health, small business development, computers, and construction to collaborate with Indian educators on developing a skills-training curriculum and career-planning video modules for people who do not know how to read or write. The 1994–95 team processed objectives and activities related to repairing air-conditioners and small machines, small business development, environmental programs, and proposal writing.

The Sinclair UDLP office has conducted a search for literature on how to train illiterate people in developing countries. Their research has provided a theoretical framework for the curriculum. Some interesting ideas about literacy and skills training that are contrary to commonly held practices in literacy training in the United States are emerging. This search for literature has validated the approach used by each project team, which is to write the skills-training curriculum according to the team's own area of expertise.

Since the CVE works mainly with the rural and urban poor, tenth-grade dropouts, women, and people who have never had an opportunity to learn skills, the curriculum is being designed in three tiers: for the illiterate, semiliterate, and literate person. For example, in small business development, the first level is for the illiterate person looking to sell wares on the street (micro-enterprise); the second level is for the semiliterate person who wants to have a small sidewalk stand or a shop in a small building (small business development); and the third level is for the literate shopkeeper seeking to enter the import-export business (formal business sector).

The teaching methodology will include pictures, simulations, and experiential exercises for the illiterate person; will add some text, arithmetic, and writing skills to the curriculum of the semiliterate person; and then add the study of laws, regulations, accounting practices, etc., for the literate person. The assumption is that illiterate people will become aware that in order to enlarge their businesses, they will need literacy skills and will thus become self-motivated to learn.

Evaluation of International Development Efforts

Evaluation documents what works and what does not work. However, if all the problems were known at the outset of an international development project, many projects would never be initiated. For both projects, it was difficult to plan specifically all the tasks ahead of time, since there were lots of issues that had to be resolved in a labor-intensive fashion. The evaluations for both projects are summative and formative and have received input from advisory board members, volunteers, and recipients of assistance.

The effectiveness of a project depends on the willingness of people to do something and on how they implement the project's goals and activities. Variability in the ways of implementing a project does not equate to lack of success but demonstrates creative problem solving, innovative ideas, and a flexible approach to working and living in another culture, which may be politically unstable during the life of the project. For example, STARFISH struggled with the peaks and valleys of the quality of work sustained by its volunteers, and the CVE's administration and staff are still grieving over the November 1993 death of the archbishop of Madras, who was a prime sponsor of CVE's activities.

Both Sinclair Community College and the CVE demonstrated their creativity and flexibility when Sinclair wrote a subcontract agreement with the CVE and instituted the transfer of funds to India—a first for the college and the CVE. Lengthy discussions were held by Sinclair and the CVE prior to a final agreement on the administrative costs and the allocation of funds to specific line items. Disappointment reigned supreme when U.S. AID would not issue a waiver to purchase a much needed non-U.S. minivan in India with U.S. AID funds. Long, exhaustive discussions finally resulted in a clear definition of the objectives and activities of the project team members. New formal validation forms for the 50 percent match were designed. Finally, an understanding of U.S. AID regulations and reporting processes now prevails.

To the extent possible, the evaluation uses objective, quantifiable measures for each area under assessment. For the Madras project, the following outcomes are expected by the end of the project (1997):

1. *Infrastructure*: The required infrastructure (a building, management systems, fiscal controls for U.S. AID funds, office equipment, an educational resource data base, etc.) will be created at the CVE, three additional CVE sites will be opened in Madras, and the Madras model will be shared at the national level.

2. *Human resource development*: At least fifteen new vocational and technical training programs will be created at the CVE through the use of the human resource development plan.

3. *Financial resource development*: Sufficient funds will be obtained annually through use of the master plan for the resource development office (which covers contract training, grants development, fund-raising, and public relations) so that the CVE will become financially self-sufficient by 1997.

For the above outcomes, an evaluation activities matrix has been outlined listing each major activity of the project, the sources of information, the measures to be used, and the time of data collection (Herbkersman and Cook 1991).

Sinclair administration will serve as on-site monitors while in Madras. They will monitor the progress of all components of the project and summarize this in a monthly report. Members of the faculty will then send reports via fax back to Sinclair. The project director will incorporate these findings into her reports to U.S. AID.

From the outset, the goal of evaluation has been to determine ways to sustain the effort so that the CVE will be a viable educational resource for many years after U.S. AID funds have ended. This will be assured by effective communication among partners (for example, when the CVE sends a monthly project report to Sinclair), regular meetings of the three advisory committees, as well as the UDLP office meeting with Sinclair administration members to discuss budgets, training programs, and the implementation of a five-year resource development plan. An international meeting of the Project Advisory Committee is held annually.

Professional and Personal Linkages: An Evaluative Component

International development projects enable community college volunteers to use their experiences to internationalize curriculum, make presentations to community groups, and obtain resources for other development projects from their professional associations. Volunteers become aware that the scope of their development initiatives represents only a small fraction of what is needed in that country, but they demonstrate their capacity to set goals and coordinate the creative use of resources in their accomplishments. And one trip, just one connection with one initiative leads to another and another. Private businesses also realize the benefits of their employees taking on community self-help development tasks. Major U.S. corporations feel that their involvement in international development adds value to the workplace and to the local community.

Although quantitative results are important (e.g., forty people trained to be brick masons or twenty sewing machines purchased), the qualitative success of these projects is more so. Many of the volunteers have never seen poverty on such a massive scale. They are forced to think about the political and social systems that have created the dietary, illiteracy, health, and transportation problems in the developing country. Many volunteers form ties with the people they meet, some of whom lead miserable existences, since they are little more than beasts of burden. As a result, volunteers return with a renewed determination that they can make a difference, and many volunteers have increased their volunteerism and philanthropy in their local communities as a result of their experiences in India and Sierra Leone. Was the experience of volunteering in a developing country worth it? Just ask them, as they enthusiastically share their experiences with their colleagues and students while simultaneously arousing their colleagues' interest in volunteering.

FUTURE ISSUES

The following are some points of advice for community colleges thinking of becoming involved with international development:

1. Consult with community colleges, funding organizations, and U.S.-based resources already engaged in international development field experiences before embarking on a program, so that you may learn from their successes and failures.
2. Establish clear reasons for getting involved in a developing country and be prepared to stay there for a long time.
3. Consult with representatives from the developing country and collaborate with indigenous nongovernmental organizations, to determine the management, direction, and resources of the program.
4. Strive to maintain a dignified sense of humility and be prepared to learn from any mistakes made in initiating an international development project.

As we prepare to move into the twenty-first century, Kennedy (1993) reminds us that the world population may reach 10 billion and thus reshape the world's borders, strain the environment, and cause politics to be remade. The "community" of the community college is now a "global village," with all the problems of overpopulation, ecology, and political upheaval.

Community colleges can address these problems by participating in international development projects, and in many instances, they need relatively few resources to do so. Any type of action is critical, especially when Kaplan (1994) tells us that "West Africa is becoming the symbol of worldwide demographic, environmental, and societal stress," "Sierra Leone is widely regarded as beyond salvage," and "Indian cities like Delhi and Bombay are ecological time bombs with much of India's economy resting on a shrinking natural-resource base."

The case studies of Sierra Leone and India demonstrate that it is indeed possible for community colleges to work on international development projects. In these projects, much has been constructed that warrants a careful review by other colleges interested in international development. One must remember, however, that community self-help international development projects involve real people who hope, dream, and work to improve their lives. You cannot be satisfied with doing an adequate job; you have to do it exceptionally well, since you are committing yourself to a cause. The challenge is real!

REFERENCES

Carnegie Commission. "Reasons for Cooperation." Report on Science, Technology, and Government. Washington, D.C.: Carnegie Commission, 1992.

Clinard, M.B. *Slums and Community Development: Experiments in Self-Help.* New York: The Free Press, 1989.

Fernando, V. "NGOs Woo Women with Water." In A. Anand (ed.). *The Power to Change.* New Delhi: Kali for Women, 1992.

Gahlot, D. "A SPARC of Hope for Slum-Dwellers." In A. Anand (ed.). *The Power to Change.* New Delhi: Kali for Women, 1992.

Herbkersman, N., and J. Cook. "A Community College Linkage to Vocational/Technical Training and Education Programs in Madras, India." Grant proposal submitted to the University Development Linkages Program of the United States Agency for International Development by Sinclair Community College. Washington, D.C., 1991.

Kaplan, R. "The Coming Anarchy." *The Atlantic Monthly* (February 1994): 46–60.

Kennedy, P. *Preparing for the Twenty-First Century.* New York: Random House, 1993.

Pfahl, N.L., and J. Cook. "A Master Plan for Resource Development for the Center for Vocational Education in Madras, India." Unpublished Report. Sinclair Community College, 1993.

Seth, S.C. "Technology-Society Nexus and Perceptions of the Future." *Futures* (October 1989): 44–76.

Society Taking Active Responsibility for International Self Help (STARFISH). *Annual Report.* Ohio, 1993.

United Nations, Department of Economic and Social Affairs. *Community Development and Related Services.* New York: United Nations Department of Economic and Social Affairs, 1960.

3 FROM AID TO TRADE

NEW TRENDS IN INTERNATIONAL EDUCATION IN CANADA

Daniel Schugurensky and Kathy Higgins

International education in Canadian community colleges is experiencing important changes in the types of activities performed and the clientele served. Indeed, activities framed in the "development education" paradigm are being replaced by those in tune with a "global marketplace" paradigm, and therefore the emphasis has shifted from providing assistance in areas such as education and health to the promotion of trade. Likewise, the focus of international education programs is shifting away from less developed countries (LDCs) and toward the Pacific Rim and Eastern Europe. While in the past an emphasis was placed on responding to the needs of "the poorest of the poor" in African, Asian, and Latin American countries, current programs are being developed to address the specific needs of students, businesses, and governments in more developed areas (Japan, Hong Kong, Singapore, the former Soviet Union, Korea, Malaysia, etc.). At the same time, there is an increasing emphasis on the role of international education in assisting the Canadian private sector. While in the past international education activities were largely funded by the state, international education offices are being increasingly pressured to generate their own sources of revenue through cost-recovery projects.

The changes underway in international education cannot be isolated from societal and institutional pressures. The economic shift from Fordism[1] to post-Fordism[2] and the implementation of market-oriented policies have influenced important transformations in the higher education system. As a result, Canadian community colleges are undergoing substantive adjustments in several areas, particularly financing, governance, and function. With regard to financing, there is a pressure on community colleges to increase their reliance on private sources of revenue, including contract services and tuition fees. With regard to governance, colleges are losing decision-making power. The government, challenging the old-time principle of autonomy and invoking the concept of accountability, is increasing its presence in higher education decision making. In relation to function, the "college-driven" model is rapidly being replaced by an "industry-driven" model based on the "needs of the economy."[3]

In summary, after decades of expansion, the present era of contraction and budget cutbacks is forcing colleges to become more particular in their selection of programs, which leads to the downsizing or elimination of those that are in insufficient demand. At the same time, colleges are pressured to adopt the managerial systems typical of industry and business and to become more entrepreneurial, selling their services and products in the market.[4]

In this chapter the implications of these social and institutional changes for international education in community colleges are explored. The chapter is organized into six sections. In the first, the shortcomings of the existing literature on Canadian community colleges in helping to comprehend the present shift of international education programs are indicated. The second section provides a framework for analyzing such a shift by considering the socioeconomic context in which it has occurred. In the third section, the institutional context is briefly reported on and the major changes experienced by Canadian community colleges are described. In the fourth section, the concept and practice of international education is analyzed and its competing rationales are examined. The fifth section presents two case studies to illustrate recent changes in international education: Grant MacEwan Community College and Mount Royal College, both located in the province of Alberta. Based on the examination of these two institutions and the new directions undertaken by the state (as expressed by key government agencies), the sixth section is a report on the conflict of paradigms in international education. The conclusion is reached that the case for the elimination of international education or for expeditiously making it a profitable enterprise (a case raised by some actors outside and inside the colleges) is myopic and shortsighted. This suggests that the imminent challenge to be faced by international education administrators will be how to find a balance between two competing rationales.

INTERNATIONAL EDUCATION IN CANADIAN COMMUNITY COLLEGES

While in the United States the examination of international education in community colleges can be traced at least to the late 1960s (see, for instance, Yarrington 1970), in Canada it is a recent issue and has not yet obtained significant academic attention. Indeed, the existing literature on Canadian community colleges consistently ignores the topic of international education.[5]

For instance, in futuristic analysis undertaken during the early 1980s, the importance of international education was largely unanticipated. In the early 1980s, the potential impact of economic globalization on community colleges was unnoticed, and there was not even one reference to international education as a possible strategy for responding to those upcoming challenges. In spite of the increasing importance of international education, the analysis of it continues to be omitted in the recent literature, as in the case of the two most influential books on Canada's community colleges: the comprehensive critical analysis of Canada's community colleges by Dennison and Gallagher (1986), which covers the ten provinces and the two territories, and the book edited by Muller (1990), which has ten chapters devoted to the analysis of relevant changes in different areas of Canada's community colleges. Unfortunately, in neither of these valuable contributions to the study of community colleges in Canada is the issue of international education addressed.

When discussing the current reorganization of Canadian community colleges, the contributors to the abovementioned books tend to focus on four major issues: structure, governance and management, curriculum, and skills training. However, we contend that in order to understand the important changes that have taken place over the last several years in community colleges, it is also important to examine the issues of function and rationale. International education provides an interesting case study in this regard.

In short, the existing literature on Canadian community colleges is insufficient to understand current changes in the area of international education. First, such literature consistently tends to overlook international education as a field of analysis. Second, changes are usually explained solely from the perspective of organizational analysis, without relating it to broader transformations in the political economy. As a matter of fact, since community colleges do not exist in a vacuum, the explanatory power of institutional analysis can be enhanced if it is complemented by a historical-structural analysis. This is the purpose of the next section.

THE SOCIOECONOMIC CONTEXT: FROM FORDISM TO FLEXIBLE ACCUMULATION

Recent reforms in international education undertaken by community colleges cannot be isolated from changes occurring in the broader socioeconomic context. During the 1990s, especially in developed countries, the Fordist techno-economic paradigm is rapidly vanishing and is being replaced by a new paradigm rooted on reducing costs and increasing the speed of moving products and information from one location of the globe to another. The welfare state, functional in the old paradigm, seems to be insufficient to respond to the challenges posed by the new paradigm of flexible accumulation.

Under the new techno-economic paradigm, economic and social life is being dramatically transformed. One of these transformations is the rise of new forces of production. The introduction of new technologies in the workplace leads to increased standardization and systematization, and therefore, industries are shifting from a factory-mechanical model based on labor to one governed by self-regulating machines. In this context, information and services are becoming more important than manufacturing and agriculture, particularly in developed countries. A second transformation is the increased flexibility in the use of the labor force. The Fordist industrial production based on a large army of blue-collar workers is declining, the hourly wage of full-time workers is being replaced by piecework remuneration, and the power of unions is being reduced because of a relaxation of labor legislation. New high-tech industries are becoming more capital-intensive, and as a result, large sections of the work force are becoming de-skilled or redundant. This situation is leading to a polarized labor market composed of a small, highly skilled and well-paid sector, on the one hand, and a large, low-skilled and low-paid sector, on the other.

A third transformation is the retrenchment of the welfare state and an increased use of market principles in public institutions. The deep fiscal crisis affecting the public sector is being addressed with adjustment programs, which include a reduction of public expenditure and an increased privatization of the state agencies (social services, health, housing, pensions, education). This leads in turn to a division of society into two sectors: the protected (or "included" by the model), on the one hand, and the unprotected (and "excluded") on the other (Newson and Buchbinder 1988).

Another important element related to the new techno-economic paradigm is the globalization of the economy, which basically means an escalation of international trade and the internationalization of the production process. The former is reflected in the increasing capacity to connect markets immediately and to move money around. Currently, 600 major multinational corporations (MNCs) control 25 percent of the world economy and 80 percent of world trade. One of the most important consequences of this economic restructuring on a global scale is the widening of the financial, technological, and cultural gap between more developed and less developed countries. Indeed, this process occurs in the context of new relations and arrangements among nations, characterized by a new international division of labor, an economic integration of national economies (common markets, free trades, etc.), the increasing concentration of power in supranational organizations (World Bank, IMF, UN, EEC, G-7, etc.), and the "internationalization" of nation-states, in the sense that their agencies and policies become increasingly adjusted to the rhythms of the new world order.

Canada has not been alien to the pressures for budgetary austerity, trade liberalization, and privatization. Under the ideology of privatization, which has faith in the natural efficiency of competition and perceives the "invisible hand" of market forces as the remedy to cure all social malaises, the state is perceived as wasteful, inefficient and unproductive, whereas the private sector is seen as efficient, effective, and responsive to the rapid changes occurring in the modern world. The urgency to curtail government expenditures has led to the dismissal of public employees and drastic cuts in social-sector programs, especially health and education.[6] The progressive withdrawal of the state from these programs implies a shift of financial burdens from government to users,[7] as well as their appropriation by private enterprises. Particularly relevant for international education are cutbacks in foreign aid. In spite of the fact that Canada's foreign aid represents merely 0.45 percent of the GNP, a much lower percentage than the 0.70 percent commitment stated by Development Assistance Committee (DAC) countries,[8] this budget is being reduced yearly: Canada's overseas development assistance to developing countries has been cut by U.S.$44 million in 1992–93 and by $225 million in 1993–94, and it will be reduced by $262 million in 1994–95 (Canadian Council for International Co-operation 1993).

The Science Council of Canada has stated that in terms of international competitiveness, Canada has been performing poorly. In this view, one of the factors undermining Canada's economic development is its low outward orientation (focus on trade and investments) in relation to other industrial countries. Interestingly, when Dennison and Gallagher addressed the issue of community colleges' contribution to enhance Canada's international competitiveness, they made exclusive reference to the local training of national human resources and made no allusion at all to international education (Dennison and Gallagher 1986, 136). However, in the late 1980s international education acquired a new profile, and specialized offices dealing with this issue were open in many community colleges.

INSTITUTIONAL CONTEXT: CURRENT CHANGES IN COMMUNITY COLLEGES

Current reforms in Canadian community colleges are highly influenced by similar reforms that have been implemented in the United States. In that country, a Business–Higher Education Forum was established in 1978 to influence postsecondary education, in an effort to align it with the business and corporate sector. The pressure on community colleges to conduct business with the marketplace was formalized in a handbook published by the

American Association of Community and Junior Colleges. This handbook, suggestively titled "Doing Business with Business," consists of a series of institutional guidelines and practical advice (from planning an office to delivering services) for colleges planning to serve commerce and industry (Hamm and Tolle-Burger 1988).

Replicating the U.S. model, a Corporate–Higher Education Forum was founded in Canada in 1983 to promote partnerships between business and higher education in a variety of areas. The impact of the initiatives emanating from this forum and other government and private agencies (such as the Business Council on National Issues) on redirecting higher education towards the market has been well documented in the recent literature.[9] Emerging trends in community colleges throughout Canada were quickly recognized by Dennison and Gallagher (1986, 81–130) and have been expanded upon by the several contributors to the book edited by Muller (1990). For instance, as Smith and Smith (1990) have described in reference to the plastic industry, colleges are moving from the "human capital approach" to the "human resource management" approach, from "occupations" to "skills," and from "student needs" to "industry needs." Changes are reported to follow a top-down approach in which the college-driven model is replaced by an industry-driven model of management "in order to serve the interests of business rather than those of working people" (Muller 1990, 13). For example, in the province of Saskatchewan, a large number of community colleges (which were originally mandated to serve the educational needs of small rural communities) and technical institutes merged in 1988 into far fewer and larger applied science and technology institutes. One policy recommendation of the forum that has shaped postsecondary reform across Canada has been its emphasis on performance-based funding allocation, in which public and private institutions compete for public funds (Cameron 1987). As a matter of fact, in Alberta the public funding of private colleges has increased.[10]

As state institutions, community colleges are highly subject to government policies. The retrenchment of the welfare state (reflected in the three R's of recession, rationalization, and restraint) is translated into budget cutbacks and the administrative restructuring of public institutions. This, in turn, results in factorylike models of education that include economies of scale (departmental merges, larger classrooms, etc.), the homogenization of teaching, a results-based curriculum, standardized tests, performance-based funding, and the like. In the new model, the goals of promoting accessibility, social criticism, cultural development, and institutional autonomy have been given lesser priority (Axelrod 1983). Instructors suffer a loss of autonomy in the control of their environment, and students are considered inputs into the "production process." In terms of financing, declining state funding is forcing colleges to become more entrepreneurial in order to generate alternative sources of revenue. This process, which is consistent with the increasing commercialization of cultural goods, means an increasing tendency for colleges to sell their services to whomever can afford them.

With declining state revenues, colleges must aggressively pursue market opportunities to remain financially viable. Obtaining these new sources of revenue has become a strategic priority in the long-term planning of many colleges, to the extent that programs failing to attract them are subject to closure (Huot 1991; Calvert and Kuehn 1993).

International Education: Functions and Rationales

Generally speaking, two major functions of international education can be distinguished in community colleges: global involvement and internationalization of the curriculum. The first refers to student study-abroad programs, student exchange programs, mini-study tours, faculty exchange programs, campus activities with an international emphasis, and consultation or support services for foreign institutions or countries, especially help in developing technical assistance programs or institutional strengthening at counterpart institutions. The second aspect refers to the integration of an international component in all programs and by all faculty. To enhance the educational experience of all students, this second aspect aims at incorporating the international dimension inherent in every course. Both aspects are supposed to be part of a broader institutionalization of the international perspective, that is, its adoption as part of the tradition and fabric of the college (Smyth 1986; Edwards and Tonkin 1990; Greenfield 1991; King and Fersh 1992).

Three main long-term rationales can be identified behind international education programs: the humanist, the political, and the economic. The humanist rationale believes that understanding other languages and cultures and contributing to the development of other countries would build world tolerance and peace and would eventually eliminate the prospect of war. The political rationale perceives international education as a pragmatic tool for national security. Finally, the economic rationale sees international education as a tool to promote international trade and as a requirement to ensure a competitive edge in the world arena (Scanlon 1990; King and Fersh 1992). While these rationales may differ in the emphasis credited to particular programs or strategies, they may also coincide in many areas. For instance, a convergence may be observed in the importance of learning foreign languages; likewise, certain types of development education can be seen simultaneously as tools for peace, for security, or for future investments. In the same vein, divergences may occur in the importance attributed to foreign aid, or in the pertinence of awareness programs.

Although the three rationales are always present, their relative weight in decision making varies in different historical conjunctures, according to the influence of structural conditions and ideological contexts. For instance, it has been argued that the economic rationale has been the main driving force behind the establishment of international education in a number of North American community colleges (Naisbitt 1982; Moore 1982; Government of Alberta 1984). Likewise, since the end of the cold war, the political rationale has rapidly decreased,[11] and an increasing clash between the remaining two rationales has emerged. Currently, under the aforementioned economic pressures, the conflict between the humanitarian and the economic rationale is reaching a turning point in which the balance of power seems to favor the latter.

The humanitarian rationale is expressed under the "development education" (Dev. Ed.) paradigm, which was introduced after World War II and has continuously evolved since. The Dev. Ed. paradigm understands the world as a system of multiple inequalities based on differential access to economic, political, and ideological power among countries and regions, as well as among people, mainly due to variables such as class, gender, and ethnicity. Dev. Ed. serves the purposes of distributive justice and socioeconomic transformation for less developed countries and cultures, and focuses on the less privileged sectors of society in developing countries, such as women, natives, peasants, street kids, etc. Covering a wide spectrum that ranges from charity-oriented projects to radical projects oriented toward consciousness raising and empowerment, Dev. Ed. attempts to raise awareness among Canadians about the living conditions of Third World peoples and to promote an improvement in these conditions, particularly in terms of health, education, and employment. It also aims at protecting values such as peace, human rights, and the environment and at achieving a greater global awareness in developed countries about issues in developing countries (global education).[12]

The economic rationale is usually expressed under the "global marketplace" paradigm, which understands the world as a harmonious system of exchange based on supply and demand. Under this paradigm, international education performs a service to the nation and assists business and industry, promoting trade and economic opportunities overseas. A restricted version of the global marketplace paradigm is the "revenue-generating" strategy based on cost-recovery or profit-oriented activities, which, in practice, consist of selling international education services to anybody who can afford them and giving the least priority to activities that do not generate revenue. While the global marketplace paradigm is based on a long-term rationale, under which international education is a means to open new markets and promote business opportunities and international trade, the revenue-generating approach constitutes a short-term strategy to keep international education activities alive in a period of drastic budget cutbacks. The argument advanced by advocates of the revenue-generating approach is that in a time of recession in the North, Canada cannot afford to provide aid to the South, because efforts and resources should be primarily directed to ameliorate the needs of people in Canada.[13]

Policies based on the global marketplace approach attempt to free higher education from the hand of the state by placing it at the disposal of industry. While the government interprets these policies as helping to unchain Prometheus, critics argue that higher education systems are "chained to a rock, with the eagles of budgetdom and intervention tearing daily at their entrails" (Neave and Vught 1991, xiv, 253).

In international education programs carried out by Albertan community colleges, the Dev. Ed. paradigm is being replaced (sometimes by consensus, sometimes by coercion) with the global marketplace paradigm and, in some occasions, by the revenue-generating approach. Therefore, the goals and activities of international education in community colleges are changing accordingly. To illustrate this shift, two cases are examined: Grant MacEwan Community College and Mount Royal College. These two institutions, located in the two largest cities of the province, have sizable enrollments and have been implementing substantive international education activities at home and abroad.

INTERNATIONAL EDUCATION IN ALBERTAN COMMUNITY COLLEGES:
TWO CASE STUDIES
Since education in Canada is provincially administered, educational institutions and their programs differ across the country. A province of 3 million inhabitants, Alberta has the highest rate of participants in postsecondary education in Canada and a labor force with the second highest percentage of postsecondary qualifications. Furthermore, its community college system is probably the closest in institutional structure and programming to the system operating in the United States.[14]

Since 1958, when the first public community college in Alberta was created (at Lethbridge), Alberta has experienced a multiplication of postsecondary institutions. This expansion was particularly evident during the 1970s, when the province enjoyed unprecedented economic growth resulting from the oil boom. Today, the higher education system of Alberta comprises an impressive spectrum: four universities, eleven public colleges, seven affiliated or degree-granting private colleges, nineteen nonaffiliated private colleges, two technical institutes, two schools of fine arts, six hospital-based schools of nursing, four vocational colleges, seventy-eight licensed private vocational schools, eighty-five further-education councils, and a variety of postsecondary educational "consortia."

The Alberta community college system has been considered the best of Canada in terms of its structure (Clarke 1983, 91). Moreover, it has been stated that Alberta's colleges have anticipated the economic crisis with much more vision than have those of other provinces, to the extent that "Alberta seems well placed to lead Canada" in terms of college-industry cooperation (Dennison and Gallagher 1986, 90). Among the eleven public colleges, the largest ones are Grant MacEwan Community College (GMCC) and Mount Royal College (MRC). The former, located in Edmonton, the capital of the province, offers over forty different diploma and certificate programs in arts and sciences, business, health and community studies, community education, and performing, visual, and communication arts. It also provides first- and second-year university transfer programs in arts, science, commerce, and nursing and a first-year program in physical education. From its three locations, the GMCC serves 26,000 students: 10,000 in credit programs and 16,000 in hundreds of career-related courses, workshops, and seminars. The MRC, located in Calgary, offers thirty-three career diploma programs, twenty career certificate programs, nine arts and sciences diploma programs, seven general and compensatory programs, and six university transfer programs. The MRC offers credit programs to more than 7,000 students per semester, and every year, the number of registrations totals more than 22,000 in continuing education and more than 9,000 in music and speech courses.

In 1986, after comprehensive research on existing international education programs in other institutions (see Smyth 1986), the GMCC established an office of international education to facilitate and coordinate all the international education activities in the college. The mandate of this office was to pursue six major goals: (a) to provide professional development opportunities for faculty, staff, and administration; (b) to prepare Alberta students to function, professionally and personally, in an interdependent world; (c) to enable students to have the opportunity to develop their full potential through participation in a wide variety of educational activities; (d) to contribute to international understanding through formal and nonformal channels; (e) to provide the college student with the opportunity to interact with students from other countries; and (f) to fulfill the college's moral obligation to contribute to international development. To achieve these goals, a number of objectives were established, including the following: "to strive for student representation from as wide a variety of countries and cultures as possible," "to develop and promote opportunity for GMCC students to participate in study/work abroad programs," "to establish linkages with foreign institutions to facilitate both student and faculty exchanges," "to promote and assist in internationalizing college curriculum," "to offer development education[15] to GMCC and the larger community," "to seek avenues to become more involved in the transfer of professional development and curriculum development expertise to institutions abroad," "to explore the need and potential for ESL instruction," and "to become involved in contract training." The office was created with the responsibility of implementing programs in four areas (services to international students, student and faculty exchanges, study or work abroad, and Dev. Ed. programs) and to facilitate the college's involvement in three areas: internationalizing the curriculum, contract education, and development assistance programs. Within this framework, the international education office implemented technical assistance activities in over twenty countries, ranging from increasing vocationalism in the curriculum in Uganda to upgrading libraries in Ecuador, training trainers in Thailand, and developing nonformal education in the Philippines. It also organized a variety of campus-based activities (such as an international awareness week, guest speakers, video presentations, etc.) to internationalize the staff, students, the curriculum, and community outreach programs.

At the MRC an international education office was established in January 1988, in an effort to coordinate existing international projects and ventures and to develop a greater presence in the international education arena. From the outset, the MRC included among its goals of international education the generation of revenue (at a minimum), the recovery of costs, and (at a maximum) the attainment of profit. Most international education activities carried out by the MRC can be classified into one of the following main areas: (a) technical assistance, (b) cost-recovery projects, (c) international students, (d) internationalization of the institution. The first area, funded mostly by the Canadian International Development Agency (CIDA), consists of human resource training and technical assistance for multifaceted projects in developing countries. Examples of these projects are a feasibility study and training for a water treatment plant in China, distance education programs and teacher training for an institute of occupational safety and health in Jordan, a rehabilitation services diploma program in the Gaza Strip, a customized training course in telecommunications for the six ASEAN bloc countries, and the development of programs for entrepreneurial education in the former Soviet Union. The second area, which consists of "business ventures," provides customized training packages and contract services to international interests and markets specialized skills abroad. Activities in this category have been predominantly concentrated on the Language Institute, which offers summer study tours and ESL courses for foreign individuals and companies, particularly from Japan and Korea. In addition to offering these "on site" programs, the MRC is now placing an increased emphasis on the expansion of technical assistance projects abroad. The third area includes the recruitment of individual international students and the provision of customized training to groups of international students on a cost-recovery basis. This includes credit students, ESL students, and international exchange students. Finally, the fourth area includes a variety of activities, from hosting visiting scholars to international-awareness festivals, faculty exchanges, and homestay programs. Among all the international education activities carried out by MRC, the most important ones in terms of number of participants and revenues have been those (mainly ESL) undertaken by the Language Institute.

In both institutions, the original mandate, the types of activities implemented, the choice of partner countries, and the profile of the clientele have been seriously affected by economic and political constraints. These constraints, expressed in government policies and budget cuts, accelerated the shift from the Dev. Ed. paradigm to the global marketplace paradigm described above, and prompted a rearrangement of priorities.

CHANGES IN COMMUNITY COLLEGE INTERNATIONAL EDUCATION: FROM "DEVELOPMENT EDUCATION" TO "GLOBAL MARKETPLACE"

During the late 1980s, the Dev. Ed. paradigm, which had dominated the ideological discourse (and in many cases, even the agenda) of international education in Canada for at least two decades, began to be challenged by a market-oriented paradigm based on international competitiveness.

A turning point in this shift can be identified as September 1988, when a provincial committee (the Alberta Colleges and Technical Institutions International Committee [ACTIIC]) was formed as a coordinating body to facilitate the delivery of education and training programs in human resource development worldwide. Concurrently, new partners emerged (Japan, Korea, Hong Kong, Ukraine, etc.) and a new language extracted from the business world started to complement (and increasingly replace) the "social reform" language of development education. For instance, in the Terms of Reference of ACTIIC, the first paragraph of the preamble states: "Alberta's colleges and institutes have a role to play in international education and in facilitating international trade and commerce and in promoting the interests of Canada and Alberta" (ACTIIC, Terms of Reference, appendix A [May 14–15, 1990]). The influence of government bodies on this turnabout cannot be ignored. A brief examination of official documents produced by the Ministry of External Affairs, Alberta Advanced Education, and the Ministry of Industry, Science and Technology, as well as of recent CIDA policies, may illustrate the direction of these changes.

First, it has been stated that the Department of External Affairs is increasingly shaping the kinds of international exchanges in which community colleges participate (Calvert and Kuehn 1993, 106). Hence, the agendas of international education offices in community colleges are largely affected by changes in Canada's foreign policy. In a leaked External Affairs document released by Valpy (1993), the government states that "the shift from global coverage to strategic intervention cannot be achieved without tough and painful choices," predicts that "in some cases, actual commitments may have to be broken," and cautions that "Canada may be perceived as backing [away] from its burden-sharing responsibilities." Since this document was leaked during the same time period of CIDA's announcement of the elimination of health and development programs in Africa, Valpy suggests that the painful choices had been already made. The dissemination of the contents of this document, as well as recent changes in actual policies, generated a strong concern among NGOs in the sense that "the Canadian government is skewing the foreign-aid budget to help business interests" and that "Canadian aid policy is shifting away from its traditional focus on long-term human development" (International News 1993, 3). This concern is accompanied by denouncements of publicly funded projects that help Canadian private companies and local elites but that are at odds with the needs of native populations and the environment (Sallot 1993). The top-down approach undertaken in the definition of the new policies has generated discontent among higher education institutions. A recent editorial in *UniWorld*, the publication of the International Division of the Association of Universities and Colleges of Canada, contends that "our government has decided to change the direction of its foreign policy without any consultation with those of us involved in delivering and designing Canada's aid" (Wasilewski 1993, 1), and calls for a participatory model based on transparent decision-making processes carried out not only by funders and executing agencies but also by the partners and participants themselves.

Second, the official policy of Alberta Advanced Education toward international education, as exposed in a recent document (AAE 1990, 1), stresses the contribution of international education to the "Province's increasing involvement in the international economic arena." In addition to supporting the establishment of academic and cultural linkages with other nations, international education should "support international trade, development and investment strategies." Likewise, international education is perceived as relevant to the achievement of economic growth and to the competitiveness of Alberta private-sector bids on international projects. In the new framework, "North and South" are replaced by a "global marketplace," "foreign aid" by "economic ties," and "assistance" by "trade," and references to poverty and underdevelopment are replaced by allusions to "successful commercial initiatives beneficial to Alberta's private sector." While the Dev. Ed. paradigm focuses on the notion of "dependency" as a continuation of colonialism and a hindrance to Third World development, the new paradigm of the global marketplace recognizes "the importance of global interdependence for economic development" (AAE 1990, 1). In this document, the government proclaims that "Alberta's emphasis on expanding international trade and investment is a major objective in our strategy for achieving further growth and diversification of the Province's economy" and makes clear that international education must become part and parcel of this strategy. In a subsequent document (AAE 1991, 1), the Minister of Advanced Education proposes a cooperative approach, which means, among other things, "developing more partnerships with business." In the same vein, in the influential *Vision for the Nineties* (Alberta Education 1991) the term *global* refers primarily to enhancing trading, commercial, and strategic interests in order to enhance Alberta's competitiveness in the world economy. For instance, schools are exhorted to develop more programs and courses on Asian and European languages and cultures to improve the ability of students "to compete successfully in the world economy" (Alberta Education 1991, 10).

The third example comes from the Ministry of Industry, Science and Technology, which notices the weakened role of CIDA as the lead government agency to identify and develop market opportunities and points out that increasing competition for international services has encouraged Canadian suppliers to explore opportunities on their own and to develop new markets for their services. This situation implies a shift from developing countries to other regions:

> As Canadian suppliers become less reliant on international development assistance programs, they are adopting more aggressive market-

ing practices and are exploring opportunities outside developing countries. For example, Middle Eastern countries have purchased Canadian expertise in school curriculum design, petroleum industry training and industrial safety training. There is also a significant potential market for Canada in Western Europe, Japan, and the United States, which have shown an interest in Canadian capabilities in technology-based training.... The potential for downstream benefits to other sectors of Canadian industry is considerable, as the provision of Canadian education and training can lead to the development of broader and long-term trading relationships. (Ministry of Industry, Science and Technology 1991, 4)

In the same document, it is pointed out that the sale of commercial education and training services in other countries can serve as a lead-in for the purchase of other Canadian services and products, and that the foreign sales potential of international education has long been recognized by Canada's major competitors, particularly Great Britain, the United States, France, Japan, and Australia. The document forecasts that "international trade in commercial education and training services through tendered contracts of IFIs (international financial institutions) is not expected to grow significantly in the near future," while "the number of non-aid related educational and training projects in many LDCs and NICs will likely continue to increase" (Ministry of Industry, Science and Technology 1991, 10). It also proclaims that the initial provision of education and training services to foreign countries results in the positive benefits of sales to foreign countries and the potential to develop broader and longer-term trading relationships.

Moreover, in 1992, a task force report on international education and marketing shows an emphasis on marketing Alberta's educational and training expertise on an international scale. In this report, the link of international education to economic goals becomes quite clear: "Now, international education activities should complement the overall provincial approach to trade promotion" (Ministerial Committee 1992, 4). The three major recommended strategies in this regard are (a) program development and delivery in Alberta, (b) international student exchanges, and (c) marketing of educational and training expertise. The task force advises that in order to successfully implement these strategies, efforts should be directed to areas of the world where the Alberta private sector is seeking to expand its market share: "Alberta must focus the limited resources on priority markets where there is the greatest potential for commercial success" (Ministerial Committee 1992, 4). This recommendation, which concentrates on exchanges in the countries of the former Soviet bloc and the Pacific Rim, could easily be associated with a similar shift from least developed countries to Eastern Europe that was undertaken at the same time by CIDA. Indeed, at the end of the 1980s, CIDA's goals still were "to help people in Africa, Asia, Latin America and the Caribbean—especially the poorest countries and people—to make social and economic progress so they can meet their own needs today and create a better future for their children" (CIDA 1988, 1).

However, in the early 1990s, CIDA ended bilateral aid to Tanzania, Rwanda, Ethiopia, Kenya, Madagascar, and Burundi, among other countries, focusing instead on the former Soviet bloc countries, which are more immediate prospects for Canadian commercial interests. CIDA's shift in the direction and content of Canada's development aid has created a great controversy across Canada.[16] The Canadian Council for International Cooperation, for instance, contends that the new policy discards the government's 1987 commitment to reduce poverty in the Third World, constitutes a huge setback to people-centered development, and drastically diminishes adult literacy, primary health care, and small-scale agriculture programs (CCIC 1993).

This shift is clearly reflected in the international endeavors of Albertan community colleges. In September 1992 the GMCC opened an office in Kiev, Ukraine, with the idea of implementing both academic and nonacademic activities. However, during the course of the first year and contrary to preliminary expectations, fifteen of the seventeen completed projects assisted Canadian industry and government in the area of business services. At the MRC, the extreme emphasis on revenue-generated international projects has prompted faculty members to warn of the risks of completely abandoning academic and development-oriented projects. Moreover, in a radical departure from what community colleges used to do, Olds College in Alberta has recently created, in conjunction with a university and two private companies, a corporation called CANED International Inc., providing agricultural-based education, training, and technology-transfer services to foreign countries. Since 1993, most international technical assistance projects undertaken by the college have been channeled through this corporation.

This gradually increasing government pressure to redirect international education toward the global marketplace paradigm has been exercised at three levels: discourse, policy, and funding. Due to their financial and political disadvantage, advocates of the Dev. Ed. paradigm usually confront those pressures at the level of discourse. In 1989 they organized a National Workshop on Development Education entitled "New Challenges for Development Education in Canada in the 1990s." Under this title, the *Journal of*

Canadian International Education devoted one entire issue in 1991 to publishing the main contributions to that workshop, in which the goals of development education were defined as follows: "to make Canadians more aware of the problems of development and to assist in the formation of attitudes and behaviors that will facilitate the constructive transformation of the many relationships between rich and poor countries" (Ariyaratne 1991, 5). In the recent literature of international education ascribing to the Dev. Ed. paradigm in Canada, the frequent mention of certain cherished values is still prevalent. The most recurrent ones are "social justice," "social change networks," "a more human world," "grass-roots organization," "compassion," "Third World perspective," "self-reliance," "new international economic order," "conscientization," "spiritual change," "individual awareness," "community work," "sustainability," "equal partnerships," "participation," "emancipation," "empowerment," "solidarity," "human rights," "working with the poor in the Third World," and "nonformal education." Recurrent references to figures such as Freire, Palme, Nyerere, or Gandhi are also noticeable (Edmonds, 1982; Toh 1987; Floresca and Toh 1989; Cronkhite 1991; James 1991; Moffat 1991; Tomlinson 1991; Choldin 1993; Toh 1993).

Development education's resistance to market-oriented policies focuses on CIDA's recent involvement in international development and the ethical priorities of the business sector. In regard to the former (although it praises CIDA for including among its priorities a partnership with Third World peoples, women's participation, environmental issues, human rights abuses, and so on), it opposes CIDA's changes in its regional priorities mentioned above. Development education also contends that CIDA "assumes uncritical support for the structural adjustment programs of the IMF and the multilateral banks," and reproaches CIDA for its emphasis on "enlarging markets for Canadian technologies and business services" (Tomlinson 1991, 77, 78). Moreover, it disapproves CIDA's tied aid, that is, the fact that roughly 80 percent of all bilateral aid[17] received by the South must be spent on the purchase of Canadian good and services (Seidel 1993).[18]

In regard to the reservations towards the private sector, Dev. Ed. advocates object to the provision of grants and loans to Canadian companies undertaking projects in developing countries, which often do not meet the normal aid standards for environmental protection, involvement of women, and so on (Hossie 1993). In the same vein, Dev. Ed advocates question "the ethics of any Canadian investment or business dealings that rely on exploited labor, including that of children" (Toh 1993, 13).[19]

The theoretical, political, and sociological contradictions between the two paradigms, together with the pressure for cost-recovery and even profit-oriented programs that results from budget cuts, has generated an intense debate in both community colleges about the mission and objectives of international education. One of the issues of the debate relates to the need to reach a balance between provincial and institutional goals (as well as between academic and scholarly benefits), on the one hand, and diplomatic and economic benefits, on the other. Another issue is the nature of the partnerships between public institutions and the private sector. A third issue is the appropriateness of marketing education as a commodity.

In the MRC, the conflict between development assistance and cost-recovery projects is addressed in several internal documents. In an evaluation conducted in July 1990, little agreement was found within the college community about the functions, goals, and objectives of its international education office and, hence, about the type of projects and activities with which it should be involved. This lack of consensus is expressed in that document as follows: "There is a tension between the pursuit of cost-recovery projects and the pursuit of development assistance projects. The goals and objectives of cost-recovery projects are incompatible with those of development assistance projects, both practically and philosophically" (Smith 1990, 31).

Consequently, the document states that clear priorities will have to be set between the two types of activities, because it is unrealistic to serve both functions. The argument for this conclusion is that given the scale of the projects and given the available resources, it is impossible to continue pursuing both types of projects unless the time and resources devoted to one of them is drastically reduced. This situation creates a dilemma, the document cautions, because on the one hand, there is a clear need for a financially self-sufficient operation, but on the other, the development projects have the widest appeal and support among college constituents and provide institutional benefits that have the widest impact. The document alleges that for international education to operate in the future, hard choices will have to be made with respect to goals and priorities. A few months later (October 31, 1990), at a Deans' Council meeting, it was reasserted that the original goals of development assistance projects and overall revenue generation are mutually exclusive, and that priorities needed to be established. Furthermore, it was pointed out that although CIDA-funded projects satisfy the ideological needed of a number of faculty, they cannot provide the college with sufficient overhead for the infrastructure to maintain them. It was also stated that "given the current economic climate, both internal and external, *plans for an International Education operation should minimize the draw on the College operating budget*" (Smith 1990, 1; emphasis in the original).[20]

At the GMCC, an evaluation of the International Education Centre conducted by Wilson (1991) pointed out the existence of similar reservations among staff. The concern raised by some interviewees was that if the center was not self-funded it would take funds from other college areas, and the question was which areas the funds could come from. Three comments quoted by Wilson may illustrate this attitude toward international education:

> First, I'd like to see the monies spent elsewhere in the college where programs are starving for basic needs to be met, then I'd like to see expansion in the international area. My major concern, and it may well be groundless, is that energy and funding for local services, which seem limited, might be directed to international causes, at the expense of our local students. Maybe what is required is reassurance that local funds are not being spent on international education. Can we afford it? What benefits accrue to the college? (Wilson 1991, 21)

Although at the GMCC international education is still well supported by the college community,[21] it is still vulnerable. Wilson reports that the increasing competition for scarce resources is creating a feeling among faculty that it takes resources from "regular" program areas.

Conclusions

Structural changes in the global economy from Fordism to flexible accumulation, the retrenchment of the welfare state, the commercialization of knowledge, a general ideological shift from worldwide social justice to international competition, and pressures to make higher education more accountable to the business sector are causing an infusion of a rapid "response"[22] in the international education programs undertaken by community colleges. New priorities in foreign aid established by CIDA, as well as institutional changes influenced by government funding and policies, are also key factors in provoking such a response.

While in the recent past international education was organized around the rationale of cooperation and aid (the Dev. Ed. paradigm), today it is increasingly organized around the notions of trade and profit (the global marketplace paradigm). Within the college community, the two paradigms are not perceived as complementary but as conflicting. In a context of scarce resources and an ideology that encourages the sale of anything that can be sold, development education is rapidly vanishing as a guiding paradigm, and is being replaced by a market-oriented strategy. Moreover, since international education is not perceived as a vital function of community colleges, it is more susceptible to cutbacks than are other areas and, hence, to pressures to implement cost-recovery programs. The two competing paradigms are simultaneously present in the international education projects undertaken by the GMCC and the MRC. Although both paradigms may sometimes enjoy peaceful coexistence, in most cases they maintain a strained relationship. Indeed, a tense conflict between the two approaches to international education has evolved in recent years. Although the final result of this struggle is still unseen, for the time being it is evident that the global market approach is controlling the agenda for discussion through political and financial means. As Neave points out, in spite of the fact that the global market model does not have popular appeal, the political influence of its proponents in most of the Western world is inversely related to their number (Neave 1991, 78).

However, the pressure towards the implementation of revenue-generating activities (in the best-case scenario) and towards the elimination of international education (in the worst-case scenario) has been severely criticized not only by advocates of development education but also by some lucid advocates of the "global marketplace" paradigm. The former contend that international education should put social justice, the environment, and the standard of living of people in developing countries before profit and commerce. The latter argue that although some international programs may not be profitable in the short term, that does not mean that they constitute an irrational investment, because they create business opportunities in the long term. Although based on differing assumptions and agendas, the defense of international education advanced by both paradigms revolves around common themes, such as the notions of the "shrinking world" and the "planetary community." From either a competitive or a collaborative standpoint, both paradigms stress the increasing interdependence of nations and the need for a global perspective in order to face today's challenges. For very different purposes, both paradigms oppose the pressure to make international education a profitable enterprise as a condition for its survival. Tsunoda (1989; 1994), for instance, contends that international education is not a luxury but a necessity. From a different perspective, Greenfield argues that international education constitutes an irrevocable function of the college.

> From an institutional point of view, international programs are not money makers. Indeed, they cost in terms of administrative and support staff time, travel, etc., but such programs may attract numbers of better students, use the entrepreneurial drives of some faculty members, enhance the employability of the students involved, lead to inter-institutional linkages, and provide opportunities for institutional and staff

renewal. Perhaps the overriding reason is a philosophical one: can the community college mission be attuned to reality if it ignores the international dimension in today's world? (Greenfield 1991, 134)

If it cannot, a less philosophical question can be posed: Is it possible to reach a compromise between the social–humanitarian and the economic–financial goals of international education? If the answer is yes, the challenge in the upcoming years will be how to harmonize these apparently incompatible rationales in a coherent program. If the answer is no, the challenge will be how to preserve the social goals of international education in a context of financial constraint. The point to consider is that short-term financial gains sometimes result in long-term misfortunes.

NOTES

1. Fordism is associated with the following features: (a) the mass production of homogeneous products and a homogenization of consumption patterns, (b) the use of inflexible technologies such as the assembly line, (c) the adoption of standardized work routines (Taylorism), (d) economies of scale, (e) de-skilling and homogenization of labor, (f) workers associations (unionism) and uniform wages, and (g) and a centralized welfare state, guided by Keynesian macroeconomic policies, which oversees collective bargaining and ensures the reproduction of the labor force through universal education and health care (Ritzer 1992).

2. Post-Fordism is associated with the flexible accumulation paradigm, which is characterized by the following: (a) a decline of interest in mass products and a growing interest in specialized products, (b) smaller, more flexible, and more productive systems, based on new technologies, (c) workers with more differentiated and greater autonomy and responsibility and equipped with better training and more diverse skills, (d) replacement of centralized and bureaucratized institutions (such as unions, political parties, and welfare) with more flexible ones responding to the needs of a more differentiated labor force and a more diverse population, and (e) more differentiated life-styles and consumption patterns (Pelaez and Holloway 1990; Ritzer 1992). The post-Fordist era has also been associated with three concurrent developments: the emergence of institutional capitalism, the retrenchment of the welfare state, and the commercialization of knowledge. For a detailed explanation of these three societal trends and their impact on postsecondary education see Raj Pannu, D. Plumb, and D. Schugurensky, "From the Autonomous to the Reflexive University: Global Restructuring and the Re-forming of Higher Education," paper presented at the Eighth World Congress of Comparative Education, Prague, Czechoslovakia (June 1992).

3. In fact, the first strategy for higher education restructuring proposed by the government of Alberta is to "focus on programs that address the needs of the economy." This means, among other things, that "industry and post-secondary institutions will be encouraged to forge stronger links with each other to ensure the relevance of education and training to the workforce and the economy." At the same time, an emphasis will be placed on "the employability of graduates and their ability to become entrepreneurs" (Government of Alberta 1994, 16).

4. According to government proposals, colleges and technical institutes should focus on short-term programs that are responsive to the labor market, including the provision of training to industry on a fee-for-service basis (Government of Alberta, 1994).

5. The limited number of available publications on international education in

Canadian community colleges in comparison to that in the United States can be attributed to the fact that these activities did not emerge until the 1980s. The first office of international education in an Alberta community college was created at Grant MacEwan in 1987.

6. This trend is evident in the province of Alberta. In 1991 this province had the highest gross domestic product per capita in Canada but spent the lowest percentage of that per-capita product on education (Russell 1993, 1).

7. In 1993 the Alberta premier proposed client fees in the health care systems and suggested that universities and hospitals should use casinos and bingo to increase self-funding.

8. The DAC is a group of twenty donor countries that belong to the Organization for Economic Co-operation and Development. According to the Canadian Council for International Co-operation (1993), only five of these countries exceeded the 0.70 percent target. Canada, with 0.45 percent, ranks seventh. The United States, with 0.20 percent, ranks second-last, with only Ireland providing less (0.19 percent).

9. See, for instance, David Langille, *The Business Council on National Issues and the Canadian State*, Studies in Political Economy No. 24 (Autumn 1987); Newson and Buchbinder 1988 and 1990; Calvert and Kuehn 1993, and David Noble, "Hijacking Higher Education," *Our Schools Our Selves* (Jan./Feb. 1993).

10. According to the Alberta Advanced Education 1990–1991 annual report, page 5, the government has the goal of funding three private colleges by 1994–95 to a level of 75 percent of the implicit average grants for public university programs in the arts and sciences.

11. Even shortly before the end of the cold war, the presence of the "national security" rationale was observable in Canadian official documents. For instance, in a document published in 1988, CIDA explains the presence of so many Canadians working for development as follows: "because Canadians believe that a fair and just world will be more stable and peaceful—and they believe it is in Canada's best interest to help to create such a world" (CIDA 1988).

12. In general, movements such as education on peace, global education, multicultural education, citizenship education, human rights education, and environmental education could be included within the Dev. Ed. paradigm.

13. This view expects that savings from foreign assistance would be redirected to the welfare state in the North, ignoring that cutbacks in foreign-aid programs directed to helping marginalized peoples in the South are correlated with similar cutbacks to programs helping marginalized peoples in the North (Seidel 1993).

14. In Alberta, unlike other provinces, community colleges have been greatly influenced by the American model since their inception. For instance, in Ontario the community college system includes applied institutes of technology, places little emphasis on general education courses, and does not offer university-transfer courses at all. In British Columbia some community colleges have obtained university status and are therefore allowed to confer degrees. In Quebec all CEGEPs offer first-year university courses and also provide technical-oriented courses.

15. Note the direct reference to "development education" as an explicit objective of international education in the mid-1980s.

16. For more information on the discussion of CIDA's change of priorities as reflected in the national media, see articles by Jeff Sallot, John Stackhouse, Richard Phinney, Michael Valpy, and Linda Hossie published in the *Globe & Mail* (Toronto), the article by Clément Trudel in *Le Devoir*, and the article by John Foster in *The London Free Press*, all from 1993.

17. The figure of 80 percent is provided by Seidel. Linda Hossie, in "Not Enough Foreign Aid Goes to Poor, Study Says: Funds from Developed Countries Often Benefit Donors' Own Domestic Industries," *Globe & Mail* (Toronto), (June 10, 1993), A1, citing a report prepared by the Canadian Council for International Co-operation produced in 1993, presents the figure of 65 percent.

18. In this regard, Seidel also argues that global markets do not operate freely and that this, together with the unequal partnership, costs the developing countries $500 billion a year—ten times what they receive in foreign assistance.

19. Although Toh refers to a "transformative" paradigm (as opposed to a "liberal-technocratic" paradigm), it has multiple ideological affinities with the Dev. Ed. paradigm as it is described in this article and, therefore, could be assimilated into it.

20. This faculty reaction was prevalent during the 1990 evaluation. Three years later, concerns about the negative implications of an overemphasis on revenue-generating projects have dissipated and the prevailing attitude is, Why aren't we making more money? (Lorna Smith, personal communication [Dec. 9, 1993]).

21. In Wilson's survey, roughly 90 percent of the faculty and staff were in support of having an international education center, and only 17 percent indicated that it was realistic to expect the center to be self-funding.

22. Following L. Cerych and P. Sabatier, *Great Expectations and Mixed Performances* (Trenham Books, 1986), a distinction can be made between "reform" and "response." Reform is something someone wants to do in relation to a set of values, whereas response is something someone must do in reaction to a situation. Although both involve change, in the first case it is active and by choice, whereas in the second it is reactive and of necessity. While the former is usually present in a period of expansion, the latter is typical of a period of contraction. In the two case studies analyzed, international education programs are based more on response than on reform, in the sense that coordinators are unable to freely select the best alternative among a range of possible choices.

REFERENCES

Alberta Advanced Education (AAE). *International Education Program. Policy, Guidelines and Procedures.* Alberta: AAE, September 1990.

———. *Alberta Advanced Education 1990–1991 Annual Report.* Alberta: AAE, March 1991.

Alberta Advanced Education and Career Development Access through Innovation. "Draft White Paper: An Agenda for Change." Alberta, March 1994.

Alberta Education, *Vision for the Nineties . . . A Plan of Action.* Alberta: Alberta Education, 1991.

Alberta Teachers' Association. "Trying to Teach." Interim report of the Committee on Public Education and Professional Practice, as approved by Provincial Executive Council for discussion at the 1993 Annual Representative Assembly. Alberta, Jan. 1993.

Ariyaratne, A.T. "Does Development Education in the More Developed World Make a Difference in the Less Developed World? *Canadian International Education* 20, no. 1 (1991): 4–12.

Axelrod, Paul. "Higher Education, Utilitarianism and the Acquisitive Society: Canada, 1930–80." Paper presented at the Canadian History of Education Society Meeting, Vancouver, 1983.

Calvert, John, and L. Kuehn. "Corporate Power, Free Trade and Canadian Education." In *Toronto: Our Schools Our Selves.* Toronto: Canadian Council for International Cooperation, 1993.

Cameron, David. *The Framework for Managing and Financing Post-Secondary Education in Canada.* Saskatoon: National Forum on Post-Secondary Education, 1987.

Canadian Council for International Co-operation (CCIC). "The Reality of Aid." *Chronicle Herald* (Feb. 4, 1993): Monograph.

Canadian International Developing Agency. *A Developing World.* Ottawa: CIDA, 1988.

Cerych, L., and P. Sabatier. *Great Expectations and Mixed Performances.* Alberta: Trenham Books, 1986.

Choldin, Earl. "The Practice of Global Education." *Global Education* 1, no. 1 (Jan. 1993): 28–30.

Clarke, John. *Alberta Community Colleges: Ten Years in Review.* M.Ed. thesis, University of Alberta, 1983.

Cronkhite, Lovella. "Development Education in Schools and Post-Secondary Institutions." *Canadian International Education* 20, no. 1 (1991): 98–113.

Dennison, John, and P. Gallagher. *Canada's Community Colleges: A Critical Analysis.* Vancouver: University of British Columbia Press, 1986.

Edmond, Edwards. "Innovation and International Education." *Canadian International Education* 11, no. 2 (Dec. 1982): 70–86.

Edwards, Jane, and H. Tonkin. "Internationalizing the Community Colleges: Strategies for the Classroom." In *Developing International Education Programs,* New Directions for Community Colleges, No. 70. San Francisco: Jossey-Bass, 1990.

Floresca, Virginia, and Toh Swee-Hin. "Peace Education: A Land of Suffering and Hope: Insights from the Philippines." *Convergence* XXII, no. 1 (1989): 11–24.

Foster, John. "Canada's Ominous Signals to Poor." *The London Free Press* (Feb. 3, 1993): 8.

Government of Alberta. Proposals for an Industrial and Science Strategy for Albertans 1985–1990. White Paper. Alberta, July 1984.

Greenfield, Richard. "Thinking Globally." In Dan Angel and M. De Vault (eds.), *Conceptualizing 2000: Proactive Planning.* Washington, D.C.: The Community College Press, 1991: 129–34.

Hamm, Russell, and L. Tolle-Burger. *Doing Business with Business: A Handbook.* Washington, D.C.: American Association of Community and Junior Colleges, 1988.

Hossie, Linda. "Not Enough Foreign Aid Goes to Poor, Study Says." *The Toronto Globe & Mail* (June 10, 1993): A1.

Huot, John. "Implications of Corporate Involvement in Ontario's Community Colleges." Unpublished paper presented at the Education Worker's Seminar, Toronto, Oct. 2 and 3, 1991.

International News Editorial. *Newsletter of the International Center of the University of Alberta, Canada* (1993): 3.

James, Susan. "Development Education in the University: Research and Praxis." *Canadian International Education* 20, no. 1 (1991): 114–23.

King, Maxwell, and S. Fersh. *Integrating the International/Intercultural Dimension in the Community College.* Washington, D.C.: Association of Community Colleges Trustees and the Community Colleges for International Development, 1992.

Langille, David. "The Business Council on National Issues and the Canadian State." *Studies in Political Economy,* no. 24 (Autumn, 1987): 41–85.

Ministerial Committee on International Representation and Strategy. *International Education and Marketing of Education and Training Services.* Task Force Report. Edmonton: Ministerial Committee on International Representation and Strategy, 1992.

Ministry of Industry, Science and Technology. Commercial Education and Training: Industry, Science and Technology Canada, 1991. Edmonton: Ministry of Industry, Science and Technology, 1991.

Moffat, Jeanne. "Networks within Canada: Partnerships Abroad: The New Challenges for Development Education." *Canadian International Education* 20, no. 1 (1991): 13–20.

Moore, B. "From Reflection to Commitment." *Canadian and International Education* 11, no. 2 (Dec. 1982): 165–69.

Muller, Jacob. "Introduction." In Jacob Muller (ed.). *Education for Work: Education* as Work: Canada's Changing Community Colleges. Toronto: Garamond Press, 1990: 13–24.

Naisbitt, J. *Megatrends*. New York: Warner Books, 1982.

Neave, Guy. "On the Cultivation of Quality, Efficiency and Enterprise: An Overview of Recent Trends in Higher Education in Western Europe, 1986–1988." *European Journal of Education* 23, no. 1/2 (1991): 7–22.

Neave, Guy, and Frans Van Vught. "Introduction." In *Prometheus Bound: The Changing Relationship between Government and Higher Education in Western Europe*. New York: Pergamon Press, 1991.

Newson, Janice, and Howard Buchbinder. *The University Means Business: Universities, Corporations and Academic Work*. Ontario: Garamond Press, 1988.

———. "Corporate-University Linkages in Canada: Transforming a Public Institution." *Higher Education* 20, no. 3 (1990): 355–79.

Noble, David. "Hijacking Higher Education." In *Toronto: Our Schools Our Selves*. Toronto: Canadian Council for International Cooperation, 1993.

Pannu, Raj, D. Schugurensky, and D. Plumb. "From the Autonomous to the Reactive University." In L. Erwin and D. MacLennan (eds.), *Sociology of Education in Canada: Critical Perspectives on Theory, Research and Practice*. Mississauga: Copp Clark Longman, 1994.

Pelaez, Eloína, and John Holloway. "Learning to Bow: Post-Fordism and Technological Determinism." *Science as Culture* 8 (1990): 15–26.

Phinney, Richard. "Foreign Aid: What's in It for Us?" *The Toronto Globe & Mail* (Feb. 1, 1993): A13.

Ritzner, George. *Contemporary Sociological Theories*. New York: McGraw-Hill, 1992.

Russell, Shelley. "Budget a 'No News' Announcement on Education." *The Alberta Teachers' Association News* (May 18, 1993): 1.

Sallot, Jeff. "The Changing Face of Foreign Aid: A Re-evaluation of Priorities for Helping Other Nations May Trigger a Battle." *The Toronto Globe & Mail* (Feb. 13, 1993): A6.

Scanlon, David. "Lessons from the Past in Developing International Education in Community Colleges." Cited in Greenfield, 1991.

Science Council of Canada. "Canadian Industrial Development: Some Policy Directions. Summary of Report 37." Ottawa, 1984.

Seidel, Rebekha. "Is Overseas Aid Helpful to the South?" *Global Education* 1, no. 1 (Jan. 1993): 39–41.

Smith, Dorothy, and G. Smith. "Re-organizing the Job Skills Training Relation: From 'Human Capital' to 'Human Resources.'" In J. Muller (ed.), *Education for Work, Education as Work: Canada's Changing Community Colleges*. Toronto: Garamond Press, 1990.

Smith, Lorna. "International Education Review." Summary presented to the Deans' Council, Mount Royal College, October 31, 1990.

Smyth, Celia. "International Education: Challenges and Responses. Final Report on the International Education Project." Alberta: Grant MacEwan Community College, May 1986.

Stackhouse, John. "Foreign Aid: Canadian Cuts Costly Setback for Ugandans." *The Toronto Globe & Mail* (March 3, 1993): A11.

Toh, Swee Hin. "Survival and Solidarity: Australia and Third World (South) Peace." *Social Alternatives* 6, no. 2 (1987): 59–66.

———. "Bringing the World into the Classroom. Global Literacy and a Question of Paradigms." *Global Education* 1, no. 1 (Jan. 1993): 9–17.

Tomlinson, Brian. "CIDA's Sharing Our Future: Analysis and Implications for Canadian Non-Governmental Organizations." *Canadian International Education* 20, no. 1 (1991): 74–85.

Trudel, Clement. "L'aide mal oriente du Canada." *Le Devoir* (February 7, 1993): 14.

Tsunoda, Joyce. "International Education Is Not a Luxury." *AACJC Journal* 59, no.

3 (Dec. 1988–Jan. 1989): 3–8.

———. "Community Colleges Lead the Way in International Education." Paper presented at the 74th Annual Convention of the American Association of Community Colleges. Washington D.C., April 6–9, 1994.

Valpy, Michael. "The Aid That Canada Will Not Be Giving." *The Toronto Globe & Mail* (March 4, 1993): A2.

Wasilewski, Ania. "From the Editor." *UniWorld, Association of Universities and Colleges of Canada* (Spring 1993): 1.

Wilson, Pat. "International Education Centre Evaluation." Grant MacEwan Community College, Alberta, Nov. 1991.

Yarrington, Roger. *International Development of the Junior College Idea.* Washington, D.C.: American Association of Junior Colleges, 1970.

4 Weaving the American Tapestry

Multicultural Education in Community Colleges

Naomi Okumura Story

Unlike the general community college curricula, which are usually bound by the traditional academic emphasis on knowledge of content or by homogenized national standards, multicultural education reflects our culture and represents diverse forms and offerings. Multicultural education in community colleges ranges from the marginalized and very conservative international food fairs to comparative studies of various cultural traits and to work that encourages the empowerment of subgroups and the promotion of social change and reform. In brief, the sophistication or maturation of multicultural education is largely dependent on the leadership and cultural environment of the faculty as well as on the vocality of the local communities. Quite often the rhetoric about ideals has not been met with the reality of standard or comprehensive multicultural educational curricula. Many cogent and compelling factors prevent a consistent and comprehensive set of standards for multicultural education. However, because the community college environment is positioned to change and revise itself to meet social, academic, and cultural needs through education, one needs to review and assess those significant efforts across the United States to evolve realistic and relevant multicultural curricula in higher education. Community colleges choose to revise their history and place in higher education continuously, as they suffer the pains of change and growth, and this too infuses the multicultural curriculum. This chapter provides a tapestry of multicultural education that several community colleges across the country have tried to weave. This tapestry contains common threads as well as unique designs.

General Goal of Multicultural Education

The notion that education is a significant route to one's productive and full participation in U.S. society is a common belief among most Americans. The amount and quality of education received are viewed by many as having a direct impact on an individual's personal and professional success. However, the value and worth of education should be reflected not only by achievements or accomplishments but also by a greater goal of perpetuating the human spirit by sustaining and enhancing our multicultural society.

Ernest L. Boyer, president of the Carnegie Foundation for the Advancement of Teaching, recognizes the role education must play in celebrating diversity and in acknowledging people's interdependency when he states:

> Educating students in a multicultural world means affirming the sacredness of every individual, celebrating the uniqueness of every culture, and acknowledging the non-uniformity that separates one person from another, the distinctiveness that makes us who we are. This is the centerpiece of education in a multicultural world.
>
> But there is another side to the equation. In our deeply divided world, students also must begin to understand that while we are unique, we do share many things in common. While we celebrate individualism in education, it is immensely important that we celebrate community, as well, and that we understand the commonalities that we share. (Boyer 1992, 1)

Thus, teaching and learning in a multicultural world require faculty and students to study the rich heritage of America's unique culture, as well as the richness of other cultures. Americans need to understand the commonalities between their communities and global society. However, the simple logic of this is not commonly accepted in our diverse educational communities. When Alexis de Tocqueville visited the United States in the 1830s, he commented that it was a positive American trait that its citizens were willing to retain a new identity and become independent, as if creating a "clean slate." When individualism is perpetuated, people forget their ancestors and begin to think of themselves in isolation. Tocqueville stated in *Democracy in America* (trans. 1969) that this fragmentation had to be countered by allowing people to look outside themselves as individuals and to become part of a larger whole.

But who defines the new community, that *whole* and its segments that were, are, and will be the United States of America? Toni Morrison (1992) says, "Race has functioned as a 'metaphor' necessary to the construction of 'Americanist': in the creation of our national identity, American has been defined as 'White.'" This perpetuates the idea that the basic culture of America is European and that "other" cultures thus become secondary ones, sometimes invisible. Ronald Takaki (1993) further suggests that our general curriculum—with its narrow, individualistic perspective—tends to be based on an *exclusive,* "Eurocentric" view of our American history rather than on the *inclusive,* multicultural reality of what America was, is, and will be.

Rhetoric and Politics

The debate on multicultural education continues to be significant among educators across the United States. Questions on what multiculturalism is and how it should be taught are posed by scholars and practitioners alike (Gaff 1992). Gaff defines multiculturalism as a "radically multidimensional" construct, which means many things to many people.

The coupling of cultural politics with educational integrity and values can exacerbate discussions on what the mission of an educational institution should be. This is especially significant within the community college system, whose basic mission is to meet its community's needs by providing postsecondary educational opportunities to all people. What does it mean to be "all things to all people"? Is the educational mission of a community college based on the social or economic demographics of the community? What is the definition of *community* in community colleges? Is teaching or learning too ethnocentric? Should it be less ethnocentric? Who decides? What multicultural education means to one group (whether community members, faculty, administrators, or students) may not be what it means to another in the community college.

The fervor of this discussion escalates when political and cultural aspects are interwoven into the intellectual and pedagogical biases of "experts" (Ogbu 1992; Estrada and McLaren 1993). Arguments over the control and definition of schooling, together with recent movements related to national educational goals and standards, have caused significant tensions among schools, community, and states, which further complicate the discussion about multicultural education (Newmann 1993). But should community college educators educate their students to understand themselves and their fellow citizens through multicultural education, or should we prepare students, through international education, to be competitive in the global and international market? Can we do both? How can standards in multicultural education be established to fit these contexts?

In higher education, the philosophical and organizational issues of multiculturalism are related to the changing needs of the new learning community and its values (Hill 1991; Bossman 1991). The discussion on educating students to live and work in a pluralistic society has centered around curricular and pedagogical reforms as well as on the creation of environments that celebrate diversity (Smith 1989). But as the academy continues to debate the "correctness" of multiculturalism and to discuss the many facets of multiculturalism (Karamcheti and Lemert 1991; Yarbough 1992), it is not clear whether the educational climate represents the multicultural context of the United States.

Community colleges are just as unclear concerning multiculturalism, especially since the demographics and needs of their communities change constantly. Multiculturalism in community colleges is often defined by the different racial or ethnic groups that live in their community or region. California community colleges, for example, place a stronger emphasis on Mexican-American and Asian-American cultures than do community colleges on the East Coast, which may focus on African-American and Latino cultural influences.

In addition, community college systems, by their nature of meeting community needs, are more flexible to change and the redefinition of their vision or mission than universities are. The paradox of allowing community input and flexibility in community college programs, such as those in multicultural education, is that when programs are criticized by individuals, they are very susceptible to being eliminated before their maturation. The politics of the community have an influence over whether programs live or "die" and they do not undergo the nurturing or refinement expected in traditional academic curricula.

Thus, the irony is that when universities incorporate "multicultural" curricular elements even though they may not be current, there are not many of them, or they may not be relevant to the community at large, the programs are sustained. Levine and Cureton (1992) specifically report that four-year institutions are ahead of two-year community colleges by 28 percent in the number of multicultural general education requirements.

Furthermore, as part of their study to examine the condition of multiculturalism in higher education, Levine and Cureton (1992) also found that 34 percent of all colleges and universities, including community colleges, have a multicultural general education requirement. However, what is striking about these general education requirements is that they primarily focus on global multiculturalism rather than on domestic diversity. This suggests that even though four-year institutions have paid greater attention to multicultural education than have two-year community colleges, their definition of it tends to reflect an international or global focus rather than one on the diversity of local communities.

Therefore, a compelling moral dilemma that community colleges now face is whether they should ignore the multicultural programs that address the critical needs and issues of their community's diverse population and follow the lead of the university and have an international perspective. To focus on the global context is politically safe when stones cannot be easily thrown from another country. An international context also suggests that the community college is establishing and providing to its students and its community's turbulent economy financial and economic access into the current and future job market. The community college can become a competitive education deliverer and help create a world-class work force.

In addition, with the new technologies available, the geographical or regional area of a community can no longer be defined. Many community colleges have satellite, networking, and other long-distance educational capabilities that provide easier and better delivery of instruction around the world.

Yet, to ignore or to forget the local community is not consistent with the community college's history or basic mission. Rural, urban, and suburban communities across the United States have critical environmental, social, health, and welfare problems that reformists as well as educators cannot escape or ignore, because of the interdependence of the various components of society's systems. As Robert Bellah et al. elaborate in *Habits of the Heart,* there is an "urgent need for community and commitment to one another," as part of the American character, and many community college leaders have begun to address this issue in recent years. This chapter, however, is not designed to add to the continuing saga of defining the context or structure of multicultural education from an academic perspective, but it is necessary to establish that the notion of multicultural education in higher education is still highly debated.

By tradition and design, the American community college focuses on the learning needs of its community and on providing exemplary teaching and learning opportunities, while four-year institutions are established to perpetuate academic research and knowledge. Thus, the type and content of the multicultural education programs in community colleges differ significantly from those at four-year institutions.

American Community Colleges: A Profile

A recent study by Cliff Adelman (1992) suggests that the myriad of roles that community colleges play reflects the current "American" culture. He states that the community college system more easily "accommodates a variety of decisions to engage in intentional learning within a formal organization" (Adelman 1992, 22) than does the four-year institution. Therefore, for the common man and woman, the community colleges represent the American Dream of access and equality in higher education.

Here are some highlights of his report that are related to the multicultural context of the American community college:

- The population usually represents the dominant ethnic population and students of all ages.
- Despite the greater ethnic diversity in the community college student population, African Americans were less likely to use the community college in their postsecondary education than were other minority groups or whites. African-American students preferred attending historically black colleges and universities (HBCUs), which are primarily four-year institutions and are in the seventeen-state Southern region. Yet, there is a popular myth that a majority of African-American students attend community colleges.
- Community colleges serve a higher percentage of students having moderate or low socioeconomic status than do other types of educational institutions.
- The proportion of minority students who are U.S. citizens is higher in community colleges (22.5 percent) than among undergraduates in four-year institutions (16.6 percent). With the reported reason of proximity to one's primary residence as the key factor in community college attendance, the community college tends to serve the white majority more than minorities. Outside the South and parts of the Southwest, rural America is heavily white, and the principal postsecondary presence in rural areas is either the community college or the state college or university system.
- Nationally, of the community college students from secondary-language backgrounds, 18 percent were Hispanic and three out of four were either white or Asian American. It should be noted that the aggregate groups of Hispanic and Asian Americans are not clarified in this class-of-1972 study.

The basic demography of race/ethnicity, proximity, and socioeconomic status thus both confirms and questions the popular notion that community colleges are largely composed of minority populations. Adelman (1992) reports that the next group in the U.S. Department of Education's longitudinal studies program of high school classes of 1982 appears to be similar. However, upon examining total enrollments (Snyder 1992) one sees that by 1990, the majority of minority students tend to attend community colleges. The data further indicate that the increase primarily occurs at community colleges that are Hispanic, and a very dramatic increase occurs in the percentage of Asian-American community college students (a group that was too small to disaggregate in the class of 1972). The figures also show a corresponding drop in the proportions of whites and African Americans in community colleges (Snyder 1992, 203).

The implications for the curriculum of the continuing growth in the percentages of ethnic and racial minorities at community colleges cannot be ignored. Carter and Wilson's *Tenth Annual Status Report on Minorities in Higher Education* (1991) indicated that the enrollment of African Americans (non-Hispanics) at two-year colleges had increased by 7.6 percent from 1988 to 1990. It also found that the rate of growth in the enrollment of Hispanics in two-year colleges was a little higher (7.8 percent) in those years. American Indians showed the largest increase (8 percent) of all groups in two-year colleges. The rate of increase was 6.5 percent for Asian Americans, while white (non-Hispanic) enrollment increased by only 5.8 percent.

The pattern of enrollment of minority students in community colleges across the country suggests that by the year 2020, they will become the majority. The ramifications of this change for the curriculum and pedagogy, as well as for organizational structures and staffing (particularly, of faculty) are obvious.

Traditional, Eurocentric notions of the vision and form of education in community colleges need to be assessed, and broad-based, systemic changes are called for. As the nature and the "faces" of our students change, institutions will need to restructure themselves to attend to their needs. For example, according to the August 25, 1993, edition of the *Chronicle of Higher Education Almanac,* only 9 percent of the faculty in two-year public institutions were minority (African American, American Indian, Asian American, and Hispanic) in 1987. Furthermore, if one looks at the data of those who received doctorates, the average percentage of minority graduates was approximately 15–18 and the rest were white (*Chronicle of Higher Education* 1993). The proportion of white (118,903) versus the aggregate proportion of minority (18,075) educational professionals (such as executives, administrators and managerial staff) is worse.

The obvious question of role models and mentors for minority students needs to be asked. However, the larger question is, who will or can change the curriculum or the system to embrace both the future majority and the future minority student population? In a lecture titled "A Different Mirror: A Multicultural History of America" and delivered at the Honor Lectures Forum of the Maricopa Community Colleges (Arizona) on April 20, 1994, Ronald Takaki said that when the minority students of Berkeley became the majority in 1987, they—the students—pressured the faculty and administration to establish a graduation requirement of studies on a comparative perspective on American cultures. This multicultural requirement is now in place, and the curricular redesign is also being taught to community college faculty at a summer institute. So, we cannot ignore demographic changes in the discussion of multicultural education in community colleges present and future.

Multiculturalism and the Community College

With service to the community as its primary mission, the community college can dynamically address the changing demographics of its population and their extensive needs. The community college system is a logical and strategic environment in which multicultural educational programs can be established. Since the cultural makeup of communities varies, the types of programs that interweave multiculturalism in their curricula and pedagogy vary as well.

Building Communities

In a report by the Commission on the Future of Community Colleges (1988), appointed by the American Association of Community and Junior Colleges (now known as the American Association of Community Colleges), the commission agreed that the central goal of community colleges is to provide excellence in teaching and learning. However, the commission extended the discussion to the larger theme of the American community college as *a builder of communities*. To build communities, the community college should provide excellence in teaching. Faculty then become the critical component in creating a climate in which both intellectual and social relationships are fostered and strengthened (a community of learning). The community college faculty and instructional staff are key factors in creating multicultural programs and services for their highly transitory and diverse student population and to meet the ever-changing demands of the private and public sectors, which hire their graduates. The community college faculty must sustain the intellectual and social environment of the college by controlling academic standards, shaping the curriculum, and helping to create a learning climate for their students. Faculty must also provide continuity to the institution by defining educational priorities and passing on traditions from one generation to another.

The commission further stated that "building of community, in its broadest and best sense, encompasses a concern for the whole, for integration and collaboration, for openness and integrity, for inclusiveness and self-renewal" (AACJC 1988, 32). This statement encourages community colleges to break down separation or barriers based on race or ethnic background, to foster collaboration and relationships with the community beyond the classroom or the institution itself, and to promote the civic education of adults. In addition, the term *community* was not restricted to a physical or service region but was meant to be a creative climate for learning. The commission recognized that community colleges have an "urgent obligation to keep students informed about people and cultures other than their own, and that the building of partnerships must be not only local and national, but global, too" (AACJC 1988, 32). Thus, the commission saw that the community college shaped society's values and educated Americans for life in an increasingly complex and changing world by creating a climate of learning. This, therefore, provides a compelling challenge for community colleges to address multiculturalism in the United States.

Creating a Climate for Multicultural Learning

Several community colleges across the nation have created and developed specific programs that are instructionally sound and successful in meeting the needs of the diverse student populations they serve and support. However, not all colleges across the nation have addressed multicultural needs systematically since the commission's report of 1988. Some community college faculty and leaders have demonstrated proactive strategies and solutions for addressing multicultural needs through the use of innovative curricula, containing the latest technologies and teaching techniques, to encourage active learning and collaboration as well as to provide enriching social and intellectual contacts among students, especially those from different ethnic and racial backgrounds.

Several community colleges have also designed services in student development and learning assistance that support the multicultural learning community. They have developed creative partnership, recruitment, retention, and outreach efforts to strengthen, increase, and maintain the success of and support among minority students. A few of the community colleges with high minority enrollment have provided special programs, such as English as a Second Language. Specific examples (Seattle Central Community College, South Mountain Community College, and the Hawai'i Community College system) are shared later in this chapter.

Community college leadership and organizational structures continue to be assessed and redefined, to establish creative ways to build strong and unified communities and establish a lifetime climate of learning. Several community college systems have multicultural agendas clearly established in their mission statements and institutional goals. Pima Community College in Tucson, for example, not only includes multiculturalism in its mission, but also assesses the success of goals related to multiculturalism and multicultural education for the college each year using outcome measures. However, community colleges like Pima are more the exception than the rule.

The Reality and the Dilemma

With the changing demographics of community colleges and with the notion that cultural pluralism and cross-cultural relations exist in all communities, it is difficult for all college systems to engage in being "all things to all people." The philosophical tone expressed in the aforementioned commission has not been readily expressed into "real" programs across the country.

The reality of multicultural education programs in community colleges is not optimistic, especially when multicultural education is not recognized as an economic value but only as one of social or intellectual significance to the community. For example, when funds are cut or "cost containment" and "fiscal responsibility" are the catch phrases of community college governing boards, programs that are highly controversial are (more often than not) scrutinized. More traditionally focused academic or occupational programs are justified and kept because they are "safe" or have been "tested" (using graduation, transfer, or employment data) to show their benefit to the community. Immediate and tangible returns are more fiscally sensible than long-term commitments to high-risk multicultural programs.

Furthermore, college leaders often see multiculturalism (especially domestic or local needs for diversity) as being "too political," especially when it requires a major shift in institutional climate. The change in paradigm occurs when not one dominant group sets the standards of instruction or the perspectives of the curriculum but people of all groups are reflected and part of the overall institutional climate and instruction. In addition, faculty are resistant to change when asked to use different teaching techniques and to establish new roles as mentors or facilitators of learning. The faculty who resist change are mostly unaware of both the mores of the multicultural population and their contribution to curricula or do not understand the importance of creating an active learning environment for different learning styles and cultural influences.

Although the ideals of multicultural education have been expressed, they have not borne a "multitude of fruit" in reality. Five years after the report of the Commission of Future Community Colleges, colleges have not assessed or clearly defined their commitment to multiculturalism. No national standards or guidelines for multicultural education in community colleges exist. Not all community colleges have consistent or shared curricular designs for multicultural education. But the varieties of and organizational support for multicultural programs in this chapter suggest an agreement on content and context.

There is no pervasive evidence across the country that demonstrates the distinct value of multiculturalism in the curriculum. More often than not, positive statements are not backed by substantive curricular integration or infusion of multicultural content. For example, textbooks for traditional courses such as English, mathematics, or U.S. history do not include a comparative or integrated multicultural context. Many community colleges include mission statements and goals that address multicultural values, yet if one looks at college catalogs, very few have programs and courses that infuse multiculturalism into the curricula.

Few colleges offer consistent or long-term support to faculty to make substantive changes in curricula or pedagogy. At conferences and meetings, presentations and workshops on multiculturalism are usually offered to community college administrators and faculty. Yet, it is common knowledge that very few faculty members incorporate new ideas or insights after these one-time, one-shot events. Several of the Maricopa Community Colleges made multiculturalism a faculty development priority for the 1993–1994 academic year. Speakers and video-conference events were offered but not required. Pockets of faculty discussed aspects of multiculturalism, but changes were reported by only one or two among over 800 faculty members. More faculty across the district were concerned about *internationalizing* the curriculum, rather than about *multiculturalizing* it, especially when special funds for international education are available. To impact the teaching and learning as well as the content of courses, faculty need time and resources, not just money. And if not supported or encouraged, most faculty members tend to gravitate to the old ways and knowledge.

Upon researching and reviewing programs that community colleges place under the rubric of multicultural education, there appears to be no agreement about, or uniformity of, components or factors. However, each of the 100 representative community colleges across the country that were surveyed and reviewed for this chapter reported at least one multicultural activity or program.

This chapter provides snapshots of current, significant multicultural education programs and activities in several community colleges representing both the local and global spectrum. The multidimensional aspect of multicultural education in community colleges today is also illustrated and discussed.

Clearly, the definition and context of multicultural education vary based on each community college's service population as well as on regional differences. Examples of philosophy, curricula, faculty, administration and leadership, teaching and learning processes, student services, and community relations, as well as partnerships with the public and private sectors, are shared and discussed in this chapter. Factors and elements that make these specific situations and examples unique and exemplary are also identified and described. Further, the implications and value of such attempts and examples are questioned and discussed.

THE MULTICULTURAL CURRICULA

Multicultural curricula in community colleges are defined from the perspective of service to clientele and tend primarily to be regionally influenced. Often, the college's chief academic officer defines a multicultural curriculum as one reflecting the diversity of the community or answering economic challenges with an educational solution in a larger, international context. Two clear facets, local and global diversity, define the multicultural curriculum. Although concepts about multicultural curricula can differ, depending on the discipline or field, both facets are reflected in academic and occupational programs, and most institutions appear to have curricula that reflect both perspectives rather than only one.

Realistically, the curriculum is influenced by its faculty and administrative leadership and by their educational priorities, as well as their notion about what interests the students. Rarely do curriculum planning teams include students in or graduates from the programs. This goes along with the traditional assumption that the institution or the faculty "knows what is best for the student." These teams may, however, include business and industry partners or colleagues in four-year institutions that receive community college graduates or transfer students.

There tends to be an overreliance on a European-centered curriculum that does not recognize contributions and insights from people from other cultures (Rendón 1990). However, it is logical to assume that if minority faculty can teach European and American literature, white faculty should be able to cover diverse and minority perspectives among the disciplines.

Local Perspectives

Multicultural programs in community colleges usually focus on addressing the characteristics and needs of, and on increasing the understanding of, the local community, which is represented by specific racial or ethnic groups. Regional characteristics also determine which populations are represented in the curricula.

ETHNIC STUDIES

The study of individual racial and ethnic groups from a cultural perspective, historical perspective, or both, is a traditional form of multicultural program. For example, African-American and Chicano studies have long been part of many institutions of higher education. Courses such as those on African-American literature or the Mexican-American child are commonly offered and are commonly taken by students who represent that individual subgroup. Whether through its literature, history, or language, each group is usually studied for its unique and sometimes enigmatic characteristics, in contrast to the comparative multicultural approach.

Several community colleges offer programs that focus on studying the specific cultures of the community. For instance, in Hawai'i—which has a large number of Asians, Pacific Islanders, and Native Hawaiians but few Hispanics, Native Americans, or African Americans—the academic and occupational curricula do not reflect the traditional representation of American minorities. There are extensive programs on Hawaiian language and culture, as well as Japanese studies, Chinese studies, Filipino studies, Korean studies, etc. The East-West Center, which is associated with the University of Hawai'i, has established a core Asian studies program, and its program director has traveled extensively across the United States to encourage community colleges to assist in developing an Asian studies program. This concept has been well received at the Maricopa Community College District in Arizona, for example, since more Asians have migrated to the state. However, tangible results have yet to be defined.

Recently, several California community college districts have had to develop programs to accommodate new immigrants from Southeast Asia and Mexico as well as the increased numbers of American-born Asians and Mexicans. For example, in order to focus specifically on Mexican-Americans, Rio Hondo Community College District (California) has a separate Mexican-American Cultural Institute within its Institute for Multicultural Programs.

As the face of the community changes, the demands of understanding the nature or unique qualities of different subgroups are addressed by the community college. Yet, it is an attempt to solve or address social needs rather than a predesigned focus that drives the development and implementation of these courses or programs. And more often than not, the enrollment in these courses is not high. The courses are often attended by people who have very special reasons (such as social or economic) for doing so.

Associate Degree Program Offerings

Degree programs in ethnic studies have been developed at community colleges, since more students have been asking for programs that address their social learning needs. These degree programs can also enhance community and faculty development and awareness of multiculturalism. For example, Fresno City Community College (California) offers two associate-in-arts degree programs in the social sciences field: one in African-American studies and another in American Indian studies. Fresno City College also has a cultural studies La Raza major toward an A.A. degree; this prepares students who wish to work with Spanish-speaking clientele. Courses for such Chicano studies are extensive and represent a two-year program of studies. According to Levine and Cureton's study (1992), 31 percent of the two-year institutions surveyed reported programs in African-American studies, 29 percent reported Hispanic-American studies, 20 percent reported Native American studies, and 25 percent reported Asian-American studies. Again, there is little demand for such programs, and if budgets are based on the number of students enrolled in programs, students may not always be able to graduate in a timely manner.

Curricula That Perpetuate Racial Identity

Multicultural curricula can also preserve cultural values and identity for the generations that follow. Salish Kootenai College, with a student population of approximately 700, is an example of a tribal community college primarily for the Native American population. At Salish Kootenai, they have a somewhat different approach to multicultural education for both Native and non-Native students. Their current enrollment is 65 percent Native American, and they offer a wide variety of Native American studies classes. All their students are required to take a course in Native American Studies titled "History of Indians in the United States." Another unique course, which their human services students are required to take, is called "Living in Two Worlds," and it explores how Native people function (successfully and unsuccessfully) in two different cultures. Such programs allow multicultural values to be perpetuated through generations and examine current societal issues and challenges that minorities must face and balance within their identities.

In Hawai'i, several curricula and programs have been established to support the academic as well as cultural development of Native and part-Native students. These programs have been funded locally and through national government funds. To deter the extinction of the Native Hawaiian culture, curricular components on Hawaiian history, land and educational issues, and political and societal structures and processes that have affected and currently actuate the Hawaiian perspective and its empowerment exist. When there is a clear mission in multicultural education, current and social dynamics are defined into special activities and opportunities that support classroom learning for students.

Curricula That Foster Improved Community Relations

Several community colleges across the country offer courses specifically designed to address issues related to racial and ethnic relations and issues. These include interpersonal and intercultural communications among and between diverse American minority populations and include gender and generational issues. These courses and programs appear to be found in the Southern, Eastern, and Midwestern states, where particular minority populations (such as African Americans) represent a large and articulate constituency or have created a long-term presence and established close enough ties with the community college system to address community relations from a proactive posture. Subaggregate groups of different races or ethnicities are not always differentiated in some institutions (i.e., the minority focus was interpreted from an African-American perspective only).

However, the proactive and collaborative nature and approach of the courses are meritable and need to be applauded. For example, Central Piedmont Community College (North Carolina) has built excellent relationships with the local African-American community. Central Piedmont's courses and programs reflect the influence of the strong African-American population in the area, as well as its educational values and cultural heritage and history. Central Piedmont, by its location, must compete for African-American students, who often choose to go to HBCUs. Yet, rather than be competitive with the local HBCUs, Central Piedmont's administration meets regularly with university leaders to discuss common issues and concerns.

CURRICULA THAT FILL A VOID IN KNOWLEDGE

Because of the regional racial or ethnic influences over the multicultural curriculum, colleges often lack courses because the local population does not have ethnic diversity. For example, in several Midwestern community colleges, the number of experts and students who are interested in Chicano or Asian-American studies may be limited. So, such courses—let alone programs—are rarely developed or taught. Yet, most community college leaders and faculty recognize this disparity and look for creative ways of and incentives for developing such courses or programs. For example, the East-West Center (Hawai'i) provides resources to support minorities establishing Asian studies programs. They award East-West Center fellowships to American Indian, Hispanic, and African-American doctoral students so that the center can expand learning opportunities for Asian and Pacific Islander students who are unfamiliar, and have little experience, with issues related to those particular American minorities.

Still, the benefit of such an institute may be small for both the college that sends delegates to the program and the college that hosts it. For one thing, one faculty member returning to a college after attending an institute may not be able to make a broad-based impact. For example, a contingent of two faculty members from the Maricopa Community Colleges attended the Asian Studies Seminar at the East-West Center. The results have not indicated a pervasive change in the Maricopa colleges' curriculum.

At a recent national conference on faculty and staff development, one of the major topics of discussion was how to reward and provide incentives to faculty who do not have a wealth of knowledge about diversity, so that courses can be redesigned from a multicultural perspective. Midwestern community colleges that lacked faculty from diverse cultural backgrounds were especially anxious to find new and creative ways of bringing in faculty from other community colleges to help design such courses. Yet, not only must the curriculum be changed, but also the faculty must be comprehensively and continuously developed to teach the courses in a different way. And once the external experts leave, to whom can the faculty turn if there is no one among them who represents a minority and who may have some background on the material?

Curricula That Provide Bilingual Teacher Aide Education

Several community colleges offer occupational programs for bilingual teacher aides. Such programs provide an opportunity for bilingual people to become productive members of their educational community, since most students who aspire to be teacher aides tend to stay within the communities in which they reside. These programs are especially beneficial if they are also tracked to the completion of an elementary education teacher certification program at the university level. Furthermore, bilingual teacher aide programs are also regionally influenced. Several colleges in the West and Southwest offer programs for the Mexican-American and Latino population on language and understanding of the Hispanic child. Through a partnership with Arizona State University and Phoenix elementary schools, Rio Salado Community College has develped a unique "grow your own faculty" program called "The Urban Teacher Corps." Elementary school teacher aides who are bilingual and also part of the local community enter this "fast track" program to complete an elementary education degree. The program includes practical teaching applications related to local communities, mentoring by teachers from the aides' home schools, and student teaching opportunities at the home schools. The notion of "growing your own" is a long-term investment for the future that focuses on developing faculty, those front-line agents of change. Similarly, Maricopa is working closely with Arizona State University to implement a program to develop minority professors for the community college district. This type of long-term nurturing has required patience and persistence, especially when two or more districts or institutions are involved. Yet, it should provide long-term systemic change.

Curricula That Help People Relate to Other Cultures

Community colleges often offer special courses and programs that broaden people's view of the difference in values and mores among minorities. Usually, these courses are offered in the social sciences or education. Child development programs, for instance, often include courses to help health care or day care workers in working with multicultural populations. Dutchess Community College (New York) offers the class "Educating Children of Color," which includes theoretical discussions on multicultural education.

Curricula That Support Interracial Issues and Agendas

Urban and metropolitan community colleges report numerous programs and courses on interracial issues and agendas. An example is the City College of Chicago (Illinois), which has a comprehensive set of course offerings and materials for the many different populations it serves. Other colleges with large minority populations across the country offer similar academic programs, which build a stronger understanding of, and stronger relationships with, local communities, especially in the social sciences and humanities. Through their community colleges, such cities as New York, Phoenix, and Dallas provide special programs that help diffuse interracial conflicts and include innovative teaching techniques and socially relevant activities. A successful example, at La Guardia Community College in New York, is the Bongo Theater course, which allows students to enact and resolve conflicts creatively through the theater.

Infusing Curricula with Multicultural Foci

Academic programs in community colleges also infuse multicultural aspects into existing courses, so that they reflect the diversity of the local population, and thereby create new and relevant curricula for students. La Guardia Community College has a program in which several multicultural aspects of society are interwoven into a multidisciplinary curriculum that includes creative, collaborative, and highly participatory interactions among students. South Mountain Community College (Phoenix)—which is considered a minority-majority college, since over 50 percent of its students are minority students—has an innovative and unique program called "Dynamic Learning." This series of courses is not only multicultural and interdisciplinary, but also incorporates nontraditional teaching and learning techniques such as dynamic group learning activities, student empowerment, alternative assessment techniques and interpersonal communication. The South Mountain program is an interdisciplinary and thematically based block program based on multicultural literature and multicultural studies. Other community colleges across the country have strong programs that are infused with the reality of multiculturalism. Over the past few years, several West Coast community colleges have developed programs for Asian immigrants. Seattle Central Community College (Washington) offers an integrated studies program based on the "learning communities" model, which is thematic and cross-disciplinary and focuses on creating relevant local learning experiences for students and faculty.

Global Perspectives

Community colleges have historically served the local geographical environment. However, as economic interests and technologies redefine the options of and access to education, territorial boundaries begin to blur and are redefined to include the global community. Thus, multicultural curricula in community colleges include international or global perspectives. Multicultural curricula are defined not only by the specific racial or ethnic makeup of the local community college environment, but also by the demands in the region for jobs and opportunity. Many colleges, especially those that have strong economic development components, are looking at a global perspective as well as a local focus, to be competitive in the education market. In the past, community colleges were geographically restricted by county or district. However, with the integration of technologies and a transitory global population, these barriers are breaking down. In one example of global learning, students in Moscow, Russia, took English 101, a freshman composition course, with students from Rio Salado Community College (Arizona). The Russian students interacted with their instructor and classmates via Internet, a computer communication network, and via the Electronic Forum, a computer conferencing system. Technology has now allowed the global classroom to become a reality. Technology begins to allow for a larger inclusionary context, which can enhance multicultural education by expanding discussion and insights about diversity.

Many community colleges have large cohorts of international students. For example, in the August 1991 *Almanac* of the *Chronicle of Higher Education*, Miami-Dade Community College (Florida) was listed as the postsecondary institution that enrolled the most foreign students (5,518) in 1989–1990, while the University of Southern California, a four-year institution, was listed second, with 3,705 students. In addition to having a large number of foreign students, Miami-Dade has a diverse listing of racial and ethnic groups. Many foreign students are from Asian and other non-Western countries and not just those from bordering countries.

The foreign-student factor is a double-edged sword for most community colleges. As more foreign languages are being used outside of class, faculty and administrators become aware about the change in demographics, and the obviousness of cultural differences are more apparent to them. However, those who have assimilated well or who are native-born citizens do not often identify with the foreign students and vice versa. Yet, most faculty and administrators from the dominant group cannot distinguish among their different needs. Broad assumptions and generalizations are often made, and stereotypes and myths may be perpetuated in programmatic decisions.

As part of its commitment to the Kellogg- and American Association of Community Colleges-sponsored Beacon project, Kapil'olani Community College (Hawai'i) hosted a 1992 conference titled "Asia, the Pacific and the Americas: Building a Community of Colleges." The event provided an exchange of a wealth of professional and programmatic ideas as well as curricular and pedagogical reforms to address the changing climates of community colleges and their communities. The faculty members who attended the conference (including many from across the Hawai'i Community Colleges) have made changes in teaching methodologies, have introduced new courses, and have established an idea-sharing network across the country. Yet, the results reported from the mainland have not been significant.

The passing of the North American Free Trade Agreement (NAFTA) is motivating many border community colleges to focus on multicultural education programs. Programs are being quickly designed by border community colleges in Texas, Arizona, and California so that students and community representatives can be competitive in global markets. The new courses are such areas as language, business, and technology and include multicultural perspectives.

As these and other internationally based agendas continue to influence our institutions, community colleges are questioning how to balance these external factors with their infrastructure and base curriculum. If multicultural and international education programs overlap, will their differences as well as their commonalities be perpetuated and exemplified? Are there assurances of balance and objectivity in the curricula? If they are separated, will there be a time, under the guise of fiscal responsibility or budgetary constraints, when one will be valued more highly than the other? Does the organizational culture know enough about each to promote each agenda well and responsibly?

Curricular Reform Efforts in Multicultural Education

Curricular reforms in which multicultural aspects are marginalized or "added onto" present courses and programs tend to be less effective and less likely to be embraced or be engaging. There are two approaches to these reforms: additive-design and contributory. Basically, the additive design trivializes the multicultural perspective as something "nice to know" but not critical to the learning objectives of the course. The contributory approach celebrates or highlights contributions by a multicultural population, but also minimizes the value of multiculturalism by only featuring a unique characteristic of that population rather than the interwoven impact of the group on others. Activities that reflect these two approaches include adding a reading or lesson on Japanese-American internment camps during World War II to a chapter or two on the war or having a multicultural food festival as part of foreign language class.

When significant issues and content are not integral to the nature of the course or program, the reform effort is insignificant in creating and promoting a climate of active learning and dynamic instruction. Debate and criticism among practitioners, researchers, and leaders continue, especially when the assessment instruments used are not appropriate to different learning styles or conditions and reflect cultural bias. For example, national placement and entrance examination assessment items are based on a general, American context of knowledge. Much like the E.D. Hirsch and Allan Bloom perspectives on common knowledge, an analogy test often includes items that refer to elements of words and phrases that assume that the test taker's experience is that of the dominant group.

Another discussion among curriculum developers is how to integrate and design cross-cultural elements that are found among different generations in a community. Social, economic, and ethical values of Asian Americans of the first generation have little in common with those of the second, third, and fourth generations, who have been assimilated into the multicultural American society. Furthermore, distinct issues occur for those of two or more distinct cultural backgrounds, such as the Amerasians or Eurasians. Distinct differences occur between cultures and are further exacerbated between generations in the same ethnic or racial group. For example, perspectives about education, society, and life may change (especially among the younger population) even though basic values may stay the same once immigrants assimilate into the United States.

It takes time and resources to allow faculty to develop programs that integrate multicultural perspectives. If faculty are not provided with opportunities to modify or develop multicultural programs, they will focus on the status quo of their content and pedagogy.

For innovations to occur in the curriculum and pedagogy, institutions have had to establish special internal grants and "carrots" for faculty. Larger community college systems appear to be addressing such needs. The Seattle Community College District and the Miami-Dade Community Colleges (through its faculty incentives programs) have motivated such changes. The Maricopa District has an internal grants source as well as a faculty coordinator for international/intercultural education to encourage and support curricular and pedagogical development among faculty. Because the distinction between international and multicultural education has not been made, those interested in multiculturalizing the curriculum also apply for and receive these funds. But naiveté about these programs could be detrimental if a choice between international and multicultural is forced.

STUDENT SUPPORT SERVICES

Multicultural education programs in the community college require comprehensive and multidimensional student support systems for both local and global perspectives to be successful within curricula. The students in such programs tend to be ill prepared in certain skills (most prominently, English language usage), and they may not understand or be aware of the dominant American group's educational mores, protocols, and behavior. Many who enter community colleges often represent the first generation in their families to have been afforded the opportunity to pursue higher education. Admissions and financial aid applications can be frustrating and disconcerting experiences for all students, and can be especially upsetting to someone who has never been asked to complete such forms.

In addition, as the economic, political, and social structures of European—especially, Eastern European—countries continue to change, more people come to the United States to begin new lives. Community college systems (such as the City Colleges of Chicago and those in the Middle Atlantic and Northeastern states) historically provide educational access and opportunities to these new immigrants. These new European immigrants may not have the same value system or economic and educational heritage of those who came to the United States in the last century.

Many community colleges offer a multitude of advisory services for multicultural groups; these include personal, social, financial, academic, and career advice. Often, multicultural advisory and support centers are developed for specific groups: Native American, Hispanic, international, Asian-American, and African-American students. Pima Community College in Tucson, Arizona, has developed an extensive program for Native American outreach and retention. The project is a highly successful and comprehensive approach to addressing the needs of Native-American students. It includes special outreach and orientation activities; assessment support; special advice and counseling by a Native-American counselor, who focuses on special academic and college survival needs and provides information on scheduling, financial aid, application forms and processes, etc.; role modeling with Native-American faculty, staff, and community leaders; and socialization opportunities not just for pleasure, but also for peer tutoring and group study.

Community colleges on the West Coast and Hawai'i address the needs of Asian and Pacific Rim immigrants. For example, California community colleges that have developed exemplary academic programs and support services for limited-English-speaking Hispanic students are having to redesign these programs for a large group of Southeast Asian, Asian, and Pacific-American students, who are not as culturally or linguistically homogeneous as the Spanish-speaking cohort.

Even among racial and ethnic subgroups, educational and cultural values differ. The perception of Asian-Americans as being the "model minority" is based on outdated stereotypes of a few select Asian groups, as well as on inaccurate data. For example, the Hmong population from Laos have lived through several decades of such disenfranchisement and turmoil that their sense of stability and their confidence in government and community is lacking. Upon arrival in the United States, Hmongs did not have a written language and did very poorly in education. Community colleges in Seattle (Washington) have had to design support services to meet the needs of this disadvantaged group. Yet, Seattle Central Community College reports that another population influx is coming from East Europe. Are they in a position to make changes in order to accommodate this group? In California's agricultural region, the State Center Community College District has been focusing on this subgroup lately in ESL programs. When this college system was addressing the needs of Mexican-Americans and migrant workers a few years ago, it found that the migrants did not only represent one culture. Many programs are not always flexible to change soon enough for the *next* cultural group. Further, as immigrant populations assimilate into American society, their needs change. Programs have not necessarily changed to meet the "second generation" issues and concerns of these people. Thus, as populations change over time, so must new programs be included to foster growth and development.

Similarly, the cultural values and behaviors of American Indians (including Native Alaskans) across the United States differ dramatically among tribes and regions. Community colleges in the state of Washington have multicultural specialists who meet regularly to discuss the changing special support needs of their Native-American and Asian-American students.

Each population's unique and diverse needs must be identified and addressed by student support and development services and cannot be generalized. However, as more communities become multiracial and multi-ethnic, cross-cultural activities must also be encouraged. Colleges—especially those with diverse groups—are beginning to recognize and create such student empowerment programs and services.

The notion that learning only occurs in the classroom is archaic. Learning centers and adjunct instructional services in community colleges are critical support mechanisms for multicultural education. GateWay Community College (Arizona), like many colleges across the country, provides academic support structures through its Learning Assistance Center. Special materials and tutoring services are designed for multicultural populations. At its various campuses, Miami-Dade Community College provides programs that build study and literacy skills, especially through computer-assisted instruction. Using government funding, Central Piedmont Community College was a primary developer of an interactive video inventory of learning styles, which incorporated multicultural elements in realistic settings.

Estrella Mountain Community College Center (Arizona) is establishing the literacy center concept from a unique perspective. Because the institution must serve several diverse communities in a highly rural area, its first-year students often come to campus with little preparation in basic skills and knowledge, which is the case with many community colleges with highly transitory populations. Estrella has designed a "walk-in, first-time" comprehensive literacy program that has all its tools and services in one location. Materials and computer-based systems are specifically designed for a "walk-in" clientele who may not enroll in school right away, but who wish to hone their skills and knowledge in a self-paced manner. The support mechanism is built around the community, and the focus is clearly to provide a comprehensive, year-round, community-based learning center.

The special student-assessment needs of a multicultural population have been established by several colleges across the country. If tests are designed for students from similar educational, cultural, political, social, or economic backgrounds, then it is logical to assume that the test items are unfair and biased. In 1988 the Mexican-American Legal Defense and Educational Fund (MALDEF) filed a class-action suit against the California community colleges, stating that their assessment instruments were biased. Although the suit was dismissed in 1991, three basic outcomes were put in place as conditions for the dismissal: the colleges were required to ensure that their assessment tools were nonbiased, regular site evaluations on assessment were expected, and detailed assessment plans needed to be established by each college.

Another questionable assessment tool is the Immigration Reform and Control Act (IRCA) Pre-enrollment Appraisal, which is used to assess the skills of limited-English speakers in terms of their placement into classes. The instrument has been criticized by many faculty for having items on citizenship and not on basic English skills and knowledge.

To assess basic skills and knowledge, several faculty members at South Mountain Community College have developed testing materials that are designed for multicultural populations. Concepts, rules, and procedures can be tested so that the context is not uniquely "American" or biased. But faculty and staff usually must spend their own time creating appropriate measures and tests, and these may not be valid or reliable, since they are not always tested themselves. In addition, the instruments for South Mountain were prepared for Spanish-speaking students and do not support the needs of other groups.

Faculty Development and Enhancement Programs

To effect long-term change and innovation in education, especially for multicultural perspectives, the development of faculty is essential. Faculty are the "front line" communicators and facilitators of knowledge and learning. Banks (1991) claims that faculty bring their own cultural perspectives, stereotypes, and misperceptions. Therefore, if they are not prepared or committed to multiculturalism, local or international programs and services will not succeed. Levine and Cureton (1992) indicated that of the two-year institutions they surveyed, 29 percent had multicultural faculty programs for recruitment and retention and 39 percent reported faculty development efforts. The value of faculty development programs does not appear to be consistent or significant for community colleges.

Through its Teaching and Learning Project, Miami-Dade Community College has developed a comprehensive agenda for faculty development. The project is linked to faculty advancement. Although the project is not specifically designed for multicultural education, the manner in which it is designed encourages constant assessment and discussion directed toward faculty enhancement and toward the improvement of the learning environment of the college's multicultural clientele. For example, the college has a Statement of Faculty Excellence, which includes not just the faculty's knowledge base but also motivation, interpersonal skills, and the application of knowledge. And because faculty advancement is tied to a comprehensive system of feedback and of assessment and development activities, change and innovation are highly likely, especially for the multicultural element of that college environment.

Professional organizations and conferences of community colleges provide numerous seminars, workshops, and events for faculty and staff to improve their knowledge and skills base for multicultural teaching and learning. The 1992 American Association of Community Colleges (AACC) national conference, with 4,000 participants, focused on "celebrating cultural diversity." Several national and local conferences for particular staff and faculty provide opportunities for exchange and dialogue. In the fall of 1992, a national teleconference sponsored by Foothill/DeAnza Community College District (California) dealt with diversity issues and successful teaching and learning practices for faculty and staff. The diversity teleconference was scheduled to continue in 1993.

The Institute on Hawaiian Values at Kapi'olani Community College in Honolulu, designed for the Hawai'i community college system, is an exemplary program for addressing the teaching and learning needs of a specific subgroup. The purpose of this institute is to provide information on Native Hawaiian students at the community colleges to faculty and counselors, so that the learning environment is conducive to the recruitment, retention, and education of Native Hawaiian students. A specific focus is placed on Hawaiian values and how they relate to the learning styles and achievement levels of Hawaiian students. Teaching strategies for more effective instruction at the college are included.

However, the vast majority of faculty nationwide do not take part in such professional development efforts; most will attend professional meetings that relate to their various disciplines. More administrators than faculty attend meetings of associations such as the AACC. Many faculty feel they do not have the time to attend activities that do not affect their particular discipline or classroom environment. Those few who seek to change the curriculum, teaching, and learning are often the ones who embrace change and innovation readily. It is also simpler and more time-efficient for many teachers to provide course content solely from textbooks, which tend to have a very limited multicultural context. Pockets of improvement in learning and instruction may occur. However, far-reaching and pervasive change and reform cannot be embedded into the curriculum or pedagogy without the permeation of tangible rewards and values throughout an institution.

PARTNERSHIPS, COLLABORATIONS, AND CONSORTIA

Community colleges respond to the changing demands of the American economy by participating actively as occupational and vocational education providers. For example, community colleges in Hawai'i, California, Washington, and other Western states have ongoing partnerships with business, industrial, and educational institutions, to make alliances with Asian and Southeast Asian countries. Trade with Mexico and with other Central and South American countries prompts Southwestern and Southern states to create programs that respond to multicultural economic demands.

Local partnerships and alliances are encouraged, especially when educational as well as business and industrial institutions are feeling budgetary constraints and have common needs for multicultural education. Through its Center for Racial Equity, the Community College of Allegheny County (Pennsylvania) has several programs with local businesses; these programs encourage diversity in the private sector and provide economic benefits to the college.

Community colleges work with local and state universities to make multicultural education inviting to community college students. There are a large number of students who transfer to four-year institutions before or after completing their associate's degree. Central Piedmont College has an informal communication forum in place with neighboring universities. Likewise, Pima College has an articulation agreement with the University of Arizona for its multicultural education courses. In addition, all community colleges in Arizona include ethnic, racial, and gender studies as a general education core requirement.

Another example of a collaborative effort is the PUENTE Project, which involves the University of California and the California Community Colleges (Halcón 1988). Targeted Mexican-American students in community colleges throughout California are placed in a comprehensive program that helps them improve their writing and gives them the confidence and motivation to continue in higher education. Writing, counseling, and mentoring are key components of this program, which includes faculty and counselors in community colleges and universities, as well as mentors from the Hispanic professional community.

COMMUNITY COLLEGE LEADERSHIP

The value and tone of multicultural education in the community college system are set by its mission statement. How the mission is articulated reflects the commitment of the institution to such programs. The Maricopa Community Colleges state that their mission is "to create accessible, effective and affordable environments for teaching and learning for the people of our communities in order that they may grow personally and become productive citizens in a changing and multicultural world." If one peruses the different college catalogs across the district, there are very few courses that represent the multicultural world.

On the other hand, while Coast Community College District (California) does not specifically identify a view of multiculturalism in its mission statement, it has two very specific multicultural goals:

- Goal 8: Develop, implement and maintain programs that address international and inter-cultural education;
- Goal 10: Increase the diversity of faculty, staff and administrative personnel so that the district's employees reflect the diversity of California's population.

How an institution assesses and continues to perpetuate its multicultural mission goal each year is a clear indication of its commitment to multicultural diversity. As earlier mentioned in this chapter, Pima Community College clearly identifies the tangible evidence it needs to find in order to consider that its goal of creating a climate responsive to its multicultural community has been achieved.

Community college leaders must create adaptable organizations and less bureaucratic models of administration and management to achieve the institution's mission and create a climate for responsive instruction and dynamic learning. New models for management suggest the need for continuous improvement, institutional assessment, and rethinking of systems to create a learning environment that instills transformation and participation among a college's faculty, administration, staff, and student and community clientele.

Related Multicultural Issues

Regular discussions occur among community college leaders about the future of multicultural issues. Coalitions such as the Urban Colleges Commission (which includes the LaGuardia, Broward [Florida], Houston [Texas], Seattle Central, and West Los Angeles [California] community colleges and other urban colleges) report on issues affecting their communities. San Diego Community College District (California), a member of the coalition, reported establishing a joint agreement with the City and County of San Diego, the University of California in San Diego, and the local school district to launch a project to create and support mechanisms in educational, health, and social services for poverty stricken, limited-English speakers from Hispanic and Asian cultures. El Paso Community College (Texas) is actively recruiting and enrolling students who are poor and homeless—as well as those who live in *colonias*, squatters' communities without any modern conveniences—so that they can learn a trade and further their education.

Thus, not only issues of educational access but also social and economic concerns need to be examined when the needs of multicultural populations are addressed. Issues of program restructuring, empowerment, social transformation, systemic change, and major paradigm shifts within and outside the community college system must also be discussed among community college leaders and theorists. If the issues are not debated and resolved within this decade in response to changing demographics, community colleges will not be well positioned to deal with multicultural student populations as well as with social, economic, and political conditions.

Multicultural Education and Budgetary Impact

When the American economy in general is shaky, the value of multicultural education is often questioned. Cost containment and budgetary constraints often threaten the existence of multicultural education, especially when institutions must "downsize" or are subject to major cuts in resources and personnel. This situation is not an unusual one in the United States today and cannot be remedied with simple methods. In the past, community colleges were able to grow through government or private funding for occupational and technical programs for large numbers of disadvantaged people, but today the tax base, as well as the "giving" base, has decreased across the nation.

Community colleges in California, for instance, are going through a major period of self-criticism and agony. California students are being asked to pay higher tuitions and fees because the state can no longer afford to carry much of the college costs. And even though the rates are dramatically below national cost averages, such increases would discourage a large number of low-SES prospective students from enrolling in classes. So once again, the people who are trying to improve themselves and move up from their current economic or social status may not escape their situation in a timely manner. Tuition and fee increases are occurring nationally and definitely affect the minority and low-income population, the mainstay of most community colleges. Therefore, it can be perceived that such actions reflect prejudice toward a specific population: those who are members of racial or ethnic groups. Racial bigotry is perceived when limited resources in financial aid prevent an individual from receiving funds or when it appears that only certain minority populations are afforded financial aid.

One blatant example of prejudice in the distribution of financial aid occurs when Asian-American subgroups are penalized under a quota system, because they are mislabeled as a "model minority." The paradox of believing that one can promote and extend oneself through education but being punished for succeeding is a reality for the Asian-American student who has suffered reverse discrimination. Policies and mechanisms to avoid such reverse discrimination are usually not planned and must be fought for by advocacy groups. When federal grant sources such as the National Science Foundation do not clearly identify that students from Asian-American groups are able to benefit from funds, questions on discrimination need to be asked.

This type of situation further divides races and ethnic groups when limited resources are available. When subgroups compete for funds and services rather than question institutional values and structures, they often attack and compete with each other. Programs and services that promote collaboration and have fair criteria for selection need to be designed and implemented. Leaving one group out by treating it as an invisible population further perpetuates wrongful discrimination.

The integrity of the community college as the postsecondary solution for communities is most certainly being questioned. If multicultural programs are eliminated or are "downsized" to the point of being insignificant, are colleges really meeting the needs of their communities? In metropolitan Phoenix, which has a substantial low-income and minority population, a major agenda that included several programs and services engaged in and integrating multicultural efforts, as well as addressing school and community needs and relations, was eliminated to solve the huge fiscal and budgetary problems of that community college in 1992–1993. Although any type of verdict on the action is premature, one of the immediate results was a significant drop in the number of students at the college in the following semesters. The question then becomes, is it better to save the college in general and foster traditional educational programs or to support the critical social needs of the community through specialized and somewhat unconventional programs?

A Final Note

The context of education is defined by its receiver. Community colleges were originally established to fill a huge postsecondary educational gap that was not being addressed by four-year colleges and universities. It is clear that the community colleges across the United States have been meeting the needs of multicultural populations with a wide variety of curricula and programs to support multicultural agendas. The community colleges have established broad-based solutions to the multidimensional challenges that multiculturalism, diversity, cross-culturalism, and pluralism bring to the forefront of this country.

Although programs may appear to be spurred by local community agendas, common threads and mechanisms are evident. To be successful, colleges cannot narrowly define multicultural education; both local and global perspectives need to be integrated or incorporated into the curricula because technological innovation and the global economy have blurred the territorial constraints of education. All students need to be empowered with exemplary tools of knowledge and skills to be competitive in global society.

To be sustained and engaging, multicultural education must be embraced by the entire community college organization as well as the local community. Faculty, staff, administrators, students, and community leaders must collaborate and communicate and must relate to the needs of the multicultural agenda. Resources and support must be available to inspire the formulation of new approaches to teaching, learning, and program development.

Finally, although it is a necessary agenda, multicultural education in community colleges is fragile, because it depends on the human spirit and on human integrity to survive. But its designs and colors are intricately woven into the American people and their future. Takaki (1993) purports that this country has a multicultural heritage and history. To ignore one or some of the different colors and threads means that we create an incomplete tapestry. Community college education—its people, processes, and programs—can weave a truly multicultural vision and purpose for our present and future generations.

As M. Crocco states:

> There is a need for curriculum to function both as Window and as Mirror . . . to reflect and reveal most accurately both a multicultural world and the student herself or himself. If the student is understood as occupying a dwelling of self, education needs to enable the student to look through the window frame . . . to see the realities of others and into mirrors . . . to see her/his own reality reflected. Knowledge of both types of framing is basic to a balanced education which is committed to affirming the essential dialogue between the self and the world. (Crocco 1988, 6)

ACKNOWLEDGMENT

The author wishes to thank the following community college leaders for their insights and contributions to this chapter: Harold Bellinger, R. Wayne Branch, Rosa Flores Carlson, Gil Dominguez, Linda M. Edington, Michael S. Engs, Bob Fouty, Mardee Jenrette, Cecelia Lopez, Sharon S. Narimatsu,

Tony J. Nevarez, Margaret Sprague, Rick Olguin, Sherrie Seymour, and Ken Yglesias. She also thanks the staff of the Maricopa Center for Learning and Instruction and the Maricopa Community Colleges for their support, as well as her editors for their insight.

REFERENCES

Adelman, C. *The Way We Are: The Community College as American Thermometer.* U.S. Department of Education. Washington, D.C.: U.S. Government Printing Office, 1992.

American Association of Community and Junior Colleges (AACJC). *Building Communities: A Vision for a New Century.* Washington, D.C.: AACJC Press, 1988.

American Council on Education and Education Commission of the States. *One-Third of a Nation: A Report of the Commission on Minority Participation in Education and American Life.* Washington, D.C.: American Council on Education and Education Commission of the States, 1988.

Banks, J.A. "Teaching Multicultural Literacy to Teachers." In *Teaching Education* 4, summer/fall (1991): 135–44.

Bellah, R.N., R. Madsen, W.M. Sullivan, A. Swidler, and S.M. Tipton. *Habits of the Heart.* Berkeley: University of California Press, 1985.

Bossman, David M. "Cross-Cultural Values for a Pluralistic Core Curriculum." *Journal of Higher Education* 62, no. 6 (1991): 661–81.

Boyer, E.L. "Curriculum, Culture and Social Cohesion." In *Leadership Abstracts.* Laguna Hills, Cal.: League for Innovation in the Community College, 1992.

Carter, D.J., and R. Wilson. *Tenth Annual Status Report on Minorities in Higher Education.* Washington, D.C.: American Council on Education, 1992.

Chronicle of Higher Education Almanac. (1991): 28.

Chronicle of Higher Education Almanac. (1993): 16, 34.

Crocco, M. "Curriculum as Window and Mirror." In *Listening for All Voices: Gender Balancing the School Curriculum.* Summit, N.J.: Oak Knoll School, 1988.

de Tocqueville, A. *Democracy in America.* George Lawrence (trans.) and J.P. Mayer (ed.). New York: Doubleday Anchor Books, 1969.

Estrada, K., and P. McLaren. "A Dialogue on Multiculturalism and Democratic Culture." *Educational Researcher* 22, no. 3 (1993).

Gaff, J.G. "Beyond Politics: The Educational Issues Inherent in Multicultural Education." *Change* 24, no. 1 (1992): 30–35.

Halcón, J.J. *Exemplary Programs for College-Bound Minority Students.* Western Interstate Commission for Higher Education (WICHE) Report. Boulder, Colo.: WICHE Information Clearinghouse, 1988.

Hill, Patrick J. "Multi-Culturalism: The Crucial Philosophical and Organizational Issues." *Change* 23, no. 1 (1991): 38–47.

Karamcheti, I., and C. Lemert. "From Silence to Silence." *Liberal Education* 77, no. 4 (1991): 14–18.

Levine, A., and J. Cureton. "The Quiet Revolution: Eleven Facts about Multiculturalism and the Curriculum." *Change* 24, no. 1 (1992): 25–29.

Morrison, Toni. *Playing in the Dark: Whiteness in the Literary Imagination.* Cambridge, Mass.: Harvard University Press, 1992.

Newmann, F.M. "Beyond Common Sense in Educational Restructuring: The Issues of Content and Linkage." *Educational Researcher* 22, no. 2 (1993): 4–13, 22.

Ogbu, J.U. "Understanding Cultural Diversity and Learning." *Educational Researcher* 21, no. 8 (1992): 5–14, 24.

Rendón, L.I. "Implementing a Diversity Restructuring Program." *Leadership Abstracts* 3, no. 18 (1990): monograph.

Smith, D.G. *The Challenge of Diversity: Involvement or Alienation in the Academy?* School of Education and Human Development Report No. 5. Washington, D.C.: George Washington University, 1989.

Snyder, T.D. *Digest of Education Statistics 1992.* National Center for Education Statistics. Washington, D.C.: U.S. Department of Education, 1992.

Takaki, Ronald. *A Different Mirror: A History of a Multicultural America.* Boston: Little, Brown and Co., 1993.

Yarbough, L. "Three Questions for the Multiculturalism Debate." *Change* 24, no. 1 (1992): 64–69.

5 INTERNATIONALIZING THE CURRICULUM

IDEALS VS. REALITY

Rosalind Latiner Raby

BLENDING OF THEORY AND PRACTICE

All segments of U.S. education, including community colleges, are beginning to acknowledge the merits of nourishing international literacy skills. International literacy is contingent upon an individual's ability to transcend a basic ignorance about international society. Since 1970, U.S. community colleges have implemented elements of curriculum internationalization by revising classes, programs, and general education requirements to include cultural and global concepts, theories, and patterns of interrelationships. This process begins when internationalism is entered into different aspects of class lectures, assignments, discussions, tests, and texts within all college programs and disciplines. The ultimate form of internationalization is when an international orientation is included as part of an A.A. degree/certificate, or a general education requirement, or both. Since community colleges educate more than half the country's adults, the impact of an internationalized curriculum on students, faculty, and the community is immense. Furthermore, since most community college students do not transfer to four-year universities, the only place where one can acquire international literacy is often the community college itself (*Guidepost* 1991; Cohen 1993).

Internationalizing the curriculum is a relatively novel phenomenon for U.S. community colleges. In the 1960s academicians and politicians conceded a high rate of international illiteracy among college students. However, community colleges were not consistently used as a medium for this type of education. In the 1980s, federal and private funding allowed community colleges to initiate innovative methodologies for internationalizing business, English, humanities, and social science classes. Many grant requirements mandated the dissemination of "how to" booklets, which facilitated the implementation of these programs nationally. Changing neighborhoods and the changing composition of student bodies, pressure from local businesses, and interest in expanding the curriculum beyond Western perspectives continue to encourage the adoption of defined programs or the initiation of components unique to a particular college. Currently some community colleges sponsor overt programs that specifically address an internationalized curriculum, while others indirectly internationalize as they respond to a world in transition. Because of its significance to the community college, internationalization maintains its popularity and withstands current economic hardships (Raby 1993, 1994).

The concepts and processes involved in internationalizing the curriculum are discussed in academic literature (Fersh 1993; King and Fersh 1992; Edwards and Humphrey 1990; Harari 1989). In this chapter the dichotomy between the ideals of internationalizing the curriculum and the reality of implementing these ideals is examined. While an emphasis is placed on California community colleges, examples are also drawn from a nationwide survey conducted by the author during the 1993–1994 academic year.[1]

Theoretical Foundation

Three educational paradigms define the development and maintenance of an internationalized curriculum. The first paradigm highlights the view that education is a perpetual focus of one's life rather than a singular element defined by occupation, mobility, or socialization. Internationalization includes education of the whole person by transcending informal, nonformal, and formal aspects of learning to encourage comprehension of the by-products of a global environment, including international and intercultural relationships. Concepts found in global, regional, peace, gender, futurist, and multicultural studies enhance these skills and augment the personality by educating students to be (a) politically prepared to participate in society, (b) economically prepared to enter tomorrow's job market, and (c) morally prepared to function in society. This holistic type of education creates a citizen who understands, participates in, and takes action regarding local political, economic, social and environmental issues, all of which require international competency (Edwards 1990; Council on Education 1984; Education for a Global Century 1981; King and Breuder 1979).

The second paradigm underscores the importance of global interrelationships. The actions of a region or country not only affect others but are also influenced by events and policies outside local control. Understanding elements that maintain international cooperation and interdependency is critical for those in pursuit of employment in business, technical, vocational, and preprofessional sectors. In California, the world's sixth-largest economic power, four out of every five jobs have international connections, and nationally over 50 percent of U.S. *Fortune* 500 corporations have international branches (Raby 1990). Community college graduates thus compete for jobs in a modern work force that requires international market economy skills. Barbara Roberts, governor of Oregon, claims that these relationships "build partnerships for better quality of life in our communities" (*AAWCC Quarterly* 1993, 3). A corollary of this paradigm is that international relationships and the exchange of knowledge perpetuate a humanitarian mission for "the repair of the world and [for] the service of our long-term national interest" (Koltai 1993, 2).

The final paradigm accentuates international competency as a means of teaching the values of diversity, sensitivity, empowerment, multicultural harmony, and tolerance. Through this paradigm, the intercultural/multicultural is blended with the international to form a revitalized campus that is responsive to the changing needs of the neighborhoods and cities in which colleges are located. The 1992 Los Angeles riots were fueled, in part, by severe cultural misunderstandings, which might have been minimized if the members of society had been internationally and interculturally/multiculturally literate. The comprehension and appreciation of differences on a global scale directly correlate with the positive interaction with ethnic variations that exist within a local area. Through global knowledge, individuals question their own prejudices and biases and safeguard themselves against parochialism. This type of education is especially important in light of recent census reports that envision that 85 percent of Los Angelenos will be Asian or Hispanic by the quickly approaching year 2000. The consequent restructuring of schools will be dependent upon their ability to build and sustain international and intercultural literacy (L.A. County Office of Education 1993; King and Fersh, 1992).

Combined, these paradigms formulate the ideal that there "should be undoubtedly strong community support for internationalizing the curriculum at the community college . . . to prepare students with a global perspective in order to function effectively in today's world" (Fersh 1993, 9).

Internationalizing the Curriculum: Ideals

For two decades, educators have expounded upon the ideals of internationalization of the curriculum. Mastering an internationalized curriculum goes beyond the mere memorization of facts, geography, and cultural traits, as depicted in Hirsch's (1988) list of 500 cultural terms. Internationalization facilitates the comprehension and use of these facts in the broader schema of life. Sjoquist eloquently asserts that "cultural literacy can do no less than increase the students' possibilities for cultural enrichment, help them cultivate a concept of civilization as it relates to the full range of human experience and foster a greater awareness of and sensitivity to the interdependence of our planet's peoples and systems" (Sjoquist 1993, 52).

Scanlon defines internationalization as a pragmatic tool necessary for ensuring national security, for stabilizing an inefficient economy, and for building world peace (Scanlon 1990, 14–15). Lamy reiterates that in their quest to gain international competency, individuals increase political skills, problem-solving skills, listening skills, and work and service skills and deepen their empathy skills (Lamy 1993, 6). Based on these ideals, internationalization creates a holistic, transcultural environment that allows faculty and students to surpass ethnocentric perceptions, perspectives, and behavior and allows the inculcation of international literacy. In essence, internationalizing the curriculum (and especially the core curriculum) makes it easier for "all students [to learn] about the human heritage and the interdependent world in which they live" (CFCC 1988, 19). The ideal perpetuates the belief that "the more we value differences, and the more we understand diversity, the greater our cohesiveness and strength will bear as a college, a community and hence a nation" (Jerry Sue Owens, quoted in Fersh 1993, 16).

The literature concerning the internationalization of the curriculum identifies three primary means through which the ideals of internationalization affect educational reform at community colleges: (a) general educational reform, (b) faculty and administration rejuvenation, and (c) student diversification.

General Educational Reform

General education reform, in all disciplines, is a critical element in the internationalization of the curriculum. Reform can be overt as well as part of the hidden curriculum. Overt reform occurs through changes in content, such as the introduction of non-Western themes into Western civilization and social science courses. Faculty and curriculum committees consistently upgrade and reform course content to ensure consistently accurate information and the relevance of their courses to a changing student body. Increasingly, such reform has international connections and consequences. Hidden reform exists in the random use of internationalized examples, techniques, and living histories to affect the way a course is taught and, therefore, what students learn. Hidden reform also occurs through the use of textbooks that have become more internationalized. Finally, the international travel, business, and life experiences of faculty members are informal guest lectures that stimulate classroom discussions and, in the process, evoke curricula reform (Raby IIP 1993).

The impetus for reform comes from internal sources (such as individual faculty, administrator, or student concerns for change) and from external sources (such as changing demographics and the local business community, which inadvertently supports international efforts by defining their necessity). Since colleges are often accountable to local businesses (potential employers), the demand for internationally competent workers often prompts and supports reform efforts.

In areas of top-down reform, internationalizing the curriculum is a key element in many colleges' revised mission and policy statements. The administration of a college is responsible for providing release time, monetary incentives for staff development (faculty enrichment grants), stipulations about hiring new teachers, and the development of new internationally themed classes. The mission statement of the Coast Community College District (California) includes strong international references, as do the individual mission statements of each of its three district colleges. Although support from the top is critical, it does not always ensure success (Raby 1990).

Success in areas of reform from below is dependent upon faculty implementation. Elements of an internationalized curriculum may first appear as internationalized examples and assignments that do not drastically alter the curriculum or as specific individual class components that purposely affect change. As faculty share innovative curricula with colleagues, entire departments become internationalized. In the process, support networks emerge that sponsor additional internationalized activities, which can become the foundation for further international efforts.

Faculty and Administration Rejuvenation

The key to successful internationalization is active support by both the faculty and administration. Staff development opportunities further solidify the combined efforts of both groups and apply to those in disciplines that are not traditionally known for internationalization efforts. Rejuvenation occurs through faculty exchanges, faculty participation in international development programs and in international seminars, and personal or professional travel. Participation in one activity often leads to other venues, as exemplified by two faculty members from the Los Angeles Community College District (LACCD) (California): one spent over a year internationalizing several English classes and eventually was part of the LACCD Fulbright faculty exchange program in Norway; the other first taught ESL classes domestically, and then taught them abroad in the district's international programs in Spain, Mexico, Guatemala, and China.[2]

A core group of supportive faculty and administrators creates the necessary enthusiasm to sustain international endeavors. As time progresses, this core influences other colleagues, and this process expands the core from year to year. Indeed, if a requirement is made for new faculty to possess some international expertise, the core is strengthened even more. Finally, leadership support—which comes from a combination of trustees, administration, academic senate members, discipline chairs, and international education committees—cements the campus's international relations.

Just as the experiences of faculty members benefit internationalization efforts, faculty apathy is the primary impediment to growth. The faculty must be encouraged through enrichment grants, sabbatical leaves, and promotional incentives to want to spend the time and energy required for quality curriculum reform. The faculty must also desire such reform and fight for it during fiscal battles. Without faculty involvement, there will be no internationalized curriculum.

Student Diversification

Students themselves are often the initiators of reform. Because of the current diversification in student backgrounds, world events, and a greater interest in ethnic and racial studies, students express greater interest in international issues and in taking classes that are culturally sensitive. Since many jobs demand international expertise, students explore careers in the international arena and participate in classes that prepare them personally as well as occupationally for such competition.[3] In addition, more and more four-year universities are forming articulation agreements with community colleges that offer A.A. degree/certificate programs in international studies, business, or both, thereby providing further incentive for students to participate in such programs.

Internationalizing the Curriculum: Reality

The transformation of ideals into reality ranges from recognizing the value of these ideals to making them a priority for implementation. Each community college has its own unique student population and agenda, and the extent to which international dimensions exist and are actually supported varies substantially. Politics, budgetary constraints, the degree of provincialism involved, and faculty knowledge influence the extent to which an internationalized curriculum thrives (Edwards and Tonkin 1990). Although a multitude of opportunities exists for institutionalizing an internationalized curriculum, reality indicates a much different picture.

Despite the proclaimed importance attached to internationalizing the curriculum, implementation is slow in occurring. In California, most community colleges have yet to evolve from the very beginning stages of recognizing that international education is an important educational component. In 1993 only fifteen California community colleges (14 percent) established international curriculum programs, the majority of them in international business. A recent Association of Professional Schools on International Affairs survey found that even fewer community colleges nationwide endorse international general education curriculum programs (Smith 1994). A dichotomy emerges, as an increasingly female and minority student body is reflected by neither curricular reform nor the college faculty, which remains predominantly white and male (California Community Colleges "Staff Data File" 1994). The following factors severely impede international curricular reform: (a) opposition by faculty and administration, (b) economic conditions, (c) disciplinary hostilities, and (d) lack of expertise.

Opposition

Despite over two decades of enlightenment, there are still many faculty members and administrators who remain ignorant about the benefits of international education. Several maintain that community colleges are for the local community, thinking of the community as an isolated phenomenon. However, as portrayed throughout this book, today's communities are not only multicultural in composition, but through economics, politics, and communication are also involved with activities worldwide. Other faculty members are suspicious of the reforms upon which internationalization is based. Tenured faculty may not be interested in complete or even partial course revision, since they are more comfortable with the familiar. Efforts at internationalization are perceived as revolutionary and, at the worst, involve more work. Many of the community college faculty are part-timers, and therefore, they may not have the time to alter courses and definitely have little if any monetary incentive to do the same. This unenlightened attitude can be overcome by education, but the process is excruciatingly slow. Despite concerted efforts, over the past eight years fewer than 300 out of 4,000 faculty members at the LACCD (7.5 percent) have participated in specific projects to internationalize the curriculum (Raby 1993).

Because internationalization supporters stem from a small core group, it is important to ensure new membership consistently. When support becomes contingent upon a few individuals, it does not become an ingrained part of the college. When these individuals leave the campus, their efforts may also be abandoned. At several California community colleges, the establishment of internationalization is dependent upon the vigorous work of a single professor. When that professor is on sabbatical or abroad, efforts on campus are severely affected (Raby CCIE 1993).

Economics

Economic shortages shake preset "ideals" to their core. Without money, new programs are neither initiated nor implemented. Faculty in-service programs, as well as the hiring of new faculty, are important for maintaining academic standards. Yet, in economically difficult times courses, programs, and entire colleges remain in jeopardy. Donald Phelps, former chancellor of the LACCD, contends that

> what has happened (in California) is the erosion of the master plan and the dream of what made California so great for so long. The state's leadership has failed to take advantage of its greatest resource, namely its institutions of higher learning. . . . State leaders really don't understand or know community colleges, which probably have a greater capability of helping to maintain the strength of the economy than the university. (CCLC Phelps 1993, 4)

The extraordinarily high California demographic rate has far surpassed the state's economic growth rate. This, in combination with a continuing severe recession and a series of natural disasters, causes economic hardships to continue to escalate (CCLC Phelps 1993). Responses to economic shortages include prohibiting faculty from conference travel; eliminating "fringe" programs such as study abroad; shifting the academic emphasis away from business, humanities, and fine arts and onto general education and basic skills while simultaneously ignoring the benefits internationalization can bring to all classes; and eliminating international education in its entirety. Lack of funding curtails faculty initiatives in support of new programs that may have an uncertain future (Raby CCIE 1994; CCLC 1994; McCurdy 1994). Finally, because of tuition increases, many students accelerate their education for quick transfer to four-year colleges or terminate education for the sake of employment (CCLC 1994). Although it is immensely important to both transfer students and those who work, the merits of internationalization are often ignored.

Nonetheless, there is evidence that precisely in times of fiscal difficulty, international programs become part of the mainstream. As unique programs become institutionalized, they avoid being subject to budget cuts and can thereby maximize their impact. James Hardt, former president of Hartnell College, asserts that this dichotomy remains true as colleges consolidate their positive forces and curtail the superfluous. During times of crisis, reform can embrace fringe programs, like international education, and allow them to become all the more ingrained within the college (ACIIE 1993). Within the past year, 10 percent of the colleges belonging to California Colleges for International Education (CCIE) have institutionalized elements of international education within their mission policies and within their college at large.

Disciplinary Hostilities

Perhaps the most devastating problem involves intracampus fighting between disciplines for funding and special allowances. Jealousy and competition prevent disciplines from working together. In various forms, such competition exists even among intercultural/multicultural, ethnic studies, and international programs. Departmentalism and provincialism can kill an international effort even before it begins. Unfortunately, as economic problems escalate, so do interdepartmental hostilities. Budget restrictions further increase hostilities and internationally oriented programs become defined as "fringes" rather than as essential components of a whole. When existing disciplines are not supportive of change, the administration is more reluctant to formulate new programs that highlight an internationalized curriculum. At one California college, the negative attitude from a small group of senior faculty prevented an entire international program from being developed.

A lack of college cohesiveness is also evident among different colleges of a multicollege district. In many cases, one district college may not know what other colleges are doing, so that activities that compete for limited students and resources actually duplicate one another. Such lack of communication has dire consequences for internationalization efforts and often escalates intracampus and intercampus hostilities (Raby CCIE 1993).

Lack of Expertise

No one person is born internationalized. She must research her field, borrow or invent creative applications and be consistently updated. This requires time, enthusiasm, and collaboration with experts in the field. The majority of faculty have not been trained through their disciplines or in graduate programs to use an international/multicultural perspective. Often they do not see nor understand the value of such knowledge. While this lack of faculty sensitivity intensifies the need for more in-service training, such training is contingent upon active staff participation. In turn, such training is negatively affected by budgetary restrictions that result from a lack of local, state, and federal funding.

Faculty who have international expertise can assist as mentors to illustrate how new perspectives can alter curricula and produce a fuller range of knowledge, which improves critical thinking and decision-making skills. Such efforts, however, take time and a considerable amount of staff development.

INTERNATIONALIZING THE CURRICULUM: TRADITIONS

Internationalization of the curriculum varies in terms of type, content, and methodology. Implementation varies with each college's needs, purposes, procedures, and personnel.

Internationalizing the Curriculum: Types

King and Fersh depict internationalization as a holistic process that encompasses the entire campus and serves to complement diverse aspects of education rather than compete with them (King and Fersh 1992). Internationalizing the curriculum takes many forms, from influencing what occurs inside the classroom to expanding the effects of education throughout the school and, in some cases, into the community.

Outside the classroom, curriculum internationalization is most dramatically shown in off-campus study-abroad programs. Study abroad encourages the development of international understanding through the observations of the participants (Mossberg 1990). However, since the number of participants in study-abroad programs remains limited, it is important to secure on-campus international curriculum efforts. The two are connected, since the experience of travel causes faculty members to revise the curriculum, which in turn inspires other internationally oriented programs (Robinson 1990). On-campus internationalization efforts may occur randomly, and there may be no connection between internationalized classes and internationalized disciplinary programs. Educational reform often hinges on each individual faculty member. Over the past ten years, the author has worked with over 450 faculty members throughout California to internationalize their classes. Internationalization also occurs through a systematic approach, which incorporates a holistic plan that includes the college mission statement and multiyear curriculum reform plans (Greene 1993; Raby 1994).

Nationally known community involvement programs include Bergen Community College's (New Jersey) monthly breakfast sessions, which encourage interaction between the local business community and the college, and Hartnell Community College's (California) promotion of ties to local businesses, its sister colleges, and the college's agricultural department. Both colleges promote short-term student-teacher exchanges or apprenticeships as well (Raby, *Comparative and International Education Society Newsletter,* 1993).

Internationalizing the Curriculum: Content

Each community college discipline (academic as well as technical) not only can but also should include international perspectives on that subject matter. No discipline is so remote that it is not influenced by international relationships, and no subject is so provincial that it cannot be viewed from an international perspective. International competence is integral to every discipline and profession, and is not a separate, isolated issue. All courses offered at the community college, from art to zoology, can and should be internationalized.

Four patterns typically emerge as U.S. community colleges internationalize their curricula. The first pattern highlights disciplines that are by their very nature international and, therefore, should already be or can easily become internationalized. These include geography, anthropology, and regional studies courses. In the latter, non-Western materials help widen the myopic perspective of Western civilization, and they also supplement area-of-concentration (i.e., Asian history), comparative (i.e., comparative religion), history, and sometimes literature courses. Effort is often directed at courses that have an almost exclusively Western orientation, to assure the representation of a significant portion of the world, whose influence on our lives is considerable. The 1993 CCIE annual report indicates that of its fifty-seven member colleges, all but two have internationalized some world history/Western civilization courses, nineteen offer specific courses in non-European history, and sixteen offer specific courses in non-European humanities.

In the second pattern, the number of foreign language programs that support academic and occupational international efforts is increased. There is also a direct correlation between the number of students enrolled in foreign language courses and the number of students in study-abroad courses. Twenty CCIE colleges support such connections.[4] The third and most popular pattern emphasizes the internationalization of business programs. Fifty CCIE colleges offer international business classes, and nine offer international business certificate/A.A. degree programs. The final pattern introduces international themes throughout the general education curriculum. This occurs in traditionally internationalized subjects such as English, humanities, political science, and the social sciences as well as in disciplines not commonly considered applicable to internationalization, such as agriculture, mathematics, nursing, physical sciences, secretarial sciences, and occupational, preprofessional, and vocational/technical disciplines. The CCIE survey confirms that this final pattern of internationalization is the most difficult to achieve and that nontraditional disciplines are the last to be addressed. Although seventeen CCIE colleges offer ethnic studies courses, twelve colleges offer courses in intercultural communications and international relations, and eleven colleges offer courses in multicultural studies (i.e., the traditional disciplines), documentation is unavailable for CCIE colleges offering nontraditional courses (Raby, CICE, 1993).

INTERNATIONAL AND INTERCULTURAL/MULTICULTURAL:
TWO SIDES OF THE SAME COIN

Although international and intercultural/multicultural studies have traditionally taken separate paths, they have more commonalities than differences. Major rifts between the intercultural/multicultural and international fields are based on a lack of departmental consensus, much of which stems from a dearth of the knowledge that fusion could provide. In the report "Building the Global Community: The Next Step," a draft policy is envisioned through which the direction of and implementation strategies for community college international and intercultural/multicultural education can be defined (Elsner, Tsunoda, and Korbel 1994). In this definitive document the terms *intercultural* and *multicultural* are used synonymously. While there are inherent differences between the two, this chapter will reiterate their similarities while leaving the discussion on their differences to Tarrow's introduction to this book. Tsunoda states that the two disciplines (international and intercultural/multicultural) form "the seamless web that many refer to as global [but also maintain] a duel terminology [that] reflects a deliberate aim to value both parts" (Elsner, Tsunoda, and Korbel 1994, 2). Merging international and intercultural (multicultural) programs and courses coordinates similar goals and activities, which often results in stimulation rather than competition; and this collaboration links "our domestic well-being to new world conditions" (ACE 1993, quoted in Elsner, Tsunoda, and Korbel 1994, 2). Fersh and Tsunoda claim that ethnicity is relevant to international and intercultural/multicultural education because "99% of us are descendants of immigrants who came here within the past 400 years from over 100 different countries" (Fersh 1993, 12; Tsunoda 1994). Tsunoda claims a need to "domesticate international education" by going beyond the outward dimension of internationalization to the application of such knowledge "back home to the communities around us" (Tsunoda 1994, quoted in Elsner, Tsunoda, and Korbel 1994, 2). Collaboration also occurs with the pairing of ethnic and international studies to realize the trajectory of race relations.

International courses provide a global scale for intercultural/multicultural studies on such issues as immigration, discrimination, prejudice, and their resulting interrelationships and conflicts. Intercultural/multicultural studies stress international events and analyze how they correlate to the many different ethnic groups in America. In addition, the knowledge gained from learning about other cultures can be applied to studies of Americans' ancestries, as well as of multiculturalism in international situations and the interrelationships that emerge from it.

The combined approach provides endless possibilities for curricula innovation without upsetting political or territorial boundaries. In California community colleges, collaboration was evident in the following staff-development workshops offered during the 1993–1994 academic year: "Valuing Differences: Initiating Change" (Cypress College), "Multicultural Symposium Coordinated with K–12 Unified and Pacific Union College (Napa Valley College), "The Hmong: Who We Are and How to Help Us" (Sacramento City College), and "Strategies for Development of the African-American Manchild" (Los Angeles Southwest College). The international elements of these multicultural topics were highlighted in each of these workshops.

Since intercultural/multicultural education became ingrained in most community colleges years before internationalization, many intercultural/multicultural proponents still regard international education with suspicion and view its programs as rivals in political and budget power struggles (Smithee 1991; King and Breuder 1979). Nonetheless, there is "a pressing need for higher education to contribute toward strengthening the social fabric of our multicultural society, toward involving our students and ourselves in service to our community and as individuals in these groups to assume greater sense of social responsibility and conscience" (Elsner, Tsunoda, and Korbel 1994, 2). The issue of conflict and consonance has yet to be resolved.

CORE REQUIREMENT

Internationalization of the core courses that all students must take for graduation (i.e., English and math) provides the foundation for building academic as well as international competency. Sjoquist states that a general education curriculum ceases to be "general" if it is bound by a single culture. In this way, the core curriculum needs to reflect a balance of cultural perspectives to "develop the kind of literacies that enhance the quality of life for all of us" (Sjoquist 1993, 58). Without the internationalization of general education core courses, students are deprived of the means of discovering their cultural heritages (CFCC 1988). Despite its importance, the institutionalization of an international core requirement is not widespread at U.S. community colleges. None of the CCIE colleges currently offer such a requirement.

A more common approach, initiated in 1980 by Broward Community College (Florida), is to require for graduation a minimum of six credit hours in international courses (Fersh and Greene 1984). Yet, six years later, a 1986–

1987 survey of 1,311 community colleges indicated that 51 percent did not require an international content in their general education curricula and the remaining 49 percent satisfied that requirement through Western civilization/history courses (72 percent), world civilization/history or culture courses (37 percent), non-Western civilization/history courses (18 percent), and other "international courses" (6 percent). (ACE 1986–1987. Participants were able to mark more than one answer.) In the 1990s considerable energy has been spent in internationalizing selected disciplines. Among CCIE colleges, internationalization efforts occur in the fields of anthropology and geography at Chaffey College, English or literature at Long Beach City College, fashion and visual merchandising and Latin American studies at the Los Angeles Community College District, and humanities at the College of the Redwoods, Golden West College, Mission College, and Saddleback College (Raby CCIE 1993). Table 3 lists the CCIE-member college classes that were "internationalized" in 1993–1994. This table does not account for the considerable internationalization that occurred in previous years.

TABLE 3. CCIE—Internationally Oriented Classes Introduced in 1993 and 1994

College	Internationally Oriented Classes
Chaffey Community College	Int'l Business Course Series; Intercultural Communications; Afro-American History; Intro. to African-American Lit.; Global Ecology; Ethnic Group Relations; Mexican History in the U.S.; Chicano Minority in the U.S.; Asian Civilization; World Religions; Intro. to Eastern Philosophy; Urban Politics—Worldwide. Internationalized aspects of ESL, anthropology and geography.
Coast Community College District	Comparative Early Childhood Education Systems; English 100; Intro. to Business; Alternative Modalities to Health; environmental studies; humanities. Coastline College stresses international business, Golden West College stresses multicultural studies, and Orange Coast College stresses international studies.
De Anza/Foothill Community College District	Complete program including nine international studies courses and forty-nine intercultural courses.
El Camino Community College	History of Non-European Architecture; Cross-Cultural Art; Introduction to International Relations. English courses were multiculturalized.
Glendale Community College	International business certificate programs.
Los Angeles Community College District	From 1987 to 1995, over 300 internationalized models were produced for individual courses. Art, civilization, geography,

College	Internationally Oriented Classes
	history, humanities, literature, and music disciplines had courses with regional focuses (China, Deaf Culture France, Germany, Israel, Italy, Korea, Latin America, and Mexico). New courses: Contemporary Latin American Short Story (in English and Spanish); Understanding Latin Americans Through Film; Cultural Awareness Through Advanced Conversation; College and Career Planning for the International Student; Communication across Cultures.
Long Beach City College	Non-Western Art (Pre-Columbian, Tribal, Asian); World Literature I and II; Asian Literature in English; Elements of Intercultural Communications.
Los Rios Community College District	California History: A Multicultural Perspective; Introduction to World Religions; History of Mexico; History of the Americas I and II.
Mission Community College	Environmental Biology; Comparative Politics; Survey of Western Art; History of Western Civilization; Graphic Arts; U.S. History.
Oxnard Community College	International business classes.
Pasadena Community College	International business curriculum.
Redwoods College	Non-European humanities through art and music appreciation; Music of the Whole Earth; Environmental Ethics.
Saddleback Community College	Humanities Department has been "internationalized."
San Francisco City College	Current Issues and Topics on the Pacific Rim; Philippines; Indonesia and PRC.
San Diego District Community College	Humanities Institute.
San Jose/ Evergreen Community College District	Pacific Rim Studies Program: Cultural Topics in Int'l Business; Building an Export Business; International Purchasing; Transportation/Distribution; International Marketing; Mexican-American Culture; Japanese People, Behavior, and Culture; Intro. to Vietnamese Culture.
Santa Barbara City College	World Literature; African and Russian History.
Santa Monica City College	Pacific Rim Studies: Arts of Asia; Asian Literature; History of of East Asia to 1600; Asian Philosophy; The Modern Far East.
Yosemite Community College District	USIA programs.

Internationalizing the Curriculum: Methodology

Many academic and technical disciplines are remiss to ignore international dimensions. The teaching of misinformation and the misuse of information become a concern, since academic quality is compromised without internationalization. Health classes that ignore the health concerns of immigrants (both in the United States and in their home countries), or ecology classes that ignore the effects of global pollution are likewise lacking. The manner in which material is taught is equally important. Fersh maintains that an internationalization that is synonymous with long lists, statistical accounts, and pronunciation guides placed at the end of a section is inadequate, for "facts, like bricks, are good for building purposes, but by themselves are not constructive" (Fersh 1993, 11). Several methodologies transcend this cycle, and all of these involve "adstructuring" and restructuring perspectives that enhance the perception of a worldview (King and Fersh 1992).

Educational reform is contingent upon motivating faculty to act and to embrace new materials and innovative teaching methodologies. Traditional staff development includes workshops and seminars specifically designed to assist faculty in using internationalized methodologies. Publishers endorse internationalization by publishing general texts (for economics, history, political science, environmental, and ESL courses) that include international components. A survey of the textbooks used at CCIE colleges indicates that the majority of books contain more international components than ever before, and these include texts published by such international public- and private-sector organizations as the World Bank, United Nations, and National Geographic Society (Raby 1993). Library expansion of books, videos, and interactive technology highlights yet another means of adding international dimensions (Harris 1992).

Student/Process/Content Methodology

Through Fersh's "Socratic method," instructors engage students in a process that requires questioning and reexamination of the highlighted content. Through the use of differing techniques, novel interpretations of content become evident, and as this occurs, the "subject of the course is not only the content; it is also concerned with the student's development and the process of learning" (King and Fersh 1992, 17). The goal is a student and faculty metamorphosis into the realm of "I never thought of that" or "I never knew that" (Fersh 1993, 7). After a recent workshop, a child development instructor gave the author the ultimate compliment that she never thought of learning from another culture to understand her own. This form of goal recognition by an individual through a series of experiences must be highlighted when one deals with faculty, administration, and students. The emphasis on self-education enables the individual to synthesize content in a holistic manner, since cognitive skills (knowledge, analysis, synthesis, and evolution) are combined with affective skills (preferences, interests, appreciation, and values) (Fersh 1993, 23).

ACTIVITY METHODOLOGY
Student participation makes learning an intimate task and helps enhance the retention of knowledge. Likewise, internationalization is intensified by both student and faculty participation. Students interact through internationally themed clubs, fairs, film series, social gatherings, displays of culturally themed artifacts, etc. Many colleges have international speakers series (sometimes planned in conjunction with events at local universities) and invite academic, political, and local community representatives to enhance current information (often not found in textbooks) and provide out-of-classroom intellectual stimulation for all students. Among CCIE-member colleges, speaker forums range from Santa Barbara City College's informal program based on individual faculty interests to American River College's formal program, which includes pre-scheduled speakers each semester.

Faculty activity falls into three distinct categories: informal, nonformal, and formal. Informally, at department meetings, faculty within the same discipline share techniques, strategies, and discipline-related information. Group brainstorming also occurs as faculty members respond to external elements that facilitate reform (such as changing textbooks or diversified student body). Nonformally, international education committees create and support programs at various stages in the institutionalization process, and international issues are frequently on the agendas of division and academic senate meetings. An inventory of the international skills and expertise of faculty members provides a built-in network of faculty who can share skills and expertise and therefore assists in the internationalization of classes.

Finally, formal activities (both optional and required) include staff development workshops and consortia affiliations that specifically highlight the internationalization of the curriculum. Staff development programs include those on campus, such as Saddleback Community College's (California) 1993 summer institute, which focused on expanding the international expertise of twenty-five members of the humanities faculty. Off-campus, universities nationwide offer staff development programs to enhance their faculties' ability to add international dimensions in their classes. Such programs include summer programs at the Far East Center in Hawaii, the Inter-Cultural Institute in Oregon, and the International Studies Summer Institutes (Community College Emphasis) at the University of California, Los Angeles. Numerous international programs (private, government, university, and community-college-sponsored) promote internationalization through faculty study-abroad ventures. For example, the LACCD International Faculty Seminar Series has included (among others) seminars in Siberia (1992), Thailand (1993), Poland (1993), and Guatemala (1994). Participation in these seminars often results in life-altering experiences, and the level of faculty enthusiasm upon completion of the seminars is often unparalleled.

Faculty workshops/seminars are viable to the internationalization of the curriculum when the knowledge learned at them is applied to curricular revision. Although it is evident from enrollment figures that community college faculties are participating more frequently in these programs, studies that follow up on their implementation are lacking. If the knowledge learned is not incorporated into the classroom or into college activities, these workshops/seminars remain an unsuccessful way of transmitting knowledge.

INFUSION METHODOLOGY

Infusion involves faculty reexamination of lecture components or class sequences and enables expansion with an international perspective. Revision of parts of or entire syllabi defines this type of programmatic reform. The basic instrument is the international master module, or lesson plan, which interjects an international perspective into an existing class. A subsequent learning package—which includes course outlines, activities, and lectures—evolves and ideally consists of a minimum of three to six lectures, roughly one to two weeks of class time. Since many community college faculty members do not have formalized pedagogical training, the terms *module, lesson plan*, or *learning package* may not be familiar ones. However, all faculty prepare their courses in advance, have a general concept of a course's structure and content, and have prepared many lectures and corresponding assignments and activities. Regardless of the terminology used, the emphasis on revision remains standard. To facilitate communication, the term *module* will be used in this section.

The content of a module must be detailed enough to offer substantial information but broad enough so that any instructor within the same discipline can adopt the ideas into his or her own class. For example, an international master module for a beginning psychology class can be incorporated by other psychology faculty members in their own courses without requiring much personal time for invention and revision. Through such a process, it becomes easier to internationalize large blocks of classes. Many faculty interns of this author maintain that modules should be introduced in the first few weeks of class to allow even those students who drop out a chance of discovering international connections. However, a distribution of modules across the curriculum remains the most effective method of their incorporation (Icochea 1984; Edwards 1990).

The benefits of modules are as follows: (1) the limits of modules coincide with those of one's imagination; (2) it is an individual process that requires no campus committees and hence can be easily implemented, although success is facilitated through the cooperation of administration and campus committees; (3) curriculum expansion results, since students gain international competency when more of their classes are internationalized; and (4) the only direct financial cost is the time that it takes for a faculty to create the module. This time can be based on individual initiative alone or can be compensated contingent upon the ability of the college to provide minigrants, release time, or promotions. Infusion involves seven approaches, which can be used individually or in combination. These approaches are described in the following paragraphs and are appropriate for all disciplines offered at community colleges.

Process Approach. The process approach highlights what students and faculty want to achieve in learning from, and want to understand about, other cultures and provides a context within which events and peoples are perceived (Fersh 1993). The emphasis is on the ability to reason from one stage to another and to learn from these transitions. For example, art and music simultaneously become windows through which students can express themselves to all cultures, and become communication devices whereby students can learn from other cultures. In English composition courses, this approach can be internalized through the development of clarity of thought about and insight from contrasting cultures. In foreign language classes, using songs from around the world and using cable or satellite TV, each student acquires a new cultural identity, which is reinforced through the attainment of language.

Area/Civilization Studies (Regional) Approach. The area/civilization studies approach involves an in-depth survey of a particular aspect of a subject as it applies to one specific country/region. This approach combines perspectives from many different disciplines (including anthropology, history, political science, and geography) and offers a comprehensive perspective that is significantly more detailed than a single-discipline approach. This culturally specific approach can be implemented in student assignments and exercises (such as country portfolios), which are expanded upon throughout the course of the semester.

Comparative Approach. The comparative approach materializes when two or more countries, regions, or cultures are compared and contrasted. This general cultural approach is applied in student assignments and activities and through class dialogue. The comparative approach is popular in that faculty do not need to obtain "expertise" in one region and can build upon student knowledge to provide the comparative edge. Furthermore, as faculty build upon their own areas of expertise, this approach is intensified.

Multidisciplinary Approach. The multidisciplinary approach integrates two or more disciplines in the process of promoting a unique perspective on an international topic. This occurs in nontraditional-style courses where more than one discipline explores a common subject. Often, this is achieved through team-teaching. For example, international languages may be combined with such academic courses such as business, nursing, and humanities and may result in "Health Professionals' Spanish," "Business Japanese," or "French for Fashion Design." In another example, political science and anthropology are combined, to allow students and faculty to learn the same material but from two different perspectives. Assuring successful pairing is contingent upon (1) a motivated faculty, (2) initiated cooperation as a means of eliminating jealousy and territorialism, and (3) increased sensitivity to the complementary rather than contradictory nature of distinct courses.

Issue Approach. In the issue approach, specific issues that are cross-cultural in their application and consequences are critically analyzed. Proponents claim that this approach allows for an in-depth focus, which helps to make courses more manageable. Examples range from discussions on the "nature of beauty" in cosmetology courses (Fersh 1993) to identifying how U.S. involvement abroad affects political science, psychology, or sociology courses. This approach is the most popular by far because one issue—be it the Olympic games, rock lyrics, environmental problems, agriculture, or race relations—can be explored using an international dimension within the confines of a single class. Many nontraditional internationalized disciplines (health, physical science, ecology, and technology) include elements that are likewise not bound by geography.

Lamy (1993) identifies five multidisciplinary issues that can be incorporated into almost every course: (1) knowledge of new forms of domestic and international organizations and alliances, (2) identification of sovereignty by exploring the meshing of international and domestic issues, (3) comprehension of human security by exploring the dichotomy between rich and poor peoples, countries, and regions, (4) perceptions about excessive nationalism, which enable people to identify and hence avoid chauvinism, and (5) appreciation of the environment and the fate of the earth. These issues may be used in an infinite variety of ways, and have infinite applications and consequences for curricula reform.

Philosophical/Theoretical Approach. The philosophical/theoretical approach critically relates the specific theories and philosophies found in various disciplines to international issues. Internationalization is equated with cultural perspectives, political understanding, and economic awareness. Lamy delineates four strategies by which the philosophical/theoretical approach can be applied in all courses: (a) ethical, (b) retrospective, (c) problem-based, and (d) forced decision making. Using this approach, interrelationships based on global sociopolitical and economic contexts can be represented in all courses. In mathematics, the application of mathematical theories to things that can be categorized (i.e., symbols and peoples) helps to promote pattern recognition, which is central to the understanding of international issues.

Technological Approach. The manner in which education is imparted is changing rapidly. Computer education, audiovisual teaching techniques, long-distance learning, and interactive television and computers expand the horizons of students and faculty through hands-on learning. Technology unleashes unlimited opportunities for what Fersh refers to as "culture transcending" (Fersh and Furlow 1993, 23). The use of long-distance learning and CD-ROMs, Internet, and the World Wide Web makes massive amounts of previously inaccessible information available to students. Likewise, courses that include computer simulation activities or satellite linkages between colleges in different regions, states, or countries reinforce the boundless nature of internationalization of the curriculum.

Problems with the Infusion Methodology. The use of the infusion methodology is not indisputable. Limitations and potential superficialities exist, since only limited portions of a class become internationalized using this approach. Infusion can translate into the mere provision of international examples, parables, or international theme assignments and does not include the in-depth study required for a student to fully comprehend a specific culture. This point may be countered by the fact that community colleges were never intended to be institutions that provided in-depth study but, rather, were designed to provide introductory courses that related to the first two years of higher education. Although this constricted methodological bias is a problem, current fiscal problems, the dwindling number of electives and the intensifying prerequisites for degrees make this methodology not only adaptable but desirable. Indeed, it is better to have some application of international themes in a class than none at all.

Another problem with this methodology is that it is time-consuming. Infusion cannot be achieved by a single workshop, and as such, the initial zeal for the process may be dampened. Time constraints cause many not to finish their "modules" or to present modules that are not of high quality. Indeed, the formidable amount of information to be undertaken in the process of infusion is enough to cause many faculty members to abandon internationalization projects and even the idea of internationalization itself.

As part of its effort to internationalize various classes, the American River College (ARC) in California gave minigrants to faculty members who committed themselves to the effort for two years. Although fewer than 50 percent actually completed their modules (twenty in total), those modules were of extremely high quality and have subsequently been used in more than one class. This remains a tremendous achievement, especially when compared to that of California State University, Long Beach (CSULB), which in 1993 finished a six-year infusion project that supported the claim that infusion was adaptable throughout the institution but that resulted in the production of only sixty-five high-quality modules.[5] Nonetheless, ARC and CSULB are offering twenty and sixty-five internationalized courses, respectively, and are offering them twice a year to approximately 60–100 students annually. The impact over time is indeed tremendous.

The quality control of modules is another area for concern. Just because an international example is used does not mean that it is used in an academic or even in a critical fashion. In addition, many faculty still define international as "Western," which severely limits the benefits of an internationalized curriculum, and the insufficient quantity and quality of the textbooks supporting internationalized courses cause problems. The final problem concerns the financial incentive for creating a module. Few incentives other than the traditional minigrant and the occasional release time exist for faculty to "internationalize."

INTERNATIONAL STUDENTS METHODOLOGY
The influx of new students (such as immigrants, refugees, and traditional international students) further internationalizes a community college's student body. Indeed, for many international students, attending community colleges is a social rite of passage into American society. Curricula reform that enhances courses and provides international dimensions to

formal and nonformalized instruction should highlight the diverse talents of these students in terms of language use, historical knowledge, and cultural expertise. It is not uncommon for community colleges to host students from over fifty countries, and such institutions as Mesa Community College (Arizona), LACCD (California), Santa Monica City College (California), and Brevard Community College (Florida) have a student body that reflects a diversity of over 100 countries (Raby 1994). Students from other countries help internationalize both the classroom and the campus because they are an on-site source of international knowledge and comparison. As Tsunoda claims, "the world isn't outside, it has arrived on our campuses. It is not a question of 'them' and 'us,' for we are all 'they'" (Tsunoda 1994, 6).

How the curriculum is influenced, however, depends on how the college perceives this variety of students. Many CCIE colleges use international students as cultural tutors (City College of San Francisco), as language tutors (American River College), as internationalization agents (Cañada College), and as research/resource magnets (Los Angeles Trade-Technical College) (Raby CCIE 1993). Regardless of how they do so, colleges need to develop strategies to deal with diversity and to foster greater sensitivity in the classroom and campuswide.

A variation of this methodology is to pair American students who have studied abroad with international students on campus. This union perpetuates the American students' international connections, causes friendships to form that can transcend the college years, and forms an internationally rich exchange. These activities affect both the formal and nonformal curricula and, through them, the campus at large.

Problems with Using International Students for Curricular Reform. There are several cautionary aspects of this methodology. First, in terms of language tutoring, just because international students are native speakers does not mean that they possess the necessary skills to teach their language to others. Indeed, teaching is an art that must be learned. However, using international students to ensure that those learning a language have someone to speak to on an informal level only enhances language retention. The second cautionary aspect is that in terms of cultural tutoring, immigrants, international students, and refugees do not speak for their country. There is a compelling reason why they are attending an U.S. college rather than one in their own country. The cultural attitude that these individuals portray, although valid, may not represent the mainstream culture felt by the majority in their home country. When placed in the proper context, the perspectives of these students remain enlightening, yet when improperly utilized, they can perpetuate prejudice, ethnocentrism, and cultural misinformation.

NEW-CLASSES METHODOLOGY
The development of new classes that specifically highlight aspects of international issues eliminates the superficial quality of the infusion methodology. New classes may be general (such as "World Literature") or specific (such as "Films of Latin America"). These classes frequently endorse multidisciplinary perspectives, and some involve pair-teaching. Examples of the latter include pairing ESL with sociology, nursing with foreign languages, and international relations with anthropology. New classes such as "Introduction to International Business," "Introduction to International Studies," and "Crosscultural Communications" often become catalysts for the initiation of a major/minor degree or certificate program.

Revision of departmental course syllabi to include international themes is another way to create new versions of old classes. The difference between this methodology and the infusion methodology is that in this methodology, an entire class is revised. Even classes whose curricula are dictated by four-year universities (for the sake of transfers) or by businesses (for the sake of employment) can become internationalized without being added to the curriculum or jeopardizing the needed course content. The ultimate form of this methodology stems from a departmental requirement that all new courses must be international in content and from the department's encouragement of the revision of existing courses so that they complement one another.

Problems with Creating New Classes. The primary problem with this method is financial. In a recession, it is difficult to propose the introduction of new courses, especially when existing courses are fighting for their own survival. In addition, new courses take time to become ingrained in a college, especially revolutionary ones such as those with an international perspective. Furthermore, once the courses are offered at the community college there remains the need to educate students, faculty, four-year universities, and businesses on the benefits and transferability of these programs. The latter has proven to be an especially difficult task.

INTERNATIONALLY THEMED A.A. DEGREE/CERTIFICATE PROGRAMS
Internationally themed certificate and/or A.A. degree programs represent a structured core of required classes plus a selection of multidisciplinary electives. The resulting holistic orientation reinforces the personal as well as occupational benefits that arise from international experiences, which (a) pro-

vide a range of employment opportunities for students, (b) foster intellectual stimulation for teachers and students, (c) advance an international perspective in instructional programs, (d) encourage teachers to use the world as their classroom, (e) stimulate staff to participate in intercultural training and instructional opportunities, (f) inspire students to participate in study-abroad programs, (g) prepare students to meet the challenges of rapid economic and political change in the world, and (h) promote ethnic and cultural diversification as an asset to future employment. A common feature of all these programs is that they allow students to take a broad range of internationalized classes within many different disciplines and therefore expose them to a range of knowledge upon which international literacy is eventually achieved.

A.A. degree and certificate programs ideally exist as an individualized department (i.e., international studies, intercultural communications, international business, etc.). More realistically they exist as part of an established department, typically business or political science. In 1994 thirty-eight CCIE-member institutions reported that they had implemented, or were in the planning stages of developing, such programs.[6] Some programs are cross-disciplinary, such as those at the American River, DeAnza, Orange Coast, and Fresno colleges. Others are rooted in a single discipline, such as political science at Santa Barbara City College, humanities at Allan Hancock College, business at Coastline College, or Latin American studies at Los Angeles Pierce College.

The majority of the A.A. international studies degree programs surveyed require twenty-seven units plus an emphasis on foreign languages. Many programs are supplemented by internationally infused general education classes; most involve selected general education courses, which are required for graduation; and nearly all offer classes that are transferable to universities. DeAnza College (California) offers advanced programs in both international and intercultural studies; these programs include nine international studies courses and forty-nine intercultural studies courses.

In California, the number of international business A.A./certificate programs is exploding. Many are modifications of Coastline College's four-part interdisciplinary approach of (a) international business studies, (b) general business management studies, (c) international culture and geography studies, and (d) foreign language studies. Some (such as the Pacific Rim Studies Program at San Jose City College or the newly proposed International Fashion and Visual Merchandising Program at Los Angeles Trade-Technical College) add unique components. Many programs include technical workshops, referral services, international student internship programs, and affiliations with local World Trade Centers organizations (*Guidepost* 1994; Hardt 1993). In 1994 twenty-four international business programs had been or were being developed at seventeen CCIE colleges.[7] Nationally, most international business certificate programs (e.g., at Oxnard, San Jose, and Portland Community Colleges) require fifteen units, while international business A.A. degree programs (e.g., at St. Louis and Pima Community Colleges) require up to seventy-one units (Raby 1994).

Although growth in the number of colleges offering A.A./certificate international programs is evident, the rate of student participation remains limited.[8] In 1993 the international studies A.A. degree program at Santa Barbara City College enrolled fifty students, the certificate program at American River College enrolled thirty-one students, the international business program at St. Louis Community College enrolled twenty-eight students, and similar programs at Glendale City, San Jose City College, and Portland enrolled twenty, thirty, and fifty students respectively. The number of annual graduates is equally small and ranges from two graduates annually at Pima College to up to twenty graduates at Portland College. Eighty percent of Portland College graduates transfer into B.A. programs, while 70 percent of the graduates at St. Louis and Pima enter or re-enter into the employment sector. Unique to this survey is Coastline Community College (California), which in 1994 enrolled over 100 students in its international business certificate program, which had 60–70 graduates (of whom 46 percent transferred to a university), and enrolled just under 100 students in its international A.A. degree program, which had 20 graduates (of whom 30 percent transferred to a university). It is important to mention that for the business programs, many students enroll for continuing education and are not officially part of either a certificate or a degree program (Raby CCIE 1993; 1994).

International and intercultural studies programs and international business programs share students and, often, a multidisciplinary curriculum of special internationalized courses. Incorporation of foreign language, cultural anthropology, and cultural geography components into different vocational areas is one example. A multidisciplinary emphasis heightens international literacy skills and helps students become more valuable in the current job market. Collaboration is exemplified in courses such as "Japanese for Business" and "Spanish for Health Professionals" and in the ESL/sociology mix. This novel integration of courses is rapidly gaining recognition and acceptance among community colleges nationally.

Problems with A.A. Degree/Certificate Programs. A.A. degree/certificate programs involve securing faculty support for radical curricula change, highlighting faculty expertise to support these programs, and identifying connections with universities (so that these programs may be articulated) and with business (so that they may accept certificates as essential components for employment). Most important, however is to ensure the necessary finances to create and sustain these programs. For many programs, the initial funding comes from federal or state grants, yet after the duration of the grant, some colleges curtail the programs because of a lack of funds. In the past decade, three Californian colleges received federal grants to develop international programs but all were forced to constrict the parameters of their programs after the initial funding ended (Raby CCIE 1993). For these types of programs to survive, they must become institutionalized as part of the college and, hence, receive funding similar to that for other disciplines.

Merging Ideals with Reality: Implications and Recommendations

In light of the data presented in this chapter, successful internationalization begins with a clear definition of what international education is and how it relates to curriculum reform. Despite decades of change, many colleges and faculty members still view international education as consisting solely of study-abroad programs. This is a narrow and confining view, since international education is considerably more, and must be addressed so that internationalized curriculum programs are built and maintained. In addition, the confusion regarding the terms *international, intercultural,* and *multicultural* must also be addressed.

With a secure definition in hand, colleges can enhance educational philosophy and mission statements so that resources, opportunities, and genuine support are given to international efforts. Indeed, the implementation of an internationalized curriculum depends on how each academic institution defines and supports international education in its mission and policy statements. To initiate and sustain internationalization, there must be an integral involvement of the college's trustees, administration, faculty, counselors, students, and community. The ultimate goal is to make the internationalized curriculum an integral part of the college by mandating that core courses be internationalized; creating a policy that identifies international activity as a criterion for promotion, tenure, salary increases, and new faculty recruitment; and receiving support from the campus staff, which is necessary for the recruitment of students for critical classes.

Institutionalization is strengthened by promotion, release time, and opportunities for first-hand experiences abroad. The most useful incentives are minigrants given to faculty to conduct international research or to participate in internationally oriented staff development programs, which are later reflected in classroom or college activities. Systematic curriculum and departmental reviews assure that internationalization efforts are of high quality, especially in introductory and core courses. Expansion of library holdings of international education texts and membership in international education consortiums aid the creation and dissemination of various reform methodologies. Finally, the orientation and support of faculty and students involved in foreign travel, work, or study further aid the correlation of these endeavors with curriculum reform.

Successful institutionalization involves the ability to overcome (a) resistance to change, (b) parochialism in educational policy, (c) an ethnocentric perception of the world, which many disciplines currently possess, and (d) faculty apathy. Curriculum reform is a slow process that often begins with a single faculty member and then spreads to others throughout the college. This slow process may be frustrating, but eventually it is quite rewarding. Overall, internationalization is impossible without the active participation of faculty. Through various outreach programs, enthusiasm can be built and maintained. However, in many instances, faculty resistance has proven to be the most difficult obstacle to overcome.

While many surveys have been administered to community colleges nationwide, few formalized evaluations relate specifically to internationalization of the curriculum. For the most part, evaluations are either part of a final stage of a grant process or part of the internal network of an individual college. Critical analysis involving the theoretical conceptualization of program content and applications is indeed lacking. Every two years in the LACCD, evaluations are given to all faculty members who have created international modules since 1989 and who are still teaching at the district. The 1992 evaluation indicated that 95 percent of faculty were still using their modules and 10 percent were participating in additional programs to enhance their modules (Raby 1992). For community colleges that have no new resources to support an internationalized curriculum, internationalization is contingent upon the efforts of a faculty enrichment committee and upon staff development. Securing a clear definition of international education to counter stereotypes and biases generates enthusiasm and support for any new programs. Finally, providing release time for coordinating programs that internationalize the curriculum can facilitate future activities.

For community colleges with limited resources that are derived from short-term grants or even from the college itself, such enticements for faculty members as minigrants, release time, promotions, and encouragement from the president are most beneficial. Limited funds can support developmental workshops that increase faculty enthusiasm and further intercultural sensitivity and knowledge of international issues. Funds can improve library holdings of books, films, and videos with an international theme, can facilitate membership in regional and national consortia, and can create as well as support A.A. degree/certificate programs. When general education requirements at four-year colleges encourage the creation of transferable courses, the support and institutionalization of these A.A. degree/certificate programs becomes even more solidified. Finally, designating a specific location for the development of an international education program office that includes a director and staff helps build a strong foundation for change.

In conclusion, an internationalized curriculum and campus promotes international competency among students, faculty, administration, and staff. Knowledge and understanding of other societies' histories, geographic environments, values, institutions, and cultural traditions are essential for comprehending our complex, interconnected world. Understanding the role of culture in shaping our policies and agendas has a direct relationship on our capacity to make personal decisions on complex international issues. Indeed, investment in internationalization of the curriculum is investment in the prevention of harm. As such, internationalization of the curriculum, as described in *Plan for Action for International Competence: A Key to America's Future*, remains central to community colleges and, hence, to our life in the next century (CAFLIS 1989).

Notes

1. There are 107 community colleges in California, and they enroll over 1.5 million students. Fifty-seven out of the 107 community colleges in the state are members of the consortium California Colleges for International Education (CCIE). Throughout this chapter, references made to California community colleges are taken from the CCIE annual report of 1993 and from the 1993–1994 report.

2. These are just two of many crossovers that have occurred over the past decade, not only at the LACCD but at community colleges throughout the country. An exact accounting has yet to be made. This crossover is what makes internationalization of the curriculum such an important part of the community college experience.

3. Jobs requiring international expertise arise in government and domestic and international business. Those who have international expertise and work in domestic business include translators, airline representatives, foreign service representatives, secretaries for international firms, journalists, and photo-journalists. There are government-oriented jobs in the Peace Corps, military, United Nations, and State Department; at embassies and consulates and in international organizations in industrialized and nonindustrialized nations. In the field of international business, there are jobs in marketing and general business, finance, media (journalism, photojournalism, broadcasting), banking, service organizations, export management companies, trading and export-import companies and administration, advertising, etc.

4. In the 1993–1994 academic year, CCIE colleges offered the following foreign language classes:

Language	No. of Colleges	Language	No. of Colleges	Language	No. of Colleges
Arabic	2	German	20	Latin	4
Armenian	2	Greek	1	Mandarin*	2
Cantonese	1	Hebrew	4	Portuguese	5
Chinese*	10	Hmong	1	Russian	14
Farsi	1	Italian	13	Spanish	25
Filipino	1	Japanese	18	Thai	1
French	21	Korean	2	Vietnamese	2

* Some colleges specifically list Mandarin as opposed to Chinese, while others list Chinese, which may include Mandarin plus other Chinese languages.

5. Presentation by Elaine Haglund of California State University, Long Beach, at the 1993 CIES Western Region Conference, Los Angeles. The following shows the number of modules per discipline:

Courses	Modules	Courses	Modules	Courses	Modules
Anthropology	4	French/Italian	1	Philosophy	6
Art	1	Geography	2	Political Science	1
Biology	1	Health care administration	1	Psychology	1
Black studies	1	Health science	1	Radio/TV/film	3
Chemistry	1	History	3	Social work	2
Comparative literature	3	Home economics	2	Sociology	3
Economics	3	Human resources management	4	Spanish	1
Electrical engineering	3	Marketing	1	Speech communication	3
Engineering	3	Mechanical engineering	1	Teacher education	1
English	3	Mexican-American studies	1	Technology and engineering	3
Finance/ real estate/law	1	Nursing	2		

6. In 1994, CCIE member institutions either had planned or were planning the following programs: A.A. degree in international Studies (5), A.A. degree in inter-

national business (7), certificate in international studies (3), certificate in international business (17), A.A. and certificate in intercultural studies (2), certificate in Pacific Rim studies: emphasis on international business (1), certificate in fashion and visual merchandising (1), certificate in Chicano studies and black studies (1), and certificate in Latin American studies (1).

7. The California International Trade Development Centers system includes the following colleges: Citrus College, Coastline College (with a high-technology emphasis), Fresno College, Los Angeles Southwest College, Merced College (with an agriculture emphasis), Oxnard College, Riverside College (with an African emphasis), Sacramento City College (with an Asian emphasis), Southwestern College, and Vista College (with an Eastern European emphasis). Other CCIE colleges that have a growing number of international business programs are Coastline, Chaffey, East Los Angeles, Glendale, Irvine Valley/Saddleback, Long Beach, Mission, Oxnard, Pasadena, San Jose, Santa Barbara, and State Center District.

8. Questions regarding student participation and the number of graduates of programs were frequently ignored in both the national and the CCIE surveys.

REFERENCES

AAWCC Quarterly. "Oregon Governor Barbara Roberts Lauds Community Colleges in Keynote Speech"; "Oregon Educational Act for the 21st Century." XVII, no. 5 (Fall 1993): 1–3.

ACIIE Newsletter (June 1993).

American Association of Community and Junior Colleges (AACJC). "Improving International Education: Is There a Role for Community Colleges?" *AACJC Journal* (Dec. 1984–Jan. 1985): 8.

American Council on Education (ACE). "Survey of Undergraduate International Studies: 1986–1987." Higher Education Panel Survey No. 76, 1988.

———. "A National Interest and International Dimensions of Higher Education in a Post War Era." *ACE Monograph Bulletin.* Washington, D.C.: ACE, 1993.

Barrows, Thomas. *College Students' Knowledge and Beliefs: A Survey of Global Understanding.* New Rochelle, N.Y.: Change Magazine Press, 1981.

Cohen, Arthur. "Talk on Community Colleges." Comparative and International Education Society Western Regional Conference, Los Angeles, 1993.

Commission on the Future of Community Colleges (CFCC). *Building Communities: A Vision for a New Century.* Report of the Commission on the Future of Community Colleges. Washington, D.C.: AACJC, 1988.

California Community Colleges. "Unduplicated Headcount." Sacramento: Chancellor's Office Management Information Services, May 3, 1994 (unpublished documentation).

———. "Staff Data File." Sacramento: Chancellor's Office Management Information System, May 3, 1994 (unpublished documentation).

Coalition for the Advancement of Foreign Language and International Studies (CAFLIS). *Plan of Action for International Competence.* Washington, D.C.: CAFLIS, 1989.

Community College League of California (CCLC). "League in Action." Sacramento: CCLC, October 1993.

———. "Interview with Donald Phelps, W.K. Kelloge Professor in the University of Texas, Austin's Community College Leadership Program." *The News* (Nov.–Dec. 1993): 3–4.

———. *The News* (March–April 1994): 1–3.

Council on Education. *What We Don't Know Can Hurt Us: The Shortfall in International Competence.* January 1984.

Ebersole, B.J. "International Education: Where and How Does It Fit in Your College?" *Community, Technical and Junior College Journal* 59, no.3 (1989): 29–31.

Education for a Global Century: Handbook of Exemplary International Programs. New Rochelle, N.Y.: Change Magazine Press, 1981.

Edwards, Jane, and Tonkin Humphrey. "Internationalizing the CC: Strategies for the Classroom." In Richard Greenfield (ed.), *Developing International Education Programs.* New Directions for Community Colleges Series No. 70. San Francisco: Jossey-Bass, 1990.

Elsner, Paul A., Joyce S. Tsunoda, and Linda A. Korbel. "Building the Global Community: The Next Step." Points of Departure for the American Council on International Intercultural Education/Stanley Foundation Leadership Retreat, Nov. 28–30, 1994.

Fersh, Seymour. "The Community College and the World Community." In *Community College Frontiers.* Springfield, Ill.: Sangamon State University, 1988.

———. *Integrating the Trans-National/Cultural Dimension.* Fastback 361, no. 104. Bloomington, Ind.: Phi Delta Kappa Educational Foundation, 1993.

Fersh, Seymour, and Richard Furlow. *The Community College and International Education: A Report of Progress.* Vol. III. Glen Ellyn, Ill.: College of DuPage, Office of International Education, 1993.

Fersh, Seymour, and William Greene (eds.). *The Community College and International Education: A Report of Progress.* Vol. II. Ft. Lauderdale, Fla.: Broward Community College Press, 1984.

Friere, Paulo. Quoted in "Radical Educator Combats Illiteracy." In *Education Exchange.* Syracuse, N.Y.: Syracuse University School of Education, Spring 1982.

Greene, William. "Area 8: The International/Intercultural General Education Requirement." *AACJC Journal* 55, no. 4 (1993): 17.

Guidepost VI, No. 1 (Jan. 1991).

Harari, Maurice. "Internationalization of Higher Education: Effecting Institutional Change in the Curriculum and Campus Ethos." Report No. 1 of Center for International Education, California State University-Long Beach (CSULB). Long Beach: CSULB, 1989.

Hardt, James. "New Innovations in International Education." Roundtable address at the Comparative and International Education Society Western Region Conference, Los Angeles, California, Nov. 1993.

Harris, Mathilda E. "Education for a Global Age." Speech delivered at the 1992 CCID Conference in Costa Mesa, California, Feb. 26, 1992.

Hirsch, E.D. Jr. *Cultural Literacy: What Every American Needs to Know.* New York: Vintage Books, 1988.

Icochea, Lynda. "Global Dimensions in an International Curriculum." In S. Fersh and W. Greene (eds.), *The Community College and International Education: A Report of Progress.* Vol. II. Fort Lauderdale, Fla.: Broward Community College Press, 1984.

King, Maxwell C., and Robert L. Breuder (eds.). *Advancing International Education.* New Directions for Community Colleges Series No. 26. San Francisco: Jossey-Bass, 1979.

King, Maxwell C., and Seymour H. Fersh. "International Education and the U.S. Community College: From Optional to Integral." *Junior College Resource Review*, Spring 1983. Los Angeles: ERIC Clearinghouse for Junior Colleges.

———. *Integrating the International/Intercultural Dimension in the Community College.* Cocoa, Fla.: Association of Community College Trustees and Community Colleges for International Development, 1992.

Koltai, Leslie. "Are There Challenges and Opportunities for American Community Colleges on the International Scene?" Keynote address at the Comparative and International Education Society, Western Region Conference, Los Angeles, California, Nov. 1993.

Lamy, Steve. "The End of the Cold War: What Do We Teach Now?" *WISC News* No. 2 (Dec. 1993): 1.

Los Angeles County Office of Education. Leadership 2000 Conference, "Restructuring for a Diverse Community." Los Angeles, California, Nov. 3–5, 1993.

McCurdy, Jack. *Broken Promises: The Impact of Budget Cuts and Fee Increases on the California Community Colleges.* Sacramento: The California Higher Education Policy Center, 1994.

Mossberg, Barbara Clarke. "Colleges Must Encourage and Reward International Exchanges." *Chronicle of Higher Education* (May 30, 1990): 22.

Raby, Rosalind Latiner. *California Colleges for International Education Annual Reports: 1988–1989; 1989–1990; 1990–1991; 1991–1992; 1992–1993; 1993–1994.* Los Angeles: CCIE, 1989; 1990; 1991; 1992; 1993; 1994 [respectively] (unpublished documentation).

———. "Internationalizing the California Community College Curriculum." *Global Pages* 8, no. 1 (Spring 1990): 13.

———. "Identity and Community through Community College International Education." *Comparative and International Education Society Newsletter* (Sept. 1993): 3.

———. "Implementation of International Education at California Community Colleges." *The News*, Community College League of California (September 1993): 8.

———. *Institute for International Programs [IIP]: 1992–1993 Annual Report.* Los Angeles: IIP, Los Angeles Community College District, 1993 (unpublished documentation).

Robinson, Brenda S. "Facilitating Faculty Exchange." In Richard Greenfield (ed.). *Developing International Education Programs.* San Francisco: Jossey-Bass, 1990.

Roueche, Suanne D. (ed.). *Innovation Abstracts* XIII, no.1. Austin: National Institute for Staff and Organizational Development, University of Texas at Austin, 1991.

Scanlon, David G. "Lessons from the Past in Developing International Education in Community Colleges." In Richard Greenfield (ed.), *Developing International Education Programs.* New Directions for Community Colleges Series No. 70. San Francisco: Jossey-Bass, 1990.

Sjoquist, Douglas P. "Globalizing General Education: Changing World, Changing Needs." In Neal A. Raisman (ed.), *Directing General Education Outcomes.* New Directions for Community Colleges Series No. 81. San Francisco: Jossey-Bass, 1993.

Smith, Kara. "Association of Professional Schools of International Affairs: 1994 Survey." Personal interview. April 1994.

Smithee, Michael. *Association of International Education* 42, no. 6 (April/May 1991): 14.

Tsunoda, Joyce. "Address to the Association of International Education Administrators Annual Conference at Tokai University." Honolulu, Hawaii, Feb. 5, 1994.

6 Study Abroad in the Pacific Islands
More Than an International Experience
Sharon Narimatsu and Robert W. Franco

Study-abroad programs provide excellent opportunities for experiencing and studying the cultures of other countries. Students who have participated in these educational programs have learned to appreciate different points of view, have gained an international perspective on issues, have developed personal confidence, and have enhanced their ability to function effectively in today's increasingly interdependent global society.

The Study Abroad in the Pacific Islands Program, created by the University of Hawai'i Community Colleges (UHCC), is unique in that it seeks to achieve all of the above outcomes but has an added focus. That focus is cultural reconnection. Through this program Native Hawaiian students are given the opportunity to reconnect with their Polynesian kin, to rediscover their Polynesian roots, and to reaffirm their Hawaiian heritage and identity. Therefore, the program is designed to be more than an international exploration of others; it is designed for self-exploration, self-discovery, and cultural perpetuation.

The initial Pacific Islands study-abroad program took thirty-three students and seven instructors, the majority of whom were Native Hawaiians, to American and Western Samoa, New Zealand (Aotearoa), and Fiji for a four-week study tour. Through this initial study-abroad project Native Hawaiian students were able to visit ancestral homelands and discover distinct historical developments and cultural transformations in Polynesia. Similar programs working with students of African, Asian, European, or Latin-American ancestry could be developed at any American community college. On the horizon, a similar, and very exciting, study-abroad project may take Vietnamese students back to their homeland.

Study Abroad: The International Dimension

Goodwin and Nacht (1988) examine policies and programs for American students venturing abroad (see also Clark and Neave 1992). In their research they visited forty diverse colleges and universities (as well as other relevant organizations and institutions) in California, Texas, Illinois, and Massachusetts. The institutions ranged from small liberal-arts and two-year colleges to major research universities. These institutions were both public and private, rural and urban, and well endowed and underfunded, and demonstrated both high and low levels of commitment to study abroad.

After considering study-abroad programs in relation to larger issues in higher education, Goodwin and Nacht delineated ten prominent educational and social goals of study-abroad programs at these representative American institutions (Goodwin and Nacht 1988). Many of the goals specified by Goodwin and Nacht were targeted in the UHCC Study Abroad in the Pacific Islands Program, and they included the following:

- *Internationalizing the educated citizenry.* Proponents of this study-abroad goal posit that an overseas experience confronts students with "difference." As a result, students become more culturally aware and sensitive and they begin to question their own national and ethnic prejudices. New perspectives are gained and personal horizons are extended.
- *Exploring our roots.* Numerous study-abroad programs have been established to help America's immigrants rediscover their historical roots, their ancestral homelands.
- *Mastering a foreign language.* Advocates of this study-abroad goal argue that language is best learned in an "immersion" context, and that language is a window to cultural perception.
- *Knowing ourselves.* Proponents of this study-abroad goal posit that we learn about ourselves by listening to new voices, that is, by being attuned to the insights of detached, objective, foreign observers.
- *Improving international relations.* The premise for this study-abroad goal is that a focused overseas experience provides students with a unique understanding of international social issues as they relate to foreign policy.

In the Study Abroad in the Pacific Islands Program, students were confronted with *differences,* but more important, they sought to understand cultural, political, and historical *similarities* among the Polynesian peoples. The goal of this unique study-abroad program was to make students more culturally aware and sensitive, and to enable them to question increasingly their own prejudices. In the process, students explored their own roots (roots too long neglected), but they also expanded their horizons to see the larger context within which Polynesian nations and territories have developed.

The program allowed students to master a language other than English. This second language is not foreign; rather, it is the language of their ancestors and their homeland, the Hawaiian language. They needed to improve their Hawaiian language after hearing cognate languages and experiencing cognate cultures in Polynesia and the broader Pacific. With a better grasp of their own language and history, they came to understand their own personal and cultural identities more fully.

With a better understanding of the geopolitical context in contemporary Polynesia, our students can consider more enlightened policies toward the emerging nations and territories of the region. Hawai'i and eastern Samoa became U.S. territories in 1899, and although Hawai'i obtained statehood in 1959, American Samoa remains an unincorporated, undefined American territory. Western Samoa gained independence from New Zealand in 1962, and Fiji achieved independence from Great Britain in 1970. Western Samoa, Fiji, and New Zealand remain self-governing members of the British Commonwealth. Thus, there is much shared history in contemporary Polynesia. Further, there is much shared concern about indigenous rights and cultural development in all the nations and territories of the region.

The UHCC Study Abroad in the Pacific Islands Program

The UHCC has an established Pacific Islands program. This program includes curriculum development, faculty exchanges, and as this chapter illustrates, study-abroad endeavors. The remainder of this chapter delineates the Study Abroad in the Pacific Islands Program, which merges international study abroad with intercultural/multicultural revitalization processes.

Historical Background

Hawai'i has a rich indigenous and multicultural history. The first Pacific Islanders arrived in the Hawaiian archipelago about A.D. 200, after 100 generations of exploring the Polynesian islands of Samoa, Tonga, Tahiti, and the Marquesas (see Franco 1987, maps 1 and 2). These Hawaiians also had ancestral connections with the Maori people of Aotearoa (New Zealand). Over a period of 1,600 years and in close harmony with the environment, Hawaiians adapted an extremely complex sociopolitical, religious, and economic system.

Hawai'i's multicultural history began in 1778 with Captain Cook's "discovery" of the Hawaiian Islands. Throughout the nineteenth century, this multicultural history continued with the arrival of more European and American explorers, missionaries, and planters. In the late nineteenth century, after the significant depopulation of, and the concomitant cultural loss among, Native Hawaiians, Asian labor was brought to Hawai'i to work the sugarcane and pineapple plantations. By 1920, the islands of Hawai'i were home to peoples tracing their ancestry to Polynesia, Europe, the Americas, and Asia. By the 1990s, Hawai'i had developed into a bustling multicultural and international bridge between East and West; and the capital, Honolulu, had become the eleventh largest urban center in the United States.

In 1993 a significant historical event was commemorated with a political fervor by, and with a resurgence of cultural awareness among, the Native Hawaiian population. It was the 100th anniversary of the overthrow of Queen Lili'uokalani, the last reigning sovereign of Hawai'i. Her dethronement by a contingent of planters and descendants of missionaries, assisted by the U.S. military, marked the end of the Hawaiian monarchy and continued the political transformation of the Hawaiian nation into a republic, then into a territory of the United States, and finally, in 1959, into the fiftieth state of the Union. Recently President Clinton formally apologized to the Native Hawaiian community for the role the U.S. military played in the 1893 overthrow.

In the highly charged context of this commemoration, faculty across the UHCC system considered what could be done to help Native Hawaiian students (who comprise approximately 10 percent of the student population) and others better understand the broader historical, geographical, and cultural context in which the overthrow occurred.

Hawai'i was among many Oceanic societies to be significantly impacted by Western powers and influences in the eighteenth and nineteenth centuries. What was needed was an opportunity for our students to learn first-hand the actions taken by the indigenous Polynesians in response to foreign pressures on their culture. In addition, students needed to understand the contemporary outcome of those actions. Through this learning process, the students could compare the transformations in the spiritual beliefs, values, political systems, and language among the Polynesians, as well as the historical and geographical factors influencing these changes.

After nine months of systemwide collaboration and numerous discussions with Pacific Island scholars in Samoa, Fiji, and Aotearoa, a three-credit study-abroad course entitled "Rediscovering Polynesian Connections" was created. The course was designed to provide an international experience *and* to enable Native Hawaiian students to receive instruction on indigenous history and cultural process from Samoan, Maori, and Fijian scholars.

The academic content of the course was developed in a collaborative effort involving UHCC faculty and faculty from the hosting institutions in Samoa, Aotearoa, and Fiji. Specifically, the curriculum addressed the following topics:

(1) Polynesian history and European contact, (2) contemporary political development, (3) language and cultural issues, (4) oratory and ceremony, (5) environmental issues, (6) health and healing, and (7) food preparation.

Students and faculty representing the seven diverse community colleges in the University of Hawai'i system were eligible to participate in the program. From the neighbor islands, Ilei Beniamina, a counselor at Kaua'i Community College, led a group of Native Hawaiian students from her campus. Ms. Beniamina is from the island of Ni'ihau, the only island in the archipelago in which Hawaiian is the primary language. Lui Hokoana, a counselor at Maui Community College, and Kamuela Chun, a counselor and expert in traditional and contemporary hula at Hawai'i Community College, led their respective student contingents.

On O'ahu, Kalani Meinecke, director of the Hawaiian-Pacific program at Windward Community College, and John Cole, coordinator of Kapi'olani's Asian-Pacific Emphasis program, led their respective student groups, as did Rob Edmondson, anthropology professor at Honolulu Community College, and Naomi Noelani Losch, Hawaiian language professor at Leeward Community College.

These faculty members, along with a cadre of UHCC international and intercultural colleagues, worked closely with Sharon Narimatsu, special assistant to UHCC chancellor Joyce Tsunoda, to develop the program's itinerary and specific program and course goals. The finalized itinerary is shown below.

PROGRAM ITINERARY

June 29–July 4, 1993: American Samoa
    Host Institution: American Samoa Community College
    Coordinator: Palauni Tuiasosopo, director of Samoan-Pacific Studies
    Accommodations: Fatuoaiga Catholic Center

July 4—July 13, 1993: Western Samoa
    Host Institution: National University of Samoa
    Coordinator: Dr. Aiono Faanafi le Tagaloa, director of Samoan Studies
    Accommodations: University of South Pacific, Alafua Branch Campus

July 14–July 23, 1993: Christchurch, Aotearoa
    Host Institution: Christchurch Polytechnic
    Coordinator: Matu Rangiuia, head of department, Maori Studies
    Accommodations: Rehua Marae and homestay

July 23–July 31, 1993: Suva, Fiji
    Host Institution: University of the South Pacific
    Coordinators: Asesela Ravuvu and Uentabo Neemia, Institute for Pacific Studies

Accommodations: Hotel Peninsula and homestay in Savu Village and Nadoria Village

Costs for the three-credit course included:

1.	Student registration fee	$195
2.	Airfare	$960
3.	Accommodations and ground transportation	$943
4.	Total	$2,098

Faculty did not pay the student registration fee. The Office of International Programs and Services at the University of Hawai'i provided substantial financial support to the faculty for their role in institutional development. The Kamehameha Schools and Bishop Estate provided generous financial support to the Native Hawaiian students, covering all but $500 of their overall costs. This $500 expenditure by the students was seen as evidence of student commitment to the course.

The faculty at the hosting institutions in Samoa and Aotearoa (New Zealand) were paid at the University of Hawai'i College of Continuing Education rate of $26 per hour. The faculty in Fiji were paid at the University of South Pacific rate of $37 per hour.

Specific Course Goals

The specific course that was designed to initiate the Study Abroad in the Pacific Islands Program was entitled "Rediscovering Polynesian Connections." The following course goals were included in the successful student funding proposal to the Kamehameha Schools and Bishop Estate:

1. To promote language proficiency and a cultural understanding of the Pacific Island nations and territories of Polynesia;
2. To reinforce links between Pacific Island peoples through a better understanding of their common historical ties and traditions;
3. To make more positive the interaction among Polynesian ethnic communities in our multicultural state.

The overall purpose is best captured in the course title, "Rediscovering Polynesian Connections." Our participants, Hawaiian and non-Hawaiian alike, hoped to learn more of Hawai'i's cultural heritage by visiting ancestral Polynesian societies. Hawaiians hoped to gain a greater appreciation of their own culture and identity, and to learn of other solutions to the problem of being at once modern people in a modern world and living heirs of an ancient Polynesian tradition.

Because of these course goals, as well as the prospect of visiting four different institutions in four different political entities, the development of the course became a united effort of faculty members at all seven community colleges. In addition, key administrators at the UHCC chancellor's office provided invaluable help in planning and coordinating this ambitious endeavor.

Participants were expected to compare their own understanding of Hawaiian culture with what they learned about other Polynesian societies. This process, it was felt, would not only enhance knowledge and initiate closer ties with Polynesian kin but would also restore the participants' awareness of their Hawaiian roots. On June 29, 1993, seven faculty members and thirty-three students departed from Honolulu on their voyage of rediscovery: a thirty-three day exploration of Samoa, Aotearoa, and Fiji.

Outcome

The following evaluation of the outcome of this study-abroad project is not based on quantitative analysis. Rather it is based on qualitative analysis, such as faculty reports and student journals and papers.

The responses of the participants clearly confirm that most of the course's goals were achieved. The student journals and papers and faculty essays are loaded with references to renewed cultural dedication, expanded visions of the future for themselves and all Polynesian peoples, and a feeling of "interconnectedness" with Pacific neighbors and kin.

One of the first things participants discovered was that in learning about Samoans and Maoris, they were also learning about themselves. There was a shared history. As Lui Hokoana remarked, "Not only did we learn about their culture, we gained a deeper understanding of our own culture." Naomi Noelani Losch remarked similarly, "We came away with a better understanding and appreciation not only of our hosts but of our own Hawaiian backgrounds." Losch and her students "discussed similarities and realized that there were many more similarities than differences." Ilei Beniamina felt that visiting Samoa was a "reaffirmation of mutual kinship that had parted ways during the migration of A.D. 400–600."

Students and faculty commented on language, cultural, and educational issues. Kalani Meinecke spoke of Maori language learning:

> I visited a Maori language immersion school. This was the only immersion school in Christchurch. I recall the effort of the Hawaiian people to hold fast for the sake of the language. So much like these Maori people. Their responsibility is to revive the native language of

the race. I am proud of the Maori as I am of the Hawaiians.... I'll treasure these insights always. Other insights from the ancestors. That was the greatest interest on this Study-abroad Tour, the pride in the wisdom from the ancestors perpetuated by the native peoples.

Davelyn Haunani Keohohu-Fukino, a student from Kaua'i Community College, observed and discussed different methods of educating children across cultures:

> The children are instructed verbally, with hands-on experiences—grasping the language, culture, and identity of who they are through interaction. Each aspect of learning is done by the entire family, through the extended family, and not just the parents. Children are taught at an early age their language and culture.... In Aotearoa, the children are immersed in their own language and culture. The educators here have developed a program that is culturally sensitive to their needs. The thought here is that the children, the future of the Maori, will have an identity by using language as a base.... I believe the Western model of early childhood education will be difficult to implement if it does not address the issue of culture and language—this is such an integral part of the individual. Culture and language help the individual child develop an identity and self-esteem.

Jean Kapi'olani Ka'ohelauli'i, a student at Honolulu Community College, commented on the environmental insights she gained:

> What I have learned from our cousins in Aotearoa, Samoa, and Fiji is the value of preserving our Hawaiian ancestral environment. My concern for nature inspires me to grow in my Hawaiian identity and to appreciate our culture, language, and arts. My identity revolves around the life of our islands, our local community, and our relationship to the land.

Albert Keomaka, another Honolulu Community College student, talked about the Polynesian reverence for the land:

> The respect for the land is an important aspect throughout the four Polynesian islands. The land is considered to be very religious and sacred.... The *atua,* or gods, protect everything. Tangaroa is the god of the ocean and its creatures within it. Tane is the god of the forest and

its creatures. Thus, all these gods are related to the land. And so traditionally, before one decided to take something of the land, one would need to do a *Karakia*, a prayer to pay homage to the land. . . . The land provides all sorts of food varieties, from the mountains to the sea.

Ululani C. Hamakua, a student from Windward Community College, discussed specific features of food preparation and ceremony:

> In America Samoa, I found the preparation of various foods very interesting. . . . I found preparing the pig quite different, especially because the pigs were young. . . . *Palusami* is made from young taro leaves and salted coconut cream, which is wrapped in a wild banana leaf and then a breadfruit leaf. . . . While in the ceremony, we visitors were expected to sit and behave with respect. For example, the women were expected to sit cross-legged. If our legs got tired, we could stretch them but needed something to cover them. It was a disgrace to the host to have someone's foot revealed.

Some students reported that they were thrilled to "see the similarities of our language, physical characteristics, and cultural practices" (Joseph Ah Sau, Maui Community College). Ms. Beniamina noted that her students were "stunned at the close cultural similarities," citing not just appearance, values, and language but also hand and facial gestures for the same thoughts and emotions. Malia Melemai from Maui Community College wrote, "What I learned was that we are just a minute part of Polynesia and that . . . Hawaiian values are not exclusive to Hawaiians. . . . The trip helped me to define more clearly what a Hawaiian is." Dellas H. Kaheakau from Honolulu Community College remarked, "I will never forget the carvings done by students from an elementary school in Christchurch, Aotearoa. The artworks are of Maori legends. . . . I was so attracted to it because my youngest son is part Maori and I had very little cultural knowledge of the Maoris."

Participants were impressed by the very open "cultural pride and sense of place that the Samoans have," especially since Hawaiian culture is not as naturally or openly practiced today (Losch). Throughout Polynesia there is much talk of "fa'a Samoa" (Samoan custom) and "Maoridom," and there is a very conscious policy of cultural perpetuation. Jon Insiong from Maui Community College remarked that in contrast to Samoan and Maori assertions of identity, "I need to consciously remind myself that I am a Hawaiian. . . . I need to constantly think about living my Hawaiian life-style. I thought how fortunate our cousins were to be practicing and living their culture."

In summing up their stay in American Samoa, many participants commented on the way Samoans "carry themselves" in a haughty or insolent manner. Those who mentioned it now express respect, and they realize that Samoan confidence arises from their close-knit families and legitimate cultural pride rather than individual arrogance. (Mr. Insiong has been wearing his Samoan *lavalava* to school this fall.)

The participants were particularly impressed with specific aspects of life in southern Polynesia. The strength of extended family connections, fluency in the native language, community spirit, and the importance of a shared land base were noted by many faculty and student writers. Language played into social relations. Those fluent in Hawaiian were able to follow speeches in Samoan and Maori; however, many of the non-Hawaiian participants experienced being the "other" or the "outsider" much of the time, even though they all had at least one semester of Hawaiian language.

Community spirit and a shared land base are closely integrated in Pacific villages from Samoa to Aotearoa to Fiji. In fact, land, language, family, community, and culture are inextricably linked in the South Pacific. Kaniela Ornellas, a Maui Community College student, hopes to become a county planner. He was "very interested in the way villages functioned" and "to see the Utopian philosophy in action. I can only imagine a place where there is no need for a welfare system, a place where the group is more important than the individual, a place where people believe that they are part of the environment." His journal is filled with designs of Samoan homes *(fale),* Maori homes *(where nui)*, and the village layout in Nadoria, Fiji. His optimism will likely affect his own planning processes. If so, he will be reviving Hawaiian as well as Samoan, Maori, and Fijian values. The villages always resonate with a warm friendliness and an amiable pace of life, which is lacking in American urban culture.

Even in the middle of Christchurch, a city "more English than England" (a frequently heard description by Christchurch residents), active Maori communal life flourished at two sacred ceremonial grounds (*marae*). Members looked after each other's families; practiced ancient traditions and rituals; learned dances, chants, arts, and crafts; and served as hosts for visitors away from home. The participants lived at Rehua Marae and grew very close to the many Maori who spent much of their free time with them, teaching them about Maori culture. Equivalent Hawaiian centers cannot be found on O'ahu, and it is hoped that the participants' experience will help inspire their creation.

Naomi Noelani Losch testified to the *marae*'s extraordinary capacity to make outsiders feel at home: "Our departure from Christchurch was the most difficult because it was like leaving family." At Rehua Marae, Ilei Beniamina heard a Maori chanter she had never met "recite my elder's name in the genealogy chant, and I was overcome with emotion." Strong emotional bonds developed between the UHCC students and faculty and their Maori hosts.

The participants often felt as if they had gone back in time as well as space. During a discussion one student noted that being in Samoa was like seeing Hawai'i fifty years ago. Jon Insiong was "impressed by the pureness of the people we visited," and favorably compared their (materially poorer) lives with the "violence and craziness" that plagues the United States. One nontraditional student, a grandmother, complained that contemporary Hawaiians were lackadaisical about their heritage and spoiled by Western culture. Not just traditionalists and Hawaiians but all participants were forced to reconsider the differences between their lives and the older Polynesian model. They were forced to reexamine the meaning of words like "need" and "want," and "wealth" and "contentment."

Follow-Up

Ten of the participants were tattooed in Western Samoa, and those images will not fade. But will the participants' resolve and intentions fade with time? Only six months after their return it is, of course, too early to tell. Most of the students have remained active in Hawaiian studies at their campuses. Three students have transferred to the University of Hawai'i, Manoa campus, and four to the University of Hawai'i, Hilo campus, to pursue baccalaureate studies in Hawaiian studies or related fields.

Follow-up on the programmatic front has already begun. In the Polynesian tradition of reciprocity, the UHCC hopes to host a return visit from faculty and students of the four South Pacific institutions. A systemwide course utilizing specific Hawaiian-Pacific scholarly expertise at each of the seven colleges is in the initial stages of development. This course proposal will be forwarded to coordinators at the South Pacific institutions, who can then determine the degree of student interest in the course. Funding is being actively sought to underwrite some of the travel expenses, since resources for such travel are scarce in the South Pacific. The UHCC chancellor's office will again play a central role in planning and coordination.

Discussions about a repeat study-abroad course are also in their initial stages. The new course will follow the same general format but will perhaps voyage off to Tahiti and French Polynesia or to the American-affiliated Pacific polities in Micronesia. "Rediscovering Polynesian Connections" gained wide publicity in Hawai'i, and many people have expressed a desire to participate in any new course. In addition, Kapi'olani Community College student Nikita Nu'uanu Lenchanko spoke for a majority of the participants when he said that he would be among the first to sign up for the next course.

Parallel activities will further strengthen connections to the South Pacific. In May 1993 Robert W. Franco, former coordinator of Kapi'olani's Asian-Pacific Emphasis program, was awarded a fellowship from the organization Community Colleges in International Development. As part of this fellowship Dr. Franco will be attempting to develop vocational training links between the UHCC and postsecondary institutions in Fiji, the Kingdom of Tonga, American Samoa, Western Samoa, and Aotearoa. These training links may result in various UHCC campuses hosting Polynesian students in their vocational training programs. In addition, further study-abroad opportunities for faculty and students may emerge from this project.

In October 1993 John Morton, provost at Kapi'olani Community College, and Sharon Narimatsu visited Christchurch Polytechnic and signed an agreement formally linking the two colleges under a long-term student and faculty study-abroad program.

The third course objective, "to make more positive the interaction between Polynesian ethnic communities in our multicultural state," has not yet been achieved. The participants expressed a strong interest in improving their understanding of and interaction with the Samoan community in Hawai'i. While in Samoa, the participants indicated that they had few Samoan friends and they knew little about the Samoan community in Honolulu. During the trip there appeared to be a unanimous desire to change this situation and, further, to work to reduce the current antagonisms between the Native Hawaiian and the Samoan communities in Hawai'i. One hopes that the Native Hawaiians' experience of Samoan culture in Samoa will provide a foundation for improved interethnic understanding in the future.

The Native Hawaiian participants will almost certainly be more active in their own communities. The powerful educational and emotional influence exerted on the participants by the Polynesian societies they visited will not soon dissipate. They have gained a new perspective on Hawaiian and Polynesian history, politics, culture, and language. In their academic endeavors, most of the participants continue to be energized by this new knowledge and a shared Polynesian spirit. Further, for these and all Native Hawaiian students, employment opportunities increasingly exist—in language instruction and education, environmental planning, health, housing, and government—where they can be of genuine service to their community.

CONCLUSION

Much work lies ahead in improving the interaction between Hawaiian and Samoan ethnic communities. However, for the vast majority of participating students and faculty, the "Rediscovering Polynesian Connections" course clearly promoted language proficiency and cultural understanding and reinforced links among Pacific Island peoples through a better understanding of the common historical ties and traditions.

Many also learned that in the South Pacific today, Polynesian orators speak with grace and wisdom, and it thus is appropriate to conclude with the words of a contemporary Hawaiian scholar, Kamuela Chun. After meeting with eighteen course participants at a recent leadership conference in Hilo, Hawaii, he remarked that he "sensed an affirmation, appreciation, and cultural pride not just in being Hawaiian but in being Polynesian. . . . The course helped to nurture both self-esteem and group esteem. . . . It renewed a sense of pride and place for those of Hawaiian ancestry."

ACKNOWLEDGMENT

The authors wish to acknowledge the contributions made by the following faculty members: Ilei Beniamina, Kamuela Chun, John Cole, Rob Edmondson, Lui Hokoana, Naomi Noelani Losch, and Kalani Meinecke.

REFERENCES

Clark, B.R., and G. Neave. *The Encyclopedia of Higher Education*. Oxford: Pergamon Press, 1992.

Franco, R. *Samoans in Hawai'i: A Demographic Profile*. Honolulu: East-West Center, 1987.

Goodwin, C.D., and M. Nacht. *Abroad and Beyond: Patterns in American Overseas Education*. Cambridge: Cambridge University Press, 1988.

7 Reform and Quality Assurance in British and American Higher Education

Ruth Burgos-Sasscer and David Collins

Colleges and universities around the world are being transformed as never before. Ready or not, like it or not, and everywhere in the industrialized world, the academy is being reshaped by forces external to it: a global economy, shifting demographics, a revolution in terms of quality and changing technologies. Even such classic institutions as historic universities in Britain and liberal arts colleges in the United States are responding in one way or another to national imperatives to produce workers and leaders who have the knowledge and skills to perform successfully in a continuously changing, competitive, and interconnected world (Newman 1985; Ball 1991; "Transatlantic Dialogue" 1993; "Dance with Change" 1994). Some faculty and administrators resent having to adjust to this new relationship between the academy and society. Nevertheless, as terms like *access, productivity, globalization,* and *accountability* are applied to the academic work setting, increasingly and universally they are beginning to understand that failure to respond appropriately puts their institutions at risk ("Transatlantic Dialogue" 1993; Scott 1993).

Furthermore, as faculty and administrators struggle with the new demands placed on them, they are discovering that traditional organizational structures and time-honored attitudes and practices are not adequate to the task. They are finding that successful responses depend on adopting broader and more flexible approaches to the educational process (Ball 1991; "Dance with Change" 1994). Not surprisingly, as they seek to make needed reforms, an increasing number of educators around the world are reaching out to each other through international conferences, exchanges, and networks ("Third Conference" 1985; Robinson 1990; Jaschik 1990; Watkins 1993).

This chapter will provide a brief description of the calls for reform in higher education in the United States and Great Britain and how each country has responded. It will then focus on the experience and results of an exchange between administrators from a U.S. community college and those from a British college of further and higher learning.

Calls for Reform in the United States

The call for educational reform was sounded loud and clear in 1983, when the National Commission on Excellence in Education, in a landmark report titled *A Nation at Risk*, warned that this nation was losing its preeminence in commerce, industry, science, and technology to competitors throughout the world and that the primary reason for this was a mediocre educational system. The commission called for greater educational rigor and a stronger international dimension in all levels of education (National Commission 1983). *A Nation at Risk* inspired a plethora of reports from other national organizations, each of which recommended greater accountability in higher education. The new reports cited the inadequate communication and critical thinking skills of college graduates as examples of the poor quality of American higher education. The authors recommended that college and university educators define the "outcomes," in terms of student performance, that they expect as a result of the courses and programs their institutions offer (National Institute 1984; Newman 1985). The most recent reports clearly call for educational outcomes that include indicators of work-force skills (U.S. Department of Labor 1991; Peterson 1993).

The idea that higher education should respond to societal needs has led to the establishment of new standards for judging the adequacy of the educational process. Accrediting and state agencies, for example, are no longer viewing faculty credentials and library resources as exclusive measures of academic excellence; their focus has shifted to student learning. In the United States, student success is now considered the most important indicator of overall institutional effectiveness (Ewell and Lisensky 1988; "Statement on Assessment" 1991; Southern Association 1992).

Calls for Reform in Great Britain

The impetus for modern reforms in British education was provided by Prime Minister Margaret Thatcher during the 1980s. Since Britain was now a member of the Common Market and she was concerned about Europe's role in the world economy, Mrs. Thatcher believed that Europe could compete successfully only if all the countries adopted uniform methods of quality control and adhered to common minimum standards of product quality. It was important, she felt, that customers receive assurance that in the new world market they could count on products that were uniform and predictable. She thus encouraged the adoption of the British industrial standards of quality (BS

5750) by all Common Market members. This initiative eventually led to the establishment of international quality standards (known as ISO 9000) for all countries. Since 1990, corporations anywhere in the world that adhere to ISO 9000 quality standards are registered by the International Organization of Standards, located in Geneva, Switzerland (Lewis and Smith 1994).

Mrs. Thatcher and other British leaders realized that if their own country was to provide high-quality products, it had to have a high-quality work force. Britain's faltering industrial and economic performance in the post–World War II period indicated that the quality of the British work force left much to be desired. They took a hard look at their educational systems and confirmed that existing vocational training programs were not providing students with the knowledge and skills required for them to compete successfully in the modern market. Furthermore, they found that not enough young people were staying in school past age 16 (when education is no longer compulsory) to receive the training and education needed to maintain a high-quality work force (Ball 1991; Lavercombe 1994).

As a result, a series of reforms were set in motion, some of which are still evolving. One of the most significant has been the integration and coordination of educational and vocational training systems, which includes the "vocationalizing" of courses at the universities and polytechnics. Traditionally in Britain, employers and a select group of educators and trainers have been responsible for the preparation of the work force. Now reformers are saying that preparing a high-quality work force is everybody's business—including the universities' (Ball 1991; Lavercombe 1994).

Another related reform is increasing the access to higher education. Unlike the United States, where approximately 42 percent of young people between the ages of 18 and 24 are in college, only 15 percent of British young people beyond age 16 continue to receive any training or education. In an effort to increase the number of students in postcompulsory education and training, the British government expanded the colleges of further and higher learning, the institutions that most closely resemble U.S. community colleges.

A recent development has been the implementation of a new series of national examinations, called General National Vocational Qualifications (GNVQs), to assess students' ability to enter the work force or to continue in higher education. In the past, students who prepared for employment and those who aspired to enter the university were tracked into separate programs and took entirely different examinations. Now the focus is on the greater integration of education and training and a more comprehensive approach to the assessment of students' knowledge and skills (Lavercombe 1994). As a result of these initiatives, enrollment in higher education doubled between 1988 and 1993. In January 1994 Britain's minister of education, John Patten, announced that for the first time in the nation's history, Britain had enrolled 1 million students in university-level programs (Walker 1994). The "massification" of education has not only increased the demand for higher education and swelled enrollments but has also irrevocably transformed the characteristics of university students in the United Kingdom (Lavercombe 1994).

Faculty and Administrative International Exchanges

Recognizing that many of the challenges they are facing are similar to those encountered by educators in other countries, college and university faculty and administrators are increasingly participating in international exchanges (Murphy 1985; Briscoe 1991; Karelis 1991). The literature suggests, however, that most of these exchanges are among faculty rather than administrators, a fact that disturbs some educational leaders. It is particularly disturbing to educators in developing countries, where administrators have minimum opportunities for professional development. At a recent meeting of the European Association for International Education, Colin N. Power, assistant director-general for education of the United Nations Educational Scientific and Cultural Organization, underscored this concern when he stated: "While higher education is in crisis throughout the world, this crisis affects institutions in the developing countries in a way that calls into question their very existence" (Desruisseaux 1994).

Follow-up studies conducted by international organizations such as the Liaison Group for International Educational Exchange indicate that faculty, student, and administrative exchanges do indeed enhance the knowledge, skills, and global perspective essential for effective leadership in the twenty-first century (Murphy 1985; Jaschik 1990; Monaghan 1993). Murphy (1984) stresses that international exchanges are particularly beneficial for administrators because administrators are the decision makers and agents of change at their institutions.

A Case Study of an American Administrative Exchange

In 1990 the Illinois Community College Presidents' Council initiated a program of exchange visits between presidents of Illinois community colleges and principals of colleges of further and higher education in Great Britain. The purpose of the program was to provide the opportunity for these CEOs to get to know each other and share their approaches to the internal and external challenges each was facing.

Among the first CEOs to participate in this exchange program were

Wallace B. Appelson, president of Harry S. Truman College (one of the City Colleges of Chicago), and Douglas Keith, principal of Sandwell College of Further and Higher Learning, West Midlands. After visiting each other's institutions, they discovered that each was finding solutions to problems with which the other was still struggling. They agreed that it would be mutually beneficial if key administrators from their respective colleges could also get together to discuss and share how each college is addressing common challenges. Thus began an exciting, enlightening, and productive relationship between two outstanding institutions.

Similar Challenges but Different Responses

Truman College and Sandwell College are similar in many important respects. They offer approximately the same levels and array of academic and occupational programs. They both serve an increasingly racially and ethnically diverse student population, many of whom are immigrants. Their faculty and staff are unionized. They are located in urban communities where economic cycles have an immediate impact on the welfare of the community. Both institutions are under pressure from the business, political, and public sectors to produce world-class workers. Finally, they are expected to use their limited resources more efficiently than they have in the past, which means that they are expected to do more with less. For example, at the time of Dr. Appelson's and Mr. Keith's visits, Truman and Sandwell Colleges were facing significant budget cuts, and their approaches to this problem were remarkably the same.

However, the CEOs identified at least three other challenges that their institutions were currently facing but meeting with different degrees of success. Mr. Keith observed that Truman was finding solutions to a problem with which Sandwell was clearly struggling (i.e., how to meet the diverse needs of students), and Dr. Appelson observed that Sandwell had found a satisfactory solution to at least two problems that Truman had not yet solved (i.e., how to provide high-quality vocational preparation and how to respond to demands for accountability). It was clear to both executives that the proposed exchanges would enable their administrators to gain new insights and perspectives that would aid them in their search for solutions to these problems.

Harry S. Truman College

In order for the reader to understand the overall nature of Harry S. Truman College, the following characteristics are defined: (a) demographics, (b) student suppport services, (c) instructional programs, (d) accountability, (e) governance and finance, and (f) quality assurance.

Demographics

With an enrollment of approximately 6,000 credit and 10,000 noncredit students, Harry S. Truman College is the largest community college in Chicago. Located in Uptown, a neighborhood that has traditionally been a place of entry for many immigrants, Truman has gradually become the most culturally and racially diverse community college in the state of Illinois. The average age of its students is 29, and over one-half are foreign-born. They come from 110 different countries and speak at least 70 different languages.

Visitors and students who enter the college through the main lobby will see a colorful display of flags from thirty different countries. Those who enter from the parking lot through a side door are greeted with a sign that says "Welcome" in fifteen languages. Throughout the building there are objects of art and posters that bear witness to a multicultural environment.

Student Support Services

One of Truman's strengths is the excellent support services it is able to provide for its multicultural students. When new groups arrive at Truman (such as 1,000 Vietnamese in 1980 and 1,200 Soviet Jews in 1990), faculty and staff immediately join ranks to respond to their special needs. For example, all new students are assessed by counselors and faculty so that they may be placed in courses at their appropriate level, and non-native speakers of English are given tests that the English as a Second Language faculty have specially designed for that population.

By drawing on resources from the community and the college itself, Truman used volunteers, personnel borrowed from local agencies, work-study students, and paid staff members to provide customized support services. Speakers of languages spoken by the largest groups of immigrant and international students are available in key service areas, such as the financial aid, testing, and registrar's offices. There are counseling centers designated for special populations, such as the handicapped, veterans, single parents, Hispanic students with limited English proficiency, African Americans, Native Americans, and recently arrived refugees. The college also provides tutors who are bilingual in various languages.

Instructional Programs

As a comprehensive community college, Truman offers a large selection of noncredit and credit courses and programs. The noncredit programs include English as a Second Language, Adult Basic Skills, and preparation for the GED. Credit transfer programs prepare students to go on to senior institutions and earn baccalaureate degrees in numerous disciplines. Occupational/technical programs lead to certificates or associate's degrees and prepare students for direct entry into the workplace. Some occupational programs are clock-hour (such as automobile repair and cosmetology) rather than credit-based and are offered through the Truman College Technical Center.

Accountability

In keeping with the academic tradition of American higher education, Truman's faculty determine the objectives and content of all courses and programs. Recent national and state mandates to provide a world-class work force have led to an increased collaboration between educators and business and industry representatives to develop vocational program curricula. However, the assessment of student academic achievement still remains the exclusive domain of faculty.

Governance and Finance

Truman College and the other six institutions that comprise the City Colleges of Chicago are governed by a board of trustees, whose members are appointed by the Mayor of Chicago. The colleges are financed by appropriations from the state, city taxes, and student tuitions and fees. Because of reduced state funding, a deficit, and increased costs, the board recently capped enrollments and raised the tuition and fees. To sustain the quantity and quality of its student services, however, Truman College has diligently sought and received additional funding from external sources.

Quality Assurance

Like most American colleges and universities, Truman College relies on inspection to determine if it is doing a good job. The college is evaluated and accredited by the North Central Association of Colleges and Schools, which traditionally has focused its inspection on the inputs of the institution, such as faculty degrees, facilities, and number of library holdings. Since 1990, however, the association is requiring institutions to produce evidence of outcomes measures, especially as they relate to student academic achievement and institutional effectiveness ("Statement on Assessment" 1991).

Sandwell College

In order for the reader to understand the overall nature of Sandwell College, the following characteristics are defined: (a) demographics, (b) instructional programs, (c) accountability, (d) governance and finance, and (e) quality assurance.

Demographics

One of the largest of Britain's 436 Colleges of Further and Higher Education, Sandwell comprises six campuses located throughout West Midlands, a heavily industrialized community near the city of Birmingham. Unlike students at Truman, who tend to be older, Sandwell's 25,000 students are primarily between 16 and 19 years of age. Like Truman, however, Sandwell's student population is culturally and racially diverse; increasingly they are immigrants from Africa, India, Pakistan, and the Caribbean.

There are signs around the six campuses that say "Sandwell College Welcomes You" in various languages. A brief statement that summarizes the college's mission, "Sandwell College is in the business of human improvement," is prominently displayed in every office and classroom.

Instructional Programs

Sandwell College offers a wide variety of academic and vocational programs in areas ranging from literacy and vocational training to university preparatory courses. Many of Sandwell's students are preparing for entrance into universities, but the majority are enrolled in programs that prepare them for immediate entry into the workplace.

Accountability

Because the responsibility for preparing the work force in Britain has traditionally rested with employers rather than with faculty, as in the United States, the objectives and content of the curricula for Sandwell's vocational programs are determined by representatives of the business sector rather than by the trainers. Before students receive credit for a particular course, they must pass National Vocational Qualifications (NVQs), which assess how well they meet the standards established by the hiring industry.

The NVQs test five different levels of competencies, with the highest (level 5) measuring management skills and techniques. Thus, students may be deemed to be competent for performing at certain levels within an industry but not at others. Those who complete the full program of instruction must pass all five levels of the NVQs before they receive full credit for their training. Students who do not pass the NVQs are expected to continue attending classes until they master the desired level of competencies. Worthy of note is the fact that passing appropriate NVQs is required for more than 80 percent of the jobs in the United Kingdom.

Students who wish to enter a university must pass A-level examinations in various academic disciplines (such as calculus, chemistry, and history). Similarly to the NVQs, these examinations are prepared by groups external to the college. In this case, however, they are prepared by educators, i.e., representatives of universities the students are likely to attend.

Because the NVQs assess workplace competencies and the A-level examinations focus on academic disciplines, there exists a dichotomy between training for the professions and training for skilled employment. To bridge the gap between professional and skilled employment preparation, British educators introduced a new series of examinations, the General National Vocational Qualifications (GNVQs), in 1992. The GNVQs are designed for those students who do not yet know whether they want to prepare for immediate employment (and the NVQs) or for the university (and the A-level examinations) and who therefore enroll in programs that train them for both. The GNVQs cover vocational as well as academic competencies and are prepared by representatives from the business and academic sectors.

Governance and Finance

British financing of public education is highly centralized. Thus, as do all Colleges of Further and Higher Education, Sandwell College receives 80 percent of its revenues from the Further Education Funding and Standards Council, a national agency. The colleges are expected to make up the 20 percent difference by competing for grants and contracts. In spite of a centralized funding source, however, the governance of the colleges and approval regarding expenditures of funds rest with locally elected boards.

Quality Assurance

A unique achievement of Sandwell College has been its implementation of a quality-assurance system encompassing the entire institution and qualifying the college to be registered as a BS 5750 firm.

In 1989, in response to criticisms that higher education was not adequately addressing business and industrial training needs, Sandwell College put into motion a plan that would assure the quality of all its programs. College leaders took International Standard of Quality Assurance ISO 9002 and part II of British Standard BS 5750, which had previously only applied to the business sector, and adapted them for higher education.

Translating industrial terms into educational jargon was not easy. Some philosophical issues had to be resolved. Everyone agreed that "customers" meant students and their future employers. However, there was a great deal of discussion regarding whether the "product" was the educational program in which a student was enrolled or the value added to the student who underwent the process of education or training. After some debate, it was decided that the "product" was in fact the value added to or the enhancement of the student in terms of skills the student developed, knowledge he or she acquired, expertise he or she gained, as well as increased self-confidence and personal development. The "process" was the delivery of the curriculum.

Everyone also agreed that in a large and diverse college such as Sandwell, it was essential that any system of quality management had to have all faculty and support staff operate as a team. To that end, the newly created Quality Assurance Unit carried out an extensive training program with small groups across the college. During May and June 1990, for example, a major staff-development exercise focused on discussions with individual academic program teams. At this stage each team was presented with a draft model procedures manual and was invited to adapt it to meet the requirements of the students and the curricula of their specific programs. The college was working towards a single system of quality assurance in which there was the possibility of considerable diversity in terms of the actual procedures used to meet the system's requirements. For example, program teams were required to obtain feedback from their students on all the courses, but could choose how they did so.

In December 1990 and again in March 1991, the quality system developing within Sandwell College was reviewed by a team of internal auditors, who represented all sectors of the college. They not only helped to prepare the institution for its external audit but also contributed to the dissemination of good practices across the college.

The result: in April 1991 the college was externally audited by three assessors from the British Standards Institution. The audit involved a rigorous inspection of the quality system and looked at procedures followed by the program teams on all six campuses. On May 1, 1991, Sandwell College became a BS 5750 registered firm, the first institution of higher education to achieve this distinction. This gives it the right to affirm that all of the education and training carried out at Sandwell College meets exacting standards of quality.

The benefits of this extraordinary achievement are too numerous to mention. At least three, however, are worthy of note. The first is that a quality-assurance ethos has been generated in which all of the issues that affect the quality of service the college provides are constantly on the college agenda. Furthermore, enrollment has increased, as have customized training contracts and, therefore, additional revenues. The Sandwell team that visited Truman financed the cost of the trip with funds generated from additional contracts.

Finally, there has also been considerable interest in the project nationally, so that well over 100 colleges in Britain are now working towards obtaining registration under the British Standards Institution. Since the standard is an international one, other countries are also beginning to express interest in the example set by Sandwell College.

Sandwell Administrators Visit Truman

In October 1991 four managers from Sandwell College traveled to Chicago. The group included co-author David Collins, who was then vice principal of Sandwell. They stayed in the homes of Truman College administrators and spent ten days interacting with staff and faculty at Truman and visiting other colleges in the Chicago area.

Prior to their arrival, the Sandwell team received and reviewed literature about Truman College and about American community colleges. Although they were interested in many aspects of American college operations, they paid special attention to student support services, since they perceived this to be Sandwell's weakest area. British educators traditionally view student support services to be a means of coddling students and, therefore, unnecessary. Needless to say, this attitude is changing in light of the changing demographics of college and university students as a result of the recent national thrust toward the massification of education.

The members of the Sandwell visiting team were anxious to see for themselves the many ways in which Truman College provides support services for its thousands of diverse students. When they left Chicago, the team had compiled a list of 100 innovative ideas, primarily in the area of student services, they were eager to share with their colleagues back home.

Truman Administrator Visits Sandwell

One year later, Truman's vice president, co-author Ruth Burgos-Sasscer, traveled to Great Britain. She too stayed in an administrator's home and interacted with managers and faculty at Sandwell College. She also met with leaders from the community and other colleges. After reviewing publications about Sandwell College and British higher education in general and picking up additional information from conversations with many individuals, the author focused on learning about the linkages between business and industry and the occupational training programs offered at Sandwell. She also wanted to learn more about how Sandwell College had responded to the challenge of accountability by incorporating industrial standards of quality assurance into all aspects of its operations, including the instructional and curricular arenas.

Interest in these areas stemmed from a growing pressure on American educators to establish closer ties between occupational programs and industry and to establish greater accountability. Colleges in Illinois now have to provide evidence of productivity (outcomes) and quality as measured by the number of students who enroll in, persist in and graduate from occupational programs and have the knowledge and skills needed for a first-class work force. Clearly, having in place a system of quality assurance similar to the one at Sandwell College would facilitate the organization, accuracy, and timeliness of responses to that state mandate.

Burgos-Sasscer knew, however, that convincing her colleagues of this would not be an easy task. Although principles of total quality management are evident in many American colleges, the idea is resisted by those who are still not convinced that business standards can or should be applied to education (Peterson 1993). Nevertheless, impressed by what she witnessed at Sandwell, the author returned to Chicago with her own list of innovative ideas and was determined to discuss the information she had learned with her colleagues at Truman College.

Results of the Exchange

Ignoring those who would accuse them of coddling students, the Sandwell College team were determined to improve the support services for students and, thus, to increase their chances for success. The team quickly developed and submitted plans for converting their library into a resource learning center, which would include computers and audiovisual materials, and when Dr. Burgos-Sasscer arrived a year later, the resource learning center was a reality. Also in place was a shop where students could buy school supplies and snacks and where the college's first student handbook was about to be published.

By 1993 Sandwell College had developed a process to assess the basic skills of new students, and they were using the results to place students in appropriate courses. The program will be fully implemented in the fall of 1994, and every new student will be required to go through this process. Because no additional resources were allocated to provide for this assessment of students, the administration decided to pay for it from savings obtained by cutting back on the hours of instruction from twenty-two to twenty hours a week.

The impact of the exchange visits was not as obvious at Truman as it was at Sandwell, but nevertheless it was notable. The presence of the Sandwell College team on the Truman campus for ten days spurred an unprecedented interest in British higher education and especially in the Colleges of Further and Higher Education. The genuine interest that the Sandwell team showed in student services was much appreciated by Truman's student service staff, a group that does not usually get attention from visitors.

Knowledge about Sandwell College's achievement as a BS 5750 registered firm strengthened a growing awareness among Truman College faculty and staff that educational institutions in other parts of the world are taking the demand for quality—as defined by the corporate world—seriously and responding accordingly. This was particularly true of faculty in the occupational and technical fields who, as a result of the Carl Perkins project and other federally funded projects, are being required to collaborate with their students' future employers. Thus, business and industry representatives not only serve on advisory committees, but also assist in assessing entry-level skills and in determining exit-level course competencies.

As expected, the resistance to considering students or employers as "customers" or to considering acquired knowledge and skills as the "product" still prevails among many faculty, especially those in the liberal arts. Many perceive a quality assurance program to be a threat to individualism and academic freedom—cherished American values. Nevertheless, there are signs that Truman's interaction with Sandwell College made a difference in attitudes and behavior. There is less resistance to listing expected competencies in course syllabi and to assessing outcomes to determine student achievement. There is now a willingness to speak about the need for team building and for continuous improvement based on assessment results. These are clearly steps in the right direction.

Probably the most important result of this exchange was that it gave the administrators of both colleges an opportunity to view each other's responses to common challenges and to view their own through the eyes of another. To the extent that they recognized that time-honored ways of doing things may no longer be appropriate or desirable, the exchange was enlightening. To the extent that they were able to influence significant changes in their institutions, the exchange was empowering.

EPILOGUE

David Collins and Ruth Burgos-Sasscer have maintained the spirit of these exchanges alive by keeping in contact via mail and telephone. They have shared their experiences with colleagues through formal presentations at various national conferences in the United States and plan to do so in Great Britain in the near future.

Coincidentally, both administrators have recently made career moves. Dr. Collins is now principal of Cheshire College of Further and Higher Education, which is smaller than but similar to Sandwell College in terms of student demographics and the type of academic programs offered. He continues to provide leadership to other British institutions (including Cheshire College) that are seeking to become BS 5750 registered firms. He also serves as a quality-management consultant to institutions in Australia, New Zealand, and Singapore.

Dr. Burgos-Sasscer is now president of San Antonio College, the largest single-campus community college in Texas. She is once again spurring a great college to heed the calls for reform so that it can better prepare its students to live and work in a changing, competitive, and interconnected world.

REFERENCES

Ball, C. *Learning Pays*. London: Royal Society for Encouragement of Arts (RSA), 1991.

Ball, R., and M. Kinnick. "Quality in Higher Education: A Cross-National Comparison between the United States and the United Kingdom." Paper presented at the 28th Annual Forum of the Association for Institutional Research, Phoenix, Ariz., May 1988.

Briscoe, K. "Broadening Horizons: Institutionalizing an International Perspective." *Educational Record* (Fall 1991): 62–64.

"Dance with Change." *Policy Perspectives: The Pew Higher Education Roundtable.* 5(3) (April 1994): 1a–12a.

Desruisseaux, P. "Looking to the Third World." *The Chronicle of Higher Education* (January 5, 1994): A49.

Ewell, P., and R. Lisensky. *Assessing Institutional Effectiveness: Redirecting the Self-Study Process*. Washington, D.C.: Consortium for the Advancement of Private Higher Education, 1988.

Jaschik, S. "Coalition Calls for Increases in Support for International-Exchange Programs." *The Chronicle of Higher Education* (April 25, 1990): A23.

Karelis, C. "Student and Faculty Exchange." *Change* (January/February, 1991): 52–53.

Lavercombe, B. "Recent Developments in Training for Work in the United Kingdom." Paper delivered at the International Seminar on Human Resources Development, Mexico City, Mexico, January 1994.

Lewis, R.G., and D.H. Smith. *Total Quality in Higher Education*. Delray Beach, Fla.: St. Lucie Press, 1994.

Murphy, P.J. "The Canadian Connection: A Co-Operative Approach to Management Development." *International Review of Education* 30, no. 2 (1984): 198–202.

———. "Preparing Education Executives for the Future: An International Undertaking." *Contemporary Education* 56, no. 2 (Winter 1985): 85–89.

Newman, F. *Higher Education and the American Resurgence*. Princeton, N.J.: The Carnegie Foundation for the Advancement of Teaching, 1985.

Monaghan, P. "North American Academic Cooperation Becomes a Higher Education Goal." *The Chronicle of Higher Education* (September 22, 1993): A39.

National Commission on Excellence in Education. *A Nation at Risk: The Imperative for Educational Reform*. Washington, D.C.: U.S. Government Printing Office, 1983.

National Institute of Education. *Involvement in Learning: Realizing the Potential of Higher Education*. Washington, D.C.: U.S. Government Printing Office, 1984.

Peterson, C.S. *Continuous Quality Assurance: Adapting TQM For Community Colleges*. Washington, D.C.: American Association of Community Colleges, 1993.

Robinson, B.S. "Facilitating Faculty Exchange." In *New Directions for Community Colleges* No. 70. San Francisco: Jossey-Bass, 1990.

Scott, P. "Reflections on the Transatlantic Dialogue." *Policy Perspectives: The Pew Higher Education Roundtable Program* 5, no. 1 (June 1993): 1B–5B.

Southern Association of Colleges and Schools. *Criteria for Accreditation*. Decatur, Ga.: Southern Association of Colleges and Schools, 1992.

"Statement on Assessment and Student Academic Achievement." *NCA Quarterly* 66, no. 2 (Fall 1991): 21–38.

"Third Conference on European Academic Mobility." *Higher Education in Europe* 10, no. 1 (January–March 1995): 131–32.

"Transatlantic Dialogue." *Policy Perspectives: The Pew Higher Education Roundtable Program* 5, no. 1 (June 1993): 1A–11A.

U.S. Department of Education. *America 2000: An Education Strategy*. Washington, D.C.: U.S. Department of Education, 1991.

U.S. Department of Labor. *What Work Requires of Schools: A SCANS Report for America 2000*. Washington, D.C.: U.S. Department of Labor, 1991.

Walker, D. "International Notes." *The Chronicle of Higher Education* (January 5, 1994): A52.

Watkins, B.T. "Push for Global Competence." *The Chronicle of Higher Education* (November 17, 1993): A48.

Wingspread Group on Higher Education. *An American Imperative*. Washington, D.C.: The Johnson Foundation, 1993.

8 Building Consensus for International and Multicultural Programs
The Role of Presidential Leadership
Evan S. Dobelle and James H. Mullen

Before beginning any discussion of consensus and international/multicultural education, it is important to understand a number of qualifications of the term *consensus*.

Consensus is always a tricky notion, particularly in academia where debate and a certain healthy intellectual contentiousness is the rule rather than the exception. Consensus in the academic world is hard-earned, often fleeting, and most often tightly circumscribed. Nowhere is this more true than in the realm of international education.

Beyond the campus as well, securing a consensus around international programs is often a delicate task. In an era of limited trust in public institutions, declining budgets, increasing tuition, and lingering suspicions that international programs draw resources away from "the three R's," an external consensus behind aggressive international efforts is far from given.

Even with such internal and external constraints, however, this chapter holds to two fundamental premises. First, international and multicultural education are essential parts of the community college mission. The demographic reality of our communities is rapidly and inexorably changing, and the world is an ever smaller and more complex place. Our students deserve a sensitive and informed voice in shaping that world to productive and peaceful ends.

Second, we believe that consensus can be developed and maintained around international education programs. This consensus must come to each college in its own time and as the result of much internal and external soul-searching.

What follows, then, are simply our reflections on lessons we have learned in attempting to build international programs at community colleges. Our primary case for illustration is Middlesex Community College, Massachusetts, where between 1988 and the present, a nationally recognized international studies program has grown from almost ground zero. Other examples are drawn from City College of San Francisco, California.

This chapter essentially focuses on practical aspects related to internal and external consensus building. While hardly intended as a "how to" primer, it seeks to bridge theory and practice while it offers one frame of reference that might assist those who face similar challenges.

Internal Consensus: Setting the Foundation

Leadership in the development of international programs at community colleges requires the ability to define and articulate why a comprehensive worldview is both inextricably linked to one's quality of life on this small and complex planet and fundamental to the long-term economic vitality of our nation.

Such leadership becomes more challenging during difficult fiscal periods, such as those that many community colleges have faced since the late 1980s. In such times, there is an inevitable push to fund only the basics and to draw back from new, less traditional programs.

It becomes particularly important in times such as these for community college faculty and staff to understand their role in the post–cold war period. As the simple dichotomies of a bipolar world fall away, nationalism and new international competition based on economic forces increasingly hold sway. Moreover, as Hispanic and Asian immigrants enter the country in larger numbers, America's demographic mix has moved inexorably away from its traditional European base. Each of these factors profoundly shapes the nature of "community" in the United States, as well as the tenor of the American workplace. Therefore, internationalization on community college campuses—those institutions by definition most closely linked to the local community and to the education of the American economy's human infrastructure—assumes particular importance.

Like any other program, international studies requires both seed capital and a steady commitment of resources. The debate around internationalization often becomes heated when those in more traditional academic programs perceive a threat to their resource base. Given the historical perception that community colleges have a career and transfer focus, this debate can be particularly contentious.

If internationalization is to succeed during such difficult times, it is essential that it be integrated into the college's existing identity and mission. Five basic conditions should exist in order for such integration to be achieved: (1) The president must be able to lead on the issue, both rhetorically and through the allocation of resources; (2) the board of trustees must understand the college's commitment to internationalization and be willing to endorse it; (3) the college's faculty and staff must accept internationalization as part of the college's mission; (4) program initiatives, particularly as they relate to curriculum, should emanate from the faculty, and wherever possible, the management of these initiatives should rest with those faculty members responsible for them; and (5) wherever possible, college initiatives related to internationalization should entail professional development for faculty and staff as well as opportunities for student enrichment. Figure 4 depicts a model for internal consensus.

FIGURE 4. Internal Consensus

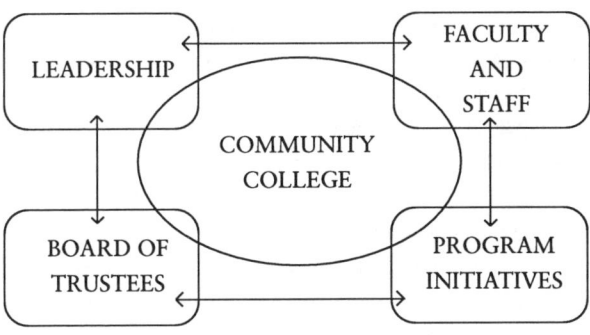

The role of the president is fundamental. Although international programs must grow strong roots throughout the college, it is the president who is uniquely positioned to plant the seeds for consensus. First, the president must play the role of both advocate and arbiter. As chief executive, he or she must clearly enunciate a vision for internationalization that extends beyond diplomatic receptions in faraway places. At the same time, he or she must encourage open debate among faculty as to the specific form that internationalization will assume on campus. This precarious balance between advocacy and dialogue requires exceptional skill and patience and is vital to sustainable long-term consensus on campus.

Second, the president must back rhetoric with resources. Starting and maintaining a successful, academically meaningful international program requires investment and necessitates faculty and staff time. In the dedication of these resources, presidents invite sure controversy.

Internally, the president must be prepared for questions from two sources. The first is the institution's governing board. Each local board is different in personality, power, and mode of appointment. Thus, each president must judge individually how to engage a local board on the issue in question.

One fallacy concerning board involvement in internationalization is the notion that trustees must travel to foreign capitals in order for programs to succeed. Those who hold to this view believe that such travel helps to earn trustee support and helps to demonstrate to foreign officials that the community college is sincere in its pursuit of such collaborative arrangements as exchanges or contract training.

Our experience has been that money spent on trustee travel is better left for investment in faculty activities. At Middlesex Community College, significant contract-training and exchange relationships have been negotiated with senior academic and government officials in Russia and the People's Republic of China without one overseas trip by a trustee. Often, the best role for a member of the governing board is to remain at home and work to build support among local business and government officials for the college's international programs. As James Henderson, chair of the Middlesex board, stated in a recent speech to the Association of Community College Trustees:

> The [Middlesex] Board has played a significant policy role in articulating the college's mission statement concerning international programs and in supporting program development. What it has not done is set individual priorities for international programming or travelled to faraway places at college expense. I am proud to say that the many successful initiatives at Middlesex have been negotiated by faculty and staff. It is, I submit, a myth that board members must travel around the globe in order for a program to succeed. In perpetuating this myth, I believe that a Board member can invite unwanted and unnecessary criticism of international programming. (Henderson 1993)

Faculty remain the key internal constituency concerning international programs. It remains an unfortunate fact that too many presidents or chancellors still believe that potentially controversial programming is best either not tried at all or accomplished in spite of, rather than in partnership with, faculty. Although no initiative can ever achieve complete consensus on campus, it remains equally true that no program can long survive without substantial and broad-based faculty support.

David M. Kalivas, associate professor of history and a leader in the development of international programs at Middlesex Community College, summarizes the need for faculty to fully support and lead the development of international programs:

Faculty need to identify global and multicultural education as a priority on their campuses. Once identified as an educational priority, an appropriate framework for professional and social development around international issues must be formed by including faculty and staff at every step of the way. Building a grass roots process is essential for the effective development of new courses, modules and programs in the areas of global and multicultural issues; otherwise this process will be diminished by concerns over territoriality. (Kalivas 1993, 1)

Faculty debate concerning international programs can take many forms. Most fundamentally, the faculty in program areas considered traditional at community colleges may question the importance of internationalization at a time when many colleges are facing severe budgetary constraints.

International-Multicultural Debates

Furthermore, campus debate over internationalization can become heated concerning the issue of "international" versus "multicultural" education. International education entails the creation of staff-development opportunities overseas, the internationalization of the curriculum, the recruitment of foreign students, and the development of international study opportunities for students. Multicultural education, on the other hand, involves understanding, recognizing, and promoting the ethnic diversity of the college population.

International education and multicultural education are not interchangeable terms. We believe, however, that it is equally true that campuses cannot easily engage one without engaging the other. The manner in which an individual college approaches internationalization and multiculturalism depends largely on the institution's identity.

For example, Middlesex Community College initially approached internationalization and multiculturalism as distinct entities. Separate committees focused on internationalization and multiculturalism, and there was only intermittent communication between the two. After several months of intensive dialogue and introspection, however, the two committees agreed to merge, believing that internationalization and multiculturalism at Middlesex could best be attained by pursuing a holistic approach. The college's success in developing international and multicultural programs emanates, at least in part, from this approach.

At City College of San Francisco, a larger and more diverse institution than Middlesex, international education and multicultural education continue to develop along separate paths. On the international front, the college has utilized funding from a federal Title VIA grant to develop and expand programs focused on the Pacific Rim, on providing international and domestic students opportunities to share their experiences on campus, and on the dissemination to all students of information concerning international events and issues.

In terms of multicultural programs, the City College board, faculty, administrators, and students have approved both a strong affirmative action plan and the development of several ethnic studies departments. For example, the college has developed strong programs in Gay and Lesbian Studies, Filipino Studies, Latin Studies, and African-American Studies.

One of the most impressive and thoughtful plans for internationalization and multiculturalization was prepared by Santa Rosa Community College, California. The college has developed an action plan that is clearly rooted in the faculty and is tied inextricably to the institution's mission and identity in its service region. The result is a challenge to faculty and administration alike to embrace diversity and multiculturalism without falling prey to divisive and ultimately destructive ideological disputes. As the summary of the action plan states:

> Fortunately, the discussion of global and intercultural studies at Santa Rosa Junior College has not generated an academic stand-off. The faculty associated with global and intercultural perspectives on the campus are to be complemented for furthering work without stimulating organized opposition. As noted earlier, past global programs have been criticized on various counts, but that criticism has been limited and not supported with developed, ideological fervor. Realizing the potential for such opposition, global and intercultural educators at Santa Rosa Junior College would be wise to consider the following safeguards to their work: refuse to buy into a liberal-conservative split over global/intercultural issues, make inclusion of the widest range of participation in courses and program offerings a guiding principle, and familiarize themselves with the debates around global/intercultural education so these very debates can become part of their courses and programs. (Santa Rosa Community College 1993)

The manner in which colleges address the international-versus-multicultural issue is less important than the fact that it is addressed. Unless a college seriously examines how internationalization and multiculturalism each enhance institutional identity, long-term internal consensus over either is unattainable.

The college's president must play a most delicate role in this self-examination. On the one hand, he or she can influence the ongoing college debate concerning mission; on the other, he or she cannot force an outcome. In the spirit of Richard Neustadt's classic work, *Presidential Power*, the college president must draw his or her powers of persuasion.

Among these powers, the president can rely most effectively on four. The first is, obviously, the power of resources. By supporting faculty initiatives in internationalization (even with small amounts), the president sends a message that international programming matters to him or her and that creativity in the area will be supported. The key here is not to support international programs in a way that is completely out of line with other programs on campus; the art is in providing enough support to send a message without creating widespread jealousy in other areas of the college.

For example, in 1988 Middlesex Community College was beginning to deal with internationalization and multiculturalization. The faculty had formed, and the president had endorsed, committees to chart the college's course on international and multicultural issues. A sum of approximately $40,000 had been set aside in the budget to hire a coordinator for international programs.

As the search for this coordinator was about to begin, however, the president suggested instead that the money be used as seed money for faculty initiatives concerning internationalization of the curriculum. Under this plan, the faculty would manage their own initiatives with the help of the existing administrators.

This model proved to be an extraordinary success at Middlesex, since the faculty used the capital to begin a series of programs in Russia and the People's Republic of China, as well as initiatives to bring students in from Ireland and South Africa. These efforts set the foundation for other programs.

Not only did the model succeed at the program level, it also provided corollary benefits. First, it drew faculty into the internationalization process. Second, it demonstrated a presidential commitment to faculty leadership over internationalization. And finally, it provided an important indication to the college's board of trustees, as well as to the community at large, that internationalization did not equate to increases in the administrative payroll at Middlesex.

A second key aspect of presidential power is visibility of office. The president is afforded countless opportunities to speak both on campus or to local businesses and civic groups. The college president has a pulpit and should use it to encourage support among key constituencies both within the campus and in the community at large.

Presidents hold the capacity to set the tone for many debates both on campus and beyond. . . . A fundamental test of leadership is the courage to be out front on issues of extraordinary long-term importance to the institutions and the regions they serve without undermining the quality of debate and dialogue that is the historic foundation of academic life. (Cowan 1993)

A third power of persuasion is the president's capacity to marshal administrative support behind innovative faculty initiatives. As faculty begin to embrace internationalization and create new curricular or program offerings, the successful president will establish administrative systems and personnel to aid such efforts quickly. As with budgetary support, a responsive administrative infrastructure demonstrates the president's capacity to back rhetoric with action.

Of particular importance in the area of administrative support are the college's grants function and its professional development program. As faculty begin to engage in internationalization, it is vital that the college have the capacity to support them quickly and effectively by assisting in the preparation of grant applications and by providing funds, release time, or both, to support their professional-growth or classroom initiatives.

At Middlesex the grant staff gave extensive support to faculty in a wide variety of disciplines (including those in the social science, humanities, business, and health careers divisions) by developing successful applications to both the Federal Title VI Program and the National Endowment for the Humanities (NEH). The funding from these grants allowed the implementation of collegewide summer workshops devoted to Asia and Latin America. These workshops, in turn, inspired an ongoing positive dialogue concerning the pedagogical challenge of integrating an Asian and Latin-American perspective into the Middlesex curriculum.

Critical support for faculty initiatives in the international arena at Middlesex also came from the college's extensive professional development program. Established by the president in 1990–91, the program provides funds for faculty initiatives related to curriculum development.

One such opportunity available to Middlesex faculty is the college's contract-training agreement with the People's Republic of China. Developed in collaboration with the Beijing Management Institute and the Chinese Academy of Science, the agreement allows two faculty members to spend up to one month in China teaching international business, accounting, economics, or international trade. The collaboration has not only permitted to the faculty an extraordinary professional growth experience but also earns revenue, which the college uses to support other international efforts.

Middlesex has also developed two programs with Russia, and they combine professional development and contract training. The first, a collaboration with the Moscow Pedagogical Institute, has focused on faculty and student visits. Developed in 1990 and the first of Middlesex's formal international collaboratives, the program brings Russian educators to the community college for pedagogical and curricular seminars as well as for cultural study. In exchange, Middlesex faculty and students visit Russia, where "homestays" are combined with cultural programs and academic study during an intense twenty-day visit.

The funding for these exchanges, as well as for other faculty exchanges with Russia, has largely come out of revenues from a series of executive training programs for Russian bankers. Combining on-site experiences at area commercial banks in the area with advanced courses in banking, the program has brought senior officers to Middlesex and has generated positive cash flows, which in turn has enabled the college to support other international and multicultural initiatives.

One of the combined international-multicultural initiatives is the Middlesex partnership with the Asian Studies Development Program (ASDP), which is co-sponsored by the University of Hawaii and the East-West Center. The ASDP supports efforts to infuse an Asian perspective into the American college curriculum. The Middlesex/ASDP partnership has brought both prestige and professional development opportunities to the community college. In 1989 and 1990 faculty and administrators from Middlesex participated in an extensive curriculum-development effort at the University of Hawaii. This effort led in 1991 to the selection of Middlesex as the first community-college ASDP satellite. With this designation, the college entered into a formal partnership that brought University of Hawaii faculty and East-West Center scholars to Middlesex, allowed Middlesex faculty members to study at the East-West Center, and provided important support for major Middlesex grant proposals (e.g., NEH and Title VI). In addition, it provided Middlesex with the opportunity to host national conferences on the teaching of Asian studies in 1994 and 1995, the latter funded through the NEH. Each of these Middlesex initiatives resulted from the placement of administrative resources (grant writing, small seed money, and staff time) at the disposal of faculty initiatives.

The fourth presidential power is the ability to bring new constituencies together. Whether through the college's formal governance and committee structures or through more informal processes, the president can draw together from various disciplines professors who share a commitment to international studies. Such allies are critical to any effort to build wide interdisciplinary support for international programs.

Outcomes

As a result of collegewide debate concerning internationalization and multiculturalization, we believe that a president can hope for at least five basic outcomes from his or her efforts to build consensus. First, the president should achieve some widespread support within a reasonable time frame. Although we believe that debate and introspection should be ongoing at any institution, it is reasonable to expect that any college can reach a consensus about an action plan for internationalization or multiculturalization within one academic year.

Second, the action plan should be faculty-driven and anchored securely in the curriculum. Moreover, the plan should include appropriate incentives (stipends, professional development monies, etc.) to encourage faculty participation. Third, the plan should clearly focus on students. Too often, colleges develop strategic plans in new areas such as internationalization, but only minimally define the benefits of such initiatives to students. At Middlesex, the action plan included a commitment to link contract-training initiatives in China and Russia to student exchanges. As Frank Falcetta, dean of economic and community development explained:

> Student involvement in international products has been a critical component in our programs since their inception. This involvement is truly reciprocal and yields significant benefit. Students assume a dual role—that of Ambassador at the host institution but, more importantly, that of envoy when they return to their homes. (Falcetta 1993)

Fourth, the plan should limit the number of new administrative appointments to the college's staff. Like any organization, colleges are prone to equate new initiatives with new staff. Although some staffing adjustments may be necessary to implement an aggressive international studies program, we are not convinced that an additional layer of bureaucracy focused on internationalism is either necessary or prudent. It is far better, in our opinion, to invest any available money as seed capital to support specific faculty initiatives than to spend it on additional staff.

Fifth, a college action plan for internationalization should look beyond state, county, or local appropriations for methods of financing. We believe that international programs can, over a three- to five-year period, become largely self-supporting. Taxpayer dollars need not be the long-term source of support for internationalization. In fact, we believe that such funds should only be used to finance pedagogical and curriculum initiatives. Travel by administrators and other nonclassroom activities should come from other sources or should not exist at all.

In conclusion, effective presidential vision and leadership, combined with meaningful institutional dialogue, can forge an internal consensus concerning international education at community colleges. And with this consensus in hand, the institution can be strengthened and the foundation for external consensus can be built and sustained.

BUILDING EXTERNAL CONSENSUS

It is impossible to discuss the internal consensus concerning internationalization without simultaneously addressing issues related to the external environment. Although external constituencies will view internationalization through different prisms from those of faculty and staff, many of the core issues debated on campus will be echoed in the community at large.

For purposes of discussion, we will consider the external constituencies to fall within four general groups: political actors, business and industry interests, the media, and the "person in the street." Any such generic listing is inherently limited, but we ask the reader's indulgence in that such groupings provide us with a rough framework for discussion. Figure 5 depicts a model for external consensus.

FIGURE 5. External Consensus

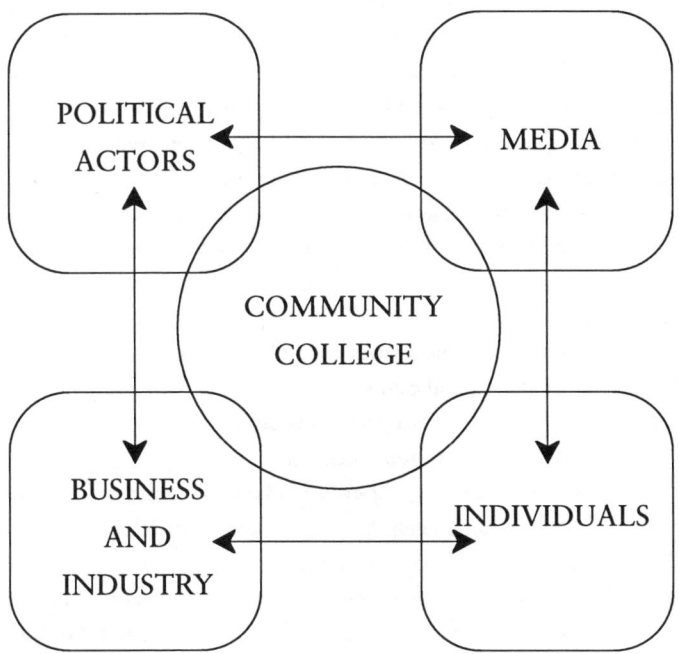

For community colleges, the most significant political actors are found at the state and local levels. State legislators, local council members, and mayors represent the clearest manifestation of the maxim that "all politics is local." By the nature of their offices, these officials are often less concerned with global affairs and the intrinsic worth of intercultural sensitivity than with ensuring voters both the maximum "bang" for their tax dollars and a public education system that provides sound basic skills.

Similarly, community colleges deal increasingly with small to medium-sized businesses. Be it a small technology-based company or a local bank, such entities tend to ask community colleges more for skilled entry-level employees than for culturally sophisticated graduates who have a knowledge of the language and culture of clients.

These predispositions on the part of political and business interests are often reinforced by the local media. Inherently skeptical of the spending methods of public colleges and increasingly focused on the limitations in the basic skills of high school graduates, local media are often dubious of community college expenditures on international programs.

Finally, while it is impossible to speak with any accuracy of "the general public" or the truly representative "person on the street," it does seem fair to say that a number of forces have combined to make much of the nation's citizenry more suspicious of programs such as international and intercultural programs at community colleges.

As the recession of the late 1980s hit communities across the country, taxpayers become particularly watchful over how their dollars were spent. This heightened sensitivity, combined with media exposure of failings in the nation's educational infrastructure and of apparent waste and corruption in government at all levels, has continued into the 1990s, as has many Americans' mistrust of government. As public institutions, community colleges are not immune to this sensitivity and therefore face a significant challenge as they move to implement nontraditional programs such as internationalization.

In this environment, presidential leadership assumes particular significance. To the general public, a college's president embodies the institution, his or her words encapsulate the college mission, and his or her behavior reflects the institution's identity.

The personalization of college identity—manifested by presidents having excessive ego, limited capacity, or both—can debilitate an institution. But for the president who is neither burdened by hubris nor short-changed in ability the potential for community leadership is extraordinary.

Nowhere is such leadership more profoundly important than in the arena of international education. For while board members and faculty can help the cause, it is ultimately the president who must make the case for internationalization in a proactive, substantively coherent manner. In making the external case, a president should keep several goals squarely in his or her sight.

First, presidents must be clear and consistent about the role of community colleges in international studies. International programs are fundamentally about providing a labor force that not only is technically proficient but also possesses sufficient cultural sensitivity to compete in world markets and to succeed in the volatile and diverse workplace of the late twentieth century. No longer can America dominate world trade simply through its size or its resources. Our nation is but one player in a global economy whose challenges are more profound every day. We cannot compete successfully by looking inward; we must engage the world sensitively, wisely, and creatively.

In *Work of Nations* Robert B. Reich writes:

> As almost every factor of production—money, technology, factories and equipment—moves effortlessly across borders, the very idea of an American economy is becoming meaningless, as are the notions of an American corporation, American capital, American products, and American technology. A similar transformation is affecting every other nation, some faster and more profoundly than others; witness Europe hurdling toward economic union. So who is "us"? The answer lies in the only aspect of a national economy that is relatively immobile internationally: the American workforce, the American people. The real economic challenge facing the United States in the years ahead—the same as that facing every other nation—is to increase the potential value of what its citizens can add to the global economy, by enhancing their skills and capacities and by improving their means of linking those skills and capacities to the world market. (Reich 1991, 8)

International and multicultural education will also provide an important foundation from which future American workers can participate in a rapidly changing work environment. Not only is technology and world competition changing American manufacturing and modes of production, the look and feel of the workplace itself is in transition. With immigration from Latin America and Asia continuing and with some estimates indicating that the population of the United States will increase by 25 percent by the year 2025, the workplace is becoming increasingly diverse. This diversity requires an American worker who is both technically competent and culturally sensitive.

For example, the city of Lowell, Massachusetts, faces both significant demographic change because of a large influx of Southeast Asian and Hispanic residents and a period of major economic adjustment. Once one of the nation's great manufacturing centers, Lowell underwent a renaissance during the 1980s through the growth of companies such as Wang Technologies and the establishment of an urban national park. Because of the economic recession of the last five years, Lowell must again adjust its economic base. To do so will require new industries that build on the city's diverse population base. With a campus in the city's downtown, Middlesex Community College has begun to play a central role both in training that population base and in encouraging intercultural sensitivity in the workplace. One part of this effort is the college's Prepare for Access to College (PAC) Program. Operated with the assistance of regional businesses, PAC assists newly arrived Americans in language training as well as in acclimation to the cultural dynamics of life in American society and in the American workplace.

Beyond the economic argument, presidents owe it to their students to articulate a second position to the external community: two-year college students deserve the opportunity to embrace other cultures and other countries simply because is intellectually fulfilling to do so.

We are all enriched when we share an understanding of and sensitivity to the many diverse cultures that comprise our nation. Conversely, when we fail to encourage international and multicultural opportunities for students at all levels of education, we limit both ourselves and our successor generations to the narrow and debilitating language of "us" and "them."

Symbiotic Relationship between Internal and External Consensus

It is important to recognize the long-term symbiotic relationship between internal and external consensus. Internal support for international and multicultural programs can enhance support from the community at large. For example, as the faculty become increasingly recognized for their interest and expertise in international matters, local media and companies will turn to them for that expertise; as students pursue international opportunities, they will become effective advocates in the community and on campus for expansion of such programs; and as board members become increasingly comfortable with the outcomes of international programs, they will become vital advocates among important external constituencies.

Conversely, external constituencies such as local business and industry or government officials have the capacity to influence the college while its commitment to internationalization and multiculturalization evolves.

This influence can take the form of requests for new programs to meet industry needs, grant opportunities for international initiatives, or the realignment of state, county, or regional budgetary resources to support program development.

For example, Middlesex has worked to develop increasingly strong ties to state governmental entities such as the Massachusetts Partners in Trade program. Partners in Trade operates under the aegis of the Massachusetts Office of Tourism and Trade and brings together major constituencies with an interest in trade issues (chambers of commerce, businesses, and academic institutions). Middlesex is the only community college to serve as a full member of this program.

Major business organizations offer community colleges another avenue for forming critical linkages. For example, chambers of commerce play a major role as voices for local and regional business. When Middlesex sent its first team to the People's Republic of China to explore contract-training and exchange opportunities, the president of one of the region's major chambers of commerce was included as part of the visiting team. This gesture had several outcomes. First, it demonstrated to the Chinese that Middlesex enjoyed the support of business leaders in its region. Second, it provided the Middlesex representatives with a significant opportunity for deepening the college's sense of partnership with a major figure in the business community. Finally, it offered the chamber-of-commerce president a chance to explore potential opportunities for members of his organization.

The college has built on this effort by developing other ties that reach deep into the region's business community. For example, the college regularly co-sponsors international business seminars with the North Suburban Chamber of Commerce (whose region includes the high-technology corridor, Route 128). In addition, the college has established a strong International Advisory Board, composed of local business leaders. The board plays an active role in helping to shape contract-training and business programs at the college, to support local companies as they engage in international opportunities and challenges. The Middlesex voice in international programming has become so strong and its ties to government and business so deep that in 1993 the governor of Massachusetts invited the college's president to join him as part of a trade mission to Latin America.

Other colleges have forged strong ties to both government and business. Among the most successful is Bergen County Community College in Paramus, New Jersey. Not only has the college built a remarkably strong faculty-driven, campuswide international program, it has also developed innovative and substantive ties to the regional business community. Through its highly regarded International Trade Round Table Association (which brings together dozens of area companies for open discussions of and expert presentations on trade issues) and through customized courses and workshops, the college has earned corporate support for its international programs. The college's success in this regard owes much to the director of its Center for International Studies, Lynda Icochea, whose understanding of the need to blend internal and external consensus is a model for internationalization.

City College of San Francisco has reached into the business community of the Bay Area to build a consensus for its international efforts. This college has found that while its constituencies may differ, the demands of building internal and external consensus concerning internationalization overlap in a number of important ways. The college's office of contract training and international business has developed a number of successful collaborative efforts with multinational corporations such as Varig Airlines and Golden Harvest. For example, Varig has supported the development of City College programs in Latin America both through reduced air fares and through introductions to other multinational firms interested in contract training.

In sum, the president must assume the ultimate responsibility for maintaining a balance of support in the internal and external communities. In both settings, it is the president who must set the tone for debate and who must demonstrate the intrinsic worth of internationalization and multiculturalization—both academically and economically.

In engaging external and internal communities on the subject of international programs, presidents should also hold to three simple rules of thumb.

1. *Avoid hubris.* Establishment of an international studies program does not transform college executives into foreign ministers. International programs need not be an excuse for presidential or board travel.
2. *Don't forget the core values that brought your college to international/multicultural programs.* Keep the program's focus on faculty, curriculum, and students. When other lofty notions intercede, take a deep breath and repeat the mantra "faculty, curriculum, students."
3. *Run lean and efficiently.* International programs should not be considered an excuse to hire more administrators, nor do they need to drain extensive taxpayer support.

CONCLUSION

Establishing a consensus for international programs demands sustained and committed presidential leadership. To succeed, the president must pursue a sustained, clear, and coherent effort to enlist both internal and external constituencies behind international studies. Internally, the president must enlist faculty and staff to support the contributions that internationalization makes to institutional core values. The president must be willing to let the faculty lead the development of a comprehensive set of programs focused on students and curriculum. Externally, the president must articulate how internationalization contributes to the fundamental educational and economic development needs of the community. Moreover, he or she must look for financing models that at once support internationalization and encourage taxpayer support of these programs.

Although the challenges inherent in such an aggressive effort are many and the risks are real, the risks of avoiding internationalism are far greater. If community colleges deny their students a worldview, history will judge them harshly, as will a generation of students unprepared to engage themselves in, much less shape, the world in which they live.

REFERENCES

Cowan, Carole A. (president, Middlesex Community College). Interview with James Mullen, October 23, 1993.

Falcetta, Frank (dean of economic and community development, Middlesex Community College). Interview with James Mullen, October 8, 1993.

Henderson, James. "Speech to the Association of Community College Trustees" (ACCT). Toronto, October 12, 1993.

Kalivas, David M. (associate professor of history, Middlesex Community College). Interview with James Mullen, November 3, 1993.

Neustadt, Richard. *Presidential Power: The Politics of Leadership from FDR to Carter.* New York: Wiley, 1980.

Reich, Robert B. *Work of Nations: Preparing Ourselves for 21st Century Capitalism.* New York: Alfred A. Knopf, 1991.

Santa Rosa Community College. *Action Plan.* Santa Rosa, Cal.: Santa Rosa Community College, 1993.

II
Dimensions of Community Colleges Abroad

Introduction to Part II

The twentieth century has witnessed a phenomenon in which "universities and university-level specialized institutions alone cannot cope with either the needs of the economy nor the social demand for higher education [and hence] the existence of a recognized alternative to traditional universities is indispensable" (Cerych 1993, 5). The resulting void left by the "demanteling of the sacred trust of traditional universities" (Kintzer 1994, 4) is being filled by an explosion of nontraditional higher education institutions offering short-cycle programs that train people in crafts, technology, and vocations, as well as offering opportunities for professional and academic growth. The nineteenth-century German *Volkhochschulen* is the prototype of these educational institutions and inspired formalized postsecondary, pre-university institutions throughout Europe and the United States. Currently there are over 4,000 short-term, short-cycle institutions, and they are found in 180 countries. They constitute "an amorphous field," which Kintzer consolidates under the rubric *nonuniversities* (Kintzer 1994, 4; Kintzer 1992, 1).

A comparative analysis of these "nonuniversities" is difficult because they differ regionally in type, duration, content, and even name.[1] A concise yet all-encompassing term that is nonelitist and nonethnocentric has yet to emerge. The 1980s description, "short-cycle short-term colleges and universities," is not concise and implies an inferior type of education.[2] The 1990s term, *nonuniversities*, while concise, conveys a negative connotation, since *non* defines absence rather than choice. Since the majority of these institutions are technical or vocational, the term *community college* is also incomplete.[3] Furthermore, the global application of the term (which is associated with the United States) elicits the accusation of U.S. ethnocentrism. However, since the "community college model" is rapidly being adopted worldwide, the term is the least deleterious of the available terms and hence is used in this text.

Cohen and Brawer (1989), Kintzer (1990; 1992; 1994), King and

Fersh (1992), and Cohen (1994) identify four basic configurations of the community college model. The first configuration is a "multipurpose" one that combines academic, pre-university, retraining, technical, vocational/occupational, remedial, sociocultural, continuing (adult), and other forms of educational instruction. The second provides a "specialized" orientation that offers two to three years of technical, vocational, or occupational programs. The third portrays a "binary" path that bridges upper-secondary, postsecondary, college, and university education. As distinct entities or as part of a university system, these configurations provide baccalaureates and other advanced degrees (both academic and occupational). The fourth configuration emphasizes lifelong learning to attain literacy or pursue cultural or social studies. Table 4 delineates the implementation of these configurations in many countries. It appears that most countries throughout the world either have developed or are in various stages of developing some form of the community college model, "with the appropriate balance between liberal and vocational education" (Koltai 1993, 6). In the process, the community college model has become unique unto itself and is gaining prominence in terms of quantity and quality throughout the world (Kintzer 1994).

The community college model has four identifiable characteristics. First, most of its students are secondary-school graduates, it exists between upper-secondary and university education, and it is able to grant only certain types of certificates or diplomas. Although included in national educational plans, many have a mission, curriculum, and budget that expresses local (regional) concerns. Many of them are accountable to local universities for providing accredited pre-university curricula and to local business for identifying curricula that relate to the community's economic and sociopolitical needs. Cohen (1994) postulates that in nations where compulsory education ends early, the community colleges serve upper-secondary, undergraduate collegiate, and paraprofessional functions and are four to five years in duration. In countries where students attend school for ten or more years, the colleges accentuate prebaccalaureate, occupational, and recurrent education studies, which are often less than two years in duration.

Second, each configuration accentuates a short-term career/personal development education that provides academic access and semiprofessional, technical, and vocational training to diverse sections of society. In this respect, the community college model presents a viable option for higher education, which was once the sole realm of the university. Third, on a global scale, the community college model is not highly regarded by governments, scholars, or the populace. As a result, it has poor financial support and is low in social status (Ishumi 1988).

TABLE 4. Community College Models

Country	Name(s)	Special Features
Countries in Africa	Regional colleges	◦ Founded in late 1970s by World Bank funding. ◦ Specialized technical/vocational programs. ◦ Accept students from middle school.
Australia	College of Advanced Education of Victoria (CAE); community colleges; Technical and Further EducationColleges (TAFEs) (120 in New South Wales alone)	◦ Multipurpose short-cycle programs. ◦ Binary short-cycle programs: bridge secondary, college, and university. ◦ CAEs have recently been granted university status.
Austria	Regional colleges	◦ Multipurpose short-cycle programs. ◦ Binary short-cycle programs: bridge secondary and short-cycle colleges.
Barbados	Community college (American model)	◦ Multipurpose short-cycle programs. ◦ Specialized technical/vocational programs.
Belarus	Community college model; *vishe skole*	◦ Multipurpose short-cycle program (emphasizes commercial cooperatives and specialist upgrading).
Britain	Colleges of further education (CFEs) (550); polytechnics	◦ Binary short-cycle programs: bridge secondary, college, and university. ◦ Founded to offer alternative to university by expanding postsecondary, work preparation, and adult education. ◦ Multipurpose short-cycle programs. ◦ CFEs are part of the 1992 educational reform movement to create free postcompulsory education for 16–18-year-olds.

Bulgaria	Community college model (40); *vishe skole*	○ Binary short-cycle programs: bridge secondary, college, and university. ○ Founded to offer alternative to university by expanding post-secondary, work preparation, and adult education. ○ Multipurpose short-cycle programs.
Canada	Community and junior colleges; Colleges of Applied Arts and Technology; Colleges d'Enseignment General et Professionnel (CEGEP) (Colleges of General and Vocational Education [Quebec])	○ Lifelong learning in social/cultural studies. ○ Technical schools are branches of universities or polytechnical colleges. ○ Multipurpose short-cycle programs. ○ Public support: federal, state, or local level.
Ceylon	Junior University College	○ Specialized technical/vocational programs.
China	Vocational University and Worker's College	○ Specialized technical/vocational programs.
Colombia	Community college (American model)	○ Multipurpose short-cycle programs. ○ Specialized technical/vocational programs.
Czech Federal Republic	Community college (based on Dutch model)	○ Specialized technical/vocational programs. ○ Multipurpose short-cycle programs. ○ Binary short-cycle programs: bridge secondary and short-cycle colleges.
Denmark	*Folkhighschool*; technical schools	○ Binary short-cycle programs: bridge secondary, college, and university. ○ Founded to offer alternative to university by expanding post-secondary, work preparation, and adult education. ○ Lifelong learning in social/cultural studies. ○ Specialized technical/vocational programs.
Eastern Europe	*Vishe skole*	○ Specialized technical/vocational programs. ○ Sometimes combined to form single upper-secondary school. ○ Public support: federal, state, or local level.

Egypt	Ma'had colleges	◦ Specialized technical/vocational programs. ◦ Little transfer to universities.
France	Instituts Universitaires Technologiques (IUTs); Higher Technician Sections (outgrowth of secondary schools)	◦ Binary short-cycle programs: bridge secondary, college, and university. ◦ Specialized technical/vocational programs. ◦ Binary short-cycle programs: bridge secondary, college, and university. ◦ Founded to offer alternative to university by expanding postsecondary, work preparation, and adult education.
Germany	*Fachhochschulen* (20 new schools since German unification); *Volkshochschulen* (900)	◦ Lifelong learning in social/cultural studies: *Volkshochschulen*. ◦ Specialized technical/vocational programs: *Fachhochschulen*. ◦ Special courses to facilitate transfer to university. ◦ Public support: federal, state, or local level.
Greece	Technological Education Institution	◦ Specialized technical/vocational programs. ◦ Public support: federal, state, or local level.
Hungary	Community college	◦ Specialized technical/vocational programs. ◦ Binary short-cycle programs: bridge secondary, college, and university. ◦ Founded in late 1970s by World Bank funding.
India	Regional colleges/community colleges; colleges of vocational studies	◦ Specialized technical/vocational programs (accept students from middle school). ◦ Lifelong learning in societal development. ◦ Binary short-cycle programs: bridge secondary, college, and university. ◦ Founded to meet expanding needs of postsecondary and adult education and founded as an alternative to the university track.
Indonesia	Technological institutes	◦ Technical/vocational base. ◦ Lifelong literacy training. ◦ Public support: federal, state, or local level.

Iran	Regional technical colleges	◦ Specialized technical/vocational programs. ◦ Lifelong literacy training.
Ireland	Regional technical colleges; polytechnics (with university degrees) in Belfast	◦ Specialized technical/vocational programs. ◦ Public support: federal, state, or local level.
Israel	Regional colleges	◦ Founded in late 1970s; World Bank funds developed 2- to 5-year schools that accept students from middle school and primarily have a vocational base.
Jamaica	Polytechnica (British model)	◦ Binary short-cycle programs: bridge secondary, college, and university. ◦ Specialized technical/vocational programs. ◦ Multipurpose short-cycle programs.
Japan	Junior colleges (561); special training schools (3,152); technical colleges (62); miscellaneous postsecondary private technical schools (3,000)	◦ Private support through student tuition. ◦ Little transfer to universities. ◦ Junior college: majority are private for women (major in humanities, home economics, and education). ◦ Special training schools: majority of students are men (major in foreign languages, business, technology or paramedical fields); some are outgrowths of secondary schools. ◦ Specialized technical/vocational programs. ◦ Public technical schools: male students who are not university-qualified and who specialize in engineering technology.
Kazakhstan	*Teknicum* (13); training institutes (21)	◦ Specialized technical/vocational programs.
Kenya	Harambee Institute of Technology (18)	◦ Specialized technical/vocational programs. ◦ Lifelong learning in cultural revitalization.

Korea	Junior technical colleges (130)	○ Specialized technical/vocational programs.
Latin America	Regional Technical Institutes of Latin America (Colegios Regionales and Institutos Technologicos) (Chile, Venezuela, Colombia—RTIs affiliated with universities)	○ Binary short-cycle programs: bridge secondary, college, and university and combine college with single upper-secondary school. ○ Lifelong literacy training. ○ Specialized technical/vocational programs. ○ Regional Colleges become University Centers, then regular University Campuses.
Malaysia	Institut Tecknologi	○ Public support: federal, state, or local level. ○ Lifelong literacy training. ○ Specialized technical/vocational programs.
Mexico	Colegio Nacional de Educacion Profesional Tecnica (CONALEP) (254)	○ Public support: federal, state, or local level. ○ Lifelong literacy training. ○ Specialized technical/vocational programs.
New Zealand	Community colleges; Vocational/technical and senior technical institutes (20)	○ Multipurpose short-cycle programs. ○ Binary short-cycle programs: bridge secondary, college, and university and combine vocational programs to form single upper-secondary school.
Norway	Regional colleges (district colleges); *folkhighschools*	○ Multipurpose short-cycle programs. ○ Binary short-cycle programs: bridge secondary, college, and university. ○ Public support: federal, state, or local level. ○ Special courses to facilitate transfer to university. ○ Lifelong learning in social/cultural studies.

Russia and newly independent states of Eurasia	*Vishe skole; Teknicum*	◦ Some private support through student tuition. ◦ Public support: federal, state, or local level. ◦ Specialized technical/vocational programs. ◦ Sometimes combined to form single upper-secondary school.
Scotland	Educational authority colleges	◦ Binary short-cycle programs: bridge secondary, college, and university. ◦ Binary short-cycle programs: bridge secondary, college, and university. ◦ Multipurpose short-cycle programs.
Singapore	Polytechnic institutes	◦ Specialized technical/vocational programs. ◦ Binary short-cycle programs.
Slovak Federal Republic	Community college (based on German *Fachhochschulen* and British polytechnical models)	◦ Specialized technical/vocational programs. ◦ Multipurpose short-cycle programs.
Sri Lanka	Regional technical institutes	◦ Specialized technical/vocational programs.
Sweden	Upper-secondary schools; technical colleges	◦ Binary short-cycle programs: bridge secondary, college, and university. ◦ Founded to meet the expanding needs of postsecondary, work preparation, and adult education, as well as other alternatives to the university track. ◦ 1960 technology/occupational program expansion to meet work needs.
Taiwan	National Taiwan Institute of Technology; junior colleges	◦ Binary short-cycle programs: bridge secondary, college, and university. ◦ Specialized technical/vocational programs. ◦ Public support: federal, state, or local level.
Tanzania	Regional Technical Institutes	◦ Specialized technical/vocational programs.
Thailand	Technological institutes; Phuket Community College of the Prince of Songkla University	◦ Specialized technical/vocational programs. ◦ Public support: federal, state, or local level. ◦ Binary short-cycle programs.

Trinidad	National Institute of Higher Education (U.S. and British models)	◦ Binary short-cycle programs: bridge secondary, college, and university. ◦ Specialized technical/vocational programs. ◦ Multipurpose short-cycle programs.
Tobago	National Institute of Higher Education (U.S. and British models)	◦ Binary short-cycle programs: bridge secondary, college, and university. ◦ Specialized technical/vocational programs. ◦ Multi-purpose short-cycle programs.
Ukraine	Junior specialist institutions (15)	◦ Specialized technical/vocational programs. ◦ Binary short-cycle programs.
Venezuela	Public pedagogical institutes; public polytechnic institutes; technological institutes (mostly public); university colleges (mostly private)	◦ Binary short-cycle programs: bridge secondary, college, and university. ◦ Multipurpose short-cycle programs. ◦ Technical schools are branches of universities or polytechnical colleges.
United States	Community colleges (1,200)	◦ Lifelong learning in social/cultural studies. ◦ Technical schools are branches of universities or polytechnical colleges. ◦ Multipurpose short-cycle programs. ◦ Public support: federal, state, or local level. ◦ Special courses to facilitate transfer to university. ◦ Potential adoption of some "binary" orientation elements.

Sources: Tables compiled from Kintzer 1990; Kintzer 1994, 6–16; Cohen 1993, 13–18.

Finally, all configurations embody the ideal that a relatively low cost means open accessibility, which in turn defines and perpetuates educational and, therefore, economic democracy. In particular, the U.S. model is believed to (a) encourage educational access to students from predominantly lower socioeconomic classes and subordinate ethnic groups, (b) assist with the transfer between secondary schools, postsecondary institutions, and employment, (c) delineate an alternative route and a second opportunity for postsecondary education, (d) provide flexibility in its programs, and in the quality of educational opportunities, and (e) help build a democratic society. Indeed, the tuition is consistently lower than that for universities, yet it may still be too expensive for many students. Private sponsorship is now required in several countries.

However, the ideal that relaxed requirements and equitable access lead to academic or vocational opportunities and that education at a community college provides the foundation for economic or political reform is dubious at best. Difficulties exist in (a) establishing sufficient communication with business and industry, to prevent a weakening of the relevancy of programs and of future job placement possibilities for students, and (b) maintaining academic autonomy while incorporating both the university and business agendas. Furthermore, the current phenomenon of privatization, a consequence of the world recession, alters the level of accessibility in configurations found in Asia, Britain, Eastern Europe and the former Soviet Union, Latin America, and New Zealand, while in the United States, increased student tuitions are actually eliminating "open access" for thousands of students.

International Development and Community College Models

For decades, developed and developing countries have used postsecondary educational reform to counter socioeconomic inequities. The community college model and the services it provides help evoke social reform, since these colleges have the "resources and expertise, especially in applied technology, that could serve well . . . in sustainable development" ("ACIIE" 1994, 1; Elsner, Tsunoda, and Korbel 1994). Western community colleges export their services either as nonprofit or for-profit ventures (the profits then are used to enhance other international programs). As vocational/technological and ESL education continues to play a pivotal role in the economic development of developing countries, debates regarding exportation are increasing (Harris 1993; Koltai 1993).

The U.S. community college model is influencing an escalating number of postsecondary institutions abroad, especially by defining open access, providing proactive methodologies, sharing technical and short-cycle career curricula, and providing U.S. certification. In the 1970s the U.S. community college model was copied in Egypt, Indonesia, Malaysia, and Mexico, and in the 1990s, Armenia, Colombia, Hungary, Kazakhstan, Russia, and South Africa are soliciting similar models[4] (Cohen 1994, 18; Koltai 1993; Raby 1993; King and Fersh 1992; Fersh and Humphrys 1992).

Theoretically, two perspectives support community college international development efforts. The "privatization" perspective views educational transfer as a money-producing venture for both the donor and the recipient colleges. This is evident in contract-education programs and in the hidden agendas of many international development projects. The "humanitarian" perspective views educational developmental assistance as a means to "apply our ideals, our sense of decency and our humanitarian impulse to the repair of the world [since] investment in development is indeed investment in prevention" (Koltai 1993, 2).[5] International development activities facilitate informational exchanges, between and within colleges, and encourage the adoption of such international and intercultural/multicultural educational programs as faculty and administrator exchanges and sister-college relationships.

Frequently, a developing country's community colleges adopt information from Western community colleges. Recently, however, similar exchanges have been occurring between community colleges within developed countries. Decentralization and the merger of occupational education with university certification into a new configuration that includes a B.A. degree are two examples of transfers of information from community colleges in Western Europe, Australia, and New Zealand to those in Canada and the United States (Eade 1993; Koltai 1993). Expanding the access to telecommunications technologies further facilitates global networking and future educational endeavors.[6]

There are three primary problems with exporting the community college modes. On the financial level, substantial difficulties exist in an economically strained period. Increased financial competition causes a "for-profit philosophy," which affects academic curricula, relationships, and the funding for nontraditional programs. The inability to maintain low cost and open access undermines the community college's basic philosophy and places its programs at risk (Immerwahr and Farkas 1993; Kintzer 1990). In California between 1992 and 1993, community college enrollment fell by 137,000 while fees increased by 40 percent. For students already possessing a bachelor's degree or higher, fees went up eightfold in 1993 alone (*Time for Decision* 1994). The question of whether privatization compromises the academic mission also applies to tuition-based models abroad and is addressed in chapters 9 and 11.

On the academic level, defining standards that are acceptable to both donor and host countries may not be easy. Cultural miscommunication may make educational assistance, academic standards, and other concepts or procedures puzzling and unacceptable to the host institution. A specialized vocational curriculum may be irrelevant if graduates succumb to chronic unemployment (Kintzer 1990). Cultural neocolonialism has positive as well as negative consequences, and the latter must not be discounted. Legal ramifications arise when both donor and host country labor unions, accreditation teams, and state legislations or ministries of education scrutinize accountability and quality factors. Overwhelming political, economic, and cultural adjustments may prevent successful international development endeavors, especially those involving the relocation of a donor college to a foreign country. Restrictions aimed at maintaining local control in Australia, Indonesia, Japan, Korea, and the Philippines are making it increasingly difficult for Western countries to establish contract education and other international development projects there. These issues are addressed in chapters 9 and 11–14.

Finally, on the philosophical level, the ideal of the community college model as a means to create and maintain democracy, as well as to continue to influence economic and social reform, is often marred by the realities of cultural colonialism and by the consequences of reinforcing economic and social dependency. The exportation of U.S. or Western education is accompanied by moral, linguistic, and cultural Westernization. The results may collide with the host country's citizenship-training program and may hinder its attempts to maintain cultural identity and autonomy in the face of world homogenization. In the transplantation of Western models abroad, the ethics of "aid," "trade," and "neocolonialism" contain nonacademic ulterior motives. Nonetheless, the fact remains that the impact of altering the overall educational structure was and remains critical. These philosophical dimensions are examined in chapters 9, 10, 12, and 14.

The phenomenon of "exporting" community college ideals and models in order to reduce cultural conflict in multicultural societies is seen as a positive value by van der Linde (chapter 10), while the same act is viewed with reservations by Harris (chapter 9), in terms of its neocolonialism. Indigenous authors explore this phenomenon in four case studies that range along a continuum: from full transfer of the U.S./Western European model, as in the case of Israel (chapter 13); to semicomplete transfer, as in the case of Egypt (chapter 12); to emulation with retention of indigenous character, as in the case of South Africa (chapter 14); to rejection of transplantation, as in the case of the Japanese branch colleges (chapter 11).

The case studies of the implementation and maintenance of the community college model are discussed in terms of indigenous uniqueness as well as worldwide support. The regions of the world that have a connection with the case studies are shown in map 3 (p. 208).

NOTES

1. This field includes, among other types of regional colleges, colleges of further education, technical institutes, *vishe skole*, *tecknicums*, junior colleges, and community colleges.

2. The term "short-cycle higher education" emerged from an OECD-sponsored conference in Grenoble, France, in 1971. At this conference, specific models from France, Norway, the United Kingdom, the United States, and Yugoslavia were compared. The similarities found there have subsequently been applied to similar institutions worldwide (OECD, 1973).

3. Indeed, the majority of these institutions (numbering over 4,000) are technical rather than academic, national rather than community, private rather than public, postcompulsory and not necessarily postsecondary, and certificate-granting rather than degree-granting. For this reason, Kinzter prefers the term *nonuniversity*.

4. International development projects require varied expertise and are very expensive, which compels community colleges to frequently use consortia to enhance their capability to perform large-scale projects. An example of these consortia are Community Colleges for International Development (CCID), College Consortium International (CCI), and International Consortium for Economic and Educational Development (ICEED).

5. In the past two decades there has been a wide variety of U.S. community college assistance, development, and contract education programs worldwide. Because of the diversity, a listing of all types of programs would take up more space than is allowed. However, examples of this type are provided below. It must be noted that not all the listed programs are successful, since many ended soon after they were initiated. The majority have affiliations with the fifty-two-member U.S. and Canadian community college consortium Community Colleges for International Development (CCID), which is led by Brevard Community College (Florida) and whose members participate in a variety of international development, international assistance, and contract education programs:

• Assistance and development type programs between CCID-member colleges and the Republic of China; TELESUR, Republic of Surinam; National Taiwan Institute of Technology; U.S. Education Foundation of India; Technical University of Bucharest; University of Budapest; Czech Technical University in Prague, Association of Colombian Universities; Supreme Council of Egyptian Universities; Neva College, St. Petersburg, Russia; and International Business School in Russia. There is an ICEED agreement between community colleges in southern United States and CONALEP (Mexico) and Canadian community colleges. Work is being planned in Australia, Guyana, Romania, and the Slovak Republic.

• Contract education programs and branch college type programs: (1) Broward Community College (Florida) and Columbo International College in Seville and Marbella, Spain; Kolej Damansara Utama (KDU), Kuala Lumpur, Malaysia; ISS International School, Singapore; Buenos Aires, Argentina; (2) Los Angeles Community College District (California) and Center for International Studies in Madrid; Tokyo-American Community College; Williams Business College in Sydney, Australia; (3) International Education Specialists, Manila; American Community College of Asturias, Northern Spain; (4) Lincoln Land Community College (Illinois) and Maktab Sains MARA Community College in Kuantan, Malaysia; (5) Bookdale Com-

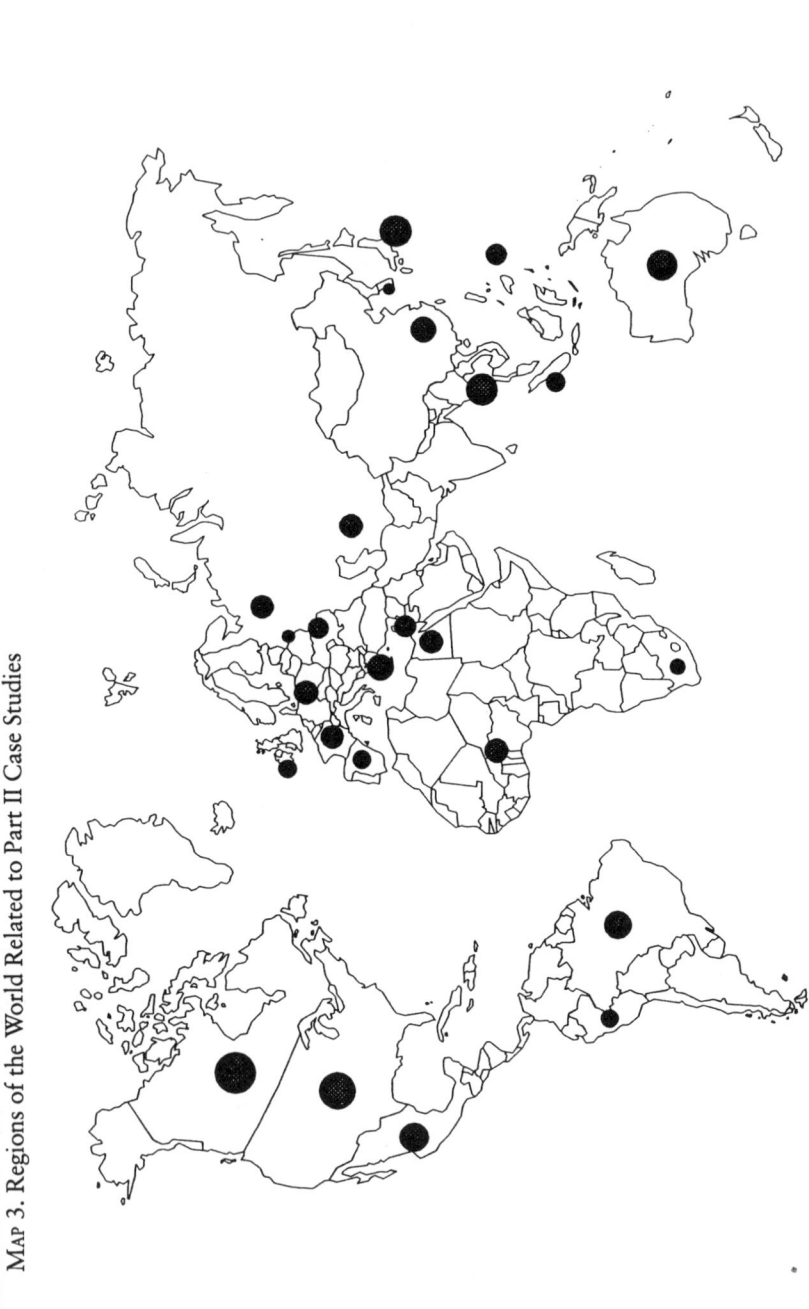

Map 3. Regions of the World Related to Part II Case Studies

munity College (New Jersey) and Guayaquil, Ecuador; (6) Edmonds Community College (Washington) and Kobe and Tokyo, Japan; (7) Ohio State University and Kazan Pedagogical Institute in Tatarstan; (8) American military bases in Europe; (9) Green River Community College (Washington) and Kanuma, Japan; (10) Mt. Hood Community College (Oregon) and Kojima, Japan; (11) Sullivan County Community College (New York) and Koyama Perfecture, Japan; (12) Middlesex Community College (Massachusetts) and China; (13) Black Hawk College (Oklahoma) and Noordlijke Hogeschool, Holland; (14) North Hennepin Community College (Minnesota) with Royal Melbourne Institute of Technology in Melbourne; (15) Miami-Dade Community College (Florida) and the American International College of Mexico; (16) Mission Community College (California) and Stamford Group in Bangkok, Thailand; (17) Consumnes River Community College (California) and Stamford Group in Kuala Lumpur; (18) Utah Valley State College and Utah Valley State College in Kiev.

6. Examples are the use of telecommunications in classroom sharing between students of the Maricopa Community College District and Moscow University and between Coast Community College District and CONALEP schools, as well as, of course, the instantaneous exchange of information via the Internet.

REFERENCES

"ACIIE Chairman Joins Washington Task Force." *ACIIE Newsletter* 1 (July/August 1994): 1.

California Higher Education Policy Center. *Time for Decision: California's Legacy and the Future of Higher Education: A Report with Recommendations.* San Jose, California Higher Education Policy Center, 1994.

Cerych, L. "The Return to Europe: Issues in Post-Community Higher Education." In A. Levine (ed.), *Higher Learning in America: 1980–2000.* Baltimore: The John Hopkins University Press, 1993.

Cohen, Arthur M. "Community Colleges." In *International Encyclopedia of Education,* 2nd ed. New York: Pergamon Press, 1994.

Cohen, Arthur, and F. Brawer. *The American Community College,* 2nd ed. San Francisco: Jossey-Bass, 1989.

Eade, David. "Keynote Presentation." Western Regional Comparative and International Education Conference, Los Angeles, 1993.

Elsner, Paul A., Joyce S. Tsunoda, and Linda A. Korbel. "Building the Global Community: The Next Step." Points of Departure for the American Council on International Intercultural Education/Stanley Foundation Leadership Retreat, November 28–30, 1994.

Fersh, Seymour, and James Humphrys (eds.). "A Report of the Caribbean Conference Mid-level Manpower Technical/Vocational Training Projects." Organization of American States, Republic of Suriname. Cocoa, Fla.: CCID, 1992.

Harris, Mathilda. "Keynote Address to the Comparative and International Education Society Western Region Conference." Los Angeles, November 5–6, 1993.

Immerwahr, John, and Steve Farkas. *The Closing Gateway: Californians Consider Their Higher Education System.* San Jose: The California Higher Education Policy Center and the Public Agenda Foundation, 1993.

Ishumi, A.G.M. "Vocational Training as an Educational and Development Strategy: Conceptual and Practical Issues." *International Journal of Educational Development* 83 (1988): 163–74.

King, Maxwell C., and Seymour H. Fersh. *Integrating the International/Intercultural Dimension in the Community College.* Cocoa, Fla.: Association of Community College Trustees and Community Colleges for International Development, Inc., 1992.

Kintzer, Frederick C. "Higher Education Approaches the 21st Century: New Perspectives on Nonuniversities." Presentation to the Nova Southeastern University, August 1994.

———. "Higher Education Beyond the U.S.: A Glimpse of Short-Cycle Higher Education in Other Countries." *Community/Junior Community College Quarterly* 16, no. 1 (1992): 58–59.

———. "Kenya's Harambee Institutes of Technology." *Community College Review* 17, no. 3 (Winter 1990): 174–76.

———. "World Adaptation of the Community College Concept." In New Directions for Community Colleges Series No. 6 (San Francisco: Jossey-Bass, 1979).

Koltai, Leslie. "Are There Challenges and Opportunities for American Community Colleges on the International Scene?" Keynote address at the Comparative and International Education Society Western Region Conference, Los Angeles, November 5–6, 1993.

Organization for Economic Co-operation and Development (OECD). "A Search for Identity." Proceedings from the OECD Conference on Short-Cycle Higher Education, Paris, 1973.

Raby, Rosalind Latiner. "Identity and Community through Community College International Education." In *Comparative and International Education Society Newsletter.* Tallahassee, Fla.: Florida State University Learning Systems Institute Press, 1993: 3.

Time for Decision: California's Legacy and the Future of Education. A Report with Recommendations San Jose: The California Higher Education Policy Center, 1994.

9 Culture, Technology, Development

Partners with a Price Tag

Mathilda Esformes Harris

By the standards of the year 2050, we are all developing nations. Rich and poor nations, powerful and weak are created almost overnight. Once, Argentina enjoyed a standard of living equal to many European countries. Two decades ago, Lebanon was a modern and prospering country. Less than fifty years ago, Germany and Japan were the destroyed losers of a world war and Israel, Singapore, Taiwan, and South Korea were poor and underdeveloped. Three years ago, the cold war ended and Russia asked Europe and the United States to assist it financially. Compound growth or compound decline makes its mark.

It is not true that rich nations all grow richer and poor nations all grow poorer; it is true that the gap between those that grow and those that do not becomes ever more cavernous, and there are many countries that have chosen to put cultural pride before growth. Labor skills and motivation, natural resources, energy supplies, peace, and an inflow of capital may each be important in explaining the success stories of Japan, the United States, Taiwan, Germany, and South Korea. A clear mission, a sense of cultural identity, education, and opportunities are also key contributors.

This chapter is based on the appropriate combination of development, culture, and technology, but it is the imbalance that is at question here. It is the imposition of external values on a developing country that is an issue, not that these very values could be adopted and incorporated into the society by internal consensus. The latter process is highly complex and often mercurial for it involves many actors, voices, and beliefs. Nevertheless, this is an issue that is very much in the forefront of the minds of many institutions and nations involved in development, especially in the developing world.

One sector that is increasingly becoming involved in development projects is U.S. higher education. It is especially noteworthy for the purpose of this chapter that one of the most recent components of postsecondary education to enter the arena of international development has been the community college. The U.S., Canadian, Australian, British, German, and French community colleges are all exporting services in the name of development. In fact, over the past decade more and more community colleges are conducting some form of international development, sister-city relationships, and technology transfers. Significant to this endeavor has been the marketing of the community college model or a version of it to developing countries. Many factors have been and are contributing to the need for community college education abroad, and they are based on the need to educate women, rural populations, underrepresented groups at the university level, and new immigrants to urban areas. Access to education for many in the developing world means access to a higher status in society. However, the majority of the population is unable to develop the necessary skills or resources to even consider a university education. Thus, the community college can indeed serve as one important means of providing education to those who cannot otherwise obtain it. The question pertaining to this chapter is how this essential component of education can best be transferred to the developing world and how community colleges in the developed world should best work abroad.

The purpose of education at all levels is to prepare for social and cultural change. However, unlike other institutions, the function of higher education is to question accepted values and to impart a global way of thinking by providing alternatives to the same values. If this is not occurring, then how can higher education develop partners abroad? These issues are explored in the context of such broader issues as the meaning of development since World War II, the essence of appropriate technology transfers, and the significance of the "technological mind" and "traditional wisdom." The critical approach taken in this chapter is not to downgrade efforts that have occurred to date, but to give insight into how they can occur in a context where individual integrity and well-being is the primary consideration. Caution, thought, and understanding are the partners proposed, for a "blind" foreign advisor can do much more harm than good or, at the very least, have little to show for his or her advice. However, an informed intermediary can offer alternatives that may or may not be incorporated in another society or culture.

CULTURE AND TECHNOLOGY

Both developed and developing countries have had to struggle with the partnership between culture and technology, which often seems harmless to the fabric of a society and culture. However, a haphazard effort in the name of economic development is far from harmless to the foundation of cultural well-being. In most cases, few societies have seriously taken into consideration the relation of technology to cultural perpetuation and growth. Technology is accepted irrespective of what it may or may not do to the psychosocial makeup of a society. It is often said, for example, that in their human behavior, the highly developed countries have imitated their machines rather than liberated themselves from the chores that have become impossible without machines. How often have we been asked to think logically and linearly, make short and concise statements, and save time—all concepts of our machines rather than what we are: human beings who often defy logic, who are cyclical rather than linear, who have the ability to dream and to speak in ways that belong to art, poetry, and literature? So much has technology impacted our lives that we ridicule these ideas, shelve them in our grandmother's closet, or deem them as stuff that wastes time and lacks purpose, discipline, a sense of competition, and the need for success. The monomania to find one "savior" in the struggle for economic success and competition has clouded cultural and human development.

The basic procedural assumption made by the technological mind is that all evidence can and must be tested, that truth has no absolute meaning or ultimate epistemological foundation, and that there is no metaphysical substructure for regarding truths known to human minds as manifestations of natural essences. In other words, the technological mind is quantitative, cumulative in the belief that constant progress is verifiable, linear, and objective. A contrary image sustains most traditional values found in developing countries and in the cultures of many minorities in the United States. The latter view of the world in subjective, holistic, symbolic, qualitative, and allegorical. Traditional cultures do not assume that there has to be a cause and effect and that every statement needs to be exemplified and demonstrated. These two worldviews hold inherently contradictory beliefs, and one has to ask whether respect for diverse ways of looking at the world can indeed occur in substance rather than as superficial window dressing, or whether multiple cultural values can be partners with technology, especially in traditional cultures.

Traditional societies possess a certain wisdom that is born from the need to articulate a meaning for their world and existence. In nontraditional societies such as the United States, the meaning of the world is, in most cases, imparted through technologically dictated, formal education. This prepares students for an uncertain and ever changing world. In traditional societies, on the other hand, wisdom is meant to guide societies away from rapid change and is used to maintain integrity. This is exemplified best by Nikos Kazantzakis's work *Zorba the Greek*, in which a Greek widow is murdered by her community because she violated her culture when she accepted a foreigner for her lover. One would agree that her punishment was appalling; however, for the Greek villagers, this transgression was the beginning of an act that, if it had not been curtailed, would have brought change and destruction to the unity of their society and culture. Similarly, in Sholom Aleichem's work *Fiddler on the Roof*, tradition is violated. However, this was inevitable, since the Jews were living in a hostile environment in which change had already been imposed upon them, and their integrity as a unified group was severely threatened from without.

In order for traditional societies to become meaningful in present conditions, their wisdom needs to be integrated with technological rationality. On the other hand, what is often ignored is another reason for such integration: to find a new meaning and make sense of the realities that can neither be comprehended nor explained by technology. It has been witnessed over and over again that an immense thirst for some type of spiritual wisdom exists in developed countries, which is matched by a thirst for scientific and technological knowledge in developing countries and among subgroups in technologically advanced societies. The thirst for spiritual growth is best exemplified in a feature article in *Newsweek* that reports that 58 percent of Americans feel the need to experience spiritual growth and that 33 percent have had a religious or mystical experience:

> "A lot has changed in the last century," says Charles Nuckolls, an anthropologist at Emory University who studies religion and healing. "We've stripped away what our ancestors saw as essential—the importance of religion and family. . . . People feel they want something they've lost. But it has left a gaping hole." That in essence, is the seeker's quest: to fill the hole with a new source of meaning. Why are we here? What is the purpose of our existence? The answers change in each generation, but the questions are eternal. (Kantrowitz et al. 1994, 55)

The thirst for scientific and technical knowledge is illustrated by the UNESCO Sixth Regional Conference of Ministers of Education and Those Responsible for Economic Planning of Member States in Latin America and the Caribbean, held in Bogota, Colombia, in 1987. Among the various recommendations to emerge during this conference were two key priorities for Latin American education: (1) science, technology, and the world of work should be incorporated at all levels of education so that students are prepared in a realistic manner for the needs of their societies; and (2) educational, scientific, and technological research "should be promoted and refocused so as to throw more light on the characteristics and problems of local communities" (UNESCO 1987, 28). In many instances, in the 1990s, it is the community college model that now fulfills this role. Yet neither in theory nor in practice is mention made of incorporating this knowledge into the fabric of the culture in such a way that the society and the individual are not damaged or traumatized by an "either/or" approach. The question that remains to be asked during this and subsequent conferences is, how can both worlds merge so that society and the individual can benefit economically and culturally?

To pursue one form of knowledge to the detriment of the other or, even worse, to impose one form on the other without synthesis and understanding leads to the damaging of the individual and the society in which he or she exists. Carl Jung describes it in terms of the conscious and subconscious mind or in terms of the rational and the spiritual and, often, unexplainable. The individual cannot grow, develop, and achieve synthesis unless he or she is able to respect and unify the two and bring them together. The same phenomenon could easily apply to societies and cultures.

It is tragic when the technologically based societies deem the traditional approaches to be inferior to the rationality of modern approaches. Hence, what is needed is the recognition that traditional societies have created a wisdom that has meaning and integrity. More often than not, sudden change to that structure creates a cultural disorientation and alienation from the group and the self. Consequently, change cannot be imposed from without, such as through the introduction of a community college approach to education in developing nations. Change can only be proposed from within and in an evolutionary rather than a revolutionary manner.

The current trend in the United States is to speak of ethnic diversity, multiculturalism, and political correctness. Unfortunately, this is done in the name of acceptance and, in harsh terms, so that one can better swallow the idiosyncrasies of the "other." Diversity is advocated for the purpose of political correctness. The traditions, values, and "soul" of the "other" are to be understood and accepted for expediency's sake rather than for the differences that might threaten the empirical understanding of the scientific mind. In a global context, we speak of augmenting our knowledge of the "other," so that we can better compete in the global marketplace, as though the world is nothing more than one huge supermarket. Under these circumstances, the relationship between the "we" and "they" is rendered impotent and relegated to the realm of continued separation between cultures and societies. The ultimate implication is the same fear that dominated the Greek villagers in *Zorba the Greek*.

The struggle to understand the "other" has to center on alternate modes of knowledge and rationality. Unfortunately, as it currently stands, there is no solid basis for defending diversity and cultural understanding. However, the struggle is between two diametrically opposed beliefs and ways of understanding the world and coping with it. Laurens Van Der Post best describes the conflict and cacophony between the two worlds as follows:

> The white man came into Africa (and Asia and America for that matter) like a one-eyed giant, bringing with him the characteristic split and blindness which were at once his strength, his torment, and his ruin. . . . The one-eyed giant had science without wisdom, and he broke in upon ancient civilization which (like the medieval West) had wisdom without science; wisdom which transcends and unites, wisdom which dwells in the body and soul together and which, more by means of myth, or rite, or contemplation, than by scientific experiment, opens the door to a life in which the individual is not lost in the cosmos and in society but found in them. Wisdom which made all life sacred and meaningful—even that which later ages came to call secular and profane. (Van Der Post 1955, 7–8)

Development

Development for those societies that have accepted the technological and scientific approaches and that have not considered, or have an inherent appreciation or understanding of, traditional cultures is defined as a process of imposing technology from without. This can only lead to simplistic thinking in which development means economic success coupled with technological knowledge. Furthermore, the very word *development* implies inequities in economic power. To achieve this power, societies must compete in the global marketplace. To compete in this arena, knowledge of capitalism, which is tightly interwoven with technology and the linear mind, is the only possibility. Technology and global economics become the arena where the major ideological problems of power, control, and economic status are played out. The current global market condemns economically challenged countries to the status of commodities. Within this context, it is quite correct to assume that the less developed world needs to be fortified in its efforts toward development so that the marketplace for the developed world can be expanded. [Rarely is it vice versa.] Were there a plan of action between both worlds to create an economic arena where developing countries can be viable players, the world might not be seeing the complete collapse of Africa, the total disorientation of Russia and many of the newly independent countries, or the dilemma of first-generation immigrants in Western societies. It is less compromising for the economically powerful countries to give aid or charity to the poor than to be threatened by their development. What is evident here is that the partners capital, technology, and profit are ideologically wedded to a social process that permeates every aspect of Western society and its institutions. It is a way of viewing the world. Competition and Social Darwinism prevail in a blind faith that defies questions and criticism. Within this context, the superimposition of these values to any and all systems is the means by which the end can be justified. The ultimate price tag in terms of individual integrity and cultural survival is high.

The point here is that no society can integrate a technological base into its structure without considering the central values and culture (or cultures) within the society. Thus, "technology policy will be soundly developmental to the extent that the vital nexus linking values to development strategy and to the criteria for technology choices is explicitly acknowledged and consistently observed" (Goulet 1980, 33). Unfortunately, many developing nations are so heterogeneous, ethnically and culturally, that it makes it very difficult for them to define the values that permeate their societies. The Balkans, Latin America, and Africa are examples of regions where one set of values is promoted at the cost of the others, leading ultimately to the disasters that the world has recently witnessed in these countries. Ethnicity is another important contributor to the struggles taking place in much of the developing world and in demographically changing Western societies. In these societies, power is defined by values and beliefs that often perplex the developed world. In common parlance, one often expresses disbelief that one group of people would slaughter another in order to maintain their identities. The corollary, however, is that in the developed world symbolic slaughtering is done in the name of economic profit and competition. A culprit in this scenario has in many instances been the exportation of unplanned and inadequately researched models of higher education.

The term *development* has been bantered about so much in the last three decades that it is now little more than a synonym for the search for money, power, and national autonomy. Its basic definition has come to mean an increase in the gross national product, productivity, and standards of living. In accordance with Darwinian biology and theories of organization, development means hierarchical survival. However, experience and research have demonstrated that what works best is the multiplication of the sources of initiative in a society, as defined by a division of labor between the centers of command and the rest of the masses. In this sense, Ithiel de Sola Pool refers to a developed system as one with a complex division of labor, where the "initiative is taken in many places and where the results can be forecast not from any one center's will but only from complex interactions in the system" (Sola Pool 1990, 168). Sola Pool's emphasis is on traditional cultural values, self-reliance, and grass-roots initiatives. Values rooted in the culture take precedence over economic and political variables. Self-development planning and execution can then evolve through popular participation, through a bottom-up rather than a top-down strategy, and with many pathways to development. In a broad sense, development encompasses the gamut of processes and means by which a society moves away from a condition of life widely perceived as unsatisfactory toward one regarded as humanely better.

The development philosophy emerged and was applied in the 1970s and 1980s. This theory identifies the following characteristics of development, which are those associated with economic growth and the modernization of Western society: industrialization, urbanization, literacy and education, mass media, political unification, differentiation and specialization of societal institutions and structure, and a break-up of traditions that retard the industrialization process. Essentially growth in one of these fields was expected to stimulate growth in others, and thus, with the popular support of the people, the country would move toward modernization. Rostow and Rogers best exemplify this approach to development, and although they have been highly criticized and rejected by many contemporary social scientists, their approach is still felt in the ways that bilateral and multilateral projects are implemented worldwide. According to their theory, the ultimate goal of development was a rapid increase in the economic productivity of a society. Productivity was the key. If national rates of economic growth per capita could be sustained at rates of 2 to 3 percent, then the country would rapidly be on its way to modernization. Of course, it is understood that this usually applies to the wealthy in the society, but according to the trickle-down effect, the benefits would reach the masses eventually. Rather than directly compete with already market-oriented societies, poor countries were encouraged to use the less demanding tactic of import substitution. Using this scheme, for some imported good in its own market, a country would substitute domestic production, thereby subsidizing fledgling industries. Eventually, companies at home would compete with foreign companies in the world markets. Through import substitution, entrepreneurs with booming businesses were expected to employ local labor. Then, the revenues collected from employer and employee would rise along with their incomes, and the government would have greater funds and sponsor more development programs.

Implied in these methods is a dichotomy between traditional and modern societies. Traditional societies were perceived as limited in their capacity to cope with their problems or master their environment, whereas modern societies were seen as coping with a wider range of internal and external problems. Ideally, a modern society should be able to expand its institutional structure continuously, increase its capacity to absorb change, and develop other characteristics of modern societies such as rationality, efficiency, and the desire for liberty. The conditions for a viable, growth-sustaining modern society were tantamount to a continuous extension of modern components. Most of these goals were directly related to the disintegration of traditional society. Thus, the traditional labor-intensive society was supposed to give way to the growth of large-scale industries using machines and capital but little labor. Given the above restrictions, the next step was to transfer technological innovations from development agencies to clients and to create an appetite for change. The thirst for Western technology was created by the mass media and advertising, while education became the silent partner with business to help developing nations to use this technology. Thus, in most cases education did not question the validity of such transfers to the culture and society and would pick up private or public contracts for specific tasks abroad. Inexperienced in international development, unable to finance their activities abroad in any other way, and wishing to increase their domestic revenue, U.S. community colleges saw these contracts as an opportunity. Although this practice is still occurring today, there is, through bitter experience, an increased understanding that the foreign advisor abroad is only one of many factors contributing to change.

One of the dangers of importing production facilities into developing countries is that they divide the population further along class lines. The local ruling classes tend to be the ones who benefit from dependent development and who are more responsive to foreign cultural patterns. Usually, members of the elite and middle class are educated in the West and are exposed to the consumer life-style of affluent societies. As a result of their past grooming, these echelons are expected to feel more receptive to foreign messages of affluence. At the same time, there is a corresponding feeling of marginalization and exclusion on the part of "other" groups. Therefore, the foreign presence affects some by bringing them under the influence of alien cultural models but subjects others to levels of existence that prevent them from exerting minimal cultural rights. The result is that the importers control the culture and politics of the developing country, which in turn put pressure on the local power centers to help strengthen their own dependent industrialization. Wielding this power, multinational corporations support a society of free enterprise. Further, despite attempts to adapt the equipment, programs, technology, etc., every form of aid sent from an industrialized country to a developing country is inherently and inescapably a transmitter of industrial consumer culture and, thus, guilty of perpetuating the cultural disorientation of the developing country.

The view that best defines the above phenomenon is cultural hegemony, suggesting that the culture of developing countries is being expropriated and shaped by a new form of imperialism in the world, which affects both foreign supply and Third World demand for Western-style technology. Examples abound in such Latin-American countries as Peru, Colombia, and Mexico, where education has been highly influenced by the United States. The same phenomenon is also seen throughout Asia and Africa. This interaction with the West—particularly in its educational form—leads to an unbalanced, one-way flow of information and technology and to what has often been defined as "culture capital."

Technological Transfers

Development and technological transfers, from the simplest to the most sophisticated, have become inseparable partners. According to the diffusion theory, a popular concept in the 1970s, technological transfers were essentially executed as a three-step process. Initially, at the invention stage, new ideas would be created or developed. Second, ideas would be communicated to members of a given social system or adapted across social structures. Finally, changes would occur in the system as a result of adopting an innovation or actively seeking to reject it. Following the example set by the Green Revolution, it was assumed that scientific research developed in the West would be imported by developing countries through education. The Green Revolution typifies the use of dissemination as an innovation, and was developed in the West, raised in Thailand, and exported to India. The reasoning was that rich countries can afford to take risks and spend extensively on research and development.

The basic idea behind the diffusion model is that some products or attitudes must be adopted in order for the developing country to reach a new level of modernization, and the receiving agent must encourage their acceptance. On a community level, an agent of change will work in the region to promote adoption of technologies by engaging in dialogue with the people to understand their needs. The agent will focus her or his efforts on encouraging people to adopt a government-approved product that will supposedly resolve the need. Further, the agent must maintain favorable relations with the local leaders, for if the leaders do not actively support the idea, the product may fail to be adopted into the community. Because villages are the most common social organization of developing countries, endorsement on a village level is essential for an innovation to be successfully accepted across the country.

Rogers and Shoemaker's (1971) description of the four steps in an individual's decision-making process explains how the long-term acceptance of a given innovation is determined. First, an individual is exposed to the existence of an innovation and gains some understanding of how it functions. Then he or she forms a favorable or an unfavorable prejudice toward the innovation, and based on this judgment, the person makes a choice whether to adopt the innovation. After the choice has been made, the individual will continue to seek reinforcement for the decision; however, this does not discount the possibility that a previous decision can be reversed if the user is exposed to new or contrary experiences. At each stage in this method, the person is continuing to collect information from various sources, but the impact of these influences depends upon the stage of a person's decision making. Once the decision is reached, a person will more likely turn to friends, family, and the interpersonal network to discuss the innovation. The exponents of the diffusion model believed that if their innovations were to be accepted, their intervention was necessary at each of the levels of change.

This development model and its application presume a myriad of elements about change in developing countries, and this leaves it open to unfavorable criticism. When analyzed critically, this paradigm not only insults poor countries but also overestimates the power of its own design. On the one hand, the paradigm lumps all poor countries into the same category. According to the dogma, the existing mind-sets of these countries are assumed to be "traditional." This argument can be perceived as insulting in two ways. It assumes that all the problems of poor countries are internal and inherent in their poverty. Furthermore, it completely ignores the centuries of colonization forced upon developing countries. To add further insult, the path to development is a path created by colonizers themselves, and finally, this kind of thinking hinders the countries' development.

On the other hand, the paradigm completely overestimates its own effectiveness and does not accurately predict the outcomes of people's efforts to follow the path of development. If ever a country could succeed in acquiring all the necessary inputs for growth, then its economy would presumably be able to sustain the same patterns of growth and the exact same rates of economic change (2 to 3 percent) as every other country, poor or rich. Once a country achieves the prescribed rate of economic growth, it is expected to continue at the same rate. In practice, this is not altogether true. Rates of growth tend to fluctuate over five to ten years, and it is not until decades later that some overall growth rate can be declared. In addition, there is no accounting for failure and no explanation of why a country may not succeed. By its silence on this matter, the paradigm faults the country for not succeeding. The greater fault of the dominant paradigm is the assumption that all poor societies are similar. Although it is possible in the paradigm to diverge from the norm in a transitional stage, dynamic forces should push the country out of this phase eventually, and once past this phase, the country should resume the same patterns as all other modernizing societies. So, every society is expected to experience almost exactly the same growth rates and patterns of change. The idea of sameness among countries challenges the evidence, which points to the contrary. Even among rich countries, no two economies are exactly the same. Despite similar circumstances (be it on the national, city, or individual level), change is not linearly predictable. Moreover, there is little mention of how the economic growth is to be distributed.

Tradition is seen as something that holds countries and groups back from modernization; from this perspective, tradition may as well be the antithesis of modernization and development. In fact, most of the characteristics of being "less developed" seem to be inherent in every poor country or group, as though there are internal elements that keep it from being able to develop without the assistance of developed societies. Yet, this idea completely overlooks the ample evidence that colonialism is a cause of underdevelopment. Instead of noticing that exploitative relationships may have crippled the poor country or group, the paradigm attributes the state of being less developed to factors within the traditional society itself. Much of the blame for this resistance to development is placed on the village or the individual; both are seen as fatalists, tradition-bound, and unresponsive to technological innovation or modern ways of thinking. A farmer is seen as the obstacle to development, especially when he is unresponsive to adopting the new innovation or attitude.

The developed nation's road to social change is implicitly understood to be synonymous with development. The results should then be free enterprise and rapid economic growth through industrialization and urbanization. This reveals an obvious disrespect for a poor country, a given region, or group by taking away all responsibility for development away from them. The necessary inputs for growth will be contributed by the developed country, and it is the developed country's prescribed goals and standards that determine when the poor country or group has graduated from one level to the next. Success and glory will belong to the West, but by design, the failures will all belong to the developing country. All possible barriers to development are characteristic of the country itself. Overall, this model of development works best as a description of what has happened in the developed country than as a predictor of change in the developing countries.

If one assumes that development was intended to transfer control of a society to its own people, then technological transfers work against this goal. The introduction of technology from the developed world can hardly be considered equivalent to legitimate development. Such a transfer does not encourage the developing society to rely on the creative energy of its own people. Even if these developing countries created their own imitations of such products, they would still have to purchase the concept. Reliance on outside influence of this kind creates a dependence on the part of the receiver, a dependence that opposes the ideas of self-control and self-reliance.

In the diffusion method, there is a silent assumption that all innovations are good and should be adopted. Yet, innovations transferred from one society may not be useful in another social context. There are many examples of adoptions of new ideas or technologies that lead to unexpected or undesirable consequences, so that the net result for the village or society is negative. For example, the introduction of agricultural innovations in the Green Revolution was capital-intensive in nature, and only relatively well-off societies could afford new seed, new fertilizers, and new machines as well as the educational knowledge to utilize these new inventions effectively. Often this created a dependence on the developed nation and divided the host country's class structure even further. In these elements is founded the dependence theory, most espoused beginning in the late 1960s and developed principally by the theorists and technocrats of developing countries. Many centers of research, such as the Center of Economics and Politics for Latin America (CEPAL), as well as major Latin American universities, attempted to create their own agricultural technology so that they would not be dependent on that of the developed world. However, they modeled these innovations after the developed world. In the case of Peru, the Agrarian University established programs for the improvement of seeds. However, these programs paralleled the approach of the University of Nebraska, mainly because Alberto Fujimori—an agronomist, the current president of Peru, and the ex-president of the university—received his training and graduated from the University of Nebraska. In this case, we continue to witness improvements that are modeled after those in the developed world. It is for this reason that such products as potatoes and corn in Peru are more expensive to produce in Peru than they are in the developed world, and that Peru currently imports industrial corn from the United States. Indigenous Peruvian and Bolivian products such as quinoa and kiwicha are being developed but at a much slower rate, because of the cost of marketing such products abroad.

The important point to be made here is that U.S. institutions of higher education—which often train the future visionaries, leaders, researchers, and policymakers of other countries—have paid little attention to creating alternative models that would apply to the needs, and contribute to the economic independence, of poorer countries. Furthermore, community colleges—which deal directly with industry, agriculture, and technology—ignore indigenous contributions. In turn, those institutions abroad requesting "assistance" perceive the value of importing such education and are doing so in increasing numbers. This is a two-way process, in that U.S. community colleges want to export education for financial reasons and developing country colleges want to import this education, which they have defined to be valuable. Examples abound, including the CONALEP (Colegio Nacional de Educación Profesional Ténica) schools in Mexico, the Central American Peace Scholarship programs that sends students to U.S. community colleges to learn agriculture technology, and the recent Japanese fiasco, in which U.S. community colleges were financed by Japanese business and individual financiers to set up U.S.-model campuses in Japan. Thus, in most cases institutions of higher education in developed countries—including the community colleges—continue to perpetuate the one and only model that worked in developed nations. Whenever the model fails, there is the spoken and unspoken assumption that somehow the indigenous and traditional approaches keep countries chained to an anachronistic past.

The community college model often resembles the technical schools model in such countries as Thailand, Nigeria, and Taiwan. Each of these countries has experimented with the U.S. community college model. Mahidol University (Thailand), a medical school that later added other disciplines, incorporated a two-year terminal and transfer program. Although it was successful in its efforts, the community college flourished best in the rural and less populated areas of the country because it served a population that could most benefit form such disciplines as technical education, nursing, and teacher training. A similar model also worked well in Taiwan, serving students who would not be going to the university. Because of its economic programs in the 1980s and 1990s, Nigeria was most interested in the U.S.

educational model, but it could not develop the community college nor find the necessary resources to do so. Thus, the traditional educational model continues to educate the few, and sadly, the four-year institutions in Nigeria remain in disarray.

With a kind of intellectual arrogance, the developed world assumes that since economic power is concentrated there, so is intellectual power (Altbach 1984; Latapi 1982). Altbach contends that such "culture capital" as research, publishing, language, and curriculum are all concentrated in the developed world and imparted to the developing world, which thus superimposes a value system that is not indigenous to the cultures of the developing world. Accordingly, language and culture are closely linked to a hierarchy of international values, and "high level . . . materials dominate most of the publications and scholarship" (Altbach 1984, 236). Again, the developed nations' road of social change is analogous with economic development. More important, partnerships between institutions of higher education are in terms of assistance rather than cooperation. This vicious circle can be represented as follows: (1) assistance = dependency and imitation; (2) dependency and imitation = needs; (3) needs = the purchasing of cultural capital or, if the developing country is unable to purchase it, the feeling of being limited in the ability to educate appropriately; and (4) limitation = frustration, loss of morale, and continued dependence on assistance.

In the past, those schools of thought that have criticized the dominant paradigm have based their critiques on a more global "structural" analysis of development called the "infrastructure approach." This approach integrates economic, political, social, technological, and cultural factors and places the human being at the *center* of all development, not at its mercy. This kind of model claims to be more self-determined and respectful of the cultural and historical specifics of societies that define their own development and the means they use. It is associated with the creation of new solidarities, with the resurgence of regional and national cultural-identity movements, with giving a voice to rural populations, and with the appearance of new agents of civil society on the political scene (women, youth, national minorities, etc.). Although it does not take responsibility as the sole bearer of social change or development, this infrastructure approach is at the center of struggles for democratic functioning in many societies.

Advocates of the infrastructure approach will argue that development is, ideally and above all, a mass phenomenon. It is a dispersion throughout society of independent judgment, self-confidence, and initiative. Development here is defined as a self-fulfilling prophecy, so that if the people in a developing country have more breadth of perception and are more future-oriented, receptive to change, and motivated to achieve, then the result will be the creation of a new citizen. Golding claims that the objectives of the infrastructure approach are to:

1. Raise awareness about specific events and the implications of such events for the masses (media as informal educators);

2. Bring social needs of the people to the attention of the government so as to provoke the government into action (media as social conscience);

3. Publicize local self-help projects by the people in order to encourage other communities to emulate the practice. (Golding 1977, 303)

In this view, it is not development if farmers use a better fertilizer or a better strain of seed just because they have been ordered to do so; it is development if they become experimental scientific farmers regardless of what fertilizer or seed they happen to choose. Development must stem from many centers; it will not succeed if it flows down the line of government channels to the people. Indeed, no government, no party, and no single authority is wise enough to decide what needs to be done in all parts of the complex system of a society. The infrastructure theorists argue that wisdom is widely dispersed, and people are more likely to be better at problem solving "on the spot" rather than with the help of an outside planner. The infrastructure approach has several virtues, including its acceptability by the people, its cultural relevance, the use of local language, its flexibility, and its ability to allow two-way communication. In this approach, decentralization plays an important role in enabling various regional identities to strengthen, and perhaps add their contributions to, the country's cultural mélange.

There were and continue to be other prevalent development theories, especially those that were espoused by the liberation-theology advocates. In the 1980s Denis Goulet best exemplified this view in the United States. Liberation theology defended the preservation of cultural identity and centered on the need for assessment and on the ideas that guide assessment in the context of development. Technological transfers, they argued, must be evaluated as part of the larger picture of their effects on environment, employment, standards of living, cultural integrity, and human rights. Goulet poses the following question: "Do all human communities enjoy a collective right to preserve their cultural identity? Scholars rarely ask whether cultural groups, like individual persons, are the subject of rights protecting their communal personality from violation. The problem arises acutely within contexts of development, because the relationship between human rights and development is itself ambiguous" (Goulet 1980, 1).

More recently, in, *Postmodern Education: Politics, Culture, and Social Criticism* (1991), Henry Giroux and Stanley Aronowitz argue that schooling is a form of cultural politics and that pedagogy needs to reflect popular culture in order to be effective to the masses. As it currently stands, for those in many developing countries and minority groups who seek an education that can be meaningful to them and their culture, there has been an array of broken promises. The hidden curriculum is geared to alienate the masses from their spiritual and cultural centers, and the result is social control and conformity to the status quo. Thus, argues Giroux, not until there is radical social change and reform in education (societal and curricular changes) and a critical theory of and rationality in citizenship education can the culture be maintained and respected. The work of Peter McLaren and, in Brazil, Jose Ribas Vieira also voices the need for radical reform in education, so that culture can be preserved and the many rather than the few can be effectively educated.

In the 1990s developing countries are becoming stronger international players. Many have entered the technological arena as importers and exporters. Over the past twenty years, such Asian countries as Taiwan, South Korea, Singapore, and Thailand, which were considered to be developing, have built industrialized and information-based economies, and they are now effectively competing in the marketplace. There were many factors that led to this achievement, two of which were their concerted efforts to promote education at all levels and their ability to adopt external technology to their own cultures rapidly. Similarly, Brazil is now exporting mass media to countries throughout the world, whereas a decade ago they were major importers of media from the United States. These are cases of countries in which development was accepted from without but adapted from within. However, the cultural alienation of many remains an important area of concern if these countries want to effectively coordinate the technological and traditional spheres.

The end of the cold war brought with it a redefinition of development assistance. Democratization and business expertise are now the key elements governing development and technology transfers. Russia and the newly independent states are looking to the developed countries to supply them with this expertise. On the other side of the coin, ethnicity and culture are the main issues that are dictating the deadly regional conflicts in this area, and ethnicity and culture are creating many of the difficult issues confronting the United States. The very elements that economists, scientists, and technocrats failed to address are now in the forefront. Cultural and ethnic issues, and not economics or modernization or democratization, are determining the failure or success of the ex–Soviet bloc countries and the Middle East and are causing the serious internal problems within many of the developed countries. In such heterogeneous societies, latent with ethnic and cultural conflicts for centuries, the priority is not democratization or business expertise but cultural and ethnic preservation.

The end of the cold war also saw the total collapse of many African countries, now left with no assistance from the superpowers. Basic necessities such as food and shelter are the current realities in the majority of African countries. Yet, this does not come as a surprise to anyone with even the slightest historical understanding of Africa. Technology transfers that were totally alien to the indigenous populations, continued exploitation, lack of respect for the cultures of rural populations, continued colonialism by the upper echelons of the society, and political and economic destabilization created by the superpowers in order to achieve control are examples of what caused the Africa of today.

Criticisms of the supply-side and demand-side approaches to cultural imperialism have revealed errors in judging the international market for culture-bearing products. One argument (Sreberny-Mohammedi 1990), looking back in time to late nineteenth-century imperialism, suggests that the very term *cultural imperialism* tends to obscure the many deep and diverse cultural effects of past imperialism, including the export of religion, educational systems, values, and European languages and administrative practices, all of which have long ago, and perhaps irretrievably, altered the cultural milieux of the colonized. Such an argument questions the utility of terms such as *authenticity* and *indignity* within a lengthy history of cultural contact, absorption, and recreation, and suggests that a cultural debate on modern technology transfers neglects other older and deeper structures, which may embody "foreign" values but may also be the pillars of modernization.

There is also a conceptual challenge to the cultural imperialism model stemming from new modes of analyzing media, and these new analyses question the "international hypodermic needle" assumption proffered by cultural imperialism. In the international communications debate, suggestions have been made that diverse audiences bring their own interpretive frameworks and sets of meaning into media texts and therefore resist, reinterpret, and reinvent any foreign "hegemonic" cultural products (Katz and Wedell 1977). Similarly in education, each student brings with him or her the student's values and culture, which reinterpret the same plots in order to reinforce the local values.

Cultural hegemony depicts an international framework in which all the major forces shaping development are determined by Western countries and motivated by an age-old pursuit to establish and maintain economic domination over economically challenged countries. This set of theories ominously suggests that far from speeding up the economic development of the Third World, technology transfers and specifically education are actually hurtling it into dependency. Since Gunder-Frank's writings on Latin America in the mid-1960s and throughout the 1970s, cultural hegemony has become a topic of intense debate, and its proposals have been refuted historically, empirically, and conceptually.

Nonetheless, cultural hegemony presents a compelling argument. It echoes the frustration of developing countries, which have been striving to speed up development by investing, in some cases, two decades' worth of resources in Western-designed products and technology. Further, it emphasizes the need for culturally sensitive methods of transforming countries in the developing world. Unlike previous perspectives on development, cultural imperialism revealed that what happens on a local level affects development just as much as events occurring on the national and even international levels do. The introduction of the concept of cultural hegemony began a debate over the true nature and intent of international relations.

HIGHER EDUCATION

To address the role that higher education in general, and the community college model in particular, can play in the conundrum of technology and culture, one would have to ask how value-free is the U.S. educational community and what success has it had in augmenting respect for ethnic and international diversity on campus. The answer lies in the way that institutions encourage international and intercultural/multicultural studies. In a survey titled "Attitudes and Activities of Full-Time Faculty Members, 1989–90" based on the responses of 35,478 faculty members at 392 colleges and universities, the September 1994 issue of the *Chronicle of Higher Education* reported that of twenty-two issues noted as being of highest or high priority at each faculty member's institution, "creating a diverse multicultural environment on campus" scored near the bottom of the list, while international studies did not even appear on the tally ("The Nation" 1994, 34). More disturbing facts are the increasing incidents of prejudice against minorities on U.S. campuses. In 1993 the Anti-Defamation League's audit of anti-Semitic acts reported that the instances of such acts on American campuses had jumped by 126 percent since 1988. "Paralleling the *Audit*'s findings for the general community, there were far more campus incidents of personal harassment, threat and assault than those involving vandalism in 1993" (Schwartz 1993, 5).

Further insight into the current educational ambience can be discerned in the curricular offerings of U.S. institutions of higher education at all levels of instruction. The reward systems of state-supported institutions can easily be seen in salaries, the departmental allocation of resources, and the level of power wielded by certain departments. According to the *Chronicle of Higher Education* (September 1994) survey of 88,733 faculty members of all ranks at 307 public four-year institutions, the highest-paid faculty are in the sciences, business, and computer information (salaries averaging approximately $55,000); while the poorest-paid faculty are in the humanities (averaging approximately $40,000) (p.36). The poor, vulnerable, and constantly harassed departments are those that pertain and are similar to traditional societies. Those in the departments of art, literature, history, classics, drama, music, languages, and, yes, international and ethnic studies are all paid much less and are vulnerable to taxpayers' whims and to further weakening by the administration. It is argued that these, after all, do not prepare students for the labor market. The persistent echo of the society from which these institutions stem is that the individual is a product for the labor market and, thus, must be objectified and validated and must resemble the machines of our time. The essence of who and what we are is all relegated to science, business, and technology.

In the *Sound and the Fury*, William Faulkner leaves the reader with the parting thought that the spirit and soul of the individual will prevail no matter how much it is violated, silenced, and trapped. In a sense what we see at our institutions of higher education is the struggle of other voices. The voices of another era continue to be heard in the halls of academe, but these are frightened, impotent voices trying to make a case to deaf ears. Those who are meant to listen are plagued with voices from without that say: "The taxpayers need accountability, workers must be trained according to the needs of industry, and industry needs specialists trained in practical fields." The budgets of these institutions, which are dictated by taxpayers and industry, strive to prepare the middle managers, the business persons, the bureaucrats, and the technocrats. The rich and private institutions, on the other hand, can give themselves and their students the luxury of contemplation, including the study of the humanities and the arts. They prepare their students to be the leaders, visionaries, and thinkers of the private and public sectors locally, nationally, and internationally. The parallel is easily made that the leaders of the profit sector, primarily educated at the elite U.S. institutions, need human labor, which serves as a commodity in their need to increase profits nationally and globally. The hall of mirrors reflects the same images for individuals, their institutions, and their countries. Again and again, machinelike terms such as "quantifiable," "human resource capacities," "labor supply," "human capital," "cheap labor," and "oversupply of labor" are applied.

The community colleges also fit within the above categories, since they are more closely tied to their communities and thus are serving human needs that are often left unanswered in other areas of higher education. The students they teach are those who often suffer or will suffer the changes in the economic system and marketplace. These changes will necessitate retraining, which these institutions now supply as what is called "lifelong learning." They also cater to the spiritually starved population through their course offerings in the arts and crafts and through lectures and support-group workshops. The number of participants in these courses is growing, and only the newest, flexible, humble, and community-based institution is meeting the societal neglect caused by the linear and technological mind.

What roles do and can community colleges play globally? Since they have experience with community-based education and since they are by their very nature flexible in their course offerings, they can serve an important global outreach purpose. However, the question is, how prepared are these institutions to serve this purpose? At this juncture of their development, they lack the commitment, the community support, the funds, and the personnel to be able to work abroad effectively. Other than having foreign students study on campus and study-abroad programs for domestic students, the role of community colleges in the global arena has yet to be defined nor accepted. For example, the tenure and promotion system does not make allowances for or encourage international involvement and research. Junior faculty are tied to the tenure clock, which does not allow for time spent on international projects. Senior faculty conditioned by the domestic agenda equally opt, for the most part, to stay at home. It is not unusual to find faculty abroad specializing in various disciplines, unable to speak the language of the country effectively, or not having traveled to that country for several years. These scholars often speak among themselves rather than with their foreign colleagues.

If higher education and, specifically, the community colleges are going to be involved in development efforts abroad, the following recommendations for change within the institution need to be given foremost consideration. The first recommendation is that there has to be a redefinition of self-interest, which needs to take place in a global context, so that the well-being and welfare of humanity are given primary consideration. Education is an important vehicle for the transmission of knowledge and culture, and it is for this reason that education should be a key factor in the redefinition of self-interest. According to Ward, the mandate for academia is "to see the world not as a nest of enemies and traitors, but as a human community" (quoted in Hamblin 1985, 17). This is a difficult task, for as Morse states: "International cooperation to help two-thirds of humanity help itself to achieve a reasonable quality of life in equitable relationships with all peoples is an idea that is still fragile, still delicate, because it is so new in the history of humanity" (Morse 1986, 8). The task does not merely involve teaching about culture, comparing educational systems, or teaching about developing countries. A much more rigorous approach needs to be taken, and it should encompass: (a) the meaning of culture in its relationship to power and economics, (b) the meaning of underdevelopment within the global political and economic context, and (c) the role of education as an active contributor to the development process of nations.

The second recommendation is to create programs of study that encompass the foregoing approaches. This can be accomplished if institutional and departmental efforts include (a) curriculum revisions; (b) faculty research abroad; (c) the establishment of long-term relationships with colleges and universities in developing nations; (d) the incorporation of the scholarship of developing nations into the curricular offerings; (e) the development of joint-degree programs with universities in developing countries, so that students can study in two out of several countries for a determined period of time; (f) field studies on Third World development for faculty and internship programs for students; and (g) the inclusion in libraries of the works of scholars from developing nations.

Curriculum

The study of development should be interdisciplinary, focusing on languages, social sciences, the humanities, and courses related to a student's major. Issues should be viewed from various cultural, political, economic, social, and literary perspectives, so that multiple conclusions are drawn from a single problem. Thus, a problem-oriented approach that coordinates and sees the links between sectors would take place. As Haag has suggested, this would lead to "a comprehensive or global way of thinking which first looks on the system to be explained as part of larger systems" (Haag 1982, 27). Development, technology, and culture would also need to be examined in the same way. "This implies knowing and explaining, among other things, how it [culture, technology, and development] is structured and for what reason" (Latapi 1982, 165). The challenge of this curriculum is to assist faculty and students to "comprehend the implications of the transnationalization [sic] of human affairs and to recognize the many interactive factors and dynamics that are fostering complexity" ("Shaping the Future" 1984, 5–6). The end result of such a curriculum will not be to create policymakers and planners for developing nations, but to create scholars and individuals who can speak with each other within a larger context that would equally apply to developing and developed nations.

Research

Although the recommendations concerning research and publications (discussed in the next section) do not necessarily apply to community colleges, there is increasing evidence that community college faculty are involved in research and publications. Accordingly, joint research is an area where the educational academic community can greatly benefit from the expertise that would be shared between scholars in developing and developed nations. Models for development would be a priority for this research, for such issues as equity, access to higher education by the underrepresented minorities, poverty, women's issues, grass-roots and community-based problems, cultural integration, and change are universal concerns; and if this research is to have any value, it should be just as applicable to, and just as important for, wealthier nations.

Publications

One of the frustrations of scholars from developing nations is that they are unable to publish their works in developed nations, even though the reverse easily takes place. Joint research would result in such publications, and more important, the research and publications from developing nations would be published and incorporated into the courses of study of U.S. institutions. If institutions of higher education are willing to be major players in the global arena, these efforts need to be supported philosophically and financially and be part of the tenure and promotion criteria.

Foreign Students

A dialogue and joint partnership must be established between U.S. institutions and developing countries so that a foreign student's education is relevant to the development process of his or her country. These partner institutions should devise a mechanism to monitor jointly the course of study offered to these students. This might be in the form of students taking courses at both institutions and being awarded joint degrees, or it may be in the form of internships whereby the student would periodically return to his or her country to apply his or her educational training.

Developing Long-Term Relationships between Institutions

Although long-term relationships between institutions of higher education do exist and are the most effective means of cooperation, this cooperation needs to be equal and should maximize the knowledge and expertise of both worlds, so that the contribution of scholars from developing nations can be just as essential and important as that from developed nations. This can occur once the redefinition of self-interest takes place, and the above educational plan becomes a comprehensive course of study for U.S. institutions. Although it is encouraging to note that some American and Canadian community colleges have adopted many of the foregoing recommendations, these colleges are still few and far between.

THE ROLE OF HIGHER EDUCATION

Since the purpose, philosophy, and function of U.S. higher education vary significantly from institution to institution, the role that each element plays abroad should reflect the institution's individual strengths. The community colleges, for example, can serve an important function in grass-roots education; lifelong learning; adult education; vocational education (when combined with transfer courses to four-year institutions); distance education; basic education in medicine, agriculture, and literacy; community education; and other programs that community colleges teach so well on their campuses. These, however, can only be applied abroad once an understanding of the implications of transferring programs from one culture to another takes place, and once these programs demonstrate a respect for the cultural milieu and fabric of the society that may be receiving them. As stated previously, a "blind" foreign advisor can do much more harm than good, but an informed intermediary can offer various alternatives that may or may not be incorporated by the host country. Success in this case is in offering alternatives within the broad context of the culture and society considering them.

The remarks of J. Brian Atwood to the Society for International Development best exemplify the theses of this chapter: "Our work is Human Development, not just 'development,' and only human development is sustainable. The improvement of society cannot be divorced from the improvement of people. We have to embrace that notion, and all the complexities it implies" (Atwood 1993, 5–6). These are difficult undertakings that surpass the perimeter of little technical niches. Atwood continues as follows:

Consider, for instance, the commitments we undertake when we endeavor to save the life of one little girl. Let's say she lives in a village, and she's the beneficiary of a program that provides inoculations against childhood diseases. What does saving her life really entail?

If you inoculate her, so she doesn't die of whooping cough or rubella, then you have to provide childhood nutrition, so her mind and body can develop.

If you feed her, then you have to provide adequate schooling so she is literate enough to understand her world.

If you educate her, then you have to provide proper housing and sanitation, so she can enter adulthood with youthful energy, and not exhausted from parasites and disease.

If you house her, then you have to provide some rural economic stability, which itself implies environmental planning and appropriate technology.

If she grows up in a stable rural environment, then you have to provide vocational training, so she can learn a skill that gives her an income and a sense of accomplishment.

If you help her acquire vocational training, then you have to address her role as a woman, including her reproductive rights, her economic rights, and her social status, so she is not isolated from the rest of society or rendered powerless.

And finally, if you do all these things, you have to help her nation build democracy, so she is not a recipient of aid, but a participant in her own development. (Atwood 1993, 5)

REFERENCES

Altbach, P.G. "The Distribution of Knowledge in the Third World: A Case Study in Neocolonialism." In P.G. Altbach and G.P. Kelly (eds.), *Education and the Colonial Experience*. New Brunswick, N.J.: Transaction Books, 1984.

Aronowitz, S., and H. Giroux. *Postmodern Education: Politics, Culture, and Social Criticism*. Minneapolis: University of Minnesota Press, 1991.

Atwood, B.J. Remarks to the Society for International Development (unpublished speech). Washington, D.C.: U.S. AID, 1993.

Eisenstadt, S.N. "The Changing Vision of Modernization and Development." In W. Schramm and D. Lerner (eds.), *Communication and Change: The Last Ten Years and the Next*. Hawaii: East-West Center Press, 1976, 33–46.

Faulkner, W. *The Sound and the Fury*. New York: Vintage Books, 1956.

Frank, A.G. *Capitalism and Underdevelopment in Latin America*. New York: Monthly Review Press, 1969.

Fuenzalida, E.F. "The Contribution of Higher Education to a New International Order." In B.C. Sanyal (ed.), *Higher Education and the New International Or-*

der. Paris: United Nations Educational, Scientific and Cultural Organization, 1982.

Fukuyama, F. *The End of History and the Last Man*. New York: The Free Press, 1992.

Golding, P. "Media Professionalism in the Third World: The Transfer of an Ideology." In J. Curran, M. Guverich, and J. Woollacott (eds.), *Mass Communication and Society*. London: Edward Arnold, in association with the Open University Press, 1977.

Goulet, D. "In Defense of Cultural Rights: Technology, Tradition and Conflicting Models of Rationality." *Human Rights Quarterly* 3, no. 4 (1981): 1–18.

———. "Development Experts: The One-Eyed Giants." *World Development* 7 no. 8 (1981): 481–89.

———. "What Price Technology?" In *Issues and Choices: The Americas in the 1980's*. Washington, D.C.: Organization of American States, 1980.

Haag, D. *The Right to Education: What Kind of Management?* Paris: United Nations Educational, Scientific and Cultural Organization, 1982.

Hamblin, F.N. *International Teacher Education. A Synthesis of Thirteen Resource Papers*. Report No. SP-026-860. Washington, D.C.: American Association of Colleges for Teacher Education for the Guidelines for International Teacher Education Project, 1985. ERIC Document Reproduction Service No. ED 265 102, 1985.

Heilbroner, R.L. *The Nature and Logic of Capitalism*. New York: W.W. Norton, 1985.

Jung, C. *Psychological Reflections*. Y. Jacobi (ed.), New York: Harper and Row, 1961.

Kantrowitz, B., P. King, D. Rosenberg, K. Springen, P. Wingert, T. Namuth, and T. Gegax. "In Search for the Sacred: America's Quest for Spiritual Meaning." *Newsweek* CXXIV, No. 2 (1994): 52–55.

Katz, E., and G. Wedell. *Broadcasting in the Third World: Promise and Performance*. Cambridge, Mass.: Boston University Press, 1977.

Kazantzakis, N. *Zorba the Greek*. New York: Simon and Schuster, 1959.

Latapi, P. "Some Lines of Action for Universities in Least Developed Countries in the Light of the New International Order." In B.C. Sanyal (ed.), *Higher Education and the New International Order*. Paris: Frances Pinter and The United National Educational, Scientific and Cultural Organization, 1982.

McLaren, P.L. "Education as Counter-Discourse." *Review of Education* 3, no. 1, (1987): 58–68.

Merton, T. *Gandhi on Non-Violence*. New York: New Directions, 1965. See also D. Goulet, "Development Experts: The One-Eyed Giants." *World Development* 7, no. 8 (1981): 37.

Morse, B. "UNDP: What It Is, What It Does. 1985—And Toward the 1990s." Annual Report of the United Nations Development Programme. New York: United Nations Development Programme, 1986.

Rogers, E.M. *Diffusion in Innovations*. New York: The Free Press, 1962.

———. "The Passing of the Dominant Paradigm—Reflection on Diffusion Research." In *Communication and Change*. Hawaii: University Press of Hawaii, 1976.

Rogers, E.M., and L. Antola. "Television Flows in Latin America." *Communication Research* 11, no. 2 (1984): 183–202.

Rogers, E.M., and F. Shoemaker. *Communication of Innovations: A Cross-Cultural Approach*. New York: The Free Press, 1971.

Rostow, W.W. *Stages of Economic Growth: A Non-Communist Manifesto*. Cambridge: Cambridge University Press, 1960.

Schwartz, A.M. (ed.), *Audit of Anti-Semitic Incidents*. New York: Anti-Defamation League, 1994.

"Shaping the Future of International Studies." Conference Report of a Wingspread Conference (Report No. SO-017-003). New York: Global Perspectives in Education. Eric Document Reproduction Service No. ED 268 027, 1984.

Sola Pool, I. de *Technologies without Boundaries*. Cambridge, Mass.: Harvard Uni-

versity Press, 1990.
Sreberny-Mohammedi, A. "The Global and the Local in International Communications." In J. Curran and M. Gurevich (eds.), *Mass Media and Society*. New York: Routledge, Chapman and Hall, 1990.
Stein, J. *Fiddler on the Roof: Based on Sholom Aleichem Stories*. New York: Limelight Editions, 1990.
"The Nation: Attitudes and Activities of Full-Time Faculty Members." *The Chronicle of Higher Education* XLI, no. 1 (1994): 34–36.
United Nations Educational, Scientific and Cultural Organization (UNESCO). *Final Report: Sixth Regional Conference of Ministers of Education and Those Responsible for Economic Planning of Member States in Latin America and the Caribbean*. Paris: UNESCO, 1987.
Van Der Post, Laurens. *The Dark Eve in Africa*. New York: William Morrow, 1955.
Vieira, J.R. *O Autoritarismo e a Ordem Constitucional No Brasil*. Rio de Janeiro: Editora Renovar, 1988.
Ward, B. *Rich Nations Poor Nations*. New York: W.W. Norton, 1962.

10 The Role of the Community College in Countering Conflict in Multicultural Societies

Cornelia H. van der Linde

In this chapter, the discussion of the role of community colleges in countering conflict in multicultural societies encompasses an examination of community colleges in the United States, Canada, Malaysia, and South Africa. The ongoing reform in U.S. community colleges provides valuable suggestions for conflict resolution in a multicultural society. Community college models in Canada and Malaysia are examined because these multicultural societies have also experienced conflict because of ethnic and other diversity. Experiential knowledge gained from community colleges in the United States, Canada, and Malaysia is also considered for application to South African community college institutions, so that they may counter conflicts during their current transition period.

For this chapter, the following assumptions apply. The better trained a person is, (a) the more employment opportunities become available to that person, (b) the less susceptible that person becomes to victimization, and (c) the better equipped that person becomes to handle friction and conflict. Thus, the community college becomes more than an academic, training, or retraining facility; it becomes an institution that offers individuals opportunities for avoiding victimization and for enhancing personal empowerment.

The New Millennium and Change

The author's premise is that the rapidly approaching advent of the new millennium will usher in a new *zeitgeist,* marking a radical departure for the intellectual and cultural history of humankind. It will demand that discrimination against class or race be finally removed from the face of the earth. In this new age, the ordinary person and his or her understanding of the world will be the focus of attention. This is already observable in the shift away from formal academic education and toward a less formal education that inculcates life skills. A person should be able to use his or her knowledge constructively in order to find worthwhile employment in a world where large-scale unemployment has become endemic.

Political, economic, and social change is taking place on a global scale, despite the vast majority of humankind's inherent and inveterate resistance to change, since "on the individual level, we will even distort evidence right in front of us in order to maintain our chosen attitudes and beliefs" (Tavris 1982, 209). This resistance toward change is due to the fear and uncertainty of those affected by it, since they increasingly feel that they are losing control of their situation as it changes. Leaders of higher education are facing problems in keeping up with accelerated change and modernization. In order to adjust to new situations, the problems associated with change should be analyzed and proactive planning should take place.

A conflict can be defined as a misunderstanding between two or more persons or groups. In conflicts, the aims, values, interests, and perceptions (i.e., culture) of one individual or group clash with those of another individual or group. The nature of conflict may vary from minor misunderstandings to a total lack of communication (Gibson and Hadgetts 1986). Since behavior may mean totally different things in different cultures, misunderstanding arises from not knowing another person or group's culture (Jacob and Jordan 1993). Because culture and education are interwoven phenomena, culture has a powerful effect on education. Conflict is heightened during times of change because parties may mistrust each other while competing for the same goals. Negative conflict can be very disruptive and may include threats, insults, arson, vandalism, strikes, demonstrations, and killing.

CONFLICT IN MULTICULTURAL SOCIETIES

The foundation for conflict in all societies is culturally defined. Therefore, for one to comprehend the reasons for—and hence, find ways to avoid—violence and other forms of conflict, cultural understanding is a prerequisite.

Culture

Culture is the spiritual programming of thought. It creates a consciousness of mind, a regulation of conduct, an understanding of the individual's place in the world, and an opportunity for transferring this knowledge to posterity (Rensburg 1992). Keesing and Keesing (1971) have a simpler definition of culture, which states that culture in its broadest sense refers to all that humans learn, in contrast to what is genetically endowed. Jacob and Jordan (1993, 16) say that patterns of behavior "are mental phenomena, meanings shared by members of a social group." According to Goodenough

(1971), a social group within a culture comprises standards for what is, standards for what can be, standards to decide what can be, other standards for deciding how one feels about what is or can be, standards for deciding what to do, and finally, standards for agreeing on how to implement decisions. It is important to keep in mind that the same behavior may mean totally different things in different cultures. People might therefore misunderstand each other completely if they do not know each other's cultures well. Jacob and Jordan (1993) also warn that it is virtually impossible to know any culture in all its subtle, multifarious variety. Since culture and education are interwoven phenomena, culture has a powerful effect on education.

Multicultural Societies and Conflict

In a multicultural society, the values of various social groups differ markedly because there is a multiplicity of religions, cultures, languages, and political views. McGehee contends that diversity may fragment societies (1991). When one culture makes contact with another, each tends to protect itself against infiltration and subversion by the other, which results in opposing camps of "us" and "them." Once this happens, the two sides are ripe for conflict, which feeds on the differences between groups. In the extreme, these differences are accentuated and raised to the level of absolutes. Conflict generates emotion, which intensifies the hostility between groups, especially when one party wants to gain at the expense of the other. A typical example of this behavior is the general practice of denying minorities access to desirable jobs and positions, as well as an equal opportunity to obtain a good education.

Ogbu refers to the relationships and mores to which black Americans were subjected for generations in the United States (Ogbu 1993). These modes of behavior were also typical of the South African educational system until recently. In Malaysia bloody riots erupted in 1969 because of the socioeconomic imbalance between the Malays and other races, such as the Chinese (Teck Ghee 1993). Inferior education is typically caused by inadequately trained teachers, different and sometimes inferior curricula, and inadequate funding, services, and facilities. Ogbu's reference to the educational practices that pertain to minorities in the United States is strongly reminiscent of the discriminatory educational system that South African blacks had to endure.

The stereotyping of minorities can provoke hatred, bitterness, violence, and other manifestations of conflict. It may also give factions in society the opportunity to use the school as a means of achieving their political aims. In South Africa the school is used by militant leaders of the community, as indicated by their slogan "liberation before education." The following statement by a black South African criticizes this movement: "Some of the very people and outfits with a hand in ruining the future of many of our youngsters with the disastrous 'liberty before education' inanity are the same people nowadays speaking about a 'lost generation.' They are the same people who misled the children into believing they could walk out of the classroom [one moment] and straight into Parliament the next" (Quelane 1992, 10). Molefe, another black South African, claims that the first black pupils in that republic demanded a free and compulsory education but that later, they demanded the release of Nelson Mandela and other political prisoners; the establishment of a state that was nonracial, unitary, and democratic; and the lifting of bans on political organisations. These black pupils were indoctrinated into seeing themselves as freedom fighters and not as future adults and thought that education was supposed to focus on the elimination of apartheid instead of on academics (Molefe 1993). Owing to historical circumstances, these black youths do not have the conventional educational qualifications they require to be recruited or promoted (Sonn 1993). Some have unrealistic expectations of equality or of what is achievable. Black illiterates or those with insufficient schooling see themselves as being on the same level, in terms of readiness for the job market, as whites of the same age, who have completed matriculation requirements.

Pupils may be alienated if they cannot see the connection between their scholastic achievement and future prospects of socioeconomic success (Du Toit 1991). This problem is reaching crisis proportions in South Africa. Since 1976, black students have taken to the streets to protest against their educational system. Because their schooling was seriously disrupted by their involvement in violent agitation against the existing system, it has been estimated that students from Soweto who sat for the 1992 matriculation examination had received only 40 percent of the schooling needed to pass (Lickindorf 1993). According to Freeman, a psychologist who has worked extensively with township youth, black youths have been in the forefront of the political struggle that has transformed South Africa over the past thirty years, but in many ways they have been denied recognition for their past endeavours. Now they stand at the sidelines and are told what to do, especially by their own leaders ("Half a Million People" 1993).

These people are called "the lost generation." A 1993 survey by the Community Agency for Social Enquiry (CASE) indicates that these students are embittered by the fact that they are uneducated, jobless, and exploited by militant leaders. These people—who are politically alienated, racially and generationally antagonistic, rebellious, angry, and confused—have a tendency to resort to or to admire crime ("Half a Million People" 1993). These people are also called "social time bombs." Traumatised after being abused, they have been hardened by conflict and exposure to violence. They do not fit in anywhere.

Quelane made a plea that they resume education, saying that no political or economic ambitions can ever be fulfilled without adequate schooling (Quelane 1993). This is very true, but it should be borne in mind that this group of bruised and battered individuals needs a caring community in which they not only receive academic education but also learn job skills and the necessary life skills. At this stage, however, these people are also involved in interracial and intraracial conflicts, which, according to the popular press ("Die kans om werk" 1993), make South Africa one of the most dangerous countries in the world. As a matter of fact, during a recent international conference in Johannesburg about multicultural conflict management in changing societies, Nieuwmeijer (1992) remarked that South Africa today is one of the best laboratories for the management of conflict in a multicultural society.

Multicultural Violence

In many multicultural societies, conflict has violent conclusions. To each of the following societies, violence has and continues to remain an important threat. It also appears that violence may be a catalyst for social change, including the reform of tertiary educational institutions, including community colleges.

REPUBLIC OF SOUTH AFRICA

The Republic of South Africa is currently experiencing drastic change. After four decades of apartheid, multicultural schools have come into being. Many schools for whites have closed, and in February 1992 it was announced that 4,000 posts for white teachers would be eliminated. Significant change in economic and social conditions can be seen. The Boipatong massacre and the African National Congress's (ANC's) reaction, the murder of Chris Hani (one of the leaders of the ANC), and the murder of the white American researcher Amy Biehl are but a few examples of the tragic consequences of racial conflict in the republic. According to the director of the Centre for Violence and Reconciliation at the University of the Witwatersrand in Johannesburg, many South Africans see violence as a legitimate means of conflict resolution for some time to come ("Die kans om werk" 1993).

United States

The United States has over 180 different ethnic groups, and ethnic-based conflict is a real and potentially explosive problem. One aspect of violent conflict stems from the socioeconomic differences between upper-, middle-, and lower-class workers in the United States. The foundation of conflict is often economic and is complicated by racial intolerance. In the United States, race is not completely an indicator of economic status, since there are African Americans and other minority groups represented in the middle and upper classes. Nonetheless, a disproportionate number of Americans of color are poorer than the white population, and many of them complain of discrimination. Discrimination plus poverty perpetuates conflict.

The United States has had problems of violence for decades, and nowadays, the national identity is still being threatened through violence. Cities such as Detroit, Washington, Miami, and Los Angeles "compete for the dubious title of murder capital of the world" (Temple 1991, 123). In all these cities, intense multicultural conflict prevails. Violence in these cities is frequently, yet not solely, the result of racial or ethnic conflict. In the city of Miami alone, there have been four incidences of racial violence in the past decade, the most recent being in 1990. The result has been 25 dead, nearly 500 injured, and more than $200 million in property damage (Booth 1993).

Canada

Samuda (1986) claims that although many Canadians are convinced that racial problems seldom occur in their country, racist ideologies have shaped immigration policies. Until the 1960s, there was extensive and undeniable discrimination against the entry of black students into certain educational institutions. Furthermore, the deepening conflict between English- and French-nationality ethnic groups threatens to split the nation in two. In addition, the schools on Indian reservations are financed and administered very differently from other Canadian schools. Discrimination, poverty, and despair characterize Canada's native people. In 1990, in an armed standoff, leaders of the Mohawk band confronted the Quebec government to protect a tribal burial ground. According to Kuptana, the chief negotiator for Canada's 37,000 Inuit, equality and justice are within their reach, since they took up arms to press their cause, and they insist that they have a right to their way of life (Serrill 1992).

Malaysia

Malaysia is divided into many ethnic, linguistic, religious, and social groups. In 1980 the population was 55.3 percent Malay, 33.8 percent Chinese, and

10.2 percent Indian (Gonzalez 1992). Prior to independence, four languages (English, Malay, Chinese, and Tamil) were used as mediums of instruction in schools. The Islamic religion is synonymous with a certain way of life, while the Malay worldview is also greatly influenced by its faith. In addition, other religious influences such as Hinduism, Buddhism, and Christianity define distinct cultural groups (Karim and Nordin 1992).

Ethnic polarization stems from the fact that while Malays dominate the political sector, non-Malays (particularly Chinese) are the leaders in the economic sector. Politically, such issues as education, job discrimination, and language use are defined along racial lines.[1] After the 1969 elections, non-Malays predominated over Malays, which aggravated feelings amongst Malays that they were no longer in control and that they would be pushed back to the *kampongs* (villages) (Ahmad 1989). The resulting riots of May 13, 1969, were initiated in Kuala Lumpur and spread to other urban centres. These violent riots resulted in a kind of catharsis, since Malay fears were brought to consciousness. The initial shock and paralysis gave birth to a political restructuring. The need for national unity was strongly supported. New educational and economic policies were introduced to redress imbalances. The 1969 riots were a culmination point that signalled change in Malaysia and prepared the role of education in the constructive handling of conflict in Malaysia.

It should be noted, however, that Malaysia—in contrast to the multicultural societies of the United States, Canada, and South Africa—is experiencing a relatively peaceful and unitary system. However, cultural tension remains, as exemplified by the April 1987 intensification of racial polarization (Ahmad 1989).

Lessons Learned from the Case Studies

Modernization creates many problems in multicultural countries, including overpopulation, poverty, and unemployment, which results from industrialization and improvements in modern technology. While modern technology robs individuals of jobs, overpopulation depletes resources. To counter conflict, society should ensure that the population lives in an environment that includes enough and good food, affordable and adequate housing, employment, and an equitable education system. Balance should be maintained. Imbalances (such as a good education and a poor job, an affordable house but a hostile neighbourhood, and a good job with an insecure future) can foster conflict. If any of the foregoing prerequisites are lacking, the environment becomes unstable, and people must devote an increasing amount of time to straightening out personal affairs. Such patterns are evident in all of the case studies.

The case studies reveal that the economic factors of unemployment and poverty lead to discrimination against certain people in terms of education and job opportunities, and this can culminate in conflict and aggression. Poor information leads to fear, which in turn can cause aggression and violence. In multicultural societies, it is imperative to maintain responsible use of resources, adequate job training and job opportunities, planned and responsible use of technology, and responsible family planning. In this regard, education can play a major role in enabling people to exercise control of the environment and to relieve themselves of the pressures of industrialization and technology.

Constructive Handling of Conflict

Conflict can be constructive, depending on how it is handled. Conflict is sometimes necessary for the implementation of adjustments and drastic changes in a society. As a matter of fact, Matlawa (1988, 15) calls it "the goose that may lay golden eggs." Conflict can also induce and foster creative ways of adapting to change. In the case studies, there are three examples of this constructive change.

In Canada there has been considerable tension between the English- and French-speaking cultural groups. In 1965 the Canadian government appointed the Bilingual and Bi-cultural Commission to investigate the relationship between people of British and French origin as well as relationships among other multicultural groups. The government decided to acknowledge the existence of a multicultural society through an official policy statement. A consequence of this was a revival in Canadian nationalism (Steyn 1989).

Conflict was handled constructively in the United States in Overtown, Florida, where more than 50 percent of the residents lived in poverty, the level of unemployment was high, and feelings of frustration and anger simmered. Three cases of race-related problems with police resulted in ethnic riots on May 17, 1980, January 16–18, 1989, and December, 1992. These incidents had a direct significance to the educational and personal lives of Miami-Dade Community College students and personnel. As a result, the college evaluated its role during a communal and physical metamorphosis of the neighbourhood. It also initiated a program that helped to transform the neighbourhood, revive a rapidly declining society, and bring about equilibrium.

Malaysian education became an important variable in the realization of an important national development goal, namely, national unity. After the 1969 riots the National Education Policy and the New Economic Policy were introduced. In the latter, education was seen as a means to raise the income levels and increase the employment opportunities of all Malaysians, so that poverty could be eradicated and the process of restructuring Malaysian community could be accelerated, to counter economic imbalances and the association of race with economic function (Aziz and Ahmad 1985). The adoption of these policies contributed to economic growth and political stability, and thus, conflict was constructively handled.

It is evident that group, class, racial, and ethnic struggles are sometimes an engine of structural change in education (Brint and Karabel 1989). In this perspective, "conflict is therefore a good to be valued, rather than a nuisance to be avoided" (Starrat 1987, 38–39).

EDUCATION'S ROLE IN COUNTERING CONFLICT

Education's role in countering conflict in multicultural societies is examined through the role of education in general and the role of the community college type of education in particular. Education's role will be exemplified by the four countries under discussion.

The Role of General Education

In the nineteenth century, Maria Montessori made the following thought-provoking comment regarding the crucial role of education in conflict situations: "All politics can do is to keep us out of war, establishing lasting peace is the work of education" (De Witt 1993, 1). Although at times education is expected to solve conflict-producing problems, few provisions are made for imparting required knowledge to emerging adults who will soon have to deal with these problems. Especially in times of change, and particularly in multicultural societies, the responsibilities of education leave very little time for the essential training of divergent groups in job skills. Also missing are life skills, which include tolerance for other cultures, cooperation with and appreciation of other values and norms, and constructive handling of conflict.

According to Aziz and Ahmad (1985), the overriding objective of the educational system in Malaysia is national unity. Malaysians believe that through a unified education system and a common curriculum, a united and harmonious nation will become a reality. Various courses in upper-secondary schools are directly related to Malaysia's personnel requirements. Practical and social skills are included in the curriculum. Attention is paid to the improvement of (among other things) the quality of education and education for nation building. The formal and informal curriculum is revitalized for the sake of developing stronger spiritual, moral, and ethical qualities in citizens and a balance between the academic, technical, and vocational spheres. Recently the increased demand for skilled and semiskilled workers has resulted in the establishment of three additional secondary vocational and polytechnical schools (Karim and Nordin 1992).

In South Africa, large numbers of the "lost generation," as well as adult illiterates or people who for some reason or other did not receive effective education, have a desperate need and desire for basic and continued schooling. The schooling received by black groups in South Africa has left much to be desired in many instances. The result is that when they enter higher education (if at all) it is with a deficiency, since they are not at the same level as their white counterparts.

The Role of the Community College

Margaret Mead described the community college as a "centre for community action . . . that takes in four generations" (Holleman 1990, 2). The community college offers equal access to tertiary education irrespective of age, sex, race, religion, and class. For some students it is also an alternative route for acquiring a B.A. degree. Community colleges are comprehensive education institutions. They provide preparatory as well as terminal education and serve as a "bridge" or a "station" between the secondary school and a four-year college or university training. Furthermore, the community college's pursuit of academic, economic, and socio-cultural objectives equips it to reduce social discrepancies and therefore promote universal tolerance. Because of their well-earned reputation for exerting an equalising effect on society, community colleges have made it possible for some social barriers to be removed because community colleges help people to understand one another better and to appreciate the contributions they can make to their country. This is evident from the following case studies.

In Quebec, Canada, during a period of political ferment and turmoil, community colleges were planned as instruments of social change for an entire society (Dennison and Gallagher 1986). The aim was to correct the divergence in educational opportunity that existed between the two linguistic groups: those who spoke English and those who spoke French. The colleges in Quebec served as an instrument through which the French Roman Catholic majority gained greater access to the two universities and the professional work force of the province (Wilson 1980). Previously, the French and Catholic educational sector was private and education was provided by the clergy. The English and Protestant sector established "public" secondary institutions as well as private schools (Dennison and Gallagher 1986). Since the "quiet revolution" in the early 1960s, community colleges have ensured equal educational opportunities in Quebec. Social barriers have been removed, and "rarely has education been used so effectively as an instrument of political policy as in that province" (Wilson 1980, 21).

In the United States, several examples are applicable. In 1988 the chancellor of the Kentucky Community College District redefined the district's mission. One key component added was the commitment to remove such barriers as poverty and racial prejudice (Horvath 1991, 74). Similarly, the Yakima Valley Community College (Washington) mission states:

> Our increasingly complex society and culturally diverse population demands accessible education as a foundation for mutual understanding, prosperity and a better quality of life. We believe in the dignity of every human being and the ability of all regardless of age, gender, ethnicity . . . to set and achieve goals which contribute to individual fulfillment and the future of the region. [The goal is to promote] student and staff self-knowledge, cultural awareness and sense of personal value by providing a positive climate of trust and mutual respect. (Yakima Valley Community College)

The stress put on education in Malaysia is accompanied by an ideology of development. This ideology gives educational issues, as well as the role of the community college, "an even greater emotional salience than they have in most developed countries" (Basham 1983, 59). The school system in Malaysia is inherited from the British system. The community college, however, was adopted from the United States. However, many Malaysians are unfamiliar with this type of institution, and not all Malaysians accept it. The reason for this is that the U.S. concept is not structurally compatible with a basically British-patterned educational system (Stedman 1986).

The U.S. influence in Malaysian community colleges is reflected in the courses offered in Malaysia by U.S. universities and colleges, such as the programme offered by Broward Community College in Florida and Kolej Damansara Utama. This influence is also reflected when private Malaysian colleges pattern their curricula so that U.S. colleges can easily identify suitable courses for transfer (Stedman 1986).

Community College Curricula for Countering Conflict

Community colleges are cultural sites whose curricula are cultural artifacts. According to Jansen (1984), a curriculum is a plan or program for teaching and learning. It is conceptualized in light of certain aims, and its content is meant to be well selected and well ordered. A programme for students in community colleges can therefore be conceptualized to counter conflict in multicultural societies. Content ranges from job skills to life skills and affects instructors, students, and the college itself.

JOB SKILLS

As the twentieth century draws to a close, community colleges have a special responsibility to train future employees and to develop a new educational and training programme for the unemployed and underemployed. In Malaysia, the needs of the work force were prioritized when community college models were established to answer the needs of skilled and semiskilled workers. In South Africa, the need for a community college model is evident, since many school graduates cannot find employment and are not in a position to start up businesses. A local newspaper reported that many school and college graduates' chances of finding employment have never been so slight. The chances were that less than 4 out of every 100 matriculants would be able to find employment in 1994 ("Die kans om werk" 1993). This has a negative effect on political stability. In the future, throughout the countries examined, community colleges will continue to help solve economic problems and to do research in this connection, as well as to provide professional staff (Atwell 1990). Yet new questions need to be addressed, and they include the following: Are community colleges becoming havens for minority education, while the universities are more segregated? Are community college graduates on an equal footing with university graduates? Do they compete for the same jobs? Are there disadvantages to community college education, and are they mirrored in the job market?

Although the Republic of South Africa is well known for its past system of apartheid, the University of South Africa (UNISA) has accepted students of all races for decades. Furthermore, all formerly "white" universities in South Africa have by now opened their doors to students of all races and cultures. Segregation at South African universities is minimal.

However, for the new community colleges in South Africa to attract more white students, the quality of the "academic subjects" needs to be high. The nature and aim of the university should be kept in mind. Community colleges, universities, and local businesses should collaborate and supplement each other.

In the United States, Gonzaga University in Spokane, Washington, joined forces with Spokane Community College and local business to develop new programmes and new services (Parnell 1990). College students joined with local engineers, college professors, and technicians to solve problems. Parnell provides two further examples from the United States, and they illustrate what industry and education can accomplish together. The first example is of the Ford Motor Company, which faced reductions in the long-term demand for manufacturing during the 1980-1982 recession. A programme was initiated with neighboring schools, colleges, and universities to retrain its labour force. The comprehensive training program included career counselling, tuition assistance, and targeted vocational retraining. By 1989 18,000 displaced Ford workers benefited from this unparalleled partnership. In the second example, each community college in Oregon managed a small business center. Long-term development assistance, short-term courses, and support services were included. Hundreds of small businesses increased their hiring quotas and benefited financially from this effort (Parnell 1990).

An example of a community college in Malaysia that contributed to national peace and unity is the MARA Community College, situated in Pahang and affiliated with Lincoln Land Community College in Springfield, Illinois. This community college was designed to train *bumiputras* (indigenous Malays) to become equal partners with other ethnic groups in industry and commerce (Stedman 1986).

In general, community colleges, companies, and businesses can form agreements to employ community college graduates. Through these agreements, the community college graduates will gain a better grounding for employment. The Kolej Damansara Utama is one of the community colleges in Malaysia that offers subjects such as economics, public affairs, and accounting, which could help increase students' chances for future employment (Stedman 1986).

Surely, university graduates will stand a good chance of securing a certain job if their training is relevant to the job and they are competent to do it. It should, however, be kept in mind that in South Africa, university graduates with B.S. and, particularly, B.A. degrees are considered "qualified" but, nonetheless, are experiencing difficulty in finding employment and need additional skills ("Die kans om werk" 1993). A person with manual skills stands a better chance of finding employment. If community college graduates are not transferred to universities, they could be trained for jobs other than those of the university graduate, who is more competent in academic skills. According to the Department of Manpower in South Africa, employment opportunities exist only for the following positions: insurance consultants, marketing agents, receptionists, typists, dispatch and administrative clerks, and security guards ("Die kans om werk" 1993).

A community college's curriculum should include education *for* work and education *about* work. Economic literacy leads to success, as exemplified by new Canadian community colleges (in Quebec, Ontario, and Manitoba) that place special emphasis on new areas of employment (Dennison and Gallagher 1986). This could also be a meaningful practice for community colleges in South Africa because of the high level of unemployment. Human resources in education "have the potential to be powerful influences for social change, towards a more equitable and just society" (Tiddy 1987, 49). It should be kept in mind that when you make it in the mainstream, victimization and conflict are gradually reduced.

LIFE SKILLS

Life skills include communication skills, an understanding of cultural diversity, and moral and civic values:

• *Communication skills* ideally allow different cultures to live together harmoniously. To achieve this goal, people should be able to communicate positively with those from different ethnic, religious, racial, and social backgrounds. This includes communication skills at the verbal and nonverbal (such as active listening skills) levels. At Valencia Community College in Orlando, Florida, graduates are required to listen, write, and speak effectively. Community colleges in Ontario, Canada, stress communication skills such as interpersonal skills and assertiveness (Dennison and Gallagher 1986). Students have to be able to deal with conflict and disagreement. Assertiveness, "I" messages, and the win-win approach are skills of utmost importance. Students should be able to understand the value of conflict. It should also be seen as a problem that can be solved through effective teamwork. In South Africa, discussions about similarities facilitate communication and bring about a fellow feeling and what is called *ubuntu* (humaneness) in the Zulu language.

• *Understanding cultural diversity*, according to McGehee, is "the aim of multicultural education [which] is to train people to like each other without becoming the same" (McGehee 1991, 3). People should be trained to value their own culture and history but also to appreciate, among other things, the culture and history of other groups. It also implies mutual respect, sensitivity, and understanding of other cultures' symbols and rituals and of their specific views.

Convergence and divergence of values are part of a continuous process, and constant adjustment on both sides is required. Certain community colleges have established goals for students to achieve by the time they complete their studies. At Valencia Community College in Orlando, Florida, graduates are expected to clarify the moral values, personal strengths, and goals that have relevance to their cultural values (Gianini and Hook 1991).

Spitzberg and Thorndike (1992) confirm that community colleges in the United States are increasingly including racial and ethnic differences in their educational programming.

- *Moral and civic values* are found in all countries in the form of laws that deal with potential violence, conflict, and insecurity. Students should be trained to fit into a society and to become law-abiding citizens having acceptable morals (Spitzberg and Thorndike 1992). It is important that community colleges be adjusted to suit the needs of a society, as was the case in Malaysia after the bloody riots that were caused by economic imbalance.

In Greenfield, California, the Los Medanos Community College provides an interdisciplinary curriculum, which embraces behavioral, social, and humanistic studies with topics such as "the nature of man in society" (Edwards and Tonkin 1990). According to Kish and Rita (1993), Bronx Community College in New York emphasizes skills that help students manage problems in their lives, job-hunting skills, and skills to improve students' performance in the workplace. The Hollard College in Charlottetown, Canada, provides opportunities for all citizens to identify personally realistic objectives, achieve socially useful goals, and rebuild their self-confidence if their previous educational performance has been handicapped because of discrimination (Dennison and Gallagher 1986).

THE CLIMATE OF THE COMMUNITY COLLEGE

According to Sergiovanni and Starrat (1988), it is often difficult to define climate because it is frequently based on subjective perceptions. The authors, however, maintain that climate is the enduring factor that typifies a certain educational institution, distinguishes it from other educational institutions, and influences the behaviour of all those in the institution. It refers to the observable effects of the people, the architecture of the buildings, the history and culture of the institution, the organizational structure, the management and leadership style, and interpersonal relations. Furthermore, it determines the attitude that the people (educators as well as students) have toward the institution. Students should be able to talk of *our* community college, *our* educators, *our* community, and *our* buildings. They should be proud of their college and should not deliberately want to destroy it. The climate of the community college is therefore of special importance. According to Kruger (1994), self-image, morale, and interpersonal relationships influence the climate in the institution. The collaboration of students in a group may contribute to the propagation of norms that are supported by the group. It could also affect relations between members of certain groups. Members of a group collaborate to attain a certain aim or reward, such as winning a rugby match. Feelings of solidarity and team spirit create opportunities for students to connect and belong in certain group settings. A sense of camaraderie and loyalty to the group creates and maintains bridges among subgroups of different backgrounds.

This collaboration between students can take place in their curricular as well as their extracurricular activities in community colleges. It could eliminate social inequality, prejudice, and discrimination toward groups of different racial or ethnic backgrounds. Furthermore, it could help students feel successful and while they are making progress, negative occurrences such as victimization, conflict, and violence often diminish.

In the process of change, the goal is for some students and some faculty to possibly be affected. Spitzberg and Thorndike provide evidence from various regions in the United States that shows that it is important to belong to the college and be part of its climate. In turn, colleges create a caring community, to which many students attribute "familylike" characteristics. At Cornell College in Iowa and Colorado College in the Rockies, a distinctive course-sequencing arrangement bonds students with faculty and the community. Whether through campus identity or through bonding, racist conflicts in a multicultural society may eventually fade away (Spitzberg and Thorndike 1992).

Sports are known as a way to erase stereotypes and prejudices in order to diminish conflict. In South Africa, police in the rural town of Delmas started a sports programme to counteract violence in a squatter camp where black violence was uncontrollable (SABC 1993). The squatters enjoyed these activities tremendously. In contrast to the past, the police are today frequently welcomed and there appears to be a spirit of affection between them and the squatters.

According to Dennison and Gallagher (1986), the philosophical framework for community colleges in Saskatchewan, Canada (created by the minister of continuing education in August 1972), includes opportunities for recreational and cultural activities. The success of these colleges is, to a large degree, due to their atmosphere of institutional unity and a climate of voluntary integration.

There is often a certain number of students whose time on campus is limited because of other responsibilities. Some of them are commuters who travel long distances. It is difficult for these students to participate in extracurricular activities and to make use of major campus services. At Piedmont Community College in Virginia, service offices remain open until 7:00 P.M. (Spitzberg and Thorndike 1992). Study and lounge areas, as well as cafeteria services, contribute to intercultural integration and create bridges between campus subgroups.

THE ROLES OF THE COLLEGE AND INSTRUCTORS

In Canada, the clarification of the role of instructors and other professional staff of community colleges is considered important (Dennison and Gallagher 1986). This is also true of community colleges in other multicultural societies. Students should analyze conflict in society critically and identify problems. The instructor needs to be creative in his or her planning, and implement societal changes through community college strategies for countering conflict.

The instructor should have a knowledge of the divergent cultures of the college students, and have a knowledge of materials and processes that reduce or eliminate prejudice and stereotyping. In a pluralistic society, leaders of the community college need to consult with a variety of groups in the community. The costs and benefits of a particular decision or policy should be debated in order to clarify and thus redefine it. "Alternative solutions should be more thoroughly explored. Conflict is therefore a good to be valued, rather than a nuisance to be avoided" (Starrat 1987, 38–39).

Fryer's advice, based on twenty-nine years of experience in seven educational institutions (principally, community colleges), is useful for college boards and community college instructors in multicultural societies, especially for the new community colleges in a conflict-torn South Africa. They should remain alert to inherent tensions in the organization, seek to resolve conflict constructively for all parties, use the first person plural rather than first person singular, and listen attentively and with sensitivity and responsiveness to students' problems (Fryer 1989).

Finally, because the education system is the main agent for socialization and change, the instructors and the board of the community college should endeavour to counter uncertainty and conflict in multicultural societies and, therefore, to bring about a just society.

The Role of the University

"That people can learn is an undeniable fact of life; that people can teach is an interesting hypothesis, but unsubstantiated" (Jacobovits, quoted in Spitzberg and Thorndike 1992, 135). Substantial progress has been made in understanding the ways in which people learn. It is unclear whether teaching at community colleges has been improved as a result.

UNISA is by far the largest university in South Africa. About one-third of South African university students are black, and one half of these people are students at UNISA. This university is one of the largest multicultural institutions in the world, and has experience and skill in teaching multicultural students. However, UNISA lecturers are faced with the problem that black first-year students are not on the same academic level as their white counterparts because of the poor standards of black education in South Africa. A desperate need, therefore, exists for community colleges in South Africa to form links with UNISA or other universities, so that community college educators can be trained. Most of the teaching staff in faculties of education in South Africa do not have experience with community colleges.

Conclusions

During South Africa's transition, higher education has been confronted with the challenge of transforming a political battlefield into an economic advantage. Increased levels of education in community colleges within multicultural societies may counteract escalating conflict. It would be naive to believe that community colleges could eliminate all conflict, but they are one of the methods that could be used. Community colleges could help bring about peace and harmony in a new millennium.

The author acknowledges in this chapter that conflict is an inherent part of many multicultural societies and that, very often, this conflict has violent repercussions. In the efforts to ease conflict and handle it constructively, education in general and community college education in particular play increasingly important roles. There is an old Chinese proverb that is relevant here: "It is far better to light a small candle than to sit passively and curse the darkness." At community colleges, we can light many candles, which, at the end of the day, will make a vast difference.

Notes

1. For example, the Alliance Party consists of the United Malay Organization, the Malayan Chinese Association, and the Malayan Indian Congress.

References

Ahmad, Z.H. "Malaysia: Quasi Democracy in a Divided Society." In L. Diamond, J.J. Linz, and S.M. Lipset (eds.), *Democracy in Developing Countries*. Boulder, Colo.: Lynn Rienner, 1989.
Atwell, R.H. "Foreword." In D. Parnell, *Dateline 2000: The New Higher Education Agenda*. Washington, D.C.: Community College Press, 1990.
Aziz, A.A., and Z.H. Ahmad. "Malaysia: A System of Education." In T. Husen, and T.N. Postlethwaite (eds.), *The International Encyclopedia of Education: Research and Studies*. Oxford: Pergamon, 1985.
Basham, R. "National Racial Policies and University Education in Malaysia." In W. McCreedy (ed.), *Culture, Ethnicity, and Identity*. New York: Academic, 1983.
Booth, C. "Miami!" *Time International* 142, no. 10 (September 1993): 28–29.
Brint, S., and J. Karabel. *The Diverted Dream: Community College and the Promise of Educational Opportunity in America 1900–1985*. New York: Oxford Uni-

versity Press, 1989.
Dennison, J.D., and P. Gallagher. *Canada's Community Colleges: A Critical Analysis.* Vancouver: University of Columbia Press, 1986.
De Witt, J.T. Unpublished manuscript. Pretoria, 1993.
"Die kans om werk te kry, is baie gering." *Beeld* (29 December 1993): 4.
Du Toit, P.J. "Leerlingaktivisme: Oorsake, Verloop en Hantering." *Die Unie* 88, no. 5 (November 1991): 105.
Edwards, J., and J.R. Tonkin. "Internationalizing the Community College: Strategies for the Classroom." In R.K. Greenfield (ed.), *Developing International Programs.* San Francisco: Jossey-Bass, 1990.
Fryer, T.W., Jr. "Governance in the High-Achieving Community College." In T. O'Banion (ed.), *Innovation in the Community College.* New York: Collier Macmillan, 1989.
Gianini, P.C., Jr., and W.M. Hook. "The Planning-Development Line." In D. Angel and M. De Vault (ed.), *Conceptualizing 2000: Pro-active Planning.* Washington: Community College Press, 1991.
Gibson, J.W., and R.W. Hadgetts. *Organizational Communication: A Managerial Perspective.* Orlando: Harcourt Brace Jovanovich, 1986.
Gonzalez, H.V. "Malaysia." In G.H. Kurian (ed.), *World Education Encyclopedia.* Oxford: Facts on File, 1992.
Goodenough, W. *Culture, Language and Society.* Reading, Mass.: Addison-Wesley, 1971.
"Half a Million People 'Lost'"; "Just Where Do They Fit In?" *Star* (Johannesburg) (21 May 1993): 11.
Holleman, W. (ed.) *The Role of the Learning Resources Centre in Instruction.* San Francisco: Jossey-Bass, 1990.
Horvath, R.J. "A Statewide Perspective." In D. Angel and M. De Vault (eds.), *Conceptualizing 2000: Pro-Active Planning.* Washington, D.C.: Community College Press, 1991.
Jacob, E., and C. Jordan. "Understanding Educational Anthropology: Concepts and Methods." In E. Jacob and C. Jordan (eds.), *Minority Education: Anthropological Perspectives.* Norwood, N.J.: Ablex, 1993.
Jansen, C.P. "'n Model van 'n Kurrikulumsentrum vir die RSA." Unpublished D.Ed. thesis. University of Pretoria, 1984.
Karim, R., and A.B. Nordin. "Malaysia." In W. Wielemans and P. Choi-Ping Chang (eds.), *Education and Culture in Industrializing Asia.* Leuven: University Press, 1992.
Keesing, R.M., and F.M. Keesing. *New Perspectives in Cultural Anthropology.* New York: Holt Rinehart and Winston, 1971.
Kish, E.R., and E.S. Rita. "The Minority Minors Program in Energy-Related Curricula." *C & U* LXVIII, No. 2 (Spring–Summer 1993): 80.
Kruger, A.G. "School Climate." ONB453-H. B.Ed. Educational Management, Tutorial Letter 103/94, Study Unit 102, School Management. Pretoria: University of South Africa, 1994.
Lickindorf, E. "Sowing the Educational Ground with Profitable Seed: The Employment Potential of the Non-Career Orientated Undergraduate Degree." *South African Journal of Higher Education* 7, no. 1 (1993): 81.
Matlawa K. "The Goose That May Lay Golden Eggs." *Popagano* 9, no. 2 (December 1988): 15.
McGehee, H. "Coming to Terms with the Multiculturalists." *The Education Digest* (December 1991): 3.
Molefe, P. "The Class of '76 Still Locked in the Grip of Crisis." *Johannesburg Star* (5 June 1993): 15.
Nieuwmeijer, L. Opening Address at the International Conference on Multicultural Conflict in Changing Societies, Johannesburg, 26 August 1992.

Ogbu, J.U. "Frameworks—Variability in Minority School Performance: A Problem in Search of an Explanation." In E. Jacob and C. Jordan (eds.), *Minority Education: Anthropological Perspectives*. New Jersey: Ablex, 1993.

Parnell, D. *Dateline 2000: The New Higher Education Agenda*. Washington: Community College Press, 1990.

Quelane, J. "Go Back to School—For All Our Sake." *Sunday Star* (Johannesburg) (26 July 1992): 10.

Rensburg, R. "Communicating Organizational Culture vs. Societal Culture." Paper delivered at the International Conference of the HSRC on Multicultural Management of Conflict in Changing Societies, Johannesburg, 28 August 1992.

Samuda, R.J. "Social and Educational Implications of Multiculturalism." *Education and Society* 4, no. 4 (1986): 65–66.

Sergiovanni, T.J., and R.J. Starrat. *Supervision: Human Perspectives*. 4th ed. New York: McGraw-Hill, 1988.

Serrill, M.S. "To Be Themselves." *Time International* 140, no. 16 (1992): A4.

Sonn, F.A. "Developing a National Education and Training Culture for a Winning Nation." Panel presentation at Competency-based Training Conference, Eskom Conference Centre, Midrand, Johannesburg, 30 November 1993.

South African Broadcasting Corporation (SABC). *Agenda: An Actuality Program on SABC* (13 December 1993).

Spitzberg, I.J., and N.V. Thorndike. *Creating Community on College Campuses*. New York: State University of New York Press, 1992.

Starrat, R.J. "Human Resource Management: Learning Our Lessons by Learning to Learn in Shaping Education." In Anderson, J. (ed.), *Shaping Education*. Victoria: Australian College of Education, 1987.

Stedman, J.B. *Malaysia: A Study of the Educational System of Malaysia*. United States: American Associates of Collegiate Registrars and Admissions, 1986.

Steyn, H.J. "The Education System of Canada." In E.I. Dekker and O.J. Van Schalkwyk (eds.), *Modern Education Systems*. Durban: Butterworths, 1989.

Tavris, C. *Anger: The Misunderstood Emotion*. New York: Simon and Schuster, 1982.

Teck Ghee, L. "Higher Education in Malaysia and Singapore: Common Roots but Differing Directions." *Higher Education Policy* 6, no. 2 (June 1993): 21.

Temple, R. "Urban Community Colleges." In D. Angel and M. De Vault (eds.), *Conceptualizing 2000: Pro-Active Planning*. Washington: Community College Press, 1991.

Tiddy, J. M. "Human Resources in Education: Strategies to Implement Equal Opportunities." In J. Anderson (ed.), *Shaping Education*. Victoria: The Australian College of Education, 1987.

Wielemants, W., and P. Choi-Ping Chang (eds.), *Education and Culture in Industrializing Asia*. Leuven: University Press, 1992.

Wilson, J. D. *Canadian Education in the 1980's*. Alberta: Detselig, 1980.

Yakima Valley Community College. "Mission Statement." 1991: 1.

11 Assessing the Relevance of American Community College Models in Japan

Tina Yamano and John N. Hawkins

Japan is widely considered to be competitive, if not dominant, in several important social sectors. The economy is the most obvious sector, but other social areas, including education, command attention as well. Just as Japanese factories produce superior manufactured products, so too, it is argued, do Japanese schools, and the one is interrelated with the other. Indeed, Japan has been without comparison as a nation that has utilized formal, nonformal, and informal education on its road to modernization. From the Fundamental Code of Education (produced in 1872) to recent reforms in higher education, the Japanese approach to providing a first-rate educational system has not gone unnoticed among the nations of the world.

The focus of this chapter is on the phenomenon of short-cycle education, including the Japanese junior college and the importation and adaptation of the community college model from the United States to Japan. This introduction of the junior and community college models to Japan is surely not the first occasion in which the Japanese have looked abroad and adopted educational forms that make sense in the Japanese context. Indeed, even the Japanese term for community college, *komyuniti kareji*, is a transliteration of the English. It is instructive, we think, to briefly review the historical context of Japanese educational development and its borrowings prior to discussing the specific examples in this chapter.

Background

It was in the mid-1800s that Japan launched a major effort to develop a modern educational system. By the 1900s the Meji government had put in place an educational system consisting of primary, middle, and normal schools and imperial universities, and this was to remain, in some respects, the basis of all other educational developments. Early on, Japan's leaders sought the educational advice of Western nations, most notably the United

States, Germany, France, and Great Britain. As Ikuo Amano has noted (1979), Japan's higher educational system was not necessarily constructed in a systematic manner, particularly regarding the use of foreign models. The principal criteria for adoption of foreign forms was how well the various models solved important human-resource problems. This approach influenced the development of junior and community colleges as well.

Thus, the faculties of law, science, and letters at Tokyo University were based generally on British and American models. The medical faculty at Todai, however, was modeled on the German system. Engineering colleges were modeled on the Swiss polytechnic system, agriculture (e.g., Sapporo Agricultural College) on the American land-grant system, and so on. The centralization of the entire system, as shown by the format of the Ministry of Education, was closer to the French than any other system. Historically, of course, China played an important role in such areas as university development and the centralized examination process. And a *laissez-faire* policy was adopted regarding the establishment of private universities.

Gradually, over time, this largely Western-influenced system was transformed into an unique Japanese hybrid model of higher education. What remained clear, however, was that there was a tradition of looking abroad for innovative forms, practices, and models that could be grafted onto the Japanese system, and this practice has continued to this day. The next major reform occurred after the U.S. occupation. A new Fundamental Law of Education and a School-of-Education Law were enacted in 1947, and they provided the framework for postwar education. A more democratic system emerged that introduced, among other innovations, the *tanki daigaku*, junior college. Although a number of these reforms were modified after 1952, the system has remained much the same to this day (Shimahara 1992). The largely meritocratic system of Japanese education has rewarded achievement, competition, and hard work, and the acquisition of credentials has been the key to employment, careers, and financial security. Although it is generally meritocratic, the higher educational system in Japan is nevertheless hierarchical and differentiated, and it is these characteristics that are critical to a discussion of the rise of junior colleges and the attempted importation of the American community college model.

HIGHER EDUCATION IN JAPAN

The Japanese system of higher education is as differentiated as any in Europe or other parts of the world; in fact, it may be more so. The vertical differentiation of the Japanese system makes the country resemble Europe more than the United States, and the system is closer to a single-tier system than to the multiple-tier system familiar to Americans (Perkin 1984). Graduate training was not emphasized or well developed in the period following the war, and junior colleges, while plentiful and increasing in numbers, did not play a major role in the overall scheme of things. The rise of private institutions has changed this picture somewhat, and in recent years a more differentiated, more American model has emerged (possibly as a result of the training that so many important Japanese educational figures received in the United States through programs such as the Fulbright exchange) (Uyeki 1993). Higher education now includes public and private universities, junior colleges, technical schools, special training schools, and miscellaneous schools. Four- and six-year programs are offered at the university level, and two-year programs at the junior college level. Admission is generally by competitive examination, recommendations from high schools and interviews, or a combination of both. In the late 1980s Japan had 460 four-year institutions, of which 350 were private universities enrolling over 70 percent of all students, 95 were national, and 34 were local-public). In addition, there were over 500 tanki daigaku (junior colleges), principally private (85 percent) and enrolling mostly female students (about 90 percent) (Shimahara 1992). The gender differentiation so prevalent at the junior college level is worth elaborating on, since it so clearly defines the two-year college experience in Japan.

Following World War II, access to all forms of higher education became legally available to both sexes, and female participation in higher education has shown tremendous growth in the past twenty-five years (Fujimura-Fanselow 1989). Despite such progress, it remains a fact that the vast majority of females participate in higher education through the two-year junior colleges rather than the more prestigious and conventional four-year institutions. Even when females do participate in the four-year institutions, they are likely to major in literature, home economics, and education.

The facts are clearly stated by Fujimura-Fanselow (1989): The expansion of women's enrollment in higher education has taken place almost exclusively at the junior college level, while males have primarily been educated at the four-year institutions; women's enrollment at the four-year institutions has in fact been declining; 30 percent of women enrolled in higher education were enrolled in all-female institutions; and women tended to enroll in the three fields mentioned (only 1 percent of the women at the junior colleges enrolled in the engineering program offered there, while 40 percent of the males did). The reasons for these facts are complex and are embedded in both the economy and the culture. There is a persistent belief among both mothers and fathers that it is less important to educate daughters than to educate sons. Sending daughters to tanki daigaku derives from the notion that the husband should be more highly educated than the wife.

It is in this context that the role of the junior college becomes important. There was no significant government program designed to increase the access of women into the more prestigious four-year universities; therefore, when women's demands for higher education increased, private junior colleges aggressively pursued this particular market. During the past three decades, hundreds of new private junior colleges have been formed catering to women. By 1981 an overwhelming proportion of women were enrolled in private junior colleges. Fujimura-Fanselow notes several reasons for this:

- The cost factor is an important consideration. The annual tuition is about the same as that for a four-year institution but needs to be paid over only two years.
- Because there are a large number of junior colleges, they are more accessible and closer to home. Because they are closer to home, parents can exert more supervision over their daughters than if they attended a large urban university.
- Employers prefer to hire women straight out of high school or with a junior college education, on the assumption that they have more work years left than does a college graduate.
- Most women do not wish to undergo the rigorous preparation necessary to compete for top university spots, and opt instead for the less rigorous junior college program (which requires interviews and recommendations but not a comprehensive examination).

There is some evidence that some changes are underway. At junior colleges there has been a decrease in the number of women studying such subjects as home economics and increases in the number of those in health- and computer-science-related fields. Women are also continuing their education beyond the junior college by attending special skills-training schools to acquire specific job-related skills (Abe 1994). This complex system has become increasingly internationalized over the past five years, since Japan has been swept by the "internationalization" movement, which has brought more foreign students, professors, and branch campuses to all levels of Japanese higher education. The community college movement has been part of this trend. One result has been a proliferation of new models of higher education, merging syncretically with Japanese patterns and producing a number of intriguing research questions. It is in this context that the international transfer of educational forms—in this case, the branch campus (*bunko*) of the American community college—will be discussed.

As had been previously discussed, Japan is no stranger to the creative borrowing and adaptation of foreign educational forms, including the American-style junior college and, later, community college. A vast literature exists not only on the development of Japanese education in an international context but also on various aspects of the role of international exchange and institutional change. Some of this literature focuses on the impact of foreign students and scholars at particular institutions, and others concentrate on the broader institutional issues themselves (Clark 1983; Clineberg 1976). Over time, the manner in which nations, including Japan, have been influenced by the educational practices and policies of other countries has changed. The evangelic, paternalistic, and colonial relationships that characterized educational transfers and borrowing during the nineteenth and early twentieth centuries have given way to relationships based on national sovereignty, with the actors playing the roles of "donors" and "recipients." The new paradigm based on cooperative and mutually beneficial interchanges suggests more equitable relations between nations, and this has clearly been the recent relationship between the United States and Japan.

The problems that continue to exist in many nations, and to some degree in Japan, can be attributed to such phenomena as lack of political will; international instability; educational systems that are dysfunctional, conventional, and tradition-bound; poorly developed delivery systems; and poor planning (Goulet 1977; Parkinson 1976; Phillips 1974). These problems have a positive aspect, since they suggest that solutions are available and that nothing is really wrong with the overall relationship between the two nations engaged in lending and borrowing.

However, there are other, less optimistic critiques that call into question the basic concept of educational transfers and make a range of charges, from invocations of dependency concepts, neocolonialism, and cultural imperialism to less strongly worded charges of inequity and lack of participation in planning the educational transfer (Berman 1979; Carnoy 1976; Tuqan 1976). It has been suggested (Hawkins 1988) that there are at least four configurations of the assertions regarding educational transfers:

1. If the models are to succeed in developing, the recipients of the models must adopt the institutional, political, and economic patterns of the lender.
2. The entire relationship between a lender and borrower is exploitative and can only take place in a neocolonialist, dominant-subordinate environment.
3. Complete autonomy is necessary if a borrowing nation is to achieve any measure of self-reliance and independence in the relationship.

4. A large degree of reciprocity and cooperative participation can exist between both lender and borrower, and from them both benefit and mutual educational advantages are gained.

As we discuss the development of the junior college and American community college in Japan, we will consider these four possible configurations and the subthemes within them in an effort to frame this relatively new phenomenon within the Japanese educational scene. For example, technical colleges were introduced in the early 1960s in response to the demand from industry for a larger number of well-trained middle-level technicians. Unlike universities or junior colleges, technical colleges require only the completion of lower-secondary schooling for admission and offer five-year programs aimed at training technicians. The lower division of the technical college is part of the secondary education system (Abe 1994). Scholars in Japan associate the technical college with similar models in France, Germany, and the United Kingdom as well as with public community colleges in the United States. There also exist special training schools, which are comparable to proprietary schools in the United States. U.S. branch colleges (bunko) of all types are legally considered and incorporated as special training schools. Thus, vocational schools of this type resemble either community colleges (if they are publicly funded and operated) or proprietary schools (if they are for profit or under private management).

The Junior College Movement in Japan and Links to the United States

Community colleges in Japan generally have small enrollments and are only able to offer a limited curriculum. In fact, the vast majority of junior colleges (about 75 percent) offer a single, concentrated curricular focus *(gakka)* in such areas as English literature, music, and art (Taira and Levine 1992). This limited curriculum often has little relevance to higher levels of education or few links to the labor force (Taira and Levine 1992) and is influenced, in part, by the American community college.

The establishment of American-style colleges and universities dates back to the 1980s. A number of factors contributed to the boom of the so-called U.S. branch schools (bunko) in Japan. First, a high demand among Japanese for higher education resulted in over 400,000 qualified high school graduates being unable to find a place in the Japanese system. Second, as U.S.-Japanese relations strengthened, interest in the United States rose proportionately. Finally, as a response to this increasing interest, the USA-Japan Committee for Promoting Trade Expansion, a private organization, was formed, and it served as the broker for the Japanese and U.S. interests concerned with establishing "branch" schools in Japan. When this initial effort demonstrated success, more offers were made by both sides so that by 1991, over thirty-five U.S. higher educational institutions of various types (only a handful of which could be called community colleges), enrolling about 10,000 students, had established some presence in Japan.

The Japanese Ministry of Education neither approves nor accredits these institutions, although most are accredited by some agency in the United States. In most cases, the physical plant is Japanese-owned and financial and other administrative matters are handled by Japanese administrators. The American side is primarily responsible for establishing the curriculum, standards, and counseling and for teaching. The "boom period" did not last long, since the colleges were hindered by a variety of adaptation problems, and the result was a decline in the total number of American institutions operating in Japan ("Japan Demystified" 1992).

The first adaptation problem was that Japanese students often did not realize the difficulty of studying in an American university and were not intellectually ready for the transition from high school to college. Second, the English-language skills of the students were not often sufficient for the coursework being offered. Third, most of the branch schools were expensive, so there was a cost factor for which Japanese parents were not prepared. Finally, the American style of higher education is not necessarily appropriate for all the Japanese who might be interested. As one scholar suggests to potential Japanese students: "Are the values of an American higher education so compelling to you that you may be willing to trade-off some of the more practical benefits of Japanese higher education?" The practical benefits include the built-in networking that is so much a part of Japanese higher education (Tanaka 1994).

What follows is a brief sketch of two of Japan's seventeen branch community colleges that were introduced as alternatives to the more conventional junior college. These two cases illustrate some of the problems facing the Japanese in their current efforts to internationalize their system through the introduction of bunko schools.

Edmonds Community College in Kobe

In late 1989, the ground was officially broken for Edmonds Community College (EDCC) in Kobe. The main campus of EDCC, which is small and suburban, is located on the outskirts of Seattle, Washington. The president of EDCC initiated an international program at the home campus in the 1980s and quickly built a reputation for infusing the curriculum with international content. Shortly thereafter, the administration was invited to Japan to explore the possibility of building a branch campus in Kobe.

The branch campus of EDCC began somewhat typically as a joint enterprise between the community college district in Washington and business interests in Japan. EDCC is accredited by the Northwest Association of Schools and Colleges and is part of the public college system of the state of Washington. The business interest involved was the Mizota group in Japan, which had responsibility for the construction and operating costs of the new facilities. EDCC had responsibility for the instructional staff and academic programs. The branch campus was designed to include an academic transfer capacity, occupational training, and an intensive English curriculum (Morgridge 1989). The college officially opened in April 1990. The basic program consists of one year of intensive English language, followed by courses leading to either the associate-of-arts-and-sciences (AAS) degree or the associate-of-technical-arts (ATT) degree in hotel hospitality, international business, and international office skills. Completion of this program normally takes two years, and classes are conducted in English. A student-exchange component of the program allows fifty American students to attend the Kobe campus (the overall enrollment is slightly over 600) and fifty Japanese students to attend the home campus in Washington.

In Japan as well as at the home campus, EDCC is heavily oriented toward international business and the general globalization of the economy. As such, it appears to serve a utilitarian function. As Morgridge has noted, "Historically the college has focused on aggressive international marketing of our home programs and services. More recently we have begun to pay attention to the preparation of domestic students as global challenges of the 21st century increasingly erode parochial complacency about the American work force and the role and responsibilities of the community college, business and industry" (Morgridge 1989, 64).

The goal for the American students in the program is clearly to gain a cross-cultural experience, acquire some degree of Japanese language training (which would be very limited if their stay is restricted to one quarter), and get course credit for courses taken at the Kobe campus. It offers Japanese students the experience of attending an American-style university, perhaps transferring to the Washington campus or some other American campus, or being trained in English-language skills in order to work in an international setting. A major goal at the outset was to prepare Japanese students desiring to study in the United States with an American-style education of a quality and rigor that would allow for an easy transition between the two systems. The president has recognized that many Japanese students transferring to American universities and colleges have a difficult time adapting to the American model; the failure rate and return rate has been quite high in general between the two systems.

In the fall of 1992 the first Japanese graduates (three in all) completed the course of study, and indeed, two were employed later by an international business in Kobe and the other transferred to a four-year university in the Pacific Northwest (EDCC 1992). EDCC appears to represent a university-transfer model that is part business-oriented and part academic. It is too early to analyze the success or failure of this effort (although clearly, the number of students involved is relatively small). However, there appears to be a degree of reciprocity involved at least on the academic front. Japanese and American students are pursuing their own interests, they are in a cross-cultural setting, funding and academic responsibility is shared, and the potential for both sides to succeed is present (although recent reports suggest that EDCC is in financial difficulty and the future is unclear).

Tokyo American Community College

Tokyo American Community College (TACC) opened in 1988 and represented a somewhat different model from EDCC. Located in Yoyogi, Tokyo, TACC was affiliated with Los Angeles City College (LACC), one of the Los Angeles Community College District's colleges. TACC's president recognized early on that there was a major problem with a number of branch campuses located in Japan. Students took a few courses, transferred to an American university, and then returned to Japan, often without a degree and with less than satisfying experiences. Hence, TACC's goal was to ensure that Japanese students were exposed to a genuinely American approach to higher education in their academic programs, to facilitate their transfer to a four-year institution in the United States.

TACC had two principal curricular components: the English as a Second Language (ESL) program and the College program. LACC provided a degree- or certificate-based, multidisciplinary curriculum accredited by the Western Association of Schools and Colleges for both these programs. The College program was transplanted intact from LACC and included instruction in English; identical grading standards, courses, and textbooks; and transferrable degrees to California universities and colleges. All program components were approved by the appropriate department chairs at LACC. Likewise, the hiring standards the TACC adopted were identical to those of the LACC and included only instructors who had extensive community college teaching experience and who had received their degrees in the United States. Japanese instructors were hired if they had a minimum of a master's degree from an American university and were approved by the LACC administration. LACC faculty who had sabbatical leave were jointly funded by LACC and TACC to teach at TACC for short periods of time. One benefit of this arrangement was that these faculty gained experience in working with Asians, whose populations are increasing in the areas served by LACC.

The TACC student body was 95 percent Japanese, who either were preparing to go to the United States or had studied in the United States but who had not finished their degrees. Students were enrolled in full-time programs and paid a tuition of U.S.$4,000 each semester. A small number of American students attended TACC for a three-week summer program to build their Japanese language skills.

Although the formation of TACC involved a fair amount of educational planning, communication problems between the American and Japanese instructors/administrators and the Japanese staff became apparent at the onset. Measures were taken to mitigate these problems by instituting a hybrid Japanese-American management style that used "bridges" (bilingual and bicultural staff) to help administrators to make and implement decisions. Another initiative to adapt the college to the Japanese environment was "component education," which allowed students the freedom to construct their own ESL or academic programs without being bound to either TACC or LACC guidelines (Takasuka 1989). The resulting custom-designed curriculum typically contained more hours in ESL than did a typical LACC program, and reflected the individual student's learning desires. The TACC admission requirements mandated that all students have a 3.2 GPA and passing scores on the Michigan Test for English. While the English requirement may have limited the number of students who could enroll in TACC, those students who were admitted experienced an American learning atmosphere much like that found in LACC or other comparable U.S. community colleges (Nozawa and Shigefume 1989).

In spite of what appeared to be a sound mixture of good academic and fiscal planning, good long-term relationships between the partners, and a flexibility in management style, TACC closed down operations in early 1994. Several problem areas were identified by TACC evaluators, including problems of communication between TACC and LACC, inability to recruit sufficient numbers of students, lack of credibility of U.S. schools in Japan, and lack of formal accreditation by the Japanese Ministry of Education (Mombusho). The latter problem had both positive and negative effects. The positive effect was that TACC and other American-style branch campuses did not need to adhere to the many regulations imposed by Mombusho on Japanese universities and thus could be more flexible in teaching and curricula. The negative effect was that without accreditation, TACC and others lacked credibility in the eyes of the Japanese press and among the public. In addition, because many branch schools were established for purely financial gain, Japanese corporations and the public viewed all branch schools with suspicion because of their low instructional quality and high dropout rates.

Yet another significant problem was that only a few Japanese students actually completed the TACC program. Once students acquired sufficient English to take regular TACC courses, many chose to transfer immediately to the United States. TACC actually encouraged this practice on the premise that a student who had completed the ESL portion and taken twelve or more units in the regular curriculum would likely survive in an American higher educational institution. Towards this end, TACC provided students departing for the United States with orientation services to help them with travel plans, U.S. checking/banking accounts, airport transportation, and housing. This emphasis on both academic preparation and ease in transfer departed from the typical Japanese approach of treating this enterprise strictly as a business.

The most critical problem, however, concerned the significant gap that exists between American-style higher education institutions (especially short-cycle institutions) and Japanese higher education. In the former, as the student progresses through a program, evaluation and screening continuously occur through course exams and other forms of evaluation. In the latter, the most significant screening occurs at the front end, and once they are in a university or college, students are not faced with continuous exams. Japanese students thus complained that the courses at TACC were too difficult and that the course load was too heavy. This misperception of what is expected in the way of performance at a community college caused many students to drop out.

Thus, a mixture of financial, administrative, perceptual, and cultural factors combined to call into question the feasibility of transferring this educational form in this particular way. The experience of these two cases provides us with a number of insights into the concept of the two-year post-high-school experience in Japan.

Conclusions and Implications

The Japanese tradition of adaptation and grafting of foreign educational forms onto existing forms has not prevented difficulties in adapting the American-style short-cycle system. It is worthwhile to review the four configurations for educational transfer referred to earlier in this chapter. Did the Japanese adopt the institutional, political, and economic patterns of the United States with respect to junior and community colleges? In some respects they did, but in general, we can conclude that when the branch community college (*bunko*) succeeds in Japan, it is precisely because it uses a uniquely Japanese structure and content. The branch community colleges encountered difficulties when they held onto their specific American character. The second configuration, which portrays an inherently exploitative dominant-subordinate relationship, is hardly applicable in the Japanese case. The Japanese borrow primarily on their own terms and mold educational transfers to suit their own purpose. Similarly, Japan's efforts to develop educational models and its years of educational interaction with many countries bely its characterization under the "complete autonomy" configuration. The fourth configuration depicts the Japanese cases best, since both the United States and Japan seek (albeit with difficulty) to establish reciprocal relations and cooperation through education. The Japanese postwar development of the junior college, with its unique orientation toward women's education, is one example of borrowing and adaptation in which the final product reveals aspects of both the U.S. and Japanese institutional and cultural characters. The more recent efforts to introduce an American-style community college (as illustrated by TACC and EDCC) meet with less success, possibly because of a more limited adaptation process, although deeper issues cannot be discounted.

It is likely that a more thorough reassessment of U.S.-Japanese educational exchanges is needed, one that focuses on the broader issues of student, faculty, scholar, and institutional interchanges and on the reasons why many of these exchanges are faltering at this time. At one time, over 120 American institutions considered setting up branch campuses in Japan, and today only a handful are fully functional. Some (like TACC) have closed, while others (like EDCC) are in jeopardy. There may be significant structural and cultural obstacles to further borrowing and adaptation. The Japanese may be creating their own unique form of junior or community college. This is a topic that deserves further investigation from both American and Japanese perspectives.

REFERENCES

Abe, Yoshia. *Japanese Education Today and Internationalization of Higher Education.* Tokyo: Tokyo University Press, 1994.

Amano, Ikuo. "Continuity and Change in the Structure of Japanese Higher Education." In William K. Cummings, Ikuo Amano, and Kazuyuki Kitamura (eds.). *Changes in the Japanese University: A Comparative Perspective.* New York: Praeger Press, 1979.

Berman, Edward H. "Foundation, United States Foreign Policy and African Education."

Harvard Educational Review 49, no. 2 (1979): 145, 179.

Carnoy, Martin. *Education as Cultural Imperialism*. New York: McKay, 1976.

Clark, Burton R. *The Higher Education System: Academic Organization in Cross-National Perspective*. Berkeley: University of California Press, 1983.

Clineberg, Otto. *International Educational Exchange*. The Hague: International Social Science Council, 1976.

Edmonds Community College (EDCC). *Kobe Campus*. "Update" International Education Division. Lynwood, Wash.: EDCC, 1992.

Fujimura-Fanselow, Kumiko. "Women's Participation in Higher Education in Japan." In James J. Shields, Jr. (ed.). *Japanese Schooling Patterns of Socialization, Equality and Political Control*. University Park: Penn. State University Press, 1989.

Goulet, Dennis. *The Uncertain Promise*. New York: IDOC, 1977.

Hawkins, John N. "Redemocratization in the Philippines: The Role of International Exchanges." In Karl Borowski (ed.). *Redemocratization in the Philippines*. Los Banos: University of the Philippines Press, 1988.

"Japan Demystified." *Japan Access* 3, no. 38 (October 5, 1992): 5.

Morgridge, G. "Choose American Style Education." In G. Morgridge (ed.), *EDCC*. Kobe: EDCC Press, 1989.

Nozawa, Satoko, and Takasuka Shigefume. "A Growing Internationalization of Education." *Daily Yomiuri* (February 9, 1989): 3.

Perkin, Harold. "The Historical Perspective." In Burton R. Clark (ed.), *Perspectives on Higher Education*. Berkeley: University of California Press, 1984.

Parkinson, Nancy. *Educational Aid and National Development*. London: Macmillan, 1976.

Philips, H.M. "The Redeployment of Education Aid." In F. Champion Ward (ed.), *Education and Development Reconsidered*. New York: Praeger, 1974.

Shimahara, Nobuo K. "Overview of Japanese Education: Policy, Structure and Current Issues." In Robert Leestma and Herbert J. Walberg (eds.), *Japanese Educational Productivity*. Ann Arbor: Michigan Papers in Japanese Studies, 1992.

Taira, Koji, and Solomon B. Levine. "Education and Labor Skills in Postwar Japan." In Robert Leetsma and Herbert L. Walberg (eds.), *Japanese Educational Productivity*. Ann Arbor: Papers in Japanese Studies, 1992.

Takasuka, Shigefumi. "Component Education Systems." *Daily Yomiuri* (February 10, 1989): 2.

Tanaka, Yoshiro. "Assessment of Branch Campuses in Japan." Unpublished manuscript. 1994.

Tuqan, I. *Education, Society and Development in Underdeveloped Societies*. The Hague: Center for the Study of Education in Changing Societies, 1976.

Uyeki, Eugene. *As Others See Us: A Comparison of Japanese and American Fulbrighters*. New York: The Institute of International Education, 1993.

12 Egyptian Community Colleges
A Case Study

Amin A. Elmallah, Kal Gezi, and Hassan Abdel Hamid Soliman

BACKGROUND

From the dawn of civilization, ancient Egyptians had their schools in the temples, where priests imparted instruction to children. The teacher's function was to produce scribes to do the clerical work of the state. Throughout the centuries that followed, it was a fact that education was used by the state as an instrument for achieving its national agenda.

The history of the two-year community educational institutes (*ma'ahed* plural; *ma'ahad* singular), which can be traced to the 1950s, attests to this fact. The 1952 coup d'état that brought President Nasser to power marked the rise of nationalism and pan-Arabism. The revolutionary government realized that there was an urgent need to prepare Egyptians in vocational and technical fields in order to replace foreign workers in Egypt and be able to help Egyptian workers to assist Arab countries in their modernization efforts. The government embarked on creating two-year, intermediate, community vocational and technical *ma'ahed mutawasitah* patterned after the British system as an extension of high school vocational education.

In the 1960s the rise of socialism in Egypt led to the nationalization of all industries and the building of state-owned factories. These efforts resulted in new ma'ahed and in the expansion of some ma'ahed to four years (*al'ali*), to allow for more advanced vocational and technical studies. Ma'ahed also became an alternate route to postsecondary education, since the universities could not cope with the increasing student demand for admission.

The distinction between the two-year and four-year ma'ahad is that the former trains students to be semiskilled technicians whereas the latter prepares students to be highly skilled technicians who could assume more advanced positions in vocational fields. The faculty of the two-year ma'ahed are predominantly temporary and consist of those who are without a doctorate but hold regular jobs in vocational fields. On the other hand, the majority of the faculty at the four-year ma'ahed have doctorates and are usually borrowed from various universities.

The two-year ma'ahed offer a diploma that is equivalent to the associate-of-arts degree granted by American community colleges. The four-year ma'ahed offer a bachelor-of-arts or bachelor-of-science degree, which is equivalent to a B.A. degree in the United States.

The Egyptian equivalent to the U.S. community college is the two-year ma'ahad, whereas the four-year ma'ahad is a hybrid institution offering degrees like a university but having lower prestige and fewer resources. Its position is somewhere between that of the university and the two-year ma'ahad.

The 1970s ushered in President Sadat's economic open-door policy (*al-infitah al-iqtisadi*), which encouraged the flow of foreign capital into Egypt, strengthened the private sector, and expanded the production of consumer goods and services. To support this policy, new ma'ahed were established specializing in tourism, hotel management, social services, and modern technology.

When President Mubarak assumed power in 1981, he initiated a policy of economic structuring that veered the economic system further toward privatization and the use of Western technology. In response to this policy, the country witnessed the growth of ma'ahed, which specialized in developing the skilled work force needed to implement Western high technology in Egypt.

As shown in figure 6, the precollege educational system in Egypt follows a 5-8-3 pattern. Graduates from secondary schools who pass a state examination are eligible for admission to a postsecondary institution. The state examination is given annually to all students and is centrally prepared, controlled, and graded. Similar to many state systems in the United States, (i.e., California and Florida), the system of higher education in Egypt is based on a three-tier structure. The top tier constitutes the major universities of Cairo, Alexandria, Ein Shams, Assiut, and Al-Azher. The latter specializes in Islamic studies. These are the original universities, which were established prior to 1952. They are the most prestigious.

The middle tier is represented by the regional universities, which were established after 1960. They are less prestigious because some of them do not offer all fields of study, they are staffed with some part-time faculty, and their housing facilities are less adequate than those of the top-tier universities.

The bottom tier is represented by the intermediate and high ma'ahed. While ma'ahed are postsecondary institutions, they are not considered part

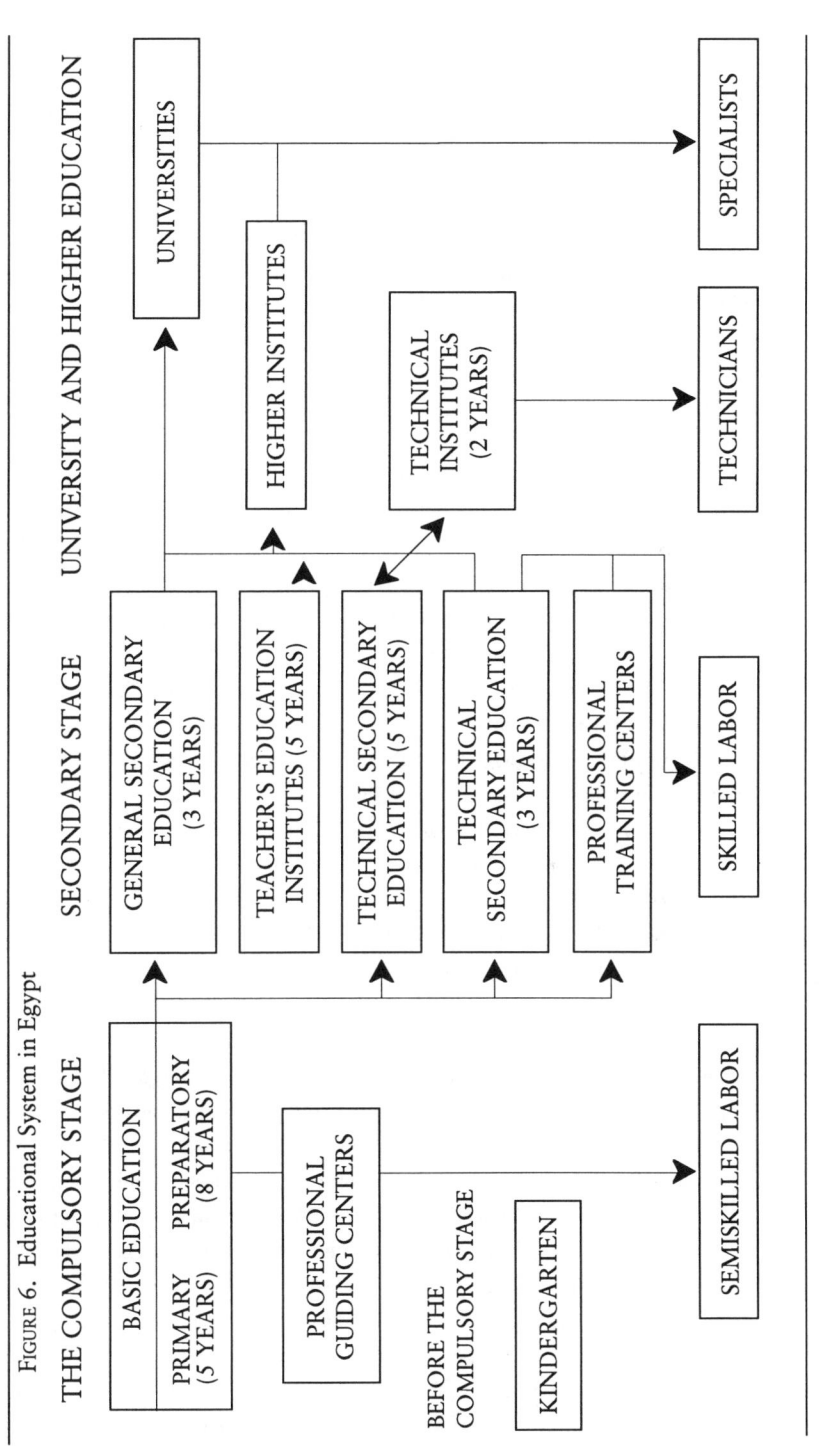

Figure 6. Educational System in Egypt

of the university system. Rather, they are small community institutions with a specialized curriculum focus on a vocational or technical field. Contrary to the U.S. model, Egyptian ma'ahed do not offer an academic program of study.

Ma'ahed are attended by students who are unable to be admitted to a university, who have failed in their university studies, or who simply are interested in a technical career. Ma'ahed share the following characteristics: (1) most are located outside of Cairo and Alexandria; (2) all emphasize technical and vocational work (unlike the U.S. models, they do not offer university-transferable academic courses); (3) all diplomas are terminal, and graduates have little chance to transfer to universities; (4) all ma'ahed are administered as a separate system by the Ministry of Higher Education and are apart from the university system and structure; (5) all are funded separately, and their per-capita funding is considerably lower than that of the university; (6) most of the facilities are inadequate, and most faculty are part-time because of the paucity of well-trained technical faculty; and (7) some are the only privately owned institutions of higher education in Egypt, since private universities are not allowed to be established.[1]

In 1992 there were eighty-seven public and private ma'ahed, which offered a range of specialized training in computers, hotel management, health, antiquities, art, agriculture, commerce, industry, social service, and secretarial work. Of these colleges, 65 were two-year ma'ahed (55 of which were public) and 22 were higher ma'ahed (10 of which were public). The focus of this discussion is on the two-year ma'ahed.

Goals and Structure

There are three broad goals for ma'ahed in Egypt. First, they are entrusted with the preparation of skilled workers and technicians in the commercial, industrial, vocational, and social service sectors. Some ma'ahed were established to offer specialized curricula (on such subjects as the hotel industry, tourism, social welfare, secretarial training, and health technology) that were not provided by the university system. Second, they are given the task of coordinating their offerings with community enterprises by being training centers for the personnel needed by local business and by providing and implementing the latest in technology to help in the improvement of community business firms. Finally, these colleges are designed to alleviate the enrollment pressures on universities. Because of the limited number of spaces in universities and the clamor for more high school graduates to pursue postsecondary education, small, specialized, and geographically accessible community institutes were established throughout the country.

In addition to these goals, each group of ma'ahed has, according to their area of specialization, a set of specific objectives. These objectives are approved by the appropriate higher council for that particular specialty. The objectives include the specification of skills, of the level of cooperation with community enterprises, and of the targeted number of graduates in each area of specialization. For example, an industrial ma'ahad may specialize in electronics and may be assigned the goal of preparing skilled workers for the community's electronics industry.

Governance

Each ma'ahad is administered by a dean, who is appointed by the minister of higher education (or by the board of directors, if it is a private institute). There are five national policy-making councils who recommend ma'ahed policies to the minister of higher education: (1) Council for Vocational and Child Education, (2) Council for Commercial Institutes, (3) Council for Higher Institutes of Technology, (4) Council for Technical and Industrial Education, and (5) Council for Higher Private Institutes. In addition, each ma'ahad has a local council, which is empowered with the implementation of the policies of the national councils and with the day-to-day operation of the institute. The membership of the local councils is composed of the dean, associate deans, department chairs, and a representative of the junior and senior faculty.

Funding

In Egypt, public higher education is, by law, free and students do not pay tuition. Students pay only minor fees for student activities, laboratory equipment, student government, and the processing of paperwork. Gifted or higher-performing students (eightieth percentile or better) in ma'ahed receive modest government stipends as an incentive for higher achievement.

The budget for each college is determined by the Ministry of Higher Education and is based on prior budgets, which are adjusted for salary increases and operating expenses to account for inflation and increased services. The capital construction and improvement budget is separate and is dealt with as part of the education building budget by the Ministry of Education.

The Ministry of Higher Education's budget for 1981–1982 and 1989–1990 (not adjusted for inflation) indicates that expenditures for salaries, operating expenses, and capital spending have increased substantially. It should be noted that the rate of inflation in Egypt is very high and is the primary cause of the increase in expenditures. The student share of the budget (higher education spending per student) increased over threefold between 1981–1982 and 1989–1990. The spending on the universities' share of the national budget increased from 2.4 percent in 1981–1982 to 3.5 percent in 1989–1990, while the expenditures on ma'ahed remained constant. Compared with the United States, community colleges get proportionately lower allocations.

CURRICULUM

The curriculum is highly structured and uniform. All first-year students enroll in freshman courses, and second-year students in specified courses. The curriculum and textbooks are determined by the Ministry of Higher Education and are reviewed by the Council on Higher Institutes. Similar ma'ahed have similar curricula. Faculty involvement in curriculum design, policy, and evaluation is minimal. Textbooks are uniform for all similar courses. However, course notes are prepared by instructors, who retain some control over course content through assignments and lectures.

The curriculum is revised infrequently, and student promotion is based on uniform examinations that are prepared for each course by department faculty and given at the same time to all students completing the course.

At the Institute of Social Service at Alexandria, for instance, students enroll in eleven courses each year. These courses require between twenty-nine and thirty-two hours for class and laboratory work (see table 5). Sample curricula from the commercial, technical-industrial, and hotel-tourism ma'ahed are depicted in tables 6–8.

TABLE 5. Ma'ahad of Social Service, Alexandria: 1992 Curriculum

First Year	Second Year
Introduction to Social Service	Service to Individuals
General Sociology	Service to Society
General Psychology	Social Organization
Introduction to Economics	Social Development
Political Science	Economic Development
Social Health	Health and Industrial Psychology
Foreign Language	Rural and Urban Sociology
Social Laws	Statistics
Islamic Laws	Communication in Social Service
Statistics	Foreign Language
Field Training	Field Training

TABLE 6. Commercial Ma'ahad, Tanta: 1992 Curriculum

First Year	Second-Year Accounting	Second-Year General
Basic Accounting	Cost Accounting	Human Relations
Introduction to Computers	Accounting	Inventory Accounting
Commercial Law	Statistics	Statistics
Office Administration	Public Sector	Public Sector
Business Administration (Management)	Private Sector	Purchasing
	Commercial Law	Commercial Law
Behavioral Sciences	Marketing and Advertising	Marketing and Advertising
Introduction to Economics		
Foreign Language	Government Accounting	Industrial Security
Business Mathematics	Foreign Language	Foreign Language

TABLE 7. Technical and Industrial Ma'ahad, Alexandria: 1992 Curriculum

First Year	Second Year
Mathematics	Operation Systems
Electronic Measurement	Industrial Organizations
Engineering Drawing	Mathematics
Electrical Engineering	Electronic Measurement and Systems
Shop Technology	Transformation Circuits
English Language	English Language
Mechanics; Introduction to Computers; Electrical Shop Resources; Control Systems	

TABLE 8. Hotel and Tourism Ma'ahad, Port Said: 1992 Curriculum

First Year	Second Year
Hotel Management A	Hotel Management B
History of Tourism	Internal Supervision and Quality Control
English and French Languages	English and French Languages
Restaurant Service, Room Service, and Hotel Decoration	Restaurant Service and Party Service
	Linen and Bedding
Linen and Bedding	Menu Preparation and Nutrition
Public Health	Hotel Culinary
Hotel Culinary	

In contrast with U.S. community colleges, none of the ma'ahed have an academic or general-education program. All curricula have a technical or vocational focus because their mission is to prepare a skilled work force and not to provide students with the courses needed for transfer to universities.

Depending on regional needs, there are some variations in the curricula offered by similar institutes. Egyptian ma'ahed place a greater emphasis on second-language competency than do their American counterparts. A foreign language is required in almost all ma'ahed. An English-language requirement is most common, followed by French. Influenced by Islamic traditions, males are more attracted to industrial education while females tend to select secretarial and nursing education. Males are considered the heads of the household and the breadwinners of the family. Females are relegated to a secondary status and perceived as homemakers or as providers of a supplementary income to the family through traditionally female occupations such as nursing, secretarial work, and primary-school teaching.

A unique aspect of the curriculum is that all courses are vocationally and technically oriented and are connected to fieldwork and practical training. Each ma'ahad has a specialized curriculum, yet courses are taught through predetermined textbooks. Universal characteristics include large classes and fieldwork components. The main method of instruction is lecturing, and the main strategy for evaluating students is examinations based on memorization. Ma'ahed hold classes in inadequate facilities, and some of them share buildings with primary or secondary schools, so that classes are held in double or triple shifts.

DEMOGRAPHIC CHARACTERISTICS OF THE PROGRAM

Based on our analysis, the profile of students who attend ma'ahed in Egypt is as follows: They have low scores on the National High School Diploma Examination, they are unable to be admitted to a university, they are from lower- to middle-class backgrounds, they live outside of the Cairo or Alexandria regions, they are older than the average university student, they have part-time work, they have technical career goals, and they have lower expectations of themselves. Many of these characterize the U.S. community college student as well.

Although university enrollments have declined, ma'ahed enrollments have increased. Several factors account for this increase. First, the population explosion in Egypt has caused a large number of high school graduates to desire the prestige of admission to a postsecondary institution. Besides, high school graduates have fewer job opportunities than do graduates of postsecondary institutions. Second, since university admission is limited to those students who score the highest on the high school national examinations, those who have lower scores on these examinations clamor to be admitted to ma'ahed. Third, even students with high scores on national tests may find it economically difficult to shoulder the costs of room and board while attending a university out of town. Location could be viewed by many students as a positive economic factor, since attendance at ma'ahed enables them to stay at home while pursuing their postsecondary education. Fourth, the government, the emerging private business sector, and the media have recently emphasized the need for technical education. Fifth, ma'ahed provide vocational training that is linked to jobs in the private sector in Egypt and throughout the Arab world. Linking training to jobs is only recently becoming common in community colleges in the United States. It is true that government jobs are the most sought after because of their security, but with the current economic recession, there are fewer government jobs available in comparison with jobs in the private sector.

As for gender, our data indicate that of the total student enrollments at public and private ma'ahed in 1992 (245,916), there were 88,220 female students (36 percent) and 157,696 male students (64 percent). While male-female statistics from previous years are sketchy, there seems to be an increase in the number of female students. Females represented almost 42 percent of the graduates of commercial ma'ahed in 1992. Some commercial institutes (such as those for secretarial training) admit women only, while the rest of the ma'ahed are coeducational. Analyzing the enrollments at two-year private ma'ahed, it is interesting to note that female students constitute about 60 percent of the student population. This may be due to the fact that most of these colleges are in the secretarial, health, and social service areas, which attract mainly women. Female students in ma'ahed have a higher dropout rate than their male counterparts. The causes for such dropouts include family problems, marriage, and the difficulty of traveling or of living away from home. In conformity with traditions, many parents shelter their daughters from the rigors of life beyond their local area.

Student access to ma'ahed is affected by socioeconomic status, urban-vs.-rural place of residence, and gender but not by religion or race. Wealthy students have more choices in higher education. They can afford to study at private colleges and universities in Egypt and abroad. Urban dwellers are close to more higher education institutions than are rural dwellers.

As for religion and race, it is important to note that even though 90 percent of Egyptians are Sunni Muslims and about 10 percent are Christians, students' religion has not been a factor in admission to ma'ahed or to the universities.

In addition to mainstream Egyptians, there are the Bedouins, who are nomadic herdspeople and traders, and Nubians, who are mostly black. The Bedouins' nomadic existence limits their access to all segments of education. Nubians, on the other hand, do not face barriers to ma'ahed because of their color. Nubians live in large cities and have a variety of occupations, which do not differ from the occupations of average Egyptians.

The influence of Islam is not seen in the curriculum or in textbooks but is shown in the conservative dress code for women and in the seating of women in the front of the class. Women do not find adequate prayer space on campus, since men and women pray separately during the five daily prayer times. Furthermore, student associations tend to be heavily dominated by Muslim traditionalists, who espouse conservative policies such as enforcement of dress codes for women.

Egyptian ma'ahed do not offer any multicultural programs. Their curricula focus on the preparation of students in specific vocational fields. Some offer courses in Islamic laws, foreign languages, and rural and urban sociology as part of the preparation of students for social service. Students who are interested in studying Islamic and Arabic culture can pursue higher studies at Al Azhar University, which focuses on Islamic studies. Many educators feel that the Egyptian culture and the culture of the rest of the Arab world are homogeneous.

Students from Arab countries who study in Egypt find little difference between their native cultures and that of Egypt. The Arabic language and Islamic traditions serve as bonds among the people of the Arab world. African students are few in number and tend to have similar social, religious, and cultural values. Thus, ma'ahed do not have students with international or intercultural experience. Egyptian students who return from study abroad usually return with B.A. or graduate degrees; hence, they are apt to enroll not at ma'ahed but at one of the major universities for advanced study.

Faced with the country's recent economic stagnation, few ma'ahad graduates find secure government jobs after graduation. Most work in the private sector in jobs related or unrelated to their training.

There is a high ratio of ma'ahad administrators to faculty, which seems to mirror the Egyptian bureaucratic practice of promoting senior staff members into the ranks of the better paid administrators. The number of ma'ahad faculty members has doubled since 1982, but the increase in the number of permanent faculty lags far behind the increase in student enrollments. In order to staff ma'ahed, the few permanent faculty are augmented by part-time faculty. In 1990 there were 2,443 administrators, 1,334 permanent faculty members, and 4,024 part-time faculty members serving all ma'ahed. Some ma'ahed, such as the secretarial and social service institutes, are staffed by part-time faculty only.

The reason for the reliance on part-time faculty is the paucity of qualified professors in most of the technical fields and the fact that part-time faculty are less costly to hire than full-time faculty. Qualified faculty members prefer to teach at universities rather than in ma'ahed.

Student Admission and Evaluation

To enter ma'ahed, students must graduate from a secondary school, pass a required test in their field of specialization, and pass a personal interview conducted by the faculty of each institute. Furthermore, students must reside in the province that is served by the desired ma'ahad, since each institute is designated a service area. Some ma'ahed have languages, some have subject or physical fitness requirements, and some are open to women only.

Students are evaluated mostly through year-end examinations, which are prepared by the faculty. If fieldwork is part of a course of instruction, its quality becomes another criterion of evaluation. Students receive a diploma, which is terminal and qualifies the graduate for technical work in the chosen field. Graduates seldom continue their studies in four- or five-year ma'ahed or at universities. For such graduates to be admitted to a university, they must attain an average score of 75 percent or more, as determined by the scores of the general high school graduating class. In addition, transfer students are accepted as sophomores not juniors, which thereby defines two years of ma'ahad studies as equal to one year of university study.

Problems Facing Ma'ahed

The first conference on higher education in Egypt, which was held in January 1993, brought together heads of all tiers of higher education, Ministry of Higher Education officials, and postsecondary education specialists. The purpose of the conference was to address the problems facing each segment of higher education and to search for viable and practical solutions.

Each ma'ahad dean was asked to prepare a paper identifying the problems faced by his or her particular institution and recommending solutions. The deans' perceptions underscore our analysis.

In our judgment, the problems faced by ma'ahed can be classified into the following four categories: cultural, governance, systemic, and economic. The deans focused mainly on the last two categories. The cultural impediments to innovation in higher education are a lack of confidence in national policies, a mistrust of people in educational leadership positions, a sense of fatalism, an unwillingness to take risks, social conformity, and apathy. A study of bureaucratic innovation and economic development in the Middle East (including Egypt) by Palmer et al. (1989) concludes "that public servants in those countries are not innovative on the job, nor inclined to try new ideas and take risks. Their apathy, which was empirically confirmed by their superiors, does not augur well for economic development" (Palmer et al. 1989, 1).

Administrators and faculty members are examples of this type of public servant. The large number of administrators in institutes means a heavy layer of bureaucracy and red tape. Faculty tend to be averse to risk taking and innovation because they do not want to jeopardize their positions or because they have given up on changing the traditional system.

Traditions in society, including education, are hard to change. As Mutchler (1990) points out, the barriers to changes in traditional behavior include fear of taking risks, fear of losing power, resistance to changes in roles and responsibilities, lack of trust, lack of task definition and clarity in tasks, inadequate resources, lack of skills, and lack of support from the top.

The Ministry of Higher Education perceives centralization as a contributor to uniformity, simplicity, speed in decision making, orderly articulation to the university, and cost reduction. But governance problems stem from the top-down model of decision making, which precludes the possibility of involvement by those who are affected by the decisions. The Ministry of Higher Education develops educational plans, allocates resources, and supervises all institutes. Within each ma'ahad, there is no shared decision making regarding the formulation of policies. Administrators make decisions, and seniority is the only basis for promotion. Policies are made at the Ministry of Higher Education and often change if there are new administrators at the ministry. Policies typically change every time there is a new minister of higher education.

The ma'ahad deans pointed out several systemic problems with which we concur. First, the faculty's instructional salaries are low. These are 30–50 percent lower than what university professors earn. Although the latter augment their salaries through the sale of textbooks that they have authored, ma'ahad faculty are not allowed to write their own textbooks, since ma'ahad textbooks are written by committees selected by the Ministry of Higher Education. The monthly salaries of these faculty members are not sufficient to pay a month's rent or a month's supply of food. That is why the majority consider their salaries to be second income. Their primary income comes from their work as technicians, construction foremen, or small-business entrepreneurs. Faculty members are paid small fees for proctoring and grading examinations. Those who serve on textbook committees are also paid book royalties. Because of the low salaries, there is a shortage of full-time faculty, and this results in a reliance on a sizable number of part-time faculty.

Second, the ma'ahad faculty and administrators are inadequately prepared for their jobs. Most of the faculty are borrowed from business, nearby universities, or industry and do not have adequate training as teachers, and because of the shortage of faculty, unqualified persons are frequently hired. There is a lack of systematic faculty development programs to assist instructors in pedagogy and to keep them abreast of developments in their fields. As for the administrators, they are mostly older instructors who are promoted to their administrative positions on the basis of seniority and political considerations. Administrators do not have administrative training or professional development programs either. Ma'ahad faculty and administrators are considered government employees and, hence, have job security and guaranteed salaries until their mandatory retirement at age sixty.

Third, outdated instructional strategies pervade ma'ahad classrooms. The lecture format is the basic teaching method. Instructional media, computers, and copying machines are scarce, and the faculty are not motivated to experiment with various instructional methodologies or rewarded for it.

Fourth, we agree with the ma'ahad deans that the curricula are limited to several technical subjects. They do not allow for sufficient practice and are slow to accommodate recent developments in the subjects they offer. The deans feel that their present curricula do not train students to work effectively in the production sector and that the coordination between ma'ahed and the job market is inadequate. Ma'ahed have failed to live up to their goal of contributing to their regions' economic growth and development.

Fifth, the examinations focus on role learning. They test students' knowledge and not their comprehension or their ability to analyze, apply, synthesize, or evaluate data. Examinations are written by a faculty committee chosen by the senior faculty and reflect what the students can remember from textbooks and lectures. Many students refrain from studying until a few weeks prior to taking their final examinations.

Sixth, ma'ahed do not have international and multicultural emphases. Each college has a narrow technical mission that excludes all other disciplines. The insufficient resources, small numbers of permanent faculty, lack of incentives for research, and lack of awareness of the emerging need for cross-cultural and global education have contributed to the exclusion of international and multicultural programs in ma'ahed.

The deans and the authors are in agreement that poor economic conditions in Egypt result in inadequate funding for ma'ahed. This is manifested in inadequate physical facilities for classrooms and laboratories and in insufficient equipment. Economic development and the job market are not keeping pace with the number of graduates. This problem is compounded by the recent decline in job opportunities for Egyptians in the Arab world. The current economic recession in Egypt has resulted in declining opportunities for self-employment and for small-business development. For government jobs, which are attractive because of their security, there is a waiting list of five years or more for applicants (Ross 1989).

RECOMMENDATIONS

The ma'ahad deans made the following recommendations for the reform of their institutions, and based on our independent research indicating the need to improve the quality of ma'ahad education, we support them.

1. Since curricula and instructional reform are designed to meet the needs of the job market, modern skills and up-to-date knowledge should be cultivated in all ma'ahed, especially in the high-technology areas.
2. Areas of specialization in each ma'ahad need to be redesigned to meet the current and future demands of the job market.
3. Stronger ties between ma'ahed and regional production and service sectors should be established. Establishments in these sectors should become training centers for ma'ahad students.
4. A plan needs to be adopted whereby administrators, faculty, and ministry officials work on reforming a few ma'ahed each year with the assurance that their goals will be implemented.
5. National and local resources need to be redirected toward the improvement of ma'ahed. Reliance on new local resources is vital to any improvement plan.
6. Prior to any reform effort, the availability of adequate facilities is a must. These include buildings, laboratories, equipment, and space for student activities.
7. Adequate preparation and compensation of faculty are significant steps toward reform.
8. The ma'ahed needs to focus their mission on providing well-trained individuals rather than on offering space for high school graduates who are unable to be admitted to a university.
9. Student admissions should be regulated in accordance with job market needs.
10. The number of years required for graduation might be increased from two to three years.

The deans sum up their recommendations by emphasizing that the availability of resources and a sufficiently qualified faculty are the key to the solution of all ma'ahad problems.

Finally, the authors believe that reform should encompass not only the economic and systemic areas but also the cultural and governance spheres. The tangled web of bureaucracy should be transformed into a clearer chart of staff functions. Centralization should be lessened gradually through increased local participation and community input. Curricula should place greater emphasis on international and multicultural educational programs, in order to prepare students to understand and value cultural diversity in a shrinking and interdependent world. This may begin with an emphasis on the multicultural dimensions of various regions in the Middle East.

Relevance of the American Community College Model

Which aspects of the American community college system are likely to enhance the Egyptian model? There are several aspects that would be helpful. First, Egypt needs to formulate a master plan for higher education, and it should articulate and clarify the mission of the university, the higher ma'ahad, and the two-year ma'ahad. The plan should clarify the relationship among these three segments and identify the means for coordination, articulation, and collaboration. Students may then be able to apply their two years of course credits at a ma'ahad to a university and therefore save the government additional expenditures. If ma'ahed can be viewed as an integral part of a master plan of higher education in Egypt, the quality of their programs would be improved and their attractiveness would be enhanced.

Second, Egyptians can use the American concept of community service to redesign their ma'ahad programs to meet community needs and build close working relationships with community establishments and local agencies. Such relationships would enhance community support and participation in the education of ma'ahad students and would provide them with opportunities for personal growth in job internships and community service.

Third, the American concept of open access for all students is the cornerstone of the democratization of education. Despite the commendable fact that education in Egypt is free, students still face several obstacles to gaining admission to ma'ahed. The foremost obstacle is passing the national examinations, which are based on rote learning. Furthermore, students still have to pay for books, course supplies, and travel and living expenses (if they come from a different region).

If admission to a local ma'ahad is based only on the student's place of residence and on the availability of space, the open-access concept can then be implemented and would transform ma'ahed into "people's colleges" and serve to promote higher education to all.

Now, let us turn to the question, which aspects of the American community college model will not translate well in Egypt?

The concept of local control, which characterizes American community colleges, cannot be implemented in the centralized educational system of Egypt, where decisions are handed down from the Ministry of Higher Education. Similarly, the concept of shared governance and management cannot translate well in Egypt because of the deep-rooted bureaucratic tradition and the zealous guarding of turf that exist there.

The limited resources available for education in Egypt will not allow drastic and costly reforms of ma'ahed to take place in the near future. Reform efforts and expansion plans have to be scaled down and phased in gradually over decades.

The American model's emphasis on experimentation, innovation, and nontraditional offerings does not have the potential for implementation in Egypt. The ma'ahad cultural ethos is one of apathy, conformity, and "don't rock the boat." This culture offers no incentive for faculty research or innovation. In fact, it condones the folk saying, "The more you work, the more errors you make."

SUMMARY

Egyptian ma'ahed have provided advanced technical education beyond the technical high schools. They have raised public awareness of the importance of technical education and have scored limited success in cooperating with community enterprises to improve the means of production and in enhancing the efficiency of Egyptian workers. Several of the more recent colleges (such as those covering hotel work, health, secretarial work, and applied technology) have made strides in achieving their goals.

Ma'ahed provide an alternate path to higher education for nontraditional students: those with low scores on the national examination, those from rural populations, and those who live in areas beyond Cairo and Alexandria. Compared to university education, ma'ahed education is less expensive for the student and for the nation. In light of the problems mentioned earlier, continual reform efforts, phased in over a period of time, are necessary for the enhancement of the institutes' effectiveness and will assist in Egypt's march into the twenty-first century.

Notes

1. The American University in Cairo is an exception, mainly because it was established prior to 1952 and has an excellent reputation.

References

Board of Governors, California Community Colleges. *The Basic Agenda.* Sacramento: Board of Governors, California Community Colleges, 1992.
"Could Egypt Be the Next Iran?" *Business Week* (July 12, 1993): 48.
Cochran, J. *Education in Egypt.* Dover, N.H.: Croom Helm, 1986.
El-Banna, R. "The Search for New Educational System." *Al-Ahram* (Cairo) (February 21, 1993).
Elmallah, A., and K. Gezi. "Educational Reform in Egypt: Practitioners' Perspectives." *Journal of Abstracts in International Education* 19, no. 2 (1992): 113.
―――. "Egypt." In R. Murray Thomas (ed.), *Education's Role in National Development Plans.* New York: Praeger, 1992.
"First Higher Education Conference Proceedings." Unpublished report. Cairo, 1993 (in Arabic).
Gezi, K. *The Educational System of the Arab Republic of Egypt.* U.S. Department of Health, Education, and Welfare. Washington, D.C.: U.S. Government Printing Office, 1979.
Kimber, P., and P. Wooford. *The Establishment of a National Center for Educational Evaluation and Examination.* Unpublished report. Washington, D.C.: The Academy of Educational Development, n.d.
Meaney, D. "Quest for Quality." *California Technology Project Quarterly* 2, no. 2 (1991): 9.
Ministry of Higher Education. *Statistics of Higher and University Education 1991/1992.* Cairo: Ministry of Higher Education, 1992.
Ministry of Education. *Education in Egypt.* Cairo: Ministry of Education, Rozalyossef New Printing, 1990.
―――. *Student Guide, Admission to Universities and Institutes.* Cairo: Cairo University Press, 1992.
―――. *Student Guide, High Institute of Social Service.* Alexandria, Egypt: University Knowledge House, 1992.
―――. *Technical Education: Proceedings of Higher Education Conference, Selected Studies.* Cairo: Ministry of Education, 1993.
Mutchler, S. *Eight Barriers to Changing Educational Policy and Practice.* Austin, Tex.: South West Educational Development Laboratory, 1990.
Palmer, M., A. Al-Hegelan, M. Abdelrahman, A. Leila, and E. Yassin. "Bureaucratic Innovation and Economic Development in the Middle East: A Study of Egypt, Saudi Arabia, and the Sudan." *Journal of Asian and African Studies* XXIV, nos. 1–2 (1989): 1.
Ross, M. "Egypt School Crisis: No Sixth Grade." *Los Angeles Times,* part I (May 8, 1989): 8.

13 MICHLALOT EZORIYOT—REGIONAL COLLEGES IN ISRAEL
CHALLENGES, PROMISES, AND PROSPECTS OF AN ALTERNATIVE MODEL IN HIGHER EDUCATION

Yaacov Iram

Higher education in Israel comprises two major sectors: universities and "other institutions of higher education." (This chapter does not deal with higher educational institutions in the West Bank and Gaza.) The seven existing universities are authorized by the Council for Higher Education (CHE) to award all types of academic degrees, while the "other institutions" provide instruction leading to professional bachelor's degrees in one specific field such as technology, administration, arts, or teaching. In addition to these two sectors, there exist eleven "regional colleges" (*michlalot ezoriyot*), which enjoy a special status and bear some of the characteristics of the other two academic sectors (CHE 1993).

The michlalot ezoriyot were established initially to serve as centers for adult education. However, since 1970, to make higher education accessible to underrepresented sectors of the population in peripheral areas (mainly Jews of North African or Asian origin, as well as Arabs and other minority groups), some regional colleges introduced an academic track. While michlalot ezoriyot are independent institutions under the jurisdiction of the Ministry of Education and Culture in their nonacademic, adult education, and enrichment programs, their academic courses are under the supervision of the universities, which prescribe their program of studies, appoint their teachers, and finally award their degrees (CHE 1993, 118–120).

Until recently the academic programs at the michlalot ezoriyot included only introductory and intermediary courses, equivalent to the first two years of the three-year baccalaureate course of study. To fulfill the requirements of the bachelor's degree, students were expected to take advanced courses and seminars at the main campus of the supervisory university. However, in light of increased demands for higher education and "in order to make higher education more accessible to broader segments of the population" (CHE 1988, 75), the Council for Higher Education appointed a special committee, in 1985, to supervise the academic courses of the michlalot ezoriyot. Indeed, the spread of regional colleges in the northern and southern parts of Israel is probably responsible for much of the increase in the number of students in higher education from underrepresented sectors of the population.

Further developments towards granting an independent and distinctive academic status to michlalot ezoriyot got underway in the 1990s, primarily as a result of demographic changes. An increased number of immigrants to Israel from the former Soviet Union has resulted in an excess of highly skilled professionals in fields such as medicine and engineering but has also caused increased demands for higher education by young immigrants whose education was interrupted or about to commence in their former countries. It was expected that these demands could be met by establishing independent nonprofessional undergraduate colleges for general studies and, particularly, by expanding the role of michlalot ezoriyot as an alternative to the specialized, traditional, undergraduate degree programs of the universities (and distinct also from the professionally oriented degree programs offered at professional colleges).

The aim of this chapter is to present and analyze the development of michlalot ezoriyot as a unique response to the changing needs of Israeli society and as an alternative model for higher education and to compare them to community colleges in the United States.

ALTERNATIVES TO UNIVERSITIES

Since the 1950s, Israel, like many developing countries, has witnessed a rapid expansion in postsecondary education. Enrollments continued to increase in the 1970s and 1980s: from 55,800 students in 1970 to 97,100 in 1980, to 117,500 in 1988, and to 153,700 in 1992 (UNESCO 1990; Central Bureau of Statistics 1993). In response to the growing demands for higher education, between 1955 and 1965 four new universities were added to the two existing higher education institutions, the Hebrew University and the Haifa Technion, which were founded before the establishment of the State of Israel.

Notwithstanding the distinct origins of the universities established in the 1950s and 60s, they tended to imitate the two veteran higher education institutions by stressing research as a measure of the strength of the institution as a whole and of particular departments (Iram 1983). Indeed, the long-standing tradition of the unity of research and teaching is responsible for the growth of research in Israeli universities, so that today it is their most important feature (Ben-David 1986). In spite of the establishment of four new universities, the dramatic growth in the number of first-degree students made it clear that traditional universities alone could not meet the educational needs of the growing number of secondary school graduates as well as the demands of the expanding Israeli economy and civil service for a trained work force. Furthermore, the Israeli universities, which followed the established path of the European traditional universities (whether Humboldtian or Oxbridge) and catered to a small group of graduates from selective secondary schools, were ill adapted to meeting the various aspirations and aptitudes of the comprehensive school graduates of the late 1960s. Indeed, Israel was approaching a transition from "elite" to "mass" higher education (Trow 1976).

Thus, sharing the concerns of some Western European countries, Israel transformed the elitist secondary schools into comprehensive high schools, increased the responsiveness and relevance of postsecondary education to a diversified clientele of graduates, and prepared them for changing employment needs. In addition, there were growing pressures for greater social equity. Indeed, demands that had been voiced during the late 1960s for equal educational opportunities were met more or less successfully by the 1968 school reform, which aimed at "secondary education for all" (Schmida 1987; Glasman 1983). This goal was also achieved by expanding the vocational education system (Iram 1986). The postsecondary reform proposals aimed to extend access to underrepresented groups according to the following categories: (1) age (more older students), (2) sex (more females), (3) ethnicity (more Orientals-Sephardim and Arabs), (4) educational and geographical background (more graduates from poorer schools in "development towns" in the northern and southern peripheries of Israel), (5) linguistic ability (more graduates of Arab high schools who were not proficient in Hebrew, the language of university instruction), and (6) local empowerment (more responsiveness to regional and local communities' needs) (Aran 1970).

To achieve these aims, there was a need, at the postsecondary level, to provide and design a wider range of vocationally oriented programs of either short-term or interim duration and at a low cost. Indeed, "short-cycle higher education" has been the term used in comparative studies to describe this phenomenon in postsecondary education, which has become prevalent since the 1960s in both developing and developed countries (Furth 1973; Duperre 1977).

Two possible strategies for introducing such changes in higher education were (1) diversification within existing (particularly the recently established) higher education institutions or (2) the establishment of separate institutions, which would be outside the universities and have distinct characteristics and purposes. The first approach favored multipurpose comprehensive universities and was adopted by Sweden (Scott 1991) and to a lesser degree by the German *Gesamthochschulen* (Cerych 1981). The second approach, represented by the American community college, was favored by most countries (Goedegebuure and Meek 1989; Gellert et al. 1991).[1]

To understand Israel's "alternatives," it is advisable to analyze them in the context of three prevalent models (Furth 1973). First is the "multipurpose" model of the American community college, which provides open access to mass higher education institutions. Community colleges offer academic, vocational, continuing, remedial, and adult short-cycle programs (Brint and Karabel 1989; Cohen and Brawer 1987, 1989). In the second model, which is common in European countries, "specialized" institutions offer short-term, vocationally oriented courses, such as those offered at Instituts Universitaires de Technologie (IUTs) in France (Lamoure 1981), *Fachhochschulen* in Germany (Teichler 1990), or Norwegian regional colleges (Kyvik 1981). Third is the "binary" model of the British polytechnics, which offer courses and qualifications that are vocationally oriented but also have authorization to offer university-level degrees (Department of Education and Science 1985; Pratt 1988).

In the 1990s European higher education is in the midst of a reconfiguration process. This is particularly evident in relation to postsecondary education, the "further education and training" (FET) sector and the "nonuniversity sector" (NUS). Changing economic markets and social demands, which were accelerated by geopolitical changes, encouraged the publication of two major reports by the Organization for Economic Cooperation and Development (OECD), which discussed these reforms in the context of "traditional" universities (OECD 1991a, 1991b).

Outside developments have caused Israel to face pressures to expand and diversify its postsecondary and higher education systems. Geopolitical and socioeconomic events during the past four-and-a-half decades of Israel's existence as an independent state (including massive immigrations from both developed and developing countries) have resulted in social inequalities between ethnic groups. In addition, periods of economic growth followed by high inflation and economic stagnation, as well as periods of conflict with its Arab neighbors, have affected the rate of growth and the direction of development of postsecondary education in Israel (Eisenstadt 1985; Iram 1992).

INSTITUTIONAL CHARACTERISTICS

Tertiary education in Israel during the past four decades underwent some major quantitative and qualitative developments. The 1950s and 1960s witnessed dramatic quantitative growth, since four new universities were founded and new programs of study and new professional schools were introduced. A major structural reform at the Hebrew University took place in 1950, when it introduced undergraduate studies and thus adopted the American three-level degree structure (B.A., M.A., and Ph.D.). This reform, which later became a structural norm for all other universities in Israel, marked a departure from the previous elitist German higher education tradition and toward that of the American comprehensive university (Ben-David 1986; Iram 1983). The 1970s brought further growth in the number of students, diversification of academic disciplines, and new programs of study (some of them interdisciplinary) at existing universities as well as in the nonuniversity sector. Indeed, the nonuniversity sector established itself with the founding of michlalot ezoriyot as an alternative to universities. The higher education system diversified further when nonuniversity institutions, particularly those geared to the paramedical professions (such as nursing, nutrition, and physiotherapy) and primary-school teaching, became more academically oriented (CHE 1975). Thus, Israel's higher education system moved in the direction of interinstitutional and intrainstitutional differentiation and democratization by adopting some "American" characteristics.

Since independence, the great demand for professional and administrative personnel in Israel has resulted in one of the highest growth rates of higher education in the world. Between 1948–49 and 1959–60, the number of students at postsecondary institutions and in universities grew by 447 percent and 567 percent respectively and between 1959–60 and 1969–70, these numbers grew by 205 percent and 381 percent, respectively. The higher education system continued to grow in the coming decades although at a slower pace and in a reverse trend, with postsecondary institutions expanding relatively more than the universities. Thus, between 1969–70 and 1979–80, the number of students in universities grew by 154 percent, while the number in postsecondary institutions increased by 213 percent. This tendency continued in the 1980s at a rate of 144 percent in universities and 163 percent in the postsecondary, nonuniversity sector (Central Bureau of Statistics 1993, 641).

In the 1990s Israel has new possibilities for economic growth, with the prospects of peaceful coexistence with its Arab neighboring states and of the massive immigration of about 750,000 people from the former Soviet Union (Central Bureau of Statistics 1993).

Employment and Social Mobility

The most manifest utilitarian link between education at all levels and, particularly, between higher education and society is its contribution to social mobility. The expectation that the graduates of Israel's higher education system would find administrative and professional employment opportunities in the expanding economy was met quite successfully during the 1950s, 1960s, and 1970s (Globerson 1978). This aim was achieved through the expansion of the educational system and by the transformation of the structure, content, and aims of higher education to meet the needs of the growing and changing labor market. Indeed, between 1980 and 1988, the proportion of employed persons engaged in the primary and secondary sectors (agriculture and production, respectively) declined by about 18 percent while the proportion of persons employed in the tertiary sector (services) rose by almost 18 percent. In the labor force, a simultaneous shift took place away from manual labor and low-status employment to professional employment, which requires a postsecondary education or higher and holds higher social prestige (Central Bureau of Statistics 1989). However, in the 1970s, it became apparent that the existing universities and the teacher-training colleges alone were not meeting the needs of significant segments of the population. Among these groups were people employed full-time and therefore unable to undertake full-time studies, people living in "development towns" in the periphery or in rural areas relatively far from the urban university centers, and women who could not leave their families. Another significant group whose aspirations for higher education could not be met were those who had not completed the high school matriculation examination and therefore lacked the prerequisite for university admission or whose grades in the matriculation certificates were low. This group was composed primarily of Jewish students of Oriental origin and Israeli Arabs.

Israel moved in three simultaneous directions to solve these needs. The first direction was to supply the needs of university education by adding four new universities in the urban centers.[2] However, the two new universities, which were founded as university colleges and not as research universities and were therefore expected to serve the special needs of clientele in the peripheral areas of the north and south, share the universities' original mission. Trow's assertion that "competition accounts for the 'drift' ... of new institutions and sectors toward the academic forms and styles, the curriculum and standards of elite institutions" (Trow 1984, 143), applies to Israel's new universities, which embraced the elitist ethos of the veteran research universities (Ben-David 1986). Thus the quantitative expansion of the system did not solve the problems of the nontraditional students, who could not afford to become full-time students or lacked formal qualifications. To meet the needs of these groups, Israel moved in the second direction of adopting the British idea of the open university and combining its two major characteristics: open admissions (namely, universal access regardless of prior formal qualifications) and correspondence courses as the main method of teaching (Halperin 1984; Rumble and Hary 1982).

The third direction was the expansion of both the postsecondary nonacademic sector and the nonuniversity institutions of higher education. The term *postsecondary* refers to about 140 small institutions for the training of technical, nursing, clerical, and business professionals as well as most of the training of primary-school teachers (Central Bureau of Statistics 1993). Some of these sectors opt to become "academic," namely, to gain a higher educational status. Although the term *higher education* distinguishes between "universities" and "other nonuniversity institutions of higher education," only universities are authorized by the Council for Higher Education to award postbaccalaureate degrees, whereas all "other institutions" provide teaching and training up to the baccalaureate level (CHE 1993). However, although the "other institutions" are authorized to teach courses leading toward professional bachelor's degrees (whether in technology or the fine arts), the regional colleges provide a host of alternatives (ranging from academic to recreational) to their students. Thus, more than other institutions, the regional colleges (michlalot ezoriyot) in Israel represent the multipurpose model of the American community college.

Each michlalot ezoriyot serves the immediate needs of the small localities in its region, and offers studies in association with existing universities. Similarly to American community colleges, the michlalot ezoriyot provide the first two years of baccalaureate studies in addition to remedial studies, occupational programs, and cultural and recreational courses. The michlalot ezoriyot were founded during the 1970s primarily as informal adult education, cultural, and recreational centers. However, over the last two decades they have developed into undergraduate institutions serving a variety of academic, vocational-technical, and artistic needs. During the last decade, the number of michlalot ezoriyot has risen to eleven, most of them in developing areas in the north (four colleges) and in the south (four colleges). In 1991 the eleven regional colleges enrolled some 30,891 students: 6,785 in academic courses leading to the bachelor's degree, 3,552 in preacademic remedial courses, 2,993 in preservice and in-service teacher-training courses, 3,211 in technological programs, 3,104 in business and civil administration, 8,942 in art programs, and the rest in general-studies and adult educational enrichment programs.

Another characteristic of the michlalot ezoriyot is their close association with the collective settlement movement. Six of the colleges were founded by the kibbutz movement to serve both their members and nearby development towns (Shpechner 1985). In 1991 21 percent of their student population came from the kibbutzim, 18 percent from rural and Arab settlements, and 22 percent from development towns (Association of Regional Colleges 1992; CHE 1993). A comparative study conducted by the National Institute for Testing and Evaluation on the profile of applicants to higher education (universities and regional colleges) cited the following characteristics of potential michlalot ezoriyot students: more female than male applicants, lower economic status, lower educational background of the students' fathers, a majority of applicants (64 percent) from Oriental (Asian-African) backgrounds (whereas Orientals constituted about one third of the university applicants) (Cohen and Oren 1986).

Oriented toward students who are also full-time employees, the michlalot ezoriyot conduct most of their classes in the evening. If necessary, the colleges reach out to their students. For example, Menashe Regional College, which operates in densely populated Arab villages and towns, teaches many of its 400 Arab students in their own villages.

Another service for the sake of social equity and integration that the michlalot ezoriyot perform derives from a unique program of "pre-academic preparatory courses." These courses offer a "second chance" to young people without matriculation certificates. A substantial number of these students are army veterans from "disadvantaged" socioeconomic backgrounds and of Oriental origin. Their tuition costs are covered by the Planning and Budgeting Committee of the Council for Higher Education, while the Ministry of Education and Culture and the Ministry of Defense cover their living expenses (CHE 1992). Considerable effort and resources are invested by the regional colleges in these projects, which in recent years have also included many new immigrants from the former Soviet Union and Ethiopia. Michlalot ezoriyot are also actively involved in absorbing immigrants into their regular programs of study, in imparting the Hebrew language, and in retraining professionals. Moreover, they are absorbing qualified immigrants into their teaching staff.

Summary

The number of students studying for the baccalaureate has increased by a factor of forty since the establishment of the state of Israel in 1948, while the population in general has grown by a factor of five. The demand for higher education continued to grow throughout the 1980s and early 1990s. Indeed, the number of undergraduate students increased by 30 percent during the 1980s and is expected to continue to grow because of massive immigrations and a higher rate of matriculation certificate holders. It was estimated by the Council for Higher Education that in 1990 more than 10,000 qualified candidates were not admitted to universities because of a lack of learning spaces. The numbers will increase with the expected immigrations. In addition, some 25,000 applicants were refused admission because they lacked qualifications, and the need for retraining or professional refresher courses is constantly growing as a result of accelerated technological developments. No doubt, all these developments call for vigorous efforts to meet the economic and social needs, as well as aspirations, of culturally diverse individuals by providing more public and governmental resources to michlalot ezoriyot, so that they can absorb more students. There are proposals under way to change the status of these regional colleges by recognizing them as independent institutions offering an alternative route to traditional higher education.

Israel is still struggling with the transition from "elite" to "mass" higher education. In terms of enrollment ratios, Israel passed the 15-percent mark, which Trow defines as the threshold of "mass" higher education. However, the participation rate of ethnic and racial minorities is still low. The most visible sign of minorities' relative lack of success is their high attrition rate because of dropouts and failures in the first year of study. Among the various potential solutions for this is the creation of a system of short-cycle courses (presumably, with easier access), as has been done in the United States and in most developed countries. This is on the national agenda and has been proposed as an amendment to the Council for Higher Education Law to be presented to the Knesset (Parliament) during 1994. Higher education in Israel appears to have performed well in serving the needs of the labor market and economy, although challenges lie ahead, since heightened expectations for higher education to serve the economy have implications for academic freedom and autonomy. It is less clear whether Israel's higher education has served the needs of all its citizens. A major challenge is to provide members of disadvantaged racial and ethnic groups with access to high-quality education. The responsibility for providing access, as well as for ensuring excellence in the education process itself, lies with the government, which provides two-thirds of the operating budget of higher education, and with individual institutions.

In its "long-term program for the development of the higher education system," the Council for Higher Education decided to strengthen the academic tracks of the michlalot ezoriyot by gradually authorizing them to grant baccalaureate degrees independently (CHE 1994). A recent OECD document concludes: "Both from social equity and from an employment perspective it seems essential that the structure and organization of studies enable students and graduates to move across sectors and institutions, allow for alteration between work and study, as well as later re-entry into higher education on the basis of a variety of learning and work experience" (OECD 1991b, 76). Indeed, the challenge of higher education in Israel and elsewhere in the twenty-first century cannot be met anymore with "more of the same."

NOTES

1. During the 1970s and 1980s, these institutions became known as the nonuniversity sector of higher education. However, in the late 1980s and 1990s, the distinction between long-cycle/university and short-cycle/nonuniversity was questioned; thus the term "alternatives to universities" was felt by researchers to be more adequate (Gellert et al. 1991).

2. Bar-Ilan University (1955), Tel-Aviv University (1956), Haifa University (1963), and Beer-Sheva University, later renamed Ben-Gurion University of the Negev (1965).

REFERENCES

Aran, L. *Government Policy toward Higher Education in Israel: Preliminary Study.* Jerusalem: Center for Policy Studies, 1970.

Association of Regional Colleges in Israel. *The Regional Colleges in Israel.* Tel Aviv: Association of Regional Colleges in Israel, ca. 1992 (in Hebrew).

Ben-David, J. "Universities in Israel: Dilemmas of Growth, Diversification and Administration." *Studies in Higher Education* 11 (1986): 105–130.

Brint, S., and J. Karabel. *The Diverted Dream: Community Colleges and the Promise of Educational Opportunity in America, 1900–1985.* New York: Oxford University Press, 1989.

Central Bureau of Statistics. *Statistical Abstract of Israel.* Jerusalem: Central Bureau of Statistics, 1989; 1993.

Cerych, L. *The German Gesamthochschule.* Paris: European Institute of Education, 1981.

Cohen, A.M., and F.B. Brawer. *The Collegiate Function of Community Colleges.* San Francisco: Jossey-Bass, 1987.

———. *The American Community College,* 2nd ed. San Francisco: Jossey-Bass, 1989.

Cohen, O., and C. Oren. *Differences between Candidates to Colleges, Preparatories and Universities.* Report No. 39. Jerusalem: National Institute for Testing and Evaluation, 1986 (in Hebrew).

Council for Higher Education (CHE). *Planning and Grants Committee, Annual Report No. 1, Academic Year 1973/74.* Jerusalem: CHE, 1975.

———. *Planning and Grants Committee Annual Report No. 14, Academic Year 1986/87.* Jerusalem: CHE, 1988.

———. *Planning and Budgeting Committee Annual Report No. 18, Academic Year 1990/91.* Jerusalem: CHE, 1992.

———. *Planning and Budgeting Committee Annual Report No. 19, Academic Year 1991/92.* Jerusalem: CHE, 1993.

———. *Planning and Budgeting Committee Bulletin, No. 6, July 1994.* Jerusalem: CHE, 1994 (in Hebrew).

Department of Education and Science. *The Development of Higher Education into the 1990s.* London: HMSO, 1985 (Cmnd 9524).

Duperre, Maurice, R. "Short-cycle Education." In A.F. Knowles (ed.), *The International Encyclopedia of Higher Education.* Vol. 8. San Francisco: Jossey-Bass, 1977.

Eisenstadt, S.N. *The Transformation of Israeli Society*. London: Weidenfeld and Nicolson, 1985.
Furth, D. (ed.). *Short-cycle Higher Education: A Search for Identity*. Paris: OECD, 1973.
Gellert, C., J. Pratt, and D. Furth. *Alternatives to Universities*. Paris: OECD, 1991.
Glasman, N.S. "Israel: Political Roots and Effects of Two Educational Decisions." In R.M. Thomas (ed.). *Politics and Education—Cases From Eleven Nations*. Oxford: Pergamon Press, 1983.
Globerson, A. *Higher Education and Employment; A Case Study of Israel*. New York: Praeger, 1978.
Goedegebuure, L., and V. Meek (eds.). *Change in Higher Education—The Non-University Sector: An International Perspective*. Culemborg: Lemma, 1989.
Halperin, S. *Any Home a Campus: Everyman's University in Israel*. Washington, D.C.: Institute for Educational Leadership and Jerusalem Center for Public Affairs, 1984.
Iram, Y. "Higher Education Traditions of Germany, England, the U.S.A and Israel: A Historical Perspective." *Paedagogica Historica* 22 (1982): 158–72.
———. "Vision and Fulfillment: The Evolution of the Hebrew University, 1901–1950." *History of Higher Education Annual* (1983): 3.
———. "Social Policy and Education for Work in Israel." *Issues in Education* 4 (1986): 259–71.
———. "Israel." In B. Clark and G. Neave (eds.), *The Encyclopedia of Higher Education*. Vol. 1 Oxford: Pergamon Press, 1992, 93–118.
Kyvik, S. *The Norwegian Regional Colleges: A Study of the Establishment and Implementation of a Reform in Higher Education*. Oslo: Norwegian Research Council for Science and the Humanities, 1981.
Lamoure, J. *Les Instituts Universitaires de Technologie en France*. Paris: Institute of Education, 1981.
Organization for Economic Cooperation and Development (OECD). *Alternatives to Universities*. Paris: OECD Publication Services, 1991.
OECD Press Division. *Intergovernmental Conference on Further Education and Training of the Labor Force*. Paris: OECD Press Division, 1991.
Pratt, J. *Alternatives to Universities in Higher Education—Country Study: United Kingdom*. Paris: OECD, 1988.
Rumble, G., and K. Hary. *The Distance Teaching Universities*. London: Croom Helm, 1982.
Schmida, M. *Equality and Excellence: Educational Reform and the Comprehensive School*. Ramat-Gan: Bar-Ilan University, 1987 (in Hebrew).
Scott, P. *Higher Education in Sweden—A Look from the Outside*. London: UHA, 1991.
Shpechner, M. "The Regional Colleges—Their Status in the Kibbutz and General Educational System." *Ofakei Haskala* (Educational Horizons) 50 (1985): 58–63 (in Hebrew).
Teichler, U. *The First Years of Study at Fachhochschulen and Universities in the Federal Republic of Germany*. Kassel: Werkstatberichte 28 Gesamthochschule, 1990.
Trow, M. "Elite Higher Education: An Endangered species?" *Minerva* 14 (1976): 355–376.
UNESCO. *Statistical Digest*. Paris: UNESCO, 1990.

14 A Review of Community College Development in South Africa

Mbuyiselwa Silas Zuma

As a result of years of concerted struggle, the political liberation of the majority people of South Africa has recently been realised. Our politicians and, indeed, the majority of South Africans need to be applauded for efforts made to transform this country into a democracy. Without active support from communities themselves, the democratic government would find it difficult to satisfy the needs and aspirations of millions of people whose skills have remained underdeveloped and who have been denied access to the type of education that could enable them to participate meaningfully in economic and social reconstruction and development. It is obvious that the economic struggle is yet to begin and will involve equipping the disadvantaged masses of this country with the necessary knowledge and skills. Any meaningful liberation should include economic and community development. While South Africans have joined in the condemnation of apartheid education, little attention has been given to the way forward.

As the country gets closer to a democratic order, most social institutions, including education, will have to undergo transformations in line with democratic ideals. There are currently no community college models in South Africa. However, educators, politicians, and the general public confirm that there is an urgent need for educational reconstruction, including the creation of a community education system based, in part, on the American community college model. The advent of a community college concept is a response to education and training needs of people who have been denied access and opportunities by the apartheid system of education.

This chapter summarises the advocacy of community colleges in South Africa and cites a few independent investigations that have confirmed this need. The chapter confirms that South Africa is already investigating a broad framework for colleges similar to American community colleges and that the foundation for implementing educational reform will exist in the near future.

Historical Overview of the South African Education System

South Africa, a country located at the southern tip of Africa, has a population of 40 million people, who are classified into four main groups: whites (16 percent), coloureds (11 percent), Indians (3 percent), and blacks (70 percent). According to this classification, there were eleven education authorities for blacks, five education authorities for whites, one for Indians, and one for coloureds; and the Department of National Education was established to set broad education policy. Figure 7 is a schematic representation of the education system in South Africa as of 1993.

Education for Whites

Prior to September 1984, education for whites was administered by five departments. The four provincial education departments provided all education except that which was defined by law as higher education. The predecessor of the Department of Education and Culture, Administration: House of Assembly was the Department of National Education, which responsible for higher education, including specialised education and education offered by technical colleges and *technikons*. (Technikons are tertiary institutions whose task is the preparation of technicians and technologists for the labour market. Programmes offered by technikons are equivalent in status to those offered by universities.) According to the terms of the Constitution of the Republic of South Africa Act (1983), all education for whites came under the Minister of Education and Culture, Administration: House of Assembly. After the provincial councils were abolished in 1986, the four provincial education departments fell under the control of this minister. Universities and technikons, historically considered to be mainly for whites, were also the responsibility of this minister.

Education for Coloureds

In the period before and during the nineteenth century, coloureds were educated mainly through the missionary societies and churches, but after 1910 the provincial education departments provided education for them. In the ensuing period, various changes in the administration of education for coloureds occurred, and from 1 June 1980, the newly formed Department of Coloured Affairs—and from 1 October 1980, the Department of Internal Affairs—administered coloured education through a directorate. In terms of the 1983 Constitution, all education for coloureds fell under the Minister of Education and Culture, Administration: House of Representatives. This included the University of the Western Cape and the Peninsula Technikon.

FIGURE 7. Schematic Representation of the Educational System in South Africa in 1993

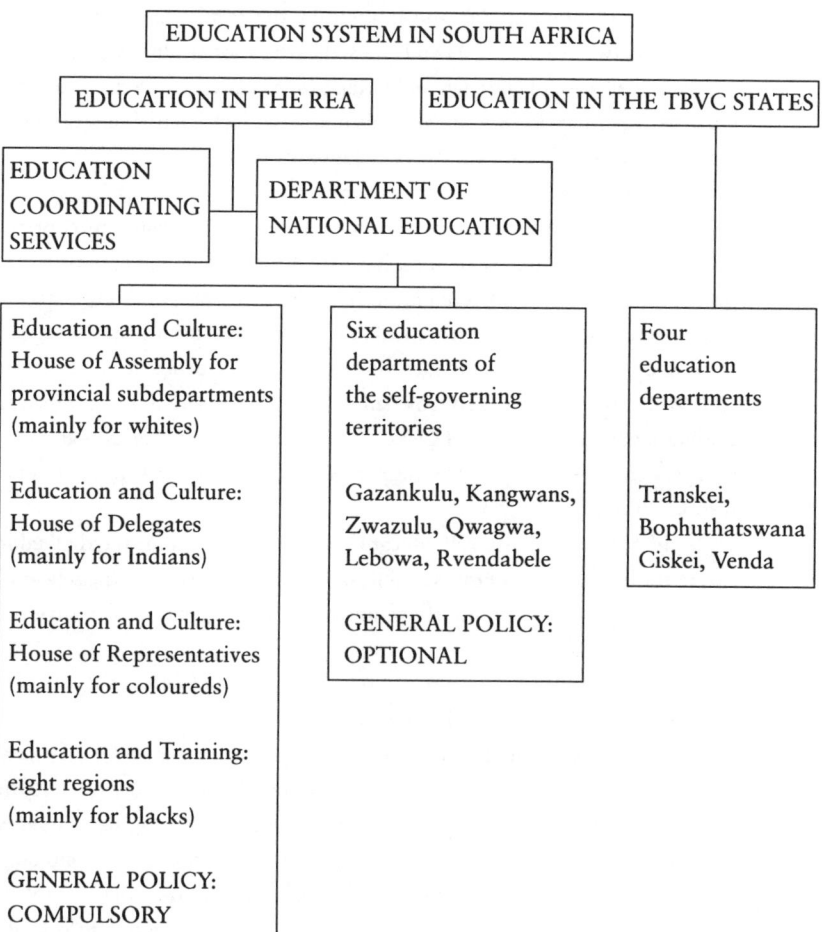

Education for Indians

Until the takeover of Indian education by the Department of Indian Affairs in 1965, provincial education departments (mainly, the Natal Provincial Administration) were responsible for Indian education. On 1 October 1980, the education of Indians became the responsibility of the Directorate of Education of the Department of Internal Affairs. With the introduction of the 1983 Constitution, all education for Indians fell under the Minister of Education and Culture, Administration: House of Delegates. This included the University of Durban Westville and the M.L. Sultan Technikon.

Education for Blacks

During the nineteenth century, the education of black persons depended mainly on voluntary efforts and funding by the missionary societies and churches. Between about 1904 and 1953, the educational administration was jointly in the hands of churches and of the provincial education departments. However, the financing and the responsibility for black education was transferred to the central government on 1 January 1954.

Since 1968, the administration of education for blacks has gradually become decentralised into regions and the self-governing territories, but close liaisons and coordination have still been maintained countrywide, particularly at the professional level. In each of the self-governing territories, a department of education, which is responsible for all education excluding university education, has been established. During the years 1976 to 1982, four of the self-governing territories—namely, Transkei, Bophuthatswana, Venda, and Ciskei, (the so-called TBVC States)—became independent states and the provision of education at all levels became their responsibility.

In 1993 the minister of education and training administered all education for black people in the Republic of South Africa (outside the self-governing territories), including those universities and technikons that were mainly for blacks.

Transition to New Educational Dispensation

With a view toward the transition to a new constitution in 1994, the government instituted the Education Coordination Service (ECS) on 1 April 1993. The purpose of the ECS was to rearrange the existing departments responsible for education provision and to introduce a nonracial, regionally based educational dispensation. The aims of the ECS are to (1) establish nonracial, regional education departments and (2) prepare part of the legislation necessary for this. It is foreseen that once the ECS has completed its task, it will cease to exist.

National Education and Training Forum

In response to the long-standing crisis that has existed within the education system in South Africa and for various reasons, the important players in education and training established the National Education and Training Forum (NETF) on 7 August 1993. Representatives of various education departments and of the Department of Manpower are members of the NETF on behalf of the State and participate fully in the work of the forum.

Mission

The mission of the NETF is to initiate, develop, and participate in projects with those involved in education, to achieve the following: (1) the resolution of crises in education, (2) the restructuring of education for a democratic South Africa, and (3) the formation of a policy that will be linked to the human, social, and economic development needs of South Africa.

Form and Structure

The NETF needs to include all national educational players. Furthermore, the forum should have a structure and procedures that ensure adequate representation and effectiveness. Accordingly, the NETF is inclusively structured to function through a Plenary and Executive Committee and through working groups.

Need for Educational Reconstruction

Most South African educators, as well as community and business leaders, agree that the apartheid system of education has brought more harm than good to the majority of the people of South Africa. Unequal distribution of the country's resources and an educational system that favoured the white minority has had adverse effects on the physical, mental, and social well-being of black South Africans.

The Workshop for National Education Nongovernmental Organisations (NGOs) and the African National Congress (ANC) Education Desk have presented the basic reasons why the present education structure is considered inappropriate.

Equity

The most important effect of the unequal education provision is that millions of people have received either no or very little formal education. Of the 40 million people living in South Africa, about 15 million adults do not have a basic formal education (National Education Coordinating Committee 1992). The following adult literacy rates for the different races within South Africa (excluding the TBVC areas) are quoted by the Development Bank of Southern Africa (DBSA) (1990): 54 percent for Africans, 66 percent for coloureds, 84 percent for Asians, and 99 percent for whites. Illiteracy rates are significantly higher in rural than in urban areas. Current adult basic education provision is extremely low in relation to the numbers of adults with little or no schooling. There are currently fewer than 100,000 adults in adult basic education in South Africa. This represents less than 1 percent of the people who have not completed basic education classes in

South Africa. The current provision can be described as small-scale, existing at multiple sites, and lacking national standards, coherence, and coordination. In the absence of a substantial national community education system, it will not be possible to redress the major educational inequalities resulting from the discriminatory provisions of the past.

Education and training have been provided primarily to young people. Older people have generally found it difficult to gain access to lifelong learning. But it is not just older people who have been prejudiced by this system; poor people, who have to earn an income from an early age, have not been able to afford the luxury of post-compulsory, full-time study. Since few apprenticeships are available, meaningful technical training has been limited to a select few. The majority of women have been excluded from education by a variety of mechanisms, such as observance of traditional roles, cultural barriers, sexist practices, and legal prohibitions. No system based on "formal" learning alone will address the problems of these disadvantaged groups and, by definition, cannot redress wrongs already suffered by those who were outside of the formal system.

Traditionally, vocational education and training are viewed separately from academic education, and yet, ironically, academic qualifications have been the best bridge into employment. Academic qualifications also give the privileged access to training and tertiary education and employment. This applies to those who make it through the traditional academic programme as well as to those few artisans (principally white males) who get apprenticeships as a result of having had a good basic education. Distinctions based on race ("separate but equal") are clearly unacceptable, but these are not the only distinctions that have to be overcome. Distinctions based on age, class, gender, location, and so on are equally unacceptable.

Many courses are based on designs developed in other countries and are unresponsive to the specific needs and context of learners. Adult courses have traditionally been based on those prepared for children—courses that are not relevant to life or to work.

Economic Efficiency

Increasingly, employers are realising the fact that the majority of their workers lack a grounding in general education. This is seen as a major constraint on growth and restructuring. The range of options for improving productivity is seriously limited.

The current levels of provisions are totally inadequate. There is a duplication of resources, particularly in materials development and teacher training, and this results in high unit costs and a general lack of cost-effectiveness; and there is no real cooperation between the different state departments involved in adult basic and further education, and there is a lack of coordination among industry-based and nongovernmental organisations. There are no national standards. The current "chaotic" and "fragmented" infrastructure does not lend itself easily to the provision of large-scale adult basic and further education.

The need to include adult education and training is not simply an equity issue. In the context of the economic crisis South Africa faces, the economy has to undergo fundamental restructuring. This will mean that large numbers of people will move from declining sectors to growth sectors (labour market mobility) and from old technologies and work organisation methods to new ones. This requires the continual upgrading of skills if employment security and growth targets, as well as job quality and productivity targets, are to be achieved. Similarly, development and infrastructure programmes aimed at raising living standards and at laying the basis for further development necessitate the broadest possible participation in lifelong education and training.

Notions of streaming (academic and vocational) serve to perpetuate the distinction between mental and manual labour. In this context, low productivity results both from the high sums spent on supervision and from problems associated with low quality. The problem extends to the unemployed. The training presently provided to unemployed people is not recognized by industry. It is too short to be meaningful. It gives three weeks of relief from unemployment, but is in no way linked to future employment possibilities. This perpetuates a downward economic cycle that remains tied to low levels of skill, low pay, low productivity, and few options for growth.

It is clear that the current systems of technical training and academic education are largely out of step with the needs for transformation, reconstruction, and growth. Education and training have been kept totally apart. Many courses are out-of-date and unable to equip South Africans to face a changing future.

Democracy

The rest of the world recognises that a basic general education is a democratic, human right and that it equips people for active participation in all spheres of life. The fact that apartheid did not deliver this ultimately contributed to its demise.

A high illiteracy rate is not just a disadvantage to some people; it is a disadvantage to the wider society. Efforts to bring about a democratic culture and strong organs of civil society are made more difficult if 15 million adults are unable to participate in the conventional forms of literate communication. Lack of literacy and wider education skills becomes a social barrier that advantages the privileged minority over the majority.

If people are to become the architects of their own future (and thereby become committed to the success of initiated programmes), they require the knowledge, skills, and power to intervene. The system will have to address the needs of those who fall outside of the compulsory learning provision. Among those who would not benefit from the present educational system are the so-called marginalised youth, the millions of semi-skilled, unskilled, and functionally illiterate people, of whom women are a significant proportion. The system's traditional response to these problems has been to provide bits and pieces of training for the employed few and little or nothing for the rest. The present system is based on a low rate of participation both economically and politically. A high level of participation is central to an economic strategy whose key component is the development of human resources.

A high level of skills, high wages, and high levels of quality and productivity are central components of the envisaged reconstruction of the economy. A high level of participation is also central to political and economic democracy. Participation needs to be based on knowledge and on an expanding influence at the workplace as well as in society at large.

COMMUNITY COLLEGE ADVOCACY IN SOUTH AFRICA

Since 1991 the Education Foundation has been a strong advocate for the establishment of community colleges in South Africa. This need has been confirmed by a number of independent studies in South Africa. Some of these studies are discussed in this section. It should be noted that no consensus has yet been reached in South Africa with respect to the appropriate name for the community college type model referred to in this chapter. The name *community college* is used to refer to a range of community-based institutions whose mission is to provide adult and continuing education. The recently formed Community College Association of South Africa has been launched to lobby for the establishment and recognition of community colleges in South Africa.

Tertiary Education Sector Assessment Report

According to South Africa's Tertiary Education Sector Assessment report, there is a strong case for the establishment of community colleges. In fact, a unique type of South African community college could perform a number of functions, including the following: (1) providing students with post-secondary and vocational qualifications, (2) undertaking remedial work in mathematics and the sciences, (3) functioning as an adult education institute, and (4) preparing students for university study. Graduation from a university preparatory course at such an institution could function as an alternative to matriculation as a university admissions requirement (U.S. AID 1992, 4.4–4.5).

Education Renewal Strategy

A study titled *Education Renewal Strategy* and conducted by the South African Department of National Education also recognises the need for the establishment of community colleges.

> As a result of the political disturbances which had a negative effect on schools for a certain period or as a result of social and economic factors, some children did not receive sufficient education to participate constructively in social, economic and normal political activities of the country. By establishing Community Colleges, this need can be addressed. Community Colleges may be institutions established by private laws which are controlled by and directed towards the needs of the local community. Basic education for adults that will include education of the marginalised youth could be offered at Community Colleges. . . . The Community College could fulfill the role of a training institution alongside the formal system, which would mean that industry and other sectors could provide inputs in respect of the training of learners. (South African Department of National Education 1992, 62)

National Education Policy Investigation

The report *National Education Policy Investigation—Post-Secondary Education* proposes that "new colleges" be introduced in the post-secondary system. Implementation of at least some of the options listed below implies that the post-secondary education system may have to be expanded by the addition of "colleges" whose primary functions would be, for example, to offer vocational education programmes and basic education programmes to adults from educationally disadvantaged backgrounds.

These new colleges could be added to the system in two ways: (1) A new kind of college (similar to the American community college) could be added to the existing structure of educational, nursing, technical, and agricultural colleges; and (2) a single kind of college could be created out of the existing colleges and the proposed community colleges, and the new colleges would offer at least some vocational programmes as well as some basic education programmes. The second option would involve rethinking the linkages between the present colleges, universities, and technikons and rethinking the different programmes that could be offered at the existing colleges (National Education Coordinating Committee 1992, 90–91).

Committee of Rectors and Deans of Teacher Education in Kwa Zulu Natal
In his paper "Community Colleges—An Alternative Model for the Tertiary Sector," Professor Andre le Roux, chairman of the Committee of Rectors and Deans of Teacher Education in Kwa Zulu Natal (CORDTEK), states:

> I believe the American Community Colleges have features which are most appropriate to our educational system. Community Colleges would be an excellent antidote to the apartheid system. No one is excluded. Some will be doing associate degrees in mathematics, physics and literature, while others are doing literacy programmes and vocational programmes such as welding, motor mechanics and book-keeping—but all will be together. This would be a means of accommodating "the lost generation," the neglected majority of maginalised youth. Community Colleges are not inferior in provision. They provide the opportunity for all people to rise to the greatest possible academic and professional heights. A modular system would enable students to build up credits and thus to move from one programme to another. Mobility could be further extended by articulation agreements between tertiary institutions without having to repeat courses. The Community College could make a meaningful contribution of wealth, power, justice and education. I believe the community college concept could also be applied to the schools system in South Africa. (le Roux 1991, 88)

Community College Feasibility Study
A feasibility study on the prospect of community colleges in South Africa was conducted in 1992 by the Tertiary Education Programme Support (TEPS), under the leadership of Professor Walter Smith. The feasibility study further confirmed the need for the establishment of community colleges in South Africa and the possibility of adapting American community college models to suite South African needs. According to Smith (1992), a national or regional plan for the development of community colleges should include the following:

1. Authorization for the establishment of comprehensive community colleges in the Republic of South Africa.
2. Authorization for the establishment of community boards of trust-

ees and advisers for each community college.

3. Authorization for the establishment of a national board of community colleges as part of the National Department of Education. This board should have the necessary responsibility to provide statewide leadership in overseeing and coordinating the individually governed public community colleges. There should continue to be maximum local autonomy in the governance and operation of individual community colleges. The national board should be subjected at all times to the overall supervision of the National Department of Education or whatever structures are developed at the national level to direct the affairs of the system.

4. Establishment of a law to ensure that students may proceed toward the completion of their educational goals as rapidly as their circumstances will allow. The law should require secondary and post-secondary education institutions to communicate and to cooperate with each other. The specific purpose of this requirement would be to improve the planning of academic programmes, improve communication among all appropriate entities, and facilitate the transfer of students from one institution to another. (This is similar to the articulation agreements between U.S. community colleges and four-year universities.)

5. Establishment of a policy to prohibit discrimination against a student or an employee in the Republic of South Africa's system of education on the basis of race, sex, or physical handicap.

6. Establishment of a nationwide office of equal educational opportunity to establish policies and guidelines, provide technical assistance and evaluate institutional compliance to equal-access policies. (Such an office exists in the United States.)

7. Establishment of the concept of a national academic support programme, in which postsecondary and tertiary preparatory courses would be designed for students who do not have the necessary academic skills to enter tertiary programmes because they were inadequately prepared in their earlier education.

The South African Committee for Higher Education (SACHED)

In a draft policy document on community learning centres, (CLCs), SACHED states:

> The development of these centres should be closely coordinated with the planned Community Colleges, which will probably be dedicated educational institutions, unlike community centers which might or might not be exclusively concerned with education. Community Colleges will do some of the same work as these centres, particularly in adult education. Colleges should be seen as an integral part of a net-

work of institutions providing adult education, and they should offer support for community centres. The precise role of Community Colleges is still being defined—there are no clear answers yet—but they are likely to be partly tertiary institutions, partly bridging and partly general adult and further education institutions. Community Colleges and centres will have a mutually beneficial relationship with each other. Centres will be able to grow into Colleges, where appropriate, and Colleges will support and collaborate with centres. Colleges might also arrange to have some of their courses run in a day even by centres. (SACHED 1993, 8)

National Institute for Community Education

The National Institute for Community Education (NICE) is a multi-stakeholder initiative aimed at developing a national framework for the provision of education and training adults, workers, and out-of-school youth who are beyond the age of compulsory schooling (+/= 16 years) and who either completed, interrupted or never attended formal schooling. NICE proposes that such provision should also cater to the physically challenged.

NICE regards the development of an effective, accessible, and relevant adult basic and further education system as central to the task of national reconstruction and development. NICE believes that the adult basic and further education system needs to be massively expanded to meet the needs of many different groups of learners: out-of-school, unemployed adults, rural inhabitants, and others.

In order for these needs to be met effectively, the developments of the adult basic and further education system must take place within a clear and coherent framework of provision. Existing resources need to be effectively mobilised and coordinated, and imaginative new forms of provision and delivery need to be put in place.

Accordingly, NICE has been engaged in an extensive process of research and consultation directed toward the development of a framework for adult basic and further education and training.

VISION AND PRINCIPLES

NICE proposes that adult basic and further education, defined as education and training outside the compulsory phase of formal schooling and ranging from basic literacy to the higher education access programmes, be regarded as a coherent field based on the following vision model:

NICE's vision of an adult basic and further education concept for South

Africa is that of education and training for adults, workers, and post-school youth which is institutionally located within the College Sector but delivered at a number of sites or venues using different modes of delivery. In this sector, community colleges with a network of community learning centres (CLCs), in close collaboration with distance education institutions, NGOs, and CBOs, should provide open access and equal opportunities for adults, workers, and post-school youth largely through partnerships with other providers, employers, and the community. Community colleges should place priority on:

- integrating education and training;
- providing high quality learning opportunities with clear learning routes so individuals can achieve their personal, education, and social goals;
- creating access to education and training for all adults, workers, and post-school youth who were previously denied it;
- targeting groups which have not been given equal opportunities, such as women, people from historically disadvantaged population groups, people with disabilities, the unemployed, or under-privileged;
- developing multiple routes for students to obtain employment and progress to qualification at the highest level;
- enabling people to progress and acquire qualifications, whether in or out of work, by means of individual learning programmes.

COMMUNITY COLLEGE

A community college is an education and training institution or a group of institutions that provides education and training of defined and agreed levels (of the NQF [National Qualification Framework]) for a defined community with emphasis on meeting the needs of adults, workers, and post-compulsory age students (+/= 16 years), the community, and other defined needs. A community college should reflect the following features:

Open Access. The community college should open its doors to all learners who are beyond the compulsory school-going age (+/= 16 years). No person should be denied admission to a community college on grounds of academic qualificaitons. However, learners would be tested on admission to determine competencies necessary for entry into programmes of their choice. These development programmes would help learners make up for their deficiencies.

Democratic Governance. The community college should be governed by a council consisting of elected representatives of the community, the main stakeholders, interest groups, and role players. Such involvement in decision making is intended to dispel the chronic alienation of large sectors of society from the education process and reduce the power of government administration to intervene where it should not.

Partnership and Cooperation. The community college should collaborate with other stakeholders and role players in the delivery of programmes. The community college should have a core full-time faculty (+/- 60%) and the other faculty members (+/- 40%) should be drawn from NGOs and/or the private sector. Such partnerships would benefit the learners a great deal. A specific partnership between distance education colleges and community colleges would enhance open learning approaches. Toward this end, a distance education support service will be dedicated to distance education technology and implementation. In collaboration with distance education institutions, the community college will train mentors and help students through their instructional material. These students will also have access to career guidance and counseling services as well as information on bursaries and loans. In addition, special arrangements will be made for distance education, so that students who need access to laboratories or workshops (including placement for the practical component of their training) will be assisted. Appropriate links will be established with distance education institutions to ensure maximum benefit to the student.

Flexible Scheduling and Delivery. The community college should operate until late in the evenings, on weekends, and during holidays. Through networks of community learning centres (CLCs), community college programmes should be offered at a number of venues or sites, such as schools after hours, work-place training centres, church buildings, universities after hours, technikons after hours, community halls, etc.

Curriculum Comprehensiveness. Community colleges should be characterised by the comprehensiveness or multipurpose dimensions of their curricula. The principle of comprehensiveness would require that they offer a mix of programmes to a mix of students with different abilities and past achievements, with a mix of educational goals within a single institutional framework. The mixes would differ from province to province, from institution to institution, from urban to rural.

NETWORK OF BRANCH CAMPUSES AND COMMUNITY LEARNING CENTRES

A community learning centre is a venue or site where education and training programmes relevant to the expressed needs of adults, workers, or post-school youth are being offered by a community college, NGO, or any other institution or organisation.

Community learning centres would be located in any public building, workplace, school, church, etc. that is easily accessible to learners and should consist of:

> The CLC manager
> A management committee
> The staff
> The learners

The community college would facilitate and support the development of a network of satellite CLCs in its district and should coordinate the accreditation of programmes offered at such CLCs.

CLCs should be divided into two types according to activity and purpose. These CLCs would be found in inner cities, townships, informal settlement, and deep rural areas and should be within walking distance from populated areas.

A single-purpose CLC should be a venue or site where a single programme is provided by a provider institution or NGO. An example is a literacy programme provided by a literacy organisation in a church hall. Single-purpose CLCs could develop into multipurpose CLCs by increasing the number of programmes offered.

A multipurpose CLC should be a venue where a number of separate programmes or activities, for example literacy and numeracy, dressmaking, art and drama, computer skills, etc. are provided by one or more provider institutions or NGOs. These programmes would have to be properly scheduled and time-tabled in order to avoid unnecessary clashes. Multipurpose CLCs could develop into community colleges by structuring their programming according to progression from the lowest to the highest level contained in the NQF.

NICE proposes the following conceptual model for South African community colleges:

The existing technical colleges, Manpower Training Centres, NGO colleges, colleges of education and colleges of agriculture in South Africa should be changed into community colleges. As community colleges, such institutions could offer a wide range of career options and study options to communities and could be enabled to respond more readily to community needs. It is accepted that such a change would require a comprehensive staff orientation and development programme, an effective institutional management system, and some additional funding.

All adult education centres or night schools should be changed into community learning centres. Community learning centres could be linked to the local community college for the purposes of programme accreditation and management support. The community college would be part of an education and training system in which each institution type has a clear mission, a defined upper level of training, and a student transfer mechanism that provides students with maximum mobility. This should enable a student to move from a school to a community college and then to a tertiary institution of his/her choice.

All prior learning should be taken into account when assessing the level at which a student should transfer, the main criterion being the student's ability to succeed at the next level, rather than trying to evaluate a one-subject match between studies completed and the higher level subjects. This means that career guidance would become a significant focus once students have been assessed.

ACCREDITATION AND ARTICULATION

Community college education is about to be newly introduced to the South African education scene; it has potential to radically change the traditional concept of education. Firstly, community education will readdress legislated past inequalities, as well as provide an education that will deal with the acute need for skilling and provide comprehensive education outside the formal system. Community college programmes should be properly accredited and well articulated to the broader system of education.

Qualification Framework

Community colleges should offer the following programmes in accordance with the NQF:

General Education Certification (GEC) (Level 1)
Prior to the GEC level there would be three nationally certified attainment levels, which would be:

- ABET Level One—equivalent to the present standard two
- ABET Level Two—equivalent to the present standard three
- ABET Level Three—equivalent to the present standard five

Some of the major principles underpinning such provisions aim at broadening of access, high-quality general education, and mechanisms for articulation.

Further Education Certification (Levels 2–4)
Education and training at this level would be characterised by a credit-based system that would allow for effective integration of education, training, articulation, and flexibility in the learning system. This would be achieved by:

o   opening and increasing access to education for most citizens;
o   providing education and training that is non-terminal and has the capability to access tertiary education;
o   preparing individuals for the world of work and social and political participation.

Post–Further Education and Training
Education and training at this level would be characterised by a credit-based system that articulates with the tertiary education system. Focus would be on career preparation with credits transferable to higher education institutions. Specific emphasis will be on a) technical and vocational programmes that increase the range of technical, vocational, and commercial courses currently offered by technical and commercial colleges; b) access programmes that allow students opportunities to upgrade their certificates to acceptable levels for eventual transfer; and c) transfer programmes that assist students who qualify for entry into universities, technikons, or colleges but who are not able to do so because of financial constraints or limited space at such tertiary institutions.

Bridging, access, and transfer programmes currently offered by some colleges, universities, and technikons would fall into this category. After due consultation and agreement between the community colleges and relevant tertiary institutions, the programme will include first-year courses leading to the relevant degrees or diplomas. After successful completion of the transfer programme, the student will enter at the second-year level of the relevant degree or diploma at a university, technikon, or college.

NICE supports representation made by organisations speaking on behalf of adult and young learners to start Level 1 at the first ABET benchmark, which would be equivalent to the end of primary education, and that the term "sub-level" be abandoned for these learners.

CURRICULUM
Community colleges would be characterised by the comprehensiveness or multipurpose dimensions of their curricula. The principle of comprehensiveness would require that colleges offer a mix of programmes to a mix of stu-

dents with different abilities and past achievements, with a mix of education goals, within a single institutional framework. The mix would differ from province to province, from institution to institution. It is assumed that communication and numeracy would be integral parts of the curriculum at all levels. The following are examples of some major curriculum areas:

A. Engineering
- Civil—bricklaying, carpentry, plumbing, etc.
- Electrical—heavy current, light current, etc.
- Mechanical—motor mechanics, general mechanics, etc.
- Chemical—analytical chemistry, biochemistry, etc.

B. Humanities
- Business Studies—marketing, business management, etc.
- Health Services—paramedics, nursing assistants, etc.
- Administration—public admin., local government admin., etc.
- Education and Training—ETD practitioner training, training of educare practitioners, etc.

C. Special Programmes

Special programmes designed to meet specific needs of specific groups should be offered at the community college. These could include:
- Youth Programmes—Matriculation finishing and upgrade programme
- School programme for never-been-to-school youth who are too old to enter school (e.g., 14 years old)
- Workers programmes—such as programmes related to labour relations and trade union movements
- Civic Education—such as programmes related to the concept of democratic society, elections and election procedures, voter education, etc.

D. Community Development
- Entrepreneurial skills development (small business development)
- Life-skills and self-help skills, such as dressmaking, hairdressing, horticulture, etc.
- Organisational development and management (CBO and NGO capacity building)
- Cultural enrichment programmes, such as performing arts, sports and leisure

Personal interest and community development programmes of cultural, recreational, or community-based character which do not carry credit toward any college diploma or certificate but which satisfy the intellectual or technical interests of individuals or groups of citizens within the community would be offered.

The above suggested curricula should be organised according to the proposed NQF.

Admission

The community college should have an open admission policy, such as: any person beyond the compulsory school-going age (11–16 years) should be admitted to the community colleges irrespective of his/her academic background. Youths younger than 6 years who cannot be admitted to formal schools because of age restrictions may also be admitted to special programmes at a community college. In short, no academic criteria should be used to keep learners out of a community college.

Specific admissions criteria should be set for each programme. Career guidance and student counseling will include the assessment of prior education or experience and of a student's potential. Pre-testing will not be conducted for screening purposes but as a pre-requisite for the determination of competencies and subsequent placement of students into relevant programmes. Developmental programmes should be offered to those students who do not satisfy criteria for admission into programmes.

Recognition of prior learning and experience (RPL) should be accepted for entry into community college programmes in instances where prospective learners do not have formal qualifications but demonstrate equivalent knowledge or skill.

A section entitled Information on Bursaries and Loans will assist needy students in securing financial support in the form of bursaries or loans. The unit will work in close collaboration with foundations, trusts, or companies that provide financial support to students or small-business developer initiatives.

Further Education

Further education programs will be available after the attainment of the general education certificate, or within the compulsory phase of schooling. Further education will be open to all adults and youth in possession of a GEC or who have appropriate prior learning or experience. Further education programmes shall include three specific programs.

The technical and vocational programmes will increase the range of technical, vocational, and commercial courses that are currently offered by technical colleges and commercial colleges. Such programmes will include subjects or modules that will ensure access to higher education (university, technikon, or college).

COMMUNITY COLLEGE DEVELOPMENT PROCESS

South Africa realizes that it has a duty to free its people from all forces of oppression. All South Africans—regardless of age, race, sex, class, or economic status—are entitled to a fair chance and to the tools for developing their minds and spirit to the utmost. This premise means that by virtue of their own efforts and adequate guidance, all South Africans can hope to attain the mature and informed judgement needed to secure gainful employment and manage their own lives, thereby serving not only their own interest but also the progress of society itself. The people of South Africa realise that individuals in their society who do not possess the levels of skills, literacy, and training essential to this new era will be effectively disenfranchised, not simply from the material rewards that accompany competent performance but also from the chance to participate fully in their national life. The resolution of unemployment, inadequate education, ill health, and other social and economic handicaps must come out of a common concern for the well-being of all our people.

All sectors of South African society—the government, commerce and industry, the professions, and community and service organisations—now realise the need to play an interactive role in making access the watchword of education and economic opportunity for all South Africans. The development plan that follows is based on the premise that the design of an effective community education system in South Africa cannot be undertaken by any single player, institution, or department or even by small groups of key players in isolation from their peers. The process must involve all the key players, stakeholders, and communities and must achieve consensus around both principle and procedure.

Development Plan

Largely influenced by the American experience, the community college debate was triggered by the need to provide education and training opportunities to all adults, workers and out-of-school youths who were denied such opportunities by the apartheid system. Ever since the community college debate started, South Africans have been opposed to any attempt to import foreign models, but have opted instead for a process that would lead to development of a South African Community College model. Indeed, a number of workshops and investigations have been undertaken to develop a framework relevant and acceptable to South Africans.

The Problem (Pre–1991)

The following statistics will give some idea of the problem:

> From a total population of about 30 million who are over 13 years of age, about 9 million (30 percent) are functionally illiterate; regional illiteracy and innumeracy vary from less than twenty percent in the Western Cape to over forty percent in the North-Western Cape (Grobbelaar).
>
> Fifty-two percent of potentially employable young people of all races between 16 and 30 are unemployed (3,000,000) (Orkin).
>
> In total about 12 million are out of school and out of work.
>
> Sixty-six percent of African youth have discontinued their studies due to lack of money (Orkin).
>
> Twenty percent of African students leave matriculation without writing the final exam. In 1992 and 1993, 400,000 failed matriculation. In 1993 only 10 percent obtained an exemption. Tertiary education absorbs only about 120,000 per annum.

No coherent framework for the provision and accreditation of education and training programmes for adults, workers, and out-of-school youth exists. Provision is characterised by fragmentation, poor quality, and no career path for educators and trainers.

The Critical Path (1991–1995)

Preinvestigation (1991–1992). A visit to U.S. community colleges was undertaken by the director of projects and planning of the Education Foundation during March and April 1991. A national workshop on community colleges was held in Durban on 23 May 1991. More than 200 bilateral discussions were held between the Education Foundation and selected business structures, NGO structures, government structures and community-based structures during 1991 and 1992. Relationships were established with community college associations in the United States, Canada, and the United Kingdom. A community college feasibility study was undertaken in the then Natal and Transvaal Provinces in 1992 by the Tertiary Education Project Support projects of U.S. AID South Africa. A National Consultative Meeting on Community Colleges was held in Johannesburg on 27 October 1992, where it was resolved that a national investigation be undertaken.

Investigation (1993–1994). A multi-stakeholder National Investigation into Community Education (NICE) was undertaken by six Working Groups under the direction of the National Steering Committee during 1993 and 1994. A discussion document entitled "A Framework for the Provision of Adult Basic and Further Education," which came out of this investigation, was discussed at a workshop in August 1994. The community college concept constituted a central feature of the report with care taken not to copy, but to adapt the American model to suit South African circumstances. The evolution of such a model could well develop into a vibrant adult education system for South Africa.

Framework (1994–1995). Main proposals of the NICE discussion document were discussed with Provincial Ministries of Education. A twenty-four-person delegation consisting of representatives of Provincial Ministries, Committee of Technical College Principals (CTCP), South African Committee for Adult Basic Education and Training (SACABET), Adult Educators and Trainers Association of South Africa (AETASA), Association of Regional Training Centres (ARTC), and Community Colleges Association of South Africa (CCASA) visited American community colleges during November and December 1994. Proposals of the NICE discussion document were given to the delegation prior to departure to enable them to test these against their own experiences. NICE, in association with the Provincial Ministries, convened workshops on community colleges during the period February to May 1995 in an attempt to seek further inputs for the framework. NICE and the College Sector Coalition in association with the National Department of Education convened a National Conference on Community Education on 5–7 July 1995 in an attempt to seek further input and adoption of the framework by stakeholders, key players, and interest groups.

Pilot Projects (1996–1998). After the National Conference, NICE proposals will be tested on the ground through relevant pilot projects. It is anticipated that appropriate existing facilities such as colleges of education, technical colleges, regional training centres, NGO colleges, etc. will be identified as core institutions around which pilot projects will be centred. A pilot project will be undertaken in each of the nine provinces. NICE will work in close cooperation with the Department of Labour in making such pilot projects a reality. Financing for such pilot projects will be sought from the government, the private sector, international agencies and communities themselves. Lessons from these pilot projects will be carefully documented and will form part of the final report. NICE proposals as well as the Interim

Implementation Plan of the College Sector Coalition will provide the necessary guidance for implementation even to those institutions that fall outside the pilot projects.

Evaluation (1997–1998). During 1997 and 1998 an independent team of evaluators commissioned by NICE will assess progress made by each province in respect to pilot projects, as well as the Interim Implementation Plan of the College Sector Coalition. Expertise of the members of the steering committee will again be vital during the evaluation phase. Gaps identified or areas needing further investigation will be subject to further research or investigation.

REFERENCES

Centre for Education Policy Development (CEPD). "A Framework for Life Long Learning." Unpublished paper. Johannesburg: CEPD, 1993.

Education Foundation. "National Investigation into Community Education—Project Description." Unpublished document. Johannesburg: Education Foundation, 1993.

le Roux, A. "Community Colleges—An Alternative Model for the Tertiary Sector." Unpublished report. Durban: Edgewood College of Education, 1991.

National Education Coordinating Committee. *National Education Policy Investigation—Post-Secondary Education.* Cape Town: Oxford, 1992.

National Investigation into Community Education (NICE) Trust. "A Framework for the Provision of Adult Basic and Further Education." Unpublished discussion document. Johannesburg: NICE Trust, 1994.

Smith, Walther. "The Community College in South Africa's Future." National Consultative Meeting on Community Colleges. Unpublished paper. Johannesburg: Education Foundation, 1992.

South African Committee for Higher Education (SACHED). "Draft Policy Paper on Community Learning Centres." Unpublished paper. Johannesburg: SACHED, 1993.

South African Department of National Education. *Education Realities in South Africa.* Pretoria: Department of National Education, 1991.

———. *Education Renewal Strategy.* Pretoria: Department of National Education, 1992.

Strauss, J.P., S.J. Plekker, and H.J. Van der Linde. *Education and Manpower Development.* Bloemfontein: RIEP, 1992.

U.S. Agency for International Development (U.S. AID). *South Africa—Tertiary Education Sector Assessment.* Washington, D.C.: Academy for Education Development (AID PDC), 1992.

Contributors

ROSALIND LATINER RABY, co-editor of this volume and author of chapters 1 and 5, is also the coordinator of the International Curriculum Project for the Institute for International Programs, Los Angeles Community College District; the editor of the newsletter of the consortium California Colleges for International Education; the coordinator of the community college curriculum for the UCLA International Seminar Series; and a part-time instructor in the Graduate School of Education at California State University, Northridge. Dr. Raby has taught graduate courses on international studies and on internationalizing the community college curriculum and, for the past nine years, has served as a consultant in international education for California community colleges.

NORMA TARROW, co-editor of this volume and author of the introduction, is a professor of education at California State University, Long Beach, where she teaches comparative and international education and intercultural/multicultural education. She is also the founder and director of the ISTE (International Student Teacher Exchange) and SIM (Semester in Mexico) programs. She presently serves the California State University system as resident director of the Bilingual Credential Program in Mexico, 1994–1996. She has taught and administered programs in Israel, England, and Spain. Her research interests include human rights and intercultural education, with a specialization in the education of indigenous minority groups.

JEAN COOK, author of chapter 2, is the project director for international education at Sinclair Community College, Ohio. She has over twenty years of teaching and administrative experience at Sinclair Community College and has professional experiences in thirteen countries, where she assists with technical skills training, experiential learning, and instructional technology.

DANIEL SCHUGURENSKY recently received his Ph.D. from the Graduate School of Education, University of Alberta. His recent research includes work in Canada, Mexico, and Argentina on topics ranging from educational restructuring to adult basic education. KATHY HIGGINS, his co-author of chapter 3, is the director of the International Education Center, Grant MacEwan Community College, Alberta, and is enrolled in the master's-of-education program in the area of comparative and international education at the University of Alberta, Edmonton.

NAOMI OKUMURA STORY, author of chapter 4, is the director of the Maricopa Center for Learning and Instruction, Maricopa Community College District, Arizona, where she provides leadership in new directions for teaching and learning agendas. In particular, she coordinates the efforts of information sharing, faculty development workshops and consultation, instructional and curricular development projects and services, and instructional innovation and experimentation. Her publications specialize in multidimensional strategies and technologies for achieving students' educational success.

SHARON NARIMATSU, primary author of chapter 6, is the assistant to the senior vice president and chancellor for the University of Hawai'i Community Colleges and handles diverse responsibilities for seven community colleges dispersed throughout the state and for one employment training center. A special assignment involves coordinating international education programs with sister colleges in Japan, China, Taiwan, and Australia. ROBERT W. FRANCO, her co-author, is an assistant professor of anthropology and the coordinator of Asian-Pacific studies at Kapil'olani Community College. He was a 1993 visiting fellow at the Program on Culture Studies at the East-West Center's Pacific Island Development Program.

RUTH BURGOS-SASSCER, co-author of chapter 7, is the president of San Antonio Community College, Texas. She has twenty years of community college administrative experience, which includes collaborating on projects with administrators from community colleges in Great Britain, Venezuela, and Mexico. DAVID COLLINS, her co-author, is the principal of the South Cheshire College for Further and Higher Learning, United Kingdom. His previous position was as vice principal at Sandwell College, where he served from 1988 to 1993.

EVAN S. DOBELLE, co-author of chapter 8, is former chancellor of the San Francisco Community College District, California; chairperson of the International/Intercultural Council (thirteen nations) of the American Association of Community and Junior Colleges; and the past president of the consortium California Colleges for International Education. Currently, Dr. Dobelle is president of Trinity College. JAMES H. MULLEN, co-author of chapter 8, is former vice president for fiscal and developmental affairs at Middlesex Community College, Massachusetts. He holds a master's degree in public policy from Harvard University and a doctorate degree in education from the University of Massachusetts at Amherst. Dr. Mullen is currently the vice president for strategic planning and government relations at Trinity College.

MATHILDA ESFORMES HARRIS, author of chapter 9, is currently director of the Center of International Development in Arlington, Virginia, and served previously as the assistant vice president of the American Association of State Colleges and Universities (Washington, D.C.). She has served as president of several international organizations and has been affiliated with community colleges nationwide for over twenty-five years. On a consulting basis, she has worked with multilateral and bilateral organizations as well as colleges and universities throughout the world. Her teaching, research, and publications focus on issues relating to development, cultural, and economic and political power.

CORNELIA H. VAN DER LINDE, author of chapter 10, is a lecturer in comparative education and educational management at the Universiteit van Suid-Afrika. She obtained her Ph.D. at the University of South Africa, has presented papers at international conferences, and is the co-author of two books. Her present interests include the training of teachers, educational management, community colleges, intercultural and multicultural education, and interactive texts in distance education. She is conducting comparative international research on teacher stress and is also involved as a team member in a qualitative research project in connection with interactive texts as they are used in distance education institutions.

TINA YAMANO, co-author of chapter 11, is a postdoctoral scholar at the University of California, Los Angeles and a specialist on education and diversity, with an emphasis on Asian Americans. She has been directly involved in the analysis of higher education and community colleges in her native Japan for several years. JOHN N. HAWKINS, her co-author, is the dean of the International Studies and Overseas Program and is a professor of education at the University of California, Los Angeles. He has written widely on issues related to higher education reform in Asia and has recently completed fieldwork throughout Asia and the Pacific Basin.

AMIN A. ELMALLAH, co-author of chapter 12, is a professor at the School of Business Administration at California State University, Sacramento. His recent scholarly research includes educational reform in his native Egypt. KAL GEZI, co-author, is a professor at the Department of Educational Administration and Policy Studies at California State University, Sacramento. His recent scholarly research includes educational development in Egypt. HASSAN ABDEL HAMID SOLIMAN, co-author, is professor of science at the Department of Geology at Assiut University, Egypt, and is involved in establishing an institute for industrial research and development, directing educational and cultural affairs, and advising government-sponsored Egyptian students in U.S. institutions.

YAACOV IRAM, author of chapter 13, is chair of the Department of Educational Foundations of the School of Education at Bar-Ilan University, Ramat Gan, Tel Aviv, Israel. He has been a postdoctoral scholar at the Graduate School of Education, University of Pennsylvania, and has lectured in various universities in the United States. His areas of research are educational policy, politics and education, multiculturalism and education, and higher education in his native Israel.

MBUYISELWA SILAS ZUMA, author of chapter 14, is the director of the National Institute of Community Education, South Africa, and is the former director of the Education Foundation in Durban, South Africa. He has been actively involved in assessing and implementing American community college models as a form of alternative educational programs in his native South Africa.

Index

administrative exchanges, xviii, 5, 12–13, 46, 159–172, 182–183
administrative support, xvii–xviii, 117, 119, 176–177
administrator role, xvii–xviii, 4, 5, 175–191
Albertan community colleges, 61–64
Allan Hancock Community College, 135
American Association of Community Colleges/American Association of Community and Junior Colleges (AACC/AACJC), xvi, 16, 17, 18, 86, 103
American Council on International/Intercultural Education (ACIIE), 12, 19, 331
American River Community College, 127, 132, 133, 135, 136
American Samoa Community College, 149
Australian community college models, 197, 212

Bergen Community College, 121, 189–190
Brevard Community College, 17, 132
British colleges of further and higher education, 161, 165–169, 171, 212, 294, 296, 297, 323
British educational reform, 160–161
Bronx Community College, 253
Broward Community College, xxviii, 25, 105, 123, 249

California Colleges for International Education (CCIE), 26–27, 135, 327, 329
Cañada Community College, 133, 232
Canadian community colleges, 53–78, 198, 234, 248–249, 251–252, 254, 255, 323

Central American Peace Scholarship program, 224
Central Piedmont Community College, 93, 101, 104
Chaffey Community College, 124
Christchurch Polytechnic, 149, 156,
City College of Chicago, 95, 99, 163, 165
City College of San Francisco, 133, 176, 180, 189
Coast Community College District, 105
Coastline Community College, 135, 136
Colegio Nacional de Educacíon Profesional Ténica (CONALEP), 224
College of DuPage, 46
College of the Redwoods, 124
Colorado College, 254
community college model, xix–xxi, xiii, 3–4, 195–207, 248–256, 259
Community College of Allegheny County, 104
Community Colleges for International Development (CCID), 17, 21, 40
community self-help development, 37–39, 40–59
conceptual partnership, xx
conflict resolution, 240–245, 246–247
consensus, 175–191
consortia, 103–104, 105
core requirement, 124
Cornell College, 254
cultural hegemony, 228–229
cultural imperialism, 206, 228, 260–261
culture, 240–241
curricular reform, 98–99, 114–115, 160–161, 232–233, 278–280, 286, 316, 319–320
Cypress Community College, 123

DeAnza Community College, 21, 135

degree, certificate programs, xxv, 17, 21, 91–92, 112, 117, 134–137, 138, 310, 318
development education model, xxi, xxii, 53, 60, 64–71, 216–220
diffusion method, 220, 244–246, 263–264
distance education, 315
Dutchess Community College, 95

Eastern Iowa Community College District, 46
Edmonds Community College, 265
Edmonds Community College in Kobe, 265–267, 270
Egyptian community colleges (*ma'ahed*), xx, 273–288
El Paso Community College, 17, 106
employment training, 250–253, 295–296, 309, 314–315
equal access, 204–205, 206, 287, 291, 293, 298–300, 307–308, 311, 312, 314, 315, 321
Estrella Mountain Community College Center, 101
ethnic studies, 90–91
ethnicity, 217
exporting model, xxi

faculty, 115–116, 118, 137–138, 159, 176– 177, 184, 255, 284–285
faculty apathy, 117, 137–138
faculty exchanges, xvii, 12–13
Foothill/DeAnza Community College District, 50, 103
Fordism, 55, 56, 71, 73n
foreign contract program, 14
foreign language instruction, 122
French community college models, 199, 294
Fresno City Community College, 92, 135
further education, 309, 319–321, 321–322

GateWay Community College, 101
general education requirements, 82, 123–124
German community college models, 195, 199, 294
Glendale Community College, 136
global education, 11, 96–97
Golden West Community College, 124
Grant MacEwan Community College, 54, 62–64, 328

Harry S. Truman College, 163–165, 169–172

Hartnell Community College, 120, 121
Hawai'i community college system, 87, 145, 147, 148, 149, 328
Hollard College, 253
Honolulu Community College, 149, 151, 152
Houston Community College, 105
humanists/humanitarian model, xxi, xxii, 6, 14, 37–51, 60, 205

in-service training/staff development, 120, 126
Indonesian community college models, 199
infusion approach, xvi, xvii, 17, 26, 95–96, 98, 128–132
intercultural, xvi, xvii, xx, xxiii, xxiv, xxv, 4, 252–253
international business, 58, 63, 114, 122
international competency, 21–22, 30, 112–113, 121, 129
international curriculum, 5, 14, 17, 18, 27, 54, 59, 89, 93, 98, 111–139, 230, 232–233
international development, xvii, xx, xxii, 5, 6, 14, 20, 37–51, 39– 40, 53–75, 181, 182–183, 204–207, 216–220, 220–229
international partnerships, 14
international/multicultural connections, xiv, 3, 4, 122–123, 179–191, 263–264, 285–286
international students, 13, 21, 25, 27, 64, 97, 100, 132–133, 231, 233–234, 263, 269
internationalizing curriculum methodology, 126–134
Israel community college model (*michlalot ezoriyot*), xix, 291–300

Japan community college model (*komyuniti kareji*), xix, 200, 224, 259–270

Kapil'olani Community College, 97, 103, 154, 155, 328
Kaua'i Community College, 149, 151
Kolej Damansara Utama, 249, 251
Korean community college models, 201

La Guardia Community College, 95, 96, 105
Leeward Community College, 149
liberation theology, 227
Lincoln Land Community College, 251
Long Beach City College, 124

Los Angeles City College, 267–268
Los Angeles Community College District, 25, 116, 118, 128, 132, 138, 267, 327
Los Angeles Pierce Community College, 135
Los Angeles Southwest Community College, 123
Los Angeles Trade-Technical Community College, 133, 135
Los Medanos Community College, 253

Malaysian community colleges, 239, 241, 245, 246–249, 251
Maricopa Community College District, 89, 91, 94, 95, 99, 105, 328
Maui Community College, 149, 152
Mesa Community College, 25, 132
Miami-Dade Community College, 97, 99, 101, 103, 246
Middlesex Community College, 175, 178–179, 181–183, 187, 189, 329
mission and policy statements, xvii, xxvii, 20, 17, 43, 44, 68, 70, 81–83, 85, 86, 105, 116, 137, 177, 180, 307
Mission Community College, 124
Mount Royal Community College, 54, 62–64
multicultural curricula, 5, 90, 92–96, 98–99
multicultural education, xvi, xvii, xxii–xxiii, xxiv–xxv, 4, 5, 12, 14–15, 17, 21–22, 79–108, 252–253, 282, 285–286, 298
multicultural faculty development, 102–103
multicultural societies, 5, 239–256
multicultural student counseling services, 164, 169
multicultural student support, 100–102

Napa Valley Community College, 123
National Association for Foreign Student Affairs (NAFSA), xviii, 15, 17
National Institute of Community Education, South Africa, 311, 314–321, 324–325, 330
New Zealand community college models, 201
Nigerian community college models, 224
Norwegian community college models, 201, 294

Orange Coast Community College, 135
Oxnard Community College, 135

partnerships, 104, 187, 315, 316, 320

Philippines community college model, 202
Piedmont Community College, 254
Pima Community College, 87, 100, 104, 105, 135, 136
Portland Community College, 135, 136
post-modernism philosophy, 227
privatization model, xxii, 6, 14, 29, 43, 53–75, 160–162, 167–169, 184, 205–206, 274

Rio Hondo Community College, 91
Rio Salado Community College, 95, 96
Rockland Community College, 17

Sacramento City College, 123
Saddleback Community College, 124, 127
Salish Kootenai Community College, 92
San Diego Community College District, 105
San Jose Community College, 134, 135
Sandwell College of Further and Higher Learning, 165–169, 328
Santa Barbara City College, 127, 135
Santa Monica Community College, 132
Santa Rosa Community College, 180
Seattle Central Community College, 87, 96, 99, 100, 105
self-development, 218, 223
short-cycle institutions, 195, 259, 291–292, 293–294
Sinclair Community College, 37–51, 327
Society Taking Active Responsibility for International Self-Help (STAR-FISH), 37–51
South Africa, 303–325
South African Community Colleges, 239, 242–243, 248, 250–251, 254–256, 303–325
South Cheshire College for Further and Higher Learning, 330
South Mountain Community College, 87, 96, 102
Spokane Community College, 46, 251
St. Louis Community College, 46, 135, 136
State Center Community College, 100
students, 99–102, 116, 126, 164, 280–282, 318
study abroad, xviii–xix, 5, 13–14, 17, 20, 27, 121, 137, 145–157, 266

Taiwanese community college models, 224
technological transfers, xix–xx, 220–229
Thai community college models, 224
Tokyo American Community College, 267–270

United States, 215, 239, 244–245, 247, 299
United States community colleges, 239, 249–250, 251, 264, 287–288, 294, 295, 297, 303, 311, 322–323, 324
University Development Linkages Project (UDLP), 37–51
University of Hawai'i Community Colleges, 145, 330

Valencia Community College, 252
vocational/technical education, 159–160, 161, 264, 273–274, 288, 308, 309, 311, 312, 317, 321

Windward Community College, 149, 152

Yakima Valley Community College, 249